Peter Norton's

Guide to Unix

Peter Norton
Harley Hahn

RANDOM HOUSE
ELECTRONIC PUBLISHING
New York

Peter Norton's Guide to Unix

Published in the United States by Random House, Inc., New York, and simultaneously in Canada by Random House of Canada, Limited.

Manufactured in the United States of America

First Edition

0 9 8 7 6 5 4

ISBN 0-679-79056-X

New York   Toronto   London   Sydney   Auckland

Dedication

To Melissa Hahn and Randy Hahn.
--H.H.

To Eileen.
--P.N.

Introduction

What This Book Is About

This book is about getting started with Unix—a computer system that runs on many different types of computers all around the world.

Unix is an operating system that was first used by two people on a small, old-fashioned computer. Today, Unix is used all around the world on computers of every size and description—from personal workstations to the world's most powerful super-computers; from PCs used by a single person to large systems that support hundreds of people at the same time.

But no matter what computer you are using, the nice thing about Unix is that it always works pretty much the same way, which is one reason why it is so popular.

In this book, we will explore the world of Unix. By the time we finish, you will understand why Unix is so important. Along the way, you will learn many practical skills that you can use in your work, or for just plain having fun with your computer.

This book is about getting started with Unix. There is no need for you to have any prior computer experience.

Unix Terminology

On our journey through the world of Unix we will encounter many new words and terms. To smooth the way, we preview each chapter with the definitions of all the new words that you will meet in that chapter. Within the chapter, we will introduce each new word by putting it in italics.

If you already know these words you may be tempted to skip the chapter. At the very least, be sure to skim the text before moving on. Unix is different from other computer systems, and you may miss a subtle point.

Unix Terminology
Words which have special Unix meanings

As a reference, we have collected all the new words into a glossary at the end of the book. It is important that you understand Unix Terminology—words for which Unix people have special meanings. Many Unix terms are English words that are used differently from what you might expect. When in doubt, check the glossary.

Special Hints

Throughout this book you will see two types of special hints. First, there are a number of ideas that we have found to be important for people learning Unix. We will draw your attention to these ideas by emphasizing them and labeling each as a "Rule for Learning Unix."

RULE   Keep in mind that Unix is fun.

Second, we recognize that many of you will have experience using a personal computer with DOS. When we explain something that can be related to your PC experience, we will call it a "Hint for DOS Users."

Hint   **DOS users:**
••••   Unix is more fun than DOS.

1

What is Unix?

Introduction

In this chapter, you will develop the background you need to understand and appreciate Unix. We will start by discussing operating systems: What are they? What do they do? From there, we move on to the basic facts about Unix: What is it? Who uses it? Who develops and maintains it?

By the time you finish this chapter, you will see that Unix is far more widespread (and more important) than most people realize.

What Is an Operating System?

By themselves, computers are lifeless lumps of metal and plastic. Unlike most machines—cars, ovens, or television sets—computers are not built to perform predetermined tasks. Rather, they are built to follow instructions.

Program:
A list of computer instructions that, when followed, achieves a desired result.

A list of instructions for the computer to follow is called a *program*. As the computer follows the instructions, we say that it *executes* or *runs* the program. You run certain programs in order to have your computer perform a desired action. A simple program might do no more than display the time and date. A

1

**Execute (or run)
a program:**
*To follow the
instructions
contained in a
program.*

Hardware:
*The physical parts
of the computer.*

Software:
Programs.

more complex program might be a full-fledged word processor
or spreadsheet.

Hardware refers to the physical parts of a computer: the
display, the keyboard, the disks (which store data), the printer,
the mouse, and so on. *Software* consists of all the programs that
you might run. Obviously, these names are misleading. Although "hard" and "soft" are opposites, hardware is not the
opposite of software. In fact, they are complementary. It is the
software—the lists of instructions—that brings the hardware to
life.

Computer hardware and software are complex—so complex
in fact, that every computer requires a special program to manage its resources. This master control program is called an *operating system.*

Unix is an operating system.

What Does an Operating System Do?

Operating System:
*The master control
program that
manages the
resources of a
computer system.*

Unix:
*An operating
system whose
variations run on
many different
types of computers.*

An operating system has two main purposes:

1. To *manage* the computer's hardware resources efficiently
2. To make it *easy* for you to use the computer

In pursuit of these goals, your operating system concerns
itself with just about every facet of your computer's operation.
It manages how programs are run, how data is stored, how
reports are printed, how words and pictures are displayed, and
on and on. In fact, one reason why operating systems even exist
is so that neither you nor your programs need to attend to the
millisecond by millisecond details necessary to manage a computer.

As you work, your operating system is always there. In fact,
you and your programs are never really on your own. The operating system watches everything you do. Many times a second,
it steps in and carries out some task on your behalf without your
even noticing it.

For example, when you run a program, it does not exist by
itself in a vacuum: it executes under the auspices of the operating system. Every time the program needs to work with the
computer's resources—for example, to read from a file—it calls
upon the operating system to perform the task.

Programs are normally not allowed to deal directly with the computer's resources. They are required to call upon the operating system to do the work. This allows the operating system to keep the strict control it needs to maintain the integrity of the entire system. For example, it is the operating system that ensures that two programs do not try to change the same file at the same time.

In the same way, your interactions with the computer are monitored by the operating system. For instance, every time you press a key, the operating system notices and displays the appropriate character on the screen.

Utility:
A program that comes with an operating system and that performs a specific task.

More directly, the operating system comes with certain programs that are there for you to use whenever you want; tools to maintain your files, send and receive messages, check out who else is using the computer, and so on. Unix has many of these programs, called *utilities*, that provide just about every type of service that you can imagine. In fact, Unix has more built-in utilities than any other operating system in the world.

What Is Unix?

As we've mentioned, Unix is an operating system—a master control program—that operates the computer on your behalf. In doing so, Unix helps programs execute and helps you do your work.

But why is Unix so important? Why do people talk about it so much? For that matter, why did we write a Unix book?

Port:
To modify a program from one computer system so that it works with a different system.

Most operating systems are used on only one type of computer. However, after Unix was invented, AT&T licensed it for free to many universities where programmers made it work on different computers. (In computer terminology, we say that the programmers *ported* Unix to different computers.) Today, Unix in one form or another works on just about any popular computer that you can think of. Not only that—there are thousands of programs available to use with Unix systems.

Multitasking:
Describes an operating system that can do more than one thing at a time.

The two most important characteristics of Unix are that it is *multitasking* and *multiuser*. Multitasking means that Unix can do more than one thing at a time. For instance, you can start a program and let it go on by itself while you work with another program. You will learn how to use this handy feature later in the book. Multiuser means that more than one person can use

Multiuser:
Describes an operating system that can be used by more than one person at a time.

the computer at the same time, sharing the resources, file space, printers, and so on.

These two facilities make Unix especially flexible. This is what makes it so important (and this is why we wrote a Unix book): Unix is a versatile system that is used on many different types of computers. When you learn to use Unix, you are learning to use one of the most important operating systems in the world.

Where Does the Name "Unix" Come From?

In the 1960s, computer scientists at MIT and Bell Labs (a part of AT&T) developed a large, ponderous operating system named Multics. The name stood for "Multiplexed Information and Computing Service." (Multiplexing combines multiple electronic signals into a single signal.)

By the late 1960s, the Bell Labs management had decided not to pursue Multics, and the AT&T researchers were pulled off the job. Some of the software developers managed to scrounge up a minicomputer (a PDP-7 made by Digital Equipment Corporation) and kept developing. They came up with a completely new operating system which they named Unix.

Why? Multics was large and complex and served many people at the same time; it had its share of problems. Unix was small and (at first) served only one person at a time. The researchers chose the name to indicate that, compared to Multics, Unix was a more workable system that devoted itself to doing *one thing at a time*. "Uni" means one, as in "unicycle."

Thus, "Unix" is a pun on "Multics."

Who Uses Unix?

There is a peculiar answer to this question. There are two types of people who use Unix: those who know they are using it and those who don't know.

First, there are many people who make use of Unix and its many utilities. They know that their computer is controlled by Unix. And, to the extent of their abilities, they use Unix to perform all kinds of tasks. Sometimes they use the built-in features and sometimes they use other software, such as a word processor or spreadsheet program.

Second, there are many other people who use computers that are already set up to perform their jobs automatically. For example, people who work in a doctor's office may be using a Unix-based computerized accounting and patient management system. All they know about is the specific office programs with which they interact. They do not care what an operating system is, nor do they care that their computer is controlled by Unix.

In fact, Unix is so widespread that we all fall into the second group more than we might suspect. Whenever we make a phone call, book an airline flight, check a computerized library catalog, or ask a government agency for information, we are, more often than not, depending on a Unix system.

Two Types of Unix Users

Another way to divide Unix users into two groups is to distinguish between those people who share a computer and those who have a computer all to themselves.

As we mentioned above, Unix is a multiuser system—that is, more than one person can use the computer at the same time. A Unix system may be as small as two or three office workers or as large as hundreds of travel agents or bank employees simultaneously accessing an enormous data repository. Such systems, regardless of size, are called *time-sharing systems*.

Time-Sharing System:
Same as a multiuser operating system.

However, many people have Unix computers all to themselves. These systems are called *standalone systems*. In such cases, the computer itself is usually called a *workstation*. This term implies that the computer is being used by only one person at a time.

Standalone:
Describes a computer system that is used by only one person at a time.

All Unix systems, no matter how large or small, require a certain amount of administration. Large time-sharing systems require the most and usually call for a full-time administrator just to see to the needs of the users and the computer. If you have your own computer, then you must act as the administrator. This makes one-person Unix systems somewhat more demanding than other small computer operating systems (such as DOS, OS/2, or the Macintosh operating system).

Workstation:
A computer that is used by only one person at a time.

Hint
••••

DOS users:
Unix requires a great deal more system administration than DOS.

What Types of Computers Run Unix?

We mentioned earlier that Unix runs on many types of computers. More specifically, Unix runs on many personal computers (such as IBM-compatible PCs and Macintoshes), midrange computers (such as DEC's VAX family), personal workstations and network servers (such as Sun's SPARC systems and IBM's RS/6000 family), mainframe computers (such as IBM's System 370) and supercomputers (such as the Cray computers).

DOS users:

You can install both DOS and Unix on a PC and start either one or the other.

With a PC version of Unix, it is possible to run DOS programs under Unix and to share both DOS and Unix files.

In fact, there are only two types of computers on which Unix is usually not available. First, most older PCs do not have the proper facilities to run such a demanding operating system. For example, Unix will not run on the low-end IBM-compatibles and Macintoshes. Second, some computer systems, which are powerful enough to run Unix, were designed for specific purposes and will probably never be adapted to the Unix environment. A good example of this is IBM's AS/400 system.

So what if you would like to have your own personal Unix computer? The most economical system is probably an IBM PS/2 or IBM-compatible. You must make sure that the processor is at least a 286 (preferably a 386 or 486). You will need a good-sized hard disk (at least 30 MB, usually 40 MB or more) and several megabytes of memory.

DOS users:

If you would like to run Unix on your PC, you should have at least a 286-based computer. For high performance, you will need a 386- or 486-based system.

Who Makes Unix?

As we mentioned, Unix was originally developed at Bell Labs, a division of AT&T. To this day, AT&T still controls the rights to Unix. Like most software, Unix is never sold, only licensed. This means that virtually any Unix that you use is based on AT&T Unix.

However, Unix very much depends on the hardware on which it is being run. This means that each type of computer needs its own variation of Unix. Most computer companies license the basic Unix from AT&T and then adapt it to work with their computers.

Many computer systems can use only one type of Unix: the one supplied by the company that made the computer. For example, IBM's RS/6000 computers can use only AIX, IBM's version of Unix.

However, some systems can run more than one variation. In particular, users of personal-computer–based systems have a choice of several Unix's, the most important of which are Santa Cruz Operation's Unix, Interactive System Corporation's Unix, and IBM's AIX PS/2.

Aside from Bell Labs, a great deal of Unix work has been done by the Computer Systems Research Group, or CSRG, at the University of California at Berkeley. In fact, CSRG distributes its own version of Unix (partially based on AT&T's) called BSD, which stands for "Berkeley Software Distribution." Among Unix people, BSD is often referred to as "Berkeley Unix." Many of the modern Unix's incorporate the BSD enhancements and, to this day, Unix development at Berkeley continues independent of AT&T.

Free Unix

There is a nonprofit organization based in Massachusetts whose purpose is to develop and provide *free* Unix all over the world. It is called the Free Software Foundation.

The Free Software Foundation was started in 1985 by Richard Stallman of MIT. The organization believes that *all* software ought to be free—at least to individuals. They are currently in the process of developing an entire Unix-like system called GNU (pronounced "G-New," with a hard "G"). The name "GNU" is a strange acronym, standing for "GNU's not Unix."

Of course, in order to be free, GNU must be written using only other free software. Eventually, the Free Software Foundation will have an operating system that is entirely independent of proprietary systems—in particular, AT&T's Unix.

By What Names Is Unix Known?

The original AT&T Unix was simply called "Unix." However, as it became popular and other companies decided to offer their own variations, AT&T was reluctant to let them use the name "Unix," which is an AT&T trademark. Thus, there arose an assortment of names, each of which describes a variation of Unix offered by a specific organization. Most, but not all, of these names are Unix-like in that they contain the letters "IX" or, at least, "X."

An important example is Xenix (pronounced "Zee-nix"), which was first developed by Microsoft as a Unix for PCs. Later on, the development was taken over by the Santa Cruz Operation company (SCO). Eventually, AT&T decided to unify Unix. Along with SCO, they resolved the technical differences and merged Xenix and Unix into one variation which was simply called "Unix." However, in the several years before that happened, the name "Xenix" was used by Microsoft, SCO, IBM, and several other companies to describe their versions of PC Unix.

Recently, AT&T has been trying to unify all the Unix variations into one family. There would be one member of the family for each important type of computer—for example, there would be one Unix for all 386- and 486-based PCs. However, at the same time, other companies have been abandoning the fold and developing their own Unix's. To be sure, these Unix's are based on AT&T Unix, but have been altered so much that their developers want to use their own name for the operating system. (And "Unix," of course, is an AT&T trademark.)

The best example of this is IBM's Unix, which IBM decided to call AIX (pronounced as three separate letters "A-I-X"). Nominally, the name stands for "Advanced Interactive Executive," but clearly the name was chosen to end with "IX" so as to be Unix-like.

Here is a list of the most important Unix names, along with the company or organization behind the Unix.

Name	Organization
AIX	IBM
ATS	Amdahl
A/UX	Apple
BSD	University of California at Berkeley
Dynix	Sequent
GNU	Free Software Foundation
HP/UX	Hewlett-Packard
OSF/1	Open Software Foundation
SunOS	Sun Microsystems
Ultrix	DEC (Digital Equipment Corporation)
Unicos	Cray Research
Unix	AT&T, ISC (Interactive Systems Corporation), SCO (Santa Cruz Operation), Sun Microsystems
Xenix	SCO

Who Controls Unix?

Most operating systems are meant to run on only one type of computer. Thus, almost all operating systems are developed and maintained by the companies that make the computers. For example, IBM developed the OS/400 operating system to run the IBM AS/400 computers; DEC's VMS operating system runs only on DEC's VAX computers.

Unix is different in that it is used on a wide variety of computer systems and is controlled by the consensus of a number of different national and international organizations, not by one computer company. These organizations fall into three categories:

1. Unix developers

2. Unix standard setters

3. Unix user groups

Although the categories are convenient, they do overlap. Figure 1.1 shows the names of some of the important Unix organizations. Let's take a quick look at the world of Unix and see who does what.

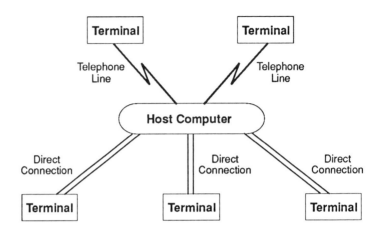

Figure 2.1   *Unix terminals connected to a host computer.*

Terminal:
A device which provides input and output facilities to the host computer.

The device that you use to do your work is called a *terminal*. A terminal consists of a display and a keyboard, along with the associated electronics. Sometimes, a terminal will also have a mouse.

Your terminal can be connected to the host in one of several ways. There may be a cable directly joining your terminal to the host; your terminal may be connected to a computer network that itself is connected to the host; or you may connect to the host over a telephone line.

Regardless of how your terminal is connected, you can picture a Unix system as it is shown in Figure 2.1. Notice that each terminal is connected to the *end* of a communications line. This is why we call them "terminals."

Types of Terminals

Dumb Terminal:
A terminal that offers only the bare minimum of facilities, a screen, and a keyboard.

There are several types of terminals that you might encounter. In its simplest incarnation, a terminal is basically a display and keyboard. Terminals such as this, that offer the bare minimum, are called *dumb terminals*. Other terminals are more sophisticated; they have memory of their own (like a computer), and they can offer more than the basic functions. These devices are

Intelligent Terminal:
A terminal that offers some memory and processing power as well as the minimum screen and keyboard.

Graphics Terminal:
A terminal that is capable of displaying pictures.

called *intelligent terminals*. Most modern terminals are intelligent terminals.

A particular type of intelligent terminal is a *graphics terminal*. A graphics terminal has special hardware that allows it to display pictures. Graphics terminals are used for such applications as computer-aided design. In Chapter 6, we will discuss a system called X-Window that allows you to work within windows. X-Window requires a special type of graphics terminal, called an X-Terminal.

The thing to remember is that, no matter how powerful it is, a terminal cannot run programs. Only the host computer runs programs. The terminal is your window into what is happening on the host.

Terminal Emulation

Emulate:
To act like a specific device by running a program that simulates that device.

Sometimes, instead of using real terminals, we use computers—usually PCs—to act as terminals. In such cases, we run a communications program that makes the PC act like an actual terminal. We say that the PC *emulates* a terminal.

The most common terminal that is emulated is the Digital Equipment Corporation's VT-100. VT-100's are not new; in fact, they are not even sold anymore. However, for most purposes, a VT-100 is fine, and it has become a de facto standard for terminal emulation. (In fact, the communications facility that comes with IBM's OS/2 operating system emulates a VT-100.)

Most of the time, PC communications programs emulate VT-100's. However, you will see a number of other terminal types. In particular, if you are working with IBM equipment, it is sometimes easier to have your PC emulate an IBM 3101 terminal.

••••

DOS users:
You can use a PC as a terminal by running a terminal emulation program.

Most terminal emulation programs emulate VT-100 terminals.

Now, PCs are more complex and expensive than most terminals. Why would anyone want to use a PC to emulate a less expensive device? Usually because a PC is available, and it is cheaper to use what you already have than to go out and buy a whole new terminal.

Moreover, a computer can be used for many purposes, while a terminal can be used only to connect to a host. Typically, you will find that such a PC is used as a terminal some of the time and as a computer the rest of the time. In fact, there are programs that will let your PC act as both a terminal and a PC at the same time. You can press a special key combination and jump back and forth between, say, a regular PC program (or DOS) and a Unix session connected to a remote host. With the proper hardware, some programs even allow you to connect to more than one Unix session at a time.

····

DOS users:
With the proper software, you can connect to a Unix host at the same time you are running DOS programs.

Dial-In Terminals

Dial-In Terminal:
A terminal which connects to a host computer over a telephone line.

Many Unix systems, especially at universities, have facilities for connecting *dial-in terminals* over the phone line.

The most common arrangement is for your computer to emulate a terminal and to use the telephone line to connect to the remote host. To connect to a remote Unix host you run a program that dials the remote computer. After making the connection, the program emulates a standard terminal (usually a VT-100, but you will probably have a choice).

All Unix systems come with this facility. If you have a DOS or Macintosh computer, you will have to obtain a communications program.

Modems

Modulation:
The process by which a computer signal is converted into a telephone signal in order to be transmitted over a telephone line.

In order to transmit data over a phone line, the information must be converted into a telephone signal. This process is called *modulation*. At the other end, this signal must be converted back into computer data. This process is called *demodulation*. The device that performs these tasks is called a *modem* and connects your phone line to your computer or terminal. (The

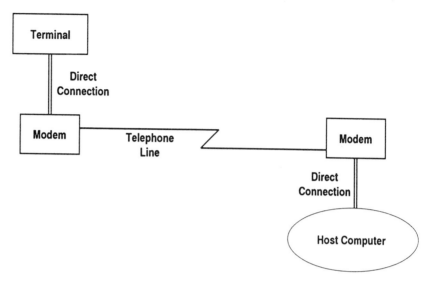

Figure 2.2   *A dial-in terminal connected to a host computer.*

Demodulation:

The process by which a telephone signal is converted to a computer signal after being received over a telephone line.

Modem (modulator/ demodulator):

A device that converts signals in both directions between a computer and the telephone line.

Console:

The main terminal that is connected to a host computer.

name stands for "modulator/demodulator.") A typical configuration is shown in Figure 2.2.

Thus, in order to communicate with a distant computer, all you need is a computer or terminal and a modem. Such connections are common in the Unix world.

The Console

Out of all the terminals that may be connected to a Unix host, there is one that has a special name—the *console*. Every Unix system has exactly one console.

The console is considered to be the main terminal and is always connected directly to the host. If a system has a full-time operator, he or she will probably use the console to administer the system. However, Unix can be administered from any terminal and, in many systems, the console is considered to be just another terminal.

Much of the time the console is actually part of the host. For example, if you are running Unix on a PC, the computer itself acts as its own console.

As you know, Unix is a multiuser system. However, many Unix systems are used exclusively by one person at a time. As we mentioned in Chapter 1, such systems are called work-stations. It may be that you are the only one who will ever use your workstation.

Regardless, think of your computer as a multiuser system with only one actual user. In such cases, you will always be working from the console: the keyboard and display that are part of your workstation. In other words, you can think of a workstation as a self-contained host plus terminal (the console).

Computer Networks

Network:
A system in which computers are connected to other computers.

Local Area Network (LAN):
A directly-connected network.

Wide Area Network (WAN):
A network in which some of the connections are indirect (via telephone lines, satellite, and so on).

Ethernet:
A local area network using an "Ethernet" arrangement.

Token-Ring:
A local area network using a "Token-Ring" arrangement.

It is common nowadays to find computers connected to other computers. When more than one computer is connected, we call it a *network*.

Computers that are connected together directly, through cabling of some type, form a *local area network* or *LAN*. Computers that are connected indirectly, over the telephone system or via satellite, form a *wide area network* or *WAN*.

LANs are usually connected using coaxial cable, twisted-pair cable (similar to the telephone wires inside your walls), or fiber-optic cable. There are a number of ways of organizing these connections. The most common system, especially with Unix, is called an *Ethernet*. Less often, you may also see *Token-Ring* systems.

Sometimes LANs are connected to other LANs, forming large networks. Many LANs have access to WANs that allow users to send data and messages to a large number of distant computers. This is common in universities, governments, and other big institutions. In fact, many of the WANs around the country are connected together.

One of our favorite Unix services is the worldwide mail system based on WANs. Using this system you can send electronic mail just about anywhere in the world—usually for free. You can also participate in any of a vast number of public discussion groups.

Unix Networks

The reason we mention networks now is that many Unix computers are connected together. In fact, Unix is often the operating system of choice for connecting computers. All Unix systems come with built-in communications facilities. Even if you are the only one using your Unix computer, you may still want to connect it other computers over a phone line. We encourage you to do so.

Within a network, each computer is called a *node* (this term is borrowed from mathematics). Each node has its own electronic address. If you know an exact address, you can send mail to someone at a particular computer, within a particular network, thousands of miles away.

Node:
A computer within a network.

Servers and Clients

Most networks have one or more computers that share resources throughout the network. Such nodes are called *servers*.

A server provides a service to the network, the most common service being file storage. In this case, the server is called a *file server*. However, there are other types of servers: a *print server* provides access to printers; a *communication server* provides access to modems to dial remote computers. Unix supports all of these activities.

When your computer makes use of a shared resource we speak of your computer as the *client*. Here is a common scenario: You are using a Unix workstation that is connected to a Unix network. Your computer has its own hard disk on which you store some of your files. However, one of the other computers on the network, a file server, has a very large hard disk, on which you keep the rest of your files.

When you use the files on your own computer the network is not involved. But when you access files on another computer, you are sharing the resources of the network. At such times, your computer is the client and the other computer is the server. If someone at another computer needs to use files on your computer then, from their point of view, their machine is the client and yours is the server.

In fact, Unix systems programmers will sometimes talk about the "client/server relationship." (Indeed, for many programmers, this is the longest lasting relationship they have ever had.)

Server:
A computer on a network that provides services or resources for the other computers.

File Server:
A server on a network that provides file storage.

Print Server:
A server on a network that provides access to printers.

Communication Server:
A server on a network that provides access to modems.

Client:
A computer on a network that makes use of a service or resource that is offered by a server.

3

A First Look at Unix

Introduction

The purpose of this chapter is to acquaint you with Unix. We will explain how you use Unix, and how you start and stop a work session. Along the way, we will introduce two important concepts: the Unix culture and the Unix language. With this chapter, you will begin to think in "Unix."

Is Unix Fun, or What?

In Chapter 1, we explained that there are many organizations that develop and standardize Unix. This observation might lead you to assume that Unix is dull and boring–the typical product of a committee or government agency.

Not at all.

In fact, all of these committees entered the world of Unix rather late in the game. By the time Unix had grown in importance to the point where the regulators sat up and took notice, most of the Unix look and feel had already been developed.

The actual Unix developers were programmers and researchers who worked alone or in small groups. These people were imaginative, creative, very intelligent and, at times, just plain weird. They created many different Unix tools, each of which was developed separately to solve a particular problem. For the most part, the programmers followed a basic philosophy. However, there are some exceptions and at odd times you will run into strange anomalies: things that are done a certain way and nobody can really explain why. Not to worry—this is just part of the charm of Unix.

Let's take a moment and consider another important operating system, OS/2. OS/2 was developed by a great many people at IBM and Microsoft. It has a master plan. It is well-designed and modern and it does a good job.

In fact, OS/2 is many things—but nobody ever accused it of being fun.

Unix was created in an ad hoc manner, by smart people *for* smart people. The marvellous thing about using Unix is that it *is* fun. In fact, it is the only major operating system that routinely comes with a selection of games. However, once you become comfortable with Unix, you will find that working with the built-in tool set is actually more fun than playing with the games.

DOS users:

Unix is a lot more fun than DOS. If you enjoy building tools with DOS, you will have a lot more fun building tools with Unix.

What Do You Do When You Use Unix?
(Entering a Command)

What do you see when you use Unix? What will you be doing from moment to moment?

Enter:

To issue a command by typing it and then pressing the <Return> key

First off, you have to start a Unix session. Once the session is started, you work by *entering* one command after another until all your work is done. You then end the session.

To enter a command, you type the command and then press the<Return> key. (On some terminals this key may be labeled <Ret> or <Enter>.) Once you press <Return>, Unix will carry out your command.

Your command may ask Unix to do something for you directly. If so, Unix will display the results of the command on your terminal. Here is an example. You enter the command

```
ls
```

The `ls` command tells Unix to list the names of your files. Unix responds by displaying, for example, the following names:

```
file1    file2    file3    file4
```

Next, you might enter

```
who
```

The **who** command tells Unix to display the names of all the people who are currently using the system. In this example, there are three people using the system. Unix displays

```
harley      console      Mar 30 12:18
addie       tty01        Mar 30 11:55
kim         tty03        Mar 30 09:28
```

(Don't worry about the details for now; we'll get back to them later.)

If you want to enter more than one command on a line, just separate them by semicolons:

```
ls; who; date
```

Sometimes, you will want to work with a program, such as a word processor or a spreadsheet. In this case, you enter the command to start the program. Usually this will be the name of the program or some abbreviation. For example, say that the name of your word processor is **wordp**. You enter

```
wordp
```

and Unix starts the word processor for you.

When Unix starts a program, it transfers partial control of your session to that program. When the program is finished, it hands control back to Unix. You can now enter another command.

Finally, you have finished all your work. You give the signal that you are done, and Unix ends your session.

Typing Ahead

Unix allows you to type as fast as you want. If your terminal cannot keep up with you, Unix will save your input and make sure that nothing is lost. Everything that you type is saved in a temporary storage area and is processed in the order it is received.

Don't worry about overflowing this storage area. It is large enough that you are unlikely to fill it, no matter how fast you type. This means that, if you want, you can enter a whole series of commands very quickly. Unix will save them and process them one at a time.

However, you should be careful if you are typing at the same time that output is being displayed. Although Unix will keep everything straight, the characters you type will be mixed in with the current output. If you find this confusing, just wait until all the output has been displayed before typing your next command.

Wheels Within Wheels

One thing about Unix that you should know—and this is something that we will see over and over again—is that anything that can be done simply can also be done with as much complexitly as you like.

If fact, let's embody that as a Rule For Learning Unix:

RULE   To learn Unix, keep in mind that anything that can be done simply, can also be done with as much complexity as you like.

In this case, we have seen how working with Unix means entering commands, one after the other, until all your work is finished. A command may be the name of a program, in which case Unix gives control to the program until it is over.

But you can issue commands within a command. For instance, with most Unix programs, you can put the program on hold temporarily and fire off another command. For instance, you might pause in the middle of using your word processor and enter a command to ask Unix what time it is. Once Unix displays the time, you are sent back to the word processor.

Think about it and you'll be able to see how important this is. Most operating systems would force you to stop and then restart the word processor just to enter a simple command.

Even more useful, if you feel like it, you could pause in your word processor, display your files, remove a couple of files that you don't need, move another file from one place to another, read your mail, check to see if one of your friends is using the system, display the time, and *then* return to the word processor.

However, with power comes the potential for complexity. Consider this scenario:

You can, if you want, pause in your word processor and start another copy of the word processor; and you can pause in that copy and start another one.

In this case, when you finally stop the third word processor you will return to the second. And when you stop the second word processor you will return to the first. And when you stop the first, original, word processor you will return back to Unix, which will be sitting patiently, waiting for another command.

But Unix can do more. Not only can you issue commands while you are in the middle of a program, you can also start a program and let it go on its own while you work on something else.

For example, say that you have a program that automatically dials your phone, connects to another computer, reads your mail, copies it back to your computer, and then disconnects. With Unix, you can start this program and let it go. While your mail is being checked you can be working on a completely different task.

Starting a Unix Session: Logging In

As we explained in Chapter 2, each Unix session begins with connecting a terminal to a host computer. If you are working on your own workstation, this happens automatically: You turn on the power, Unix starts itself, and your terminal (that is, your keyboard and display) is automatically connected.

On a dial-in system you will have to dial the phone. When the host answers the phone, its modem will communicate with your modem and establish the connection. If you are using a PC to access the host, you will run a communications program that will dial your phone and emulate a terminal.

(If you think about an old typewriter, you will remember that to type capital letters, you held down the shift key. This caused the letters on the top part of the key, the *upper* case, to print. As a matter of fact, computer keyboards still have a <Shift> key, even though when you hold it down nothing actually shifts.)

So, to state the rule precisely: Unix distinguishes between upper and lower case.

Remember this when you make up names for your files: In Unix, `document-1` and `Document-1` are two completely different names.

Stopping a Unix Session: Logging Out

When you have finished working with Unix, you stop the session by logging out. There are two ways to log out, depending on what shell you are using.

What is a shell? Well, we will go into the details later, in Chapter 5. For now, let's say that the shell is the command processor—the part of Unix that reads your commands and carries them out. (If you are a DOS user, you can think of COMMAND.COM as being like a Unix shell.)

DOS users:

A Unix shell is similar to the DOS command processor, COMMAND.COM

As we'll discuss in Chapters 5 and 6, the two most common shells are the Bourne shell and the C-shell. Here is how you can tell which shell you are using.

When the shell is ready to read a command it prompts you by displaying a special character. (We will cover this in more detail in Chapter 5.) If you are using the Bourne shell, the prompt will be the dollar sign ($). In this case you can log out by pressing <Ctrl-D>. That is, you hold down the <Ctrl> key and press the <D> key.

If you are using the C-shell, the prompt will be the percent sign (%). In this case, you can log out by entering the `logout` command. The `logout` command will issue the <Ctrl-D> signal for you.

Here are two examples. Each one starts with the shell displaying its prompt.

Logging out from within the Bourne shell, you press <Ctrl-D>:

```
$ <Ctrl-D>
```

Logging out from within the C-shell, you enter the `logout` command:

```
% logout <Return>
```

Starting and Stopping a Session: A Summary

Once your terminal connects to the host computer, Unix will display

```
login:
```

You enter your login name. Unix will then display

```
Password:
```

You enter your password. Your session will now start.

You enter one command after another, until all your work is done. Each time you press <Return> the shell (the command processor) will carry out the command.

There are two common shells that you might use. The Bourne shell will prompt you for a command by displaying

```
$
```

The C-shell will prompt you for a command by displaying

```
%
```

You start a program or use a command by entering its name. From within a program or command, you can pause in what you are doing and enter a new command. You can even start another program.

You can also start a program or command and have it carry on independently while you are working on something else.

When you are finished, you end your session by logging out. If you are using the Bourne shell, you log out by pressing <Ctrl-D>:

$ <Ctrl-D>

If you are using the C-shell, you log out by entering the `logout` command.

% logout <Return>

4

How Unix Stores and Displays Information

Introduction

One of the most mysterious things about operating systems is how they actually store and manipulate data. Although Unix works on a wide variety of computers, all Unix systems use data in pretty much the same way. In this chapter, we will lay the groundwork for more advanced work by exploring the ways in which Unix displays and stores data.

Two Ways of Displaying Data: Text and Graphics

Text:
Data in the form of separate characters.

Graphics:
Data in the form of pictures composed of small dots.

Character Terminal:
A terminal that displays only text, not graphics.

There are two ways in which Unix can display data: as *text* or as *graphics*. Text refers to separate characters, like letters and numbers. Graphics refers to pictures.

When Unix displays text, each character has a code. To display a specific character, Unix sends the appropriate code to your terminal. The terminal interprets the code and displays the appropriate symbol. We refer to such terminals as *character terminals*. The characters which Unix uses are the letters of the alphabet (a–z and A–Z), the numerals (0–9), and the special characters (@ # $ % and so on).

33

When Unix works with graphics, it draws everything—including characters—out of small dots. This means that Unix can display boxes, curves, and other pictures as well as characters.

As we mentioned in Chapter 2, graphics require a special type of terminal. Moreover, such terminals must receive a great deal more data from the host computer (since the terminal must display many, many dots).

Because of this, graphics terminals are usually connected directly to the host—a phone connection is just not fast enough. This means that if you access Unix over a telephone you will probably be using a character terminal. This also holds true if you are using a PC to emulate the terminal (even though the PC does support graphics when it runs its own programs).

DOS users:

If you are accessing a Unix system over a phone line, you will not be able to use graphics.

If you are using Unix on a workstation or a PC, the console (the built-in terminal, see Chapter 2) will consist of your computer's keyboard and display. In this case your computer can act as a graphics terminal.

However, many Unix systems use multiple terminals to access a host. An important consideration is that graphics terminals are more expensive than character terminals. For this reason, most Unix terminals are character-based.

The Unix Character Set: ASCII

ASCII (American Standard Code for Information Interchange):
A standard coding scheme used by Unix for representing a character as a pattern of 8 bits.

As we mentioned in the last section, each character has its own code. These codes are used for more than sending output to terminals. Unix uses these same codes to store text in files.

Each code requires 8 bits which is 1 byte (see below). Thus, storing 2,000 characters of textual data requires 2,000 bytes of storage space.

The code that Unix uses is an old one. It is called ASCII, which stands for "American Standard Code for Information Interchange." ASCII contains 128 different codes. These are used for lower-case letters (a–z), upper-case letters (A–Z), numerals (0–9), the `space` character (which you get by pressing the <Space> bar), and the following special characters:

```
!   "   #   $   %   &   '   (   )   *   +
,   -   .   /   :   ;   <   =   >   ?   @
[   \   ]   ^   _   `   {   |   }   ~
```

ASCII also contains codes for several important characters that do not have symbols, but which do have keys on the keyboard. Here is a list, along with corresponding keys:

`tab`   the <Tab> key
`escape`   the <Esc> key (called the <Escape> key on some terminals)
`return`   the <Return> key (called the <Enter> key on some terminals)

The entire ASCII code is shown in a table in Appendix A in the back of the book.

The Return Character

Electric typewriters have a "return" key which physically returns the carriage or the typeball to the left-hand margin. The first video terminals mimicked these typewriters in having a <Return> key, even though there was nothing that physically returned to the left margin. These were the types of terminals that were used when Unix was invented.

As computers developed, it became clear that the <Return> key usually provided an "Enter" function. Most modern computers now have an <Enter> key, although there are still several terminals that call it the <Return> key.

To Unix, however, it's all the same. Pressing the key, whatever its name, sends the **return** signal. Indeed, Unix gets even more anachronistic: Unix literature often refers to this character as a "carriage return," even though it's been years since people used Unix with a carriage that actually returned.

We will discuss this topic in detail in Chapter 9.

5

User Interfaces

Introduction

How you interact with an operating system is an important issue. It is this interaction—what you see and what you do—that gives each system its own personality.

In this chapter, we explore the various ways that have been developed to work with Unix. You will see that there is a variety: ranging from simple command-driven systems, where you enter one command after another, to sophisticated desktop managers in which you manipulate pictures of the objects you want to use.

Understanding and Appreciating User Interfaces

Interface:
Hardware or software that bridges a gap.

An *interface* is something—a program or a device—that bridges a gap. We often think of an interface as connecting two pieces of hardware. In Chapter 2, for example, we saw how a modem acts as the interface between your computer and the telephone system.

A more personal example would be your keyboard, mouse, display and printer. These devices act as an interface between you and the rest of your computer or terminal.

However, when we work with Unix we use interfaces that involve more than just the hardware. Here is why:

Interactive:
Describes a computer system that responds immediately to your commands.

Unix is called an *interactive* system because it responds immediately to your commands. Not all computer systems are interactive. For instance, the telephone company has various computers that control the switching of signals and that generate the monthly bills. Neither of these systems is interactive—they work on their own.

The important idea about interactive computer systems is that by themselves, they do nothing. They exist only as a vehicle for allowing people (users) to work with tools (programs) that have been designed by other people (programmers). Because Unix *is* interactive, there is more to working with it than what your fingers touch and what your eyes see.

If we were to make a diagram of you working with Unix, we would draw a keyboard, perhaps a mouse, a display, a printer, a connection to the host computer, and the host itself. However we must be careful not to leave out the two most important parts: your mind interacting with the Unix programs (see Figure 5.1). The only reason all this computer hardware exists at all is to allow your mind to work with the Unix tools.

User Interface:
The set of commands and responses associated with a particular program.

Your keyboard and display form the interface that bridges the gap between you and the hardware. But the important interface is the one between you and the programs. This is called the *user interface*, and it describes what Unix looks like and how it feels when you use it.

When we discuss a user interface, we are discussing how the programmers intended for you to use Unix. The user interface that you choose—and there are a variety—will greatly affect how you think as you use Unix to do your work. Let's think of this idea as a Rule for Learning Unix.

RULE	Your user interface influences how you think when you use Unix.

Types of User Interfaces

Menu:
A list of choices.

Unix has a number of user interfaces: some are character-based and some are graphical. The simplest interfaces are *menus*. A

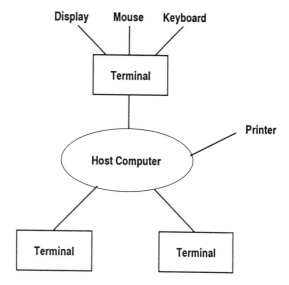

Figure 5.1 *The principal components of a Unix system.*

menu is a list of choices. You make a selection and the menu program carries it out for you.

Menu interfaces are especially popular in environments where the people using the computer have a fixed number of choices. For instance, it is common to find Unix-based menu systems in business offices. Such systems are easy to learn and easy to use, but they are limited in what they can do.

The basic Unix interfaces are the shells that we mentioned in Chapter 3. These shells are character-based. The two most common shells are the Bourne shell and the C-shell. We will discuss them in detail in Chapter 6 and throughout the book. All versions of Unix come with one or both of these shells.

When you use the shell, you enter commands which the shell will carry out. For example, if you want to see the time and date, you would enter

```
date
```

The shell would process your command and you would see something like this:

```
Sat Mar 30 12:23:03 CST 1990
```

Scrolling:
A method used to display data on a screen such that lines move up as new lines appear.

Graphical User Interface (GUI):
A user interface, based on graphics, that is especially easy to use.

Window:
A rectangular box, displayed by a graphical user interface, in which the output of a particular task is displayed.

Each line of output consists of characters written to the bottom of your screen. Every time a new line is displayed, all the other lines are moved up and the line at the top disappears. This is called *scrolling* or, more precisely, vertical scrolling, since the lines move up. Since the shells are character-based all you will see are the standard text characters.

In the past few years, terminals have been developed that have far more capabilities than simple character display and scrolling. In particular, there are graphics terminals, capable of displaying anything that can be formed out of tiny dots.

To fully exploit such terminals, you use a *graphical user interface*, often referred to as a GUI, pronounced "goo-ee."

GUI's display rectangular boxes called *windows*, in which you work. While you work, you use a mouse to move a pointer around the screen and to make selections. You may have used a GUI before. It is the type of system used on a Macintosh or on a PC running OS/2 or Microsoft Windows. GUI's do not come standard with Unix although they are readily available.

DOS users:

If you have used Microsoft Windows or the OS/2 Presentation Manager, you will find it easy to learn how to use a Unix graphical user interface.

Desktop Manager:
A sophisticated graphical interface, in which you work with objects represented by pictures.

Shell:
An interactive program, usually text-based, that reads and interprets a wide variety of commands.

Finally, there is a sophisticated type of graphical interface, built on a GUI, called a *desktop manager*. This type of interface allows you to use the mouse to work with programs and data files that are represented as pictures.

What Is a Shell?

When you use Unix you hear a great deal about "the shell"—the shell does this, the shell does that. What is a shell?

There are two answers.

First, the standard answer: a *shell* is a program whose purpose is to read and interpret your commands. Right after you log in, Unix starts a shell for you. The shell then waits for you to start entering your commands. Every person who logs in gets his or her own copy of a shell.

As you know, your work with Unix consists of entering one command after another. It is the shell that reads, interprets and processes your commands. If you want to run a program, the shell will start it for you and pause temporarily. When the program finishes, the shell will restart.

In other words, the shell is your interface to Unix. If you are a DOS user, you can think of the shell as being similar to COMMAND.COM, the DOS command processor (although the shell is much more powerful).

DOS users:
Unix shells are much more powerful and complex than the DOS command processor.

That's the standard answer as to what is a shell. With this standard answer, you usually get an explanation of where the name "shell" comes from: Think of Unix as an oyster. The hard outer surface, the shell, surrounds the insides—protecting them from the outside world. The Unix shell, being an interface, hides the Unix internals from prying eyes.

However, there is more to the shell; the shell is nothing less than a way of thinking. It is your window into the vastness of the Unix system.

Moreover, as you know, there are several different shells. (We will describe them in Chapter 6.) For the most part, they are similar, although they each have their own personality. You can use whichever one you like as long as it is available on your system. But, at all times, whenever you are typing commands, you are talking to a shell.

As you read this book and as you practice, you will gain more and more insight as to what the shell really is and what it can do for you. The shell is more powerful and much more complex than most people realize. For example, each shell has its own programming language. You can write programs without even using a standard computer language, such as C or Pascal.

The beauty of the shell is that it has depth. If you want, you can do nothing more than enter simple commands; on the other hand, you can spend hours building complex systems—and it can all be done within the shell.

Let's summarize all of this as a Rule For Learning Unix:

RULE	The shell is Unix's command processor. It has a large number of powerful features that you will come to appreciate as your experience with Unix grows.

What Happens When You Press a Key?

When you use a computer, whatever you type is displayed on the screen. For instance, when you press the <A> key an "A" appears on the screen. It seems as if your keyboard is connected directly to your display.

Looks are deceiving—it doesn't work that way.

When you press a key, the shell receives the code for the key that you pressed. For instance, when you press the <A> key, the shell receives the "A" signal. Once the shell receives this signal, it sends the code for the appropriate character to your terminal. We say that the shell *echos* the character to the screen.

Most of the time this happens so fast that it seems instantaneous. However, if you use a Unix system over a slow telephone line, you can sometimes notice a delay, especially when the system is busy. You press a key and it may take a moment for the character to be echoed.

Here is an interesting experiment we once ran. Unix has a built-in command to allow you to log in to another Unix system. As long as the two computers are connected, you can access a remote computer just as if you had dialed in directly.

We logged in to a computer in Texas via a phone line. From this computer, we logged in to a computer in Wisconsin. From Wisconsin, we logged in to a computer in California. At this point, we were working with a shell running on a computer in California. All outgoing signals had to travel from our terminal to Texas, to Wisconsin, and to California. Signals from the shell traveled on the reverse path.

Thus, whenever we pressed a key, the signal traveled through two computers and several thousand miles. The shell in California would recognize the signal and send the code to display the appropriate character. This code would first travel to Wisconsin, then to Texas, and finally to our terminal.

The point is, when you press a key a signal has to travel all the way to the shell and back before a character is echoed to the screen. During our experiment, there were times when it took a few seconds for us to see a character after pressing a key.

The Shell Prompt

Prompt:

A signal displayed by an interactive program to indicate that the program is waiting for input.

The shell signals that it is ready for you to enter a command by displaying a *prompt*. This can be anything you want. For example, you could have the shell display

```
Hello Peter, please enter a command:
```

every time it is ready for input.

This might seem sort of cute at first (especially if your name is Peter), but you would tire of it quickly. Traditionally, people use less expressive prompts, often just a single character. If you do not set your prompt, the shell will automatically use a single character: the Bourne shell will use $ (the dollar sign); the C-shell will use % (the percent sign). Actually, this is the best way to discover quickly which shell is active—simply look at the prompt.

Defaults

Default:

A choice that is made for you automatically.

Throughout our work with Unix we will encounter many situations in which you can specify something: a prompt, the name of a file, the name of a program, whatever. Much of the time, Unix will not require you to make a choice. If you don't, Unix will choose for you. Unix's choice is called a *default*.

Within Unix, this word is used in three related ways: as a noun:

If you don't set your prompt, the shell will use a single character as a default.

as an adjective:

The default shell prompt is a single character.

and as a verb:

The shell prompt defaults to a single character.

Unix, and the shell, and all the Unix commands have many defaults. Most of the time, you will use them without even knowing they are there.

Aside from the built-in Unix defaults, there are also defaults that are set by the person administering your particular Unix system (which may be you). For example, Unix has a built-in electronic mail system, and all the mail that you receive will be stored in a file until you get around to reading it. Your administrator may decide that, on your Unix system, mail should be stored in a file with a particular name.

Here is another Unix term: We describe "your system" as being the *local* system. So, we might say

On our local system, mail is kept in a file named `mailfile`.

Sometimes, the word "local" is used to indicate a location:

The use of the file name `mailfile` is local to our system.

Override:
To specify your own choice rather than accept a default.

The last term we want to explain concerning defaults is used when you decide to specify your own choice. In this case, we say that you *override* the default. For instance

In order to hide his mail from the Unix administrator, Harley decided to override the local default and choose a file name that no one else would recognize.

Graphical User Interfaces

As we mentioned earlier in this chapter, graphics terminals can support graphical user interfaces, or GUIs.

The Apple Macintosh computer has made the window-mouse-icon interface popular. (An icon is a small picture.) In the PC world, we find similar interfaces with Microsoft Windows, the OS/2 operating system, and Hewlett-Packard's New Wave.

GUIs are fashionable in the sense that people talk about them. However, most Unix users still use the traditional character-based interfaces: shells or menu systems.

GUIs do have advantages—the most important being that you can work with several windows at the same time. Within each window, you can work on a specific task. For example, you might have two windows that contain sessions with the shell, one window that holds a clock, and one window that is running a word processor. You can overlap windows, hide windows, change their size and location, and shrink them down to icons (small pictures).

Using your mouse, you can move from one window to another. Whichever window you select becomes active. Whatever you type goes into that window.

The thing about GUIs, however, is that they require special equipment. You will need a mouse with either a graphics terminal or a standalone workstation, as well as the GUI software (which often costs extra).

The important thing to appreciate is that even if you use a GUI, you still need to understand all about Unix and how to use it. You may have several windows on your screen, but all you can put in them are shell sessions or programs. In fact, you might think of a regular character-based system as being one large window.

The Various Graphical User Interfaces

Most GUIs are based on the X-Window System developed at MIT. (Here is where the name comes from: Programmers at Stanford University developed an operating system called V—the letter "V." To go with V, they developed a windowing system called W. Later, the W system was reprogrammed at MIT to work with different hardware. This new system was christened X.)

X-Window is a system for supporting GUIs. Thus, GUIs are built "on top of" X-Window. X-Window itself does come with a rudimentary GUI. However, most of the GUIs you will encounter will be based on X-Window but will have their own look and feel.

The two most important X-Window–based GUIs are Motif from the Open Software Foundation and Open Look from AT&T. One of these GUIs is available on virtually every major Unix system.

The only important Unix GUI that is not based on X-Window is Nextstep, which was developed for the Next computer. Aside from the Next computer, Nextstep is offered on a few other systems, including the IBM RISC System/6000.

Desktop Managers

The final user interface that we will mention—the desktop manager—is a special type of program that is built on a GUI. A desktop manager provides a simplified, graphical working environment in which you use your mouse to manipulate pictures of objects. You work by pointing and clicking with only a minimal amount of typing. A common example is clicking the "keys" on a picture of a calculator to perform arithmetic.

Within a desktop manager, you still have access to traditional Unix tools. For example, you can always open a new window and start a shell or run a program.

Desktop managers are not all that common because they require GUIs. Three of the more important desktop managers are X.desktop from IXI Limited, Open Windows from AT&T and Sun Microsystems, and Looking Glass from Visix Software.

X.desktop and Looking Glass are based on the Motif GUI; Open Windows is based on the Open Look GUI.

A special case is Nextstep, the user interface developed for the Next computer. Nextstep is both a GUI and a desktop manager. Moreover, it is the only major GUI that is not based on the X-Window system.

6

The Unix Shells

Introduction

Unlike most other operating systems, Unix offers several command processors, or "shells," to act as your primary interface. We will examine the most important of these shells and show you sample sessions and programs.

The Various Shells

There are a variety of shells that you might find on Unix systems. The two basic shells, as we mentioned earlier, are the Bourne shell and the C-shell. However, there are a few other shells that are based on these two.

Just about everything that we do and say in this book will hold true for all the shells. As a basis, however, we will use the Bourne shell. In a few places, we will point out differences with the C-shell.

The other shells (see below) have important advantages over the basic shells. As you get more advanced, you may want to start using one of these other shells if it is available on your system.

The Korn Shell

The Korn shell is named after its developer, David Korn, a researcher at AT&T Bell Laboratories. The Korn shell was first introduced in 1983 and released publicly in 1986.

This shell is an upward-compatible extension to the standard Bourne shell. Anything that works with the Bourne shell will work the same way with the Korn shell. In particular, what you learn in this book will work with either shell.

The Korn shell adds new features to the Bourne shell. The most important of these features are similar to those that we described above for the C-shell: a history mechanism, job control, and aliasing. However, there are differences in the way that these shells provide these facilities.

Many Unix systems routinely use the Korn shell instead of the Bourne shell. Many users have no idea they are using an extension to the standard shell until they start to use some of the advanced features.

The name of the Korn shell program is `ksh`. As with the Bourne shell, there is a restricted version of the Korn shell for setting up special user environments. The restricted Korn shell is called `rksh`.

The Bourne Again Shell

The Bourne Again shell is a product of the Free Software Foundation. As we explained in Chapter 1, this organization is a nonprofit company devoted to providing free Unix software. Their shell, `bash`, was written by Brian Fox and was first released in 1989. As the name "Bourne again" implies, `bash` extends the capabilities of the Bourne shell in a manner similar to the Korn shell.

The `tcsh` Shell

The `tcsh` is an extended version of the C-shell. The `tcsh` does not have any formal name—it is only known by the name of the actual program, which is usually pronounced "tee-see-shell." The "t" stands for "Tenex," the name of one of the operating systems used to run the old PDP-10 computers. It was on a Tenex system that the first work was done that eventually led to the `tcsh` shell.

This shell was developed over a number of years by various people from all over the country, each of whom contributed different features at different times. (Many important Unix programs were developed in the same way.)

The origin of the `tcsh` starts with work done by Ken Greer in 1975 at Carnegie Mellon University. In 1981, he added several extensions to the C-shell, based on this work. For the next several years, a few other people continued to develop enhanced shell facilities. In 1987, Paul Placeway, then of Ohio State University, took these facilities, added some important work of his own, and released the whole thing as a complete shell under the name `tcsh`. Since then, other programmers have continued to add new features.

As you might have guessed, the development and distribution of the `tcsh` is somewhat informal. However, the advanced features of the `tcsh` were developed by expert Unix people. If you are a programmer, you will probably find the `tcsh` a useful addition to your toolbox.

The `tcsh` adds a number of interesting facilities to the C-shell. Mostly these fall into two main categories: First, the `tcsh` makes it possible to recall, edit, and resubmit previously entered commands. Second, when you are typing a command, it is possible to type only part of a file name. The shell will look at the list of your files and complete the name for you. Similarly, if you type the name of a command incorrectly, the `tcsh` tries to figure out what you meant, displays it for you, and asks if that is what you really wanted.

The `tcsh` is widely available at universities but is not seen much in the business world. If it is available where you use Unix, you might want to give it a try.

Pseudo Shells

Unfortunately, there are a number of programs that are called "shells" but are not full command processors. Here are the names of three of them:

`rsh`	remote shell
`msh`	mail shell
`mush`	mail user's shell

The remote shell is used on some networks to execute commands on a remote computer. The two other programs are used to process electronic mail.

These are all important programs. It's just that they shouldn't have been called "shells." Don't be confused—especially by rsh, which has the same name as the restricted shell we described above.

A Sample Session Using the Bourne Shell

In the last few sections we have described several shells. But remember, the principal Unix shells are the Bourne shell and, to a lesser extent, the C-shell. In the next two sections, we will present sample sessions using these shells. These examples will give you an idea of what it looks like to work with Unix.

First, a short session with the Bourne shell. Take a look at the example in Figure 6.2 and then read the explanation that follows. To make it easy for you to follow the discussion below, we have numbered the lines. We have also indicated, by arrows, the lines on which we typed something. These numbers and arrows, of course, would not appear on your screen.

This session used a telephone line to connect a PC emulating a terminal to the host Unix computer. To start the session, we had our modem dial the remote system. Once we were connected, we saw the login prompt on line 1. We typed our user name (harley) and pressed the <Return> key. Unix responded by asking for our password on line 2. Notice that, for security reasons, Unix did not echo the password as we typed it.

Once our user name and password were verified, Unix displayed some general information on lines 3 and 4. This type of information will vary from system to system. However, what we see in this example is representative.

First, we saw the type of Unix we are using—Unix System V/386 Release 3.2. Next, we were reminded of the last time we logged in. This is handy if you suspect someone has been using your Unix account without your permission.

Once the login procedure was completed, Unix started our shell and we saw the shell prompt on line 5. Since we saw a $, we knew that we were using the Bourne shell. At this point, just to see what would happen, we pressed <Return> without typing

```
 1 →    login: harley
 2 →    password:
 3      UNIX System V/386 Release 3.2
 4      Login last uses: Fri Mar 30 11:57:56
 5 →    $
 6 →    $ who
 7      addie     console  Mar 30 09:28
 8      kim       tty01    Mar 30 11:55
 9      harley    tty02    Mar 30 12:18
10      murray    tty03    Mar 30 08:59
11      marilyn   tty04    Mar 30 11:58
12      randolph  tty05    Mar 30 12:09
13      melissa   tty08    Mar 30 10:23
14      hilary    tty07    Mar 30 12:14
15      mitchell  tty00    Mar 30 12:21
16      misty     tty02    Mar 29 10:33
17 →    $ mailx
18      No mail for harley
19 →    $ date
20      Fri Mar 30 12:23:03 CST 1990
21 →    $ ls
22      file1    file2    file3    file4
23 →    $
24      NO CARRIER
```

Figure 6.2   *A sample Unix session using the Bourne shell.*

a command. The shell responded as simply as possible by displaying another prompt.

At this prompt, line 6, we entered the **who** command to ask Unix to show us the names of all the users logged in to the system. As you can see, there were ten users, including us. Along with the user names, **who** displayed the name of the terminal and the time of the log in. When the **who** command finished, control returned to the shell which displayed another prompt.

At this prompt, line 17, we entered the name of the mail program, **mailx**, to check for messages. As you can see in line 18, there were no messages.

On line 19, we entered the **date** command to display the time and date, and on line 21, we used the **ls** command to list our files. In this case, we had only four files with simple names.

Finally, on line 23, we logged out by pressing <Ctrl-d>. The shell ended and Unix terminated our session. The message "NO CARRIER" means that the phone line was disconnected. This message came from our modem, not from Unix.

A Sample Session Using the C-Shell

In the last section we saw a sample Unix session using the Bourne shell. Figure 6.3 shows a similar session using the C-shell.

The biggest thing that we want you to notice is that not much is different. In fact, in this example, there are only two differences due to our using the C-shell. First, as you can see in lines 5, 10, 12, 14, and 16, the prompt is % rather than $. Second, to log out (line 16) we enter the logout command rather than pressing <Ctrl-d>.

As above, we have included line numbers and arrows that you would not normally see on your display. The arrows indicate the lines on which we typed something.

Most of what we see here is similar to the Bourne shell example in the last section. However, for this example we connected to a different Unix host. In line 4, you can see that this computer uses the Ultrix form of Unix. Ultrix is the Unix used on Digital Equipment Corporation computers.

Programming the Shell: Shell Scripts

Shell Script:
A list of commands that are to be executed, one by one, by a shell.

Interpret:
To execute a list of commands, one by one.

Script:
A list of commands that are to be executed, one by one, by a specific program.

So far, we have seen how the shell, our user interface, acts as a command processor. A second important facility that the shell provides is that it runs programs. Each shell has a built-in computer language. You can use this computer language to write a program which you store in a file. When you enter the name of the file, the shell will process your program.

In Unix terminology, such a program is called a *shell script*. Think of a movie actor following a script, line by line. As the shell executes the script, we say that it *interprets* each line. Thus, the shell is sometimes called a "command interpreter." The Unix term *script* is used to refer to any file of commands that is executed by an interpreter. Later in the book, we will see

```
 1 →     login: harley
 2 →     Password:
 3       Last login: Fri Mar 30 13:24:03 from ttyp2
 4       Ultrix Worksystem V2.1 Tue Jan 23 09:54:08 CST 1990
 5 →     % who
 6       bart      ttyp0    Mar 15 23:32
 7       bart      ttyp1    Mar 30 09:32
 8       peter     ttyp2    Mar 30 13:24
 9       kevin     ttyp3    Mar 30 09:37
10 →     % mail
11       No mail for harley
12 →     % date
13       Fri Mar 30 13:24:43 CST 1990
14 →     % ls
15       doc1      doc2     doc3     doc4
16 →     % logout
17       NO CARRIER
```

Figure 6.3 *A sample Unix session using the C-shell.*

that you can also write scripts for other Unix interpreters, such as the Unix text editing programs.

A shell script can be a simple list of commands, similar to what you might enter directly from your terminal. For example, a simple shell script might contain

```
who
mail
date
```

When you execute this script, the shell will perform these three commands.

But as we mentioned, the shell has a built-in programming language which you can use to write scripts that are full-fledged programs. If you are a DOS user, you can think of shell scripts as being similar to batch files. However, the DOS command processor, COMMAND.COM, is not nearly as powerful as the Unix shells and you will find that Unix shells scripts can be much more useful than DOS batch files.

7
The Unix Universe

Introduction

Most of us think about computer systems as consisting of machinery (hardware), programs (software), and people (users). With Unix, however, this view is too limited. After all, it is not at all difficult to find two completely different Unix systems. Somehow, even though they have different hardware, different software, and different users, the two systems are still both Unix.

How can this be?

The answer is that Unix is not really machinery, programs, and people. Of course, all computer systems need machinery, programs, and people in order to exist—but Unix itself is what happens when all this comes together.

In this chapter we discuss the real players, the inhabitants of the Unix universe.

Users and Userids

Userid (pronounced "user-eye-dee"): *A name, registered with a Unix system, that is used to identify a particular user.*

In the computer world we talk a great deal about *users*, the people who use the computers. Believe it or not, within a Unix system, there are no users. Instead, there are *userids*.

A userid, pronounced "user-eye-dee," is a user identification name. It is the name that you use when you log in. A userid can be any letters or numbers you want up to 8 characters. As a rule, most people use only lower-case letters.

Most of the time, you will choose each userid to identify the person who is using it. Common examples are names and initials. For example, for Peter Norton you might see userids like `peter`, `petern`, `pnorton`, `norton`, or `pfn`.

So, within Unix, there are no people. As far as Unix is concerned it is userids, not users, that log in to the system. For instance, electronic mail is not sent from one person to another; it is sent from one userid to another userid.

At first, this may seem like a silly distinction. However, everything in Unix is oriented toward userids, so that is really the best way to think about it. Your userid serves as your universal name within Unix.

Here is an example: In Chapter 16 we will talk about Unix files. You will see that a file is "owned" (controlled) by whoever created it. On our system Harley Hahn has created some files. However, as far as Unix is concerned, Harley Hahn does not own these files—they are owned by userid `harley`. Similarly, Peter Norton's files are owned by userid `peter`.

When you log in, Unix has no way of determining who you really are. If you tell someone your password, he will be able to log in with your userid—userids are not secret. As far as Unix is concerned this person will have all the privileges associated with your userid. For instance, anyone logged as userid `harley` could remove all of the files owned by `harley`. Be careful with your password!

Unix will let you log in from different terminals using the same userid. This can come in handy if you have two terminals, say one in your office and one at home, and you want to keep them both logged in all the time. Logging in on several terminals with the same userid is also helpful when you are experimenting with a system. You will be able to try different tests from each terminal.

Finding Out Who Is Logged In: The who Command

At any time, you can ask Unix to show you all the userids that are currently logged in by entering the who command:

```
who
```

You will see something like:

```
bart      ttyp0     Mar 15 23:32
bart      ttyp1     Mar 30 09:32
peter     ttyp2     Mar 30 13:24
kevin     ttyp3     Mar 30 09:37
```

Some Unix systems will display more information.

In this example you see each userid, the name of the terminal it is using, and the time of the login. Notice that Unix uses a 24-hour clock: "23:32" is 11:32 pm and "13:24" is 1:24 pm.

This particular example was taken from one of the sample sessions we looked at in Chapter 6. In this case, userid `bart` is logged in to two different terminals. Userids `peter` and `kevin` are each logged in to one terminal.

Make sure that you understand that the `who` command does not tell you which people are actually using the system. It may be that one person has logged in to all four terminals using three different userids. Or it may be that two different people each logged in using the userid `bart`.

Probably, someone named Bart logged in to two terminals and two people, Peter and Kevin, each logged in to one terminal. But if you need strict security on your system, be careful.

Notice that one of the terminals at which `bart` is logged in has been connected for a long time. In this case, it happens that Bart is in charge of the system and he keeps a permanently logged in terminal in his office.

On some systems, especially those connected to a network, it is important that each computer have a name. When you use such a computer the `who` command may display the name of the computer as well as the userid.

Here is an example. Notice that the ! character is used to separate the computer name from the userid.

```
asiago!harley ttyp3 Apr 6 17:17
```

In this case, the name of the computer is `asiago`. (This particular machine is in the Computer Sciences Department at the

University of Wisconsin, where many of the computers are named after types of cheese.)

In Chapter 2, we mentioned that in a network each computer is called a node. In this example, we would say that the name of the node is `asiago`.

We will describe the `who` command more formally in Chapter 12.

Who Are You? The `who am i` and `logname` Commands

At any time, you can find out the userid that is logged in to the terminal you are using by entering a variation of the `who` command:

```
who am i
```

If it makes you feel more comfortable, you can capitalize the "I":

```
who am I
```

The output of this command will look something like this:

```
harley    console    Apr  6 17:12
```

In this case, you can see the userid is `harley`, and the name of the terminal is `console`. This userid logged in at 5:12 pm on April 6. (Remember, Unix uses a 24-hour clock.)

An alternative command is `logname`. This command displays only the userid. For example, if you enter

```
logname
```

you might see

```
harley
```

We will describe the `logname` command more formally in Chapter 12.

The Superuser: Userid `root`

In a Unix system all userids are not equal. There is one userid, `root`, that has extra privileges. (In the next section, we will explain where this name comes from.)

The `root` userid is used by the person whose job it is to maintain the system. This person is called the *system manager* or *system administrator*.

When someone is logged in as `root`, we refer to the person as the *superuser*. The `root` userid allows the superuser to do just about anything he wants. He can look at and modify anybody's files, he can add or remove userids, he can install new software, he can change other userids' passwords, and so on. The superuser can also shut down the Unix system when necessary. Moreover, there are certain administrative commands that only the superuser is allowed to use.

These privileges must be used carefully. Unix makes it easy to cause damage accidentally. For example, the superuser can wipe out all the files on the entire computer with one short command.

To guard against inadvertent catastrophes, it is a good idea to use the `root` userid only when necessary. Even then, you should use it for as short a time as possible.

Here is an example: The system manager for a particular system is named Melissa. She has two userids. For system administration, she uses `root`; for regular work, she uses `melissa`, an ordinary userid with no special privileges.

Most of the time, she logs in as `melissa`. When she needs to perform an administrative task, she logs in as `root`, but as soon as the work is done she logs out.

In Chapter 13, we will learn how to use the `su` (substitute userid) command to change temporarily to superuser.

Why Is the Superuser Userid Named `root`?

In Chapter 17, we will discuss the organization of the Unix file system. We will see that files are kept in directories and that directories are organized into a hierarchy that can be described as being "tree-structured." The main directory is called the "root directory," like the root of a tree.

The superuser userid, `root`, is named after the root directory—the most important directory in the file system.

System Manager:
The person whose job it is to maintain a Unix system.

System Administrator:
Same as system manager.

Superuser:
A user who is logged in to a system using a userid that gives him special privileges.

The Superuser Prompt: #

As we mentioned, it's easy to make a mistake and cause damage when you are logged in as superuser. For this reason, it is vital that you know when you *are* the superuser. You don't want to be in the situation where you forget and cause an accident.

Of course, you can always use the who am i or logname commands, but it is better not to take chances.

To help you, the shell will display a special prompt whenever you log in as root. As we explained in Chapter 5, the usual shell prompt—unless you change it—is $ for the Bourne shell and % for the C-shell. When you log in as the superuser, the shell will use a prompt of # (the number sign). As long as you are logged in as the superuser, you will see the # prompt, regardless of which shell you are using.

Who Is the System Manager?

Some types of computer systems will run themselves once they are set up. This is particularly true of single-user systems, such as Macintosh computers or PCs running DOS or OS/2.

Unix, however is more complex. *All* Unix systems require routine system maintenance. It only makes sense that a system that serves multiple users will need more management than a single-user system.

DOS users:

Unlike DOS, Unix requires routine system maintenance. If you are using a standalone Unix system, you will be your own system manager.

Every Unix system must have a system manager, sometimes called the system administrator. If you are using a standalone system—that is, if you are the only one using your system—you will be the system manager. This means that you will occasionally have to log in using the root (superuser) userid to perform maintenance tasks. Your system will come with a manual that explains what needs to be done and how to do it. Some Unix systems have a menu-driven program to make system administration as easy as possible.

Multiuser systems have a designated system manager, usually an experienced Unix programmer. Large systems often require a full-time manager. In fact, very large systems may have a complete staff to assist the manager.

Hint

••••

DOS users:

The amount of time and effort required to manage a multiuser Unix system is comparable to what is required to manage a DOS-based local area network.

Some systems divide up the management workload among several userids. One userid may be used to register new users, another userid may be used to backup the system (copy files to tape for safekeeping), and so on.

If you are using a large system you can always send mail to the system manager when you have a question. If you are not sure what userid your system manager uses, send mail to `root`. (We will discuss the mail system in Chapter 15.)

Terminals—The `tty` Command

TTY (pronounced "tee-tee-why"):
A terminal; the name "tty" is derived from the name "teletype."

As we explained in Chapter 2, Unix uses a host computer to which terminals are connected. In Unix language, a terminal is often referred to as a *TTY* (pronounced "tee-tee-why"). The name "tty" is derived from the name "teletype."

A teletype is an old typewriter-like machine that sent and received messages. In the olden days (the 1970s), these machines were sometimes used as Unix terminals.

To this day, each terminal which is connected to a Unix system is given a name starting with "tty." For instance, in one of the examples of the `who` command earlier in this chapter, we saw that userid `harley` was logged in to terminal `ttyi5`.

If you want to find out the name of your terminal, enter the `tty` command:

```
tty
```

The output will look like this:

```
/dev/tty01
```

In this example, the name of the terminal is `tty01`. The `tty` command actually displays the name of the file—`/dev/tty01`—that contains the system interface to this terminal. This is called a "special file" and is explained in Chapter 16.

We will describe the `tty` command more formally in Chapter 12.

Processes—The `ps` Command

Process:
A program that has started to execute.

Programs are stored in files. In order for a program to do anything, it must be read from its file, loaded into memory, and started. Once it starts, the program becomes a *process*.

Make sure you understand this point: By itself a program is lifeless. It is only when a program becomes a process—that is, when it begins to execute—that anything happens.

Processid (pronounced "process-eye-dee"):
A unique identifier describing a process.

Every time Unix starts a program, it gives the resulting process a unique identification number called a *processid* (pronounced "process-eye-dee"). You use the processid whenever you need to refer to a specific process. For example, later in the book we will discuss how to use the `kill` command to stop a process that is out of control. To do so, you will have to specify the processid of the process you wish to stop.

In order to find out what processes are currently active in your session, you can enter the `ps` (process status) command:

```
ps
```

You will see something like

```
PID TTY        TIME COMMAND
 89 console   0:01 sh
551 console   0:00 ps
```

In this example, there are two processes. The processids are **89** and **551**. These processes are executing within a session connected to the console. The first process has been executing for 1 second. The execution time for the second is so small that it registers as 0 minutes and 00 seconds. The first process is executing the Bourne shell, `sh`, and the second process is executing the `ps` command.

If you use the `ps` command by itself, you will see the status of only those processes that are associated with your terminal. If you want to see the status of all the processes in the system, enter

```
ps -a
```

The "a" stands for "all." If you are using a multiuser system, you may be surprised at how many processes there actually are.

If you want to display the processes associated with a particular terminal, specify -t followed by the name of the terminal. Use the terminal name as the **ps** command would display it. For example,

```
ps -ttty01
```

will display information about the processes associated with terminal **tty01**.

We will describe the **ps** command more formally in Chapter 12.

Daemons

The most exotic inhabitants of the Unix universe are the *daemons*. A daemon is a process that executes in the background in order to be available at all times. For example, there is a mail daemon that is constantly on the lookout for messages that need to be delivered.

(When we refer to a "background" process, we are using a Unix term. It means that the process can run by itself without input from a terminal. We explain more about such processes and how to control them later in the book.)

Unix systems have all kinds of daemons. Some, like the mail daemon, are always running, waiting to serve you. Others, like the **cron** daemon, which we mention below, are usually sleeping. They wake up at intervals to see if there is any work for them.

Most daemons are programs that are started automatically as part of the system initialization. These daemons provide services of general interest. Occasionally, people will program their own daemons to provide a purely personal service.

If you want to see what system-wide daemons live in your computer, enter the following version of the **ps** (process status) command:

```
ps -t"?"
```

The `-t"?"` tells `ps` to display information about all the processes that are not associated with a terminal, that is, those processes that are associated with terminal `?`. (You need to use the double quotes because `?` is a special character.)

You may be surprised: there are often more daemons than you might anticipate, especially if you are using a large system.

The two most common daemons that you will see are

`cron`	automatically runs commands at specified times
`lpsched`	manages the line printer (line printer daemon)

("Line printer" is the Unix term for a printer.)

You may also see the following daemons that perform system maintenance functions:

`sched`	schedules memory usage
`vhand`	virtual memory handler
`bdflush`	block device flusher
`UEdaemon`	maintains the Norton Utility UnErase facility

(Virtual memory uses disk storage to simulate large amounts of regular memory. The block device flusher makes sure that certain data that is stored in memory is "flushed" out to its destination device. The UnErase daemon is a part of the Norton Utilites for System V. UnErase allows you to recover data that has been erased by accident.)

Different versions of Unix use different daemons with a variety of names. In particular, if your computer is connected to a network, you may find a gaggle of daemons whose jobs involve data transmission, file sharing, and remote program execution.

The daemons we described above are what you will see if your system is based on AT&T's System V Unix. If you are using a type of Unix based on BSD, from U.C. Berkeley, you will see different deamons. (These two types of Unix are discussed in Chapter 1). The BSD daemons are

`cron`	automatically runs commands at specified times
`lpsched`	manages the line printer (line printer daemon)
`syslog`	logs error messages to the system log file
`update`	periodically updates the file system
`pagedaemon`	helps manage system memory
`swapper`	helps manage system memory

(In Unix, memory is organized into chunks called "pages" that are "swapped" back and forth from the disk as necessary.)

By the way, note that we have spelled "daemon" with an "a." This is the traditional spelling. Some versions of Unix drop the "a" and use "demon."

The Inhabitants of the Unix Universe

To conclude this chapter, let us pause for a moment and think about the question, What is Unix? We have already discussed this topic in Chapter 1. However, in this chapter, we answered the same question in a completely different way.

Unix is a dynamic system that requires hardware, software, and users in order to exist. However, what characterizes Unix can be explained by describing the inhabitants of the Unix universe.

To capture this idea succinctly, we will now state what we call the Fundamental Equation of Unix:

Host + Terminals + Userids + Files + Processes = UNIX

(Remember: Processes are the only entities in a Unix system that actually do anything. Daemons are a type of process.)

This equation is *one* of the answers to the question, What is Unix? By now, you should realize that there are a number of answers to this question.

Let us end this chapter by summarizing the composition of the Unix universe as a Rule for Learning Unix.

The Fundamental Equation of Unix shows what objects compose a Unix system:

```
    Host
 +  Terminals
 +  Userids
 +  Files
 +  Processes
 ─────────────
    UNIX
```

8

Preparing to Use Unix

Introduction

In Part I of this book we introduced you to Unix. By now, you should have a good idea of what Unix is and how it works. In Chapter 3, we covered how to log in and log out, and how to enter commands.

With this chapter, we get down to the business of using Unix in our day-to-day work. We will start by explaining how to make sure that Unix is ready to use. Along the way, we'll pick up some useful terminology and an understanding of how Unix manages a wide variety of terminals.

Single-User and Multiuser Modes

Mode:
One of a number of specific ways in which a program can behave.

When a program can act in more than one distinct manner, we sometimes describe each type of behavior as a *mode*.

Here is an example that you will recognize if you have ever used a word processor or text editor: When you are typing in "insert mode," the characters that are already on the screen are moved to the right to make room for the new characters. When you are typing in "replace mode," the new characters that you type overwrite the existing characters. In both cases, you are using the same program; it's just that it can run in two different modes.

As you work with Unix, you use programs that work in more than one mode. The reason we mention this now is that Unix itself runs in two different modes, which you may encounter when you start up your system.

Single-User Mode:

A special mode of operation for Unix, used for system maintenance, in which only the superuser is logged in.

Multiuser Mode:

The normal mode of operation for Unix, in which all userids may log in and use the system.

System Maintenance Mode:

Same as single-user mode.

Unix can run in either *single-user mode* or *multiuser mode*. Single-user mode is used only for special system maintenance by the superuser. In fact, this mode is sometimes referred to as *system maintenance mode*. Within this mode, only the superuser is logged in. This is necessary only occasionally, when work needs to be done that precludes other people from using the system at the same time.

Most of the time, Unix operates in multiuser mode in which people are free to log in and to work as they please. This is the normal mode of operation.

Some Unix systems are used by many people and are never turned off unless something goes wrong. On these systems, Unix will constantly be in multiuser mode. If the system manager needs to enter single-user mode to do special work, he will send a message to the users requesting them to log off. Once they do, he will enter a special command to switch from multiuser mode to single-user mode. When he is finished, he will switch back to multiuser mode.

A good system manager will minimize such maintenance time. Whenever possible, he will bring down the system only during times of low use—such as late at night or on the weekend. Fortunately, most system management can be done by logging in as superuser in the regular multiuser mode. It is only infrequently that a system manager is forced to put Unix in single-user mode.

If you are using a standalone Unix system, in which only one person uses the computer at a time, you will be your own system manager. This will be the case if you are running Unix on your own PC.

With such systems, it is common to turn off the computer when you are finished working. Unlike most PC operating systems, such as DOS, with Unix you cannot just turn off the computer. You must switch to superuser and enter a special command. This allows Unix to wrap things up gracefully. The command varies from system to system, but it is often named shutdown or haltsys.

DOS users:
If you are managing your own system, remember to enter the special shutdown command before turning off the power.

When you turn your computer back on, Unix will restart automatically. With many systems, Unix will give you the chance to enter single-user mode right away. Typically, you would do this by entering the superuser password.

Unless you need to perform special maintenance, opt for the normal multiuser mode. Even though you may be the only person using the computer, it is a poor idea to actually work in single-user mode. Remember, in single-user mode you are logged in as superuser and it is easy to cause damage accidentally. Even more important, Unix does not completely set up the entire system in single-user mode. Switch to multiuser mode before you start work.

How Does Unix Handle Different Terminals?
The termcap File

When you start to work with Unix, one of the first things you need to do is make sure that Unix knows what type of terminal you are using. Before we tell you how to do that, we need to take a few moments and discuss how Unix handles different terminals.

The first terminals that were used with Unix were simple teletype-like devices. These terminals did nothing more than print all the characters they received, except for about 5 or 6 special control codes. (We will discuss these early terminals further in Chapter 9.) Today, we use many different types of video display terminals, some of them quite sophisticated.

Each terminal responds to certain codes that control how information is displayed on the screen. For example, there are code sequences to clear the screen, move the cursor, and scroll the display. Most terminals also have special keys that send signals back to the host computer.

As Unix increased in popularity, it became evident that people needed to be able to use any terminal that happened to be handy. This meant that Unix had to be able to work with a great many types of terminals. Moreover, there had to be a mechanism to allow people to use new terminals as they became available.

The problem is that each type of terminal uses its own set of codes. For instance, the code that you send to one terminal to tell it to clear the screen may be completely different from the code for another terminal. Clearly, you could not ask programmers to make sure that every Unix program understood the codes for every possible terminal. And even if programs were written that way—a Herculean task—what happens when some company comes out with a new terminal?

To solve this problem, the designers of Unix created a collection of terminal descriptions. These descriptions are kept in a system file named `termcap` ("terminal capabilities").

When you log in, Unix determines what type of terminal you are using (this is discussed below). When a program needs to interact with your terminal, it finds out the name from Unix and looks up the codes it needs in the `termcap` file.

The `termcap` file contains a description—usually referred to as an "entry"—for each type of terminal. Each entry specifies what signals are sent and received by that type of terminal. For example, within each `termcap` entry, the control signal for "clear the screen" is specified.

When a new terminal becomes available, all that is needed is for someone to write a description for it and add it to `termcap`.

A Sample `termcap` Description

Defining and using a `termcap` description is highly technical and not something most people want to get involved with. However, you might find it interesting to look at least one such description.

Figure 8.1 shows the `termcap` entry for a Digital Equipment Corporation VT-100 terminal. We might point out, by the way, that VT-100's have long since been replaced by more modern terminals. However, the VT-100 has become a de facto standard.

```
# VT-100 terminal description
d0|vt100|vt100-am|vt100:\
   :am:\
   :bl=^G:\
   :bs:\
   :cd=50\E[J:\
   :ce=3\E[K:\
   :cl=50\E[;H\E[2J:\
   :cm=5\E[%i%d;%dH:\
   :co#80:\
   :cr=^M:\
   :cs=\E[%i%d;%dr:\
   :do=^J:\
   :ho=\E[H:\
   :is=\E[1;24r\E[24;1H:\
   :k1=\EOP:\
   :k2=\EOQ:\
   :k3=\EOR:\
   :k4=\EOS:\
   :kb=^H:\
   :kd=\EOB:\
   :ke=\E[?1l\E>:\
   :kl=\EOD:\
   :kr=\EOC:\
   :ks=\E[?1h\E=:\
   :ku=\EOA:\
   :le=^H:\
   :li#24:\
   :mb=2\E[5m:\
   :md=2\E[1m:\
   :me=2\E[m:\
   :mr=2\E[7m:\
   :nd=2\E[C:\
   :nl=^J:\
   :pt:\
   :rc=\E8:\
   :rs=\E>\E[?3l\E[?4l\E[?5l\E[?7h\E[?8h:\
   :sc=\E7:\
   :se=2\E[m:\
   :so=2\E[7m:\
   :sr=5\EM:\
   :ta=^I:\
```

Figure 8.1   *A sample* `termcap` *entry, describing the VT-100 terminal.*

```
:ue=2\E[m:\
:up=2\E[A:\
:us=2\E[4m:\
:vt#3:\
:xn:
```

Figure 8.1   *continued*

As we mentioned in Chapter 2, many terminal emulation programs emulate VT-100's, so all Unix `termcap` files contain a VT-100 description.

Don't worry if you don't understand all the abbreviations—most people don't. In the unlikely event that you ever need to know what the codes mean you can look them up in a manual.

RULE

When you run into something that has many technical details, do not avoid it and do not try to memorize it all. Instead, try to make sure you understand the overall concepts. Later, if you need the details, you can look them up in the manual.

Out of interest, let's take a look at one code, `cl`, the one for clearing the screen. The part following the `cl=`, `50\E[;H\E[2J`, is what you would send to a VT-100 terminal to clear the screen. The `\E` stands for the `escape` character (a special character that we will discuss in Chapter 9).

As you can see, a terminal description is full of technical abbreviations. It is not important to understand what each abbreviation means, but we will make a few general remarks.

1. Lines that start with # (like the first line) are comments and are not counted as part of the actual description.

2. The beginning of a `termcap` description lists several names by which the terminal might be known. The first is a two-letter abbreviation that is used only with older Unix systems. The second is the usual name of the terminal. This may be followed by several alternate names. The last is a full descriptive name.

3. A `termcap` description is actually one long string of characters. In fact, it must be no longer than 1,024 characters. Although this example looks like 47 separate lines, it is really one long line. The backslash characters at the end of all but the final line tell Unix that the next line is really just a continuation.

A Newer Method of Describing Terminals: The `terminfo` Files

The `termcap` system has some shortcomings: the entries are all stored in one big file, they take up a fair amount of space, and each entry is limited in size. To overcome these problems, a new system, `terminfo`, was devised for AT&T's System V version of Unix. We won't go into the details here. Suffice to say that, for the most part, `terminfo` entries look like `termcap` entries. However, `terminfo` has several advantages.

First, while all the `termcap` entries are stored in one large file, `terminfo` entries are categorized alphabetically and stored in a series of directories. (We will discuss directories in Chapter 13.) Each terminal description is stored in its own file. This makes it faster for a program to find and access a particular description.

Second, `terminfo` entries can be longer than 1,024 characters. This is important for some especially complex terminals.

Third, `terminfo` entries are stored in a special compressed format that takes up less space and is faster for programs to access. Unfortunately, this means that you can't browse through the `terminfo` entries the way you can with the `termcap` entries.

Although there is no need to be a `termcap` and `terminfo` expert, it's good to appreciate how it all works. From time to time, you may have trouble getting Unix to work with a particular terminal. At such times, you will find it important to understand what is happening.

To make life easier for programmers, there is a library of programs that can be used to access the `terminfo` or `termcap` files. This library is called `curses`, because a great part of controlling a terminal involves manipulating the cursor.

The beauty of this system is that a program does not need to know how to work with all types of terminals. Instead, the programmer uses the `curses` library to build his program. As the program executes, it accesses the appropriate `terminfo` or `termcap` description to make sure that the correct codes get sent to the terminal.

How Does Unix Know What Terminal You Are Using?

Regardless of whether your system uses `termcap` or `terminfo`, most of the work goes on automatically, behind the scenes. However, this can only happen if Unix knows what type of terminal you are using. But how does Unix know?

There are two answers: First, when you log in Unix guesses which type of terminal you are using. Second, if you are not sure that Unix has made the right choice, you can specify your terminal type directly.

Port:

A connecting point at which data flows in or out of a computer.

In Chapter 2, we explained how terminals are connected to a host computer. Each terminal attaches to the host through what is called a *port*. Think of a port as being the place where data flows in and out of the host, much as an airport is the place where airplanes fly in and out of a city.

Before anyone can log in, the system manager must register each port. This involves specifying items such as how fast the port will send and receive data. One of the items that must be specified is the type of terminal that will attach to the port.

Environment:

An area of memory in which Unix and other programs can store data common to all processes executing within a session.

When you log in, Unix can make a pretty good guess at what type of terminal you are using by checking the information associated with your port. Unix then stores your terminal type in a special area of memory called the *environment*.

The Environment

Each userid that logs in has its own environment. This is an area of memory where Unix and other programs can store data that needs to be accessible to all the userid's processes. The information in the environment is stored as strings of characters of the form

```
name=value
```

Variable:

A named quantity whose value is stored in the environment.

"name" is a descriptive name and is called a *variable*. "value" represents the contents of the variable.

Here is an example:

```
TERM=vt100
```

In this case, the variable TERM has the value vt100.

Whenever you log in, Unix looks at the information that describes your port and sets the value of TERM to your terminal type.

Global Variable:
A variable that is accessible to all the processes executing within a session.

When a variable, such as TERM, is accessible to all the processes executing within a session, it is called a *global variable*. The convention is for global variables to use names that are in upper-case letters only, to help them stand out. This is one of the few places in Unix where lower-case letters are not used in a name.

All processes have access to the TERM variable at all times. When a program needs to determine what type of terminal you are using, all it has to do is check this variable.

Checking Your Terminal Type

Some people use a terminal that is connected directly to the host computer. In this case, the terminal is always attached to the same port and the terminal type is set permanently. This will be the case if you are using a standalone workstation. Your terminal will always be the console and its terminal type will be built-in.

However, if you are using a system where different terminals can attach to the same port, you cannot be sure that Unix has set the TERM variable correctly. This is especially important if you connect to the host computer using a phone line. There is no way to know in advance what type of terminal each person will be using. The system manager makes the best guess he can when he sets up the port.

If your terminal type is incorrect, things will probably be okay when you are entering simple commands. But as soon as you use a program that manipulates the display screen—such as the vi editor that we discuss later in this book—you will have trouble. In fact, the most common cause of terminal problems is having the TERM variable set incorrectly.

In many cases then, you will want to specify your terminal type directly. This is actually quite easy—all you have to do is set the **TERM** variable.

First off, you may want to display the value of **TERM** just to check it out. How you do this depends on what shell you are using. With the Bourne shell (the shell that displays the $ prompt), enter

```
echo $TERM
```

You will see whatever terminal name **TERM** is currently set to, for example,

```
vt100
```

If you want to see the settings of all your global variables, enter

```
set
```

If you are using the C-shell (the shell that displays the % prompt), you can see the value of the TERM variable by entering the same **echo** command:

```
echo $TERM
```

To see all your global variables, enter the **env** (environment) command:

```
env
```

Some versions of the C-shell do not have an **env** command. Instead, you would use **printenv** or **setenv**.

Specifying Your Terminal Type

As we mentioned above, to specify your terminal type all you need to do is set the **TERM** variable. If you are using the Bourne shell, you need to use two commands:

```
set TERM terminal-name
export TERM
```

Export:
To make available the value of a variable to all subsequent processes.

The first command, `set`, defines the value of TERM; the second command, `export`, tells the shell to make this value accessible to all subsequent processes. This is called *exporting* the value of the variable.

Here is an example of how to use these two commands to specify a VT100 terminal:

```
set TERM vt100
export TERM
```

If you want, the shell allows you to enter more than one command on a line. Just separate each command by a semicolon:

```
set TERM vt100; export TERM
```

If you are using the C-shell, you need only one command:

```
setenv TERM terminal-name
```

The `setenv` command both sets and exports a variable. Here is an example that specifies a VT100 terminal:

```
setenv TERM vt100
```

Specifying Your Terminal Type Automatically

As you might imagine, it is inconvenient to have to specify your terminal type each time you log in. As a matter of fact, you will find that it is handy to have the shell execute a whole list of commands each time you start work. These commands can set up your working environment to suit your preferences.

For this reason, there is an initialization file that the shell will execute for you each time you log in. With the Bourne shell, the file is called `.profile`; with the C-shell, the file is called `.login`.

Notice that these names begin with a . (period). The . is part of the name. The reason is that when you list the names of your files, names that begin with a . are not displayed unless you ask for them explicitly. We will discuss this in Chapter 21.

The . is pronounced "dot." Thus, a Unix person might talk about your "dot-profile" or your "dot-login" file.

Whatever commands you place in your .profile or .login file will be executed by the shell each time you log in. When your userid was added to the system, Unix automatically created a .profile or .login file for you. (Some systems create both files, in case you want to use either shell.)

If you are a DOS user you can think of these files as corresponding to your AUTOEXEC.BAT file.

DOS users:

The .profile file (Bourne shell) and the .login file (C-shell) perform the same types of initialization functions as the AUTOEXEC.BAT file.

All you need to do is add the terminal specification commands to the appropriate file. For example, if you use the Bourne shell and you put the commands

```
set TERM vt100; export TERM
```

in your .profile or .login file, your terminal type will be set to vt100 every time you log in.

However, we have a problem here. How do you add lines to a file? In order to do so you will need to use an editor program.

The editor that comes with all Unix systems is called vi (pronounced "vee-eye"). But vi is not simple. In fact, we will spend most of Part IV of this book discussing vi. Until then, the best advice we can give you is to ask someone else to add the commands to your initialization file for you; either that or type the commands each time you log in. Sorry.

9

Using the Keyboard

Introduction

Let's review where we are at this point in our work with Unix: We have made sure that our system is in multiuser mode (Chapter 8); we have logged in (Chapter 3); and we have specified our terminal type by making sure the value of the global variable TERM is set correctly (Chapter 8).

Are we ready to start work? Almost. We just need to make sure that the keys we use will act the way we want. In a moment we will do just that by using the stty command. But first, we need to take a tour of the Unix keyboard.

To start, it would be helpful to have an explanation of how your keyboard works with Unix, that is, how each one of the keys on *your* keyboard is used. Unfortunately, we can't give you such an explanation. There are all kinds of terminals and all kinds of different keyboard designs.

What we *can* do is explain how Unix works with keyboards in general. Then, we will describe the various keys and how you will use them. Finally, we will show you how to use the stty command to see how the keys are used with your Unix system, and how to change them to suit your preference.

The Ancestors of Unix Terminals: Teletypes

The best way to understand how Unix uses the keyboard is to put yourself in the place of the early Unix developers. When they first developed Unix, the programmers used terminals that were patterned after teletype machines.

Teletype:

An electro-mechanical device that was used to send messages from one location to another.

The *teletype* was an electromechanical device that was used to send messages from one location to another. You could type in a message which would be sent over a wire to another teletype. At the other end, your message would print on paper. The only keys that printed were the letters of the alphabet, numerals, and standard punctuation. There was also a space bar. But there were no function keys, backspace keys, or any of the other ancillary keys that we find on modern terminals and computers.

However, there was a Control key. By holding down <Control> and pressing another key you could send a special signal. These signals were used to control the operation of the system. For example, Control-G rang the bell. If you sent a Control-G at the end of the message the bell would alert the operator at the other end that the message was finished.

Another important signal was Control-M. This signal, called "carriage return," caused the receiving teletype to return its printing element to the beginning of a new line. A companion signal, Control-J or "line feed," caused the teletype to move the paper up one line. Thus, each line of text might end with a Control-M, Control-J—carriage return, line feed. This would position the paper just right to print the next line.

There were a number of other control signals. In fact, all the alphabetic keys could be used with the Control key—from Control-A to Control-Z—and they all had their own functions. Most of these functions are not important to us now. The only two other ones we would like to mention are Control-H and Control-I.

Control-H sent the "backspace" signal. This moved the printing element one space to the left. This could be handy for printing one character on top of the other. Control-I sent the "tab" signal. Using tabs to move across the paper was often faster than sending a series of spaces.

Why "Print" Means "Display"

Print:
To display data on the screen; less often in Unix, to print data on paper.

The first Unix terminals resembled teletypes. Their keyboards were similar and they printed on paper. Because of this, it only made sense to talk about printing output. Unix is fraught with tradition and, to this day, the word *print* is still used—only now it is a synonym for "display."

For example, in the section on checking your terminal type, we saw that for some versions of the C-shell, the command `printenv` *displays* information about the environment.

A more common example is the `pwd` command that we will meet in Chapter 18. This command *displays* the name of your working directory even though the name `pwd` stands for "*print* working directory." Unix is full of examples like this.

Line Printer:
The Unix term for a regular printer that prints data on paper.

When Unix refers to an actual printer, it is often called a *line printer*. (This is the type of printer that was used by the early Unix developers.) For example, the command to print a file is `lpr`.

The Special Codes

The design of the early terminals placed important limitations on the way that Unix could use the keyboard. Like the older teletypes, these terminals had only the standard letters and numbers, the space bar, the punctuation characters, and a <Control> key. There was also a <Shift> key to type the upper-case letters and some of the punctuation. To this day, these are still the only keys you need to use Unix.

As Unix developed, the characteristics of these early terminals influenced how the keyboard was controlled. The Unix programmers decided to adopt all of the standard and control keys and define a number of special ones. The special keys were defined as sending certain codes. A particular terminal could send these codes using whatever key combination made the best use of its keyboard.

Here are the most important of the special codes:

```
eof        quit
erase      return
esc        space
intr       start
kill       stop
lnext      tab
newline    werase
```

At first, the list seems discouragingly long. "My goodness," we hear you saying, "do I really have to memorize what all these codes are?"

Well . . . yes.

But it's not as bad as it looks. We will divide the list into groups and you will see that it all makes sense.

RULE	Take some time and learn about the Unix special codes:

`eof`, `erase`, `esc`, `intr`, `kill`, `lnext`, `newline`, `quit`, `return`, `space`, `start`, `stop`, `tab`, `werase` |

Codes That Represent Characters

The codes that represent characters are

`eof`, `esc`, `newline`, `return`, `space`, `tab`

`eof`, "end of file," is the code that indicates the end of a file. `eof` is the same as Control-D. When a program reads data from the terminal, you press Control-D to tell the program that there is no more input. We discuss this code in more detail below.

`esc` is a general-purpose "escape character." We will discuss this in detail later in the chapter. You generate the `esc` code by pressing the <Esc> key.

`newline` is the same as Control-J, the "line feed" that was used with teletypes. Within a file of text, a `newline` is used to mark the end of each line. When you create a file using an editing program, it will put a `newline` at the end of each line for you.

`return` is the same as Control-M, the "carriage return" that was used with teletypes. You generate the `return` code by pressing the <Return> key. On some terminals, it is named <Ret> or <Enter>. When you read Unix books and manuals, you will sometimes see the `return` code referred to as <CR> or <cr>.

Unix handles the `return` and `newline` codes with great care. We discuss these codes in detail below.

`space` is the character that is generated when you press the <Space> bar. It is important that you appreciate that, although you can't see a `space`, it is a real character. Occasionally, you may read some instructions in which the presence of a `space` is crucial. This may be indicated by showing the **space** characters explicitly,<Space>like<Space>this.

tab is the same as Control-I, the "tab" character that was used with teletypes. You generate this character by pressing the <Tab> key. By default, Unix assumes that there is a tab set at every 8th position. If your terminal has changeable tabs, you can set them to whatever you want. However, you would have to describe the tab settings to Unix by modifying the description of your terminal in the **termcap** or **terminfo** file. Most people don't bother.

Codes to Help You Type

The codes that help you type are

erase, kill, lnext, werase

erase is the character that you use to indicate that the last character you typed was a mistake. With the original early terminals that printed, the **erase** character was **#** (the pound sign).

Whenever you make a typing mistake, you can correct it by typing the **erase** character. For example, say that you make a mistake entering the **date** command (to display the time and date). You might enter

```
daq#te
```

The **#** tells the shell to ignore the erroneous q. If you type more than one bad character, you can enter more than one **erase**:

```
daqqq###te
```

Or even,

```
daqqq###twwwww#####e
```

With modern display terminals, **erase** is usually set to the <Backspace> key. <Backspace> is the same as Control-H, as with a teletype. Either key will do.

Using the <Backspace> key makes more sense than using **#**. When you press <Backspace> it will move the cursor one position to the left and actually erase the previous character.

Remember, # was used with printing terminals that could not erase characters. If you had typed <Backspace> to move the printing element to the left, the new characters would be obscured by what was already there.

With some Unix systems, `erase` is still set to #. If this is true with your system, you can change `erase` to <Backspace> by using the `stty` command which we discuss later in this chapter.

`kill` is used to indicate that you want to cancel a command completely. On an old terminal that printed, `kill` was the @ (at sign). If you had corrected so many mistakes with # that it was hard to read the line, you could cancel the whole thing with @:

```
daq#sw##hste####@
date
```

In this case, we made several mistakes trying to enter the `date` command. We pressed @ and then entered the command correctly on a fresh line.

On a printing terminal, it is important that `kill` be a printable character so that you can be sure which lines were canceled. On modern video display terminals, `kill` is usually set to Control-X or Control-U. This means that you don't have to give up @ as a legitimate character.

Even today, `kill` is still an important character, especially if you connect to a Unix system over the phone. From time to time, you will be typing a command when some electrical noise will generate a bunch of spurious characters. When this happens, simply press the `kill` key and retype the line.

From time to time, you will want to enter a control character as a legitimate character. For example, you might want to actually enter a Control-M. However, if you do, Unix will interpret it as a `return`, just as if you had pressed the <Return> key. The `lnext` code tells Unix that the next character is to be treated literally and not as a special code.

On most systems, you press Control-V to get an `lnext` code. So, if you want to type an actual Control-M, you would press Control-V Control-M. If you want to type an actual Control-V, just use Control-V Control-V.

The last code that you use for typing is `werase`, which you generate by pressing Control-W. This code erases the last word that you typed. This is helpful if you want to retype just one word or two words. In such cases, it is faster to use Control-W than `erase`, which erases only one character at a time, or `kill`, which cancels the entire line.

Some systems do not support the `werase` code. To check your system, use the `stty` command, explained later in this chapter.

RULE Get in the habit of using all three typing codes

`erase`	<Backspace>
`kill`	Control-X or Control-U
`werase`	Control-W

instead of relying only on <Backspace>.

Codes to Help You Control Programs

The codes that help you control programs are

`intr, quit`

The `intr` code is used to cancel programs. For example, say that you enter a command that is taking much longer than you expected. You may have made a mistake and entered something that went astray.

For whatever reason, you can use `intr` to stop the program. The name "intr" stands for "interrupt." On some systems, you generate `intr` by pressing Control-C (think of "cancel"). On other systems, you press the <Delete> key (also an appropriate choice). In any case, if you don't like your setting you can change it with the `stty` command. Both the <Delete> key and the `stty` command are explained later in the chapter.

Be sure that you do not confuse `intr` with `kill`. The `kill` code has nothing to do with controlling programs—it simply cancels the line you are currently typing.

RULE Do not confuse the `intr` code with the `kill` code.

`intr`	(interrupt) stops a program that is executing.
`kill`	cancels the line you are currently typing.

Like `intr`, the `quit` code stops the current program. However, after the program stops, `quit` generates a memory dump. This is a representation of the contents of the program's memory at the time the program stopped.

As you might imagine, a memory dump is useful in certain cases but only for advanced programmers trying to solve particularly tricky problems. It is unlikely that you will ever need to use `quit`.

If you do use `quit`, perhaps by accident, Unix will save the memory dump in a file called `core` (an old term for computer memory). If you find a `core` file you can safely erase it.

The key that you press for `quit` varies. On some systems you press Control-\ (backslash); on other systems, Control-| (vertical bar). To be sure, you can have the `stty` command display all your code settings.

Codes to Help You Display Output

The codes that help you display output are

`start, stop`

From time to time, you will find that Unix is displaying text faster than you can read it. As lines are added to the bottom of the screen, the lines on the top scroll out of sight before you can read them.

There are programs, which we will learn about in Chapter 23, that can display data, one screenful at a time. But for convenience, it is helpful to be able to make the screen display pause whenever you want.

The `stop` code does just that. To generate the `stop` code you press Control-S. Although it is convenient to remember that the "S" stands for "stop," it is more correct to think of it as a "pause output" key.

Be aware that pressing Control-S does not stop the program that is executing. The program will keep going and will still generate output. But Unix will make the screen display pause and will store the output so that none of it will be lost.

To restart the screen display, press Control-Q to generate the `start` code. If you have trouble remembering, think of "S" for "stop" and "Q" for "Qontinue."

If you are a DOS user, you can think of stop as working like the <Pause> key. (On older PC keyboards this is Control-NumLock.) The difference is that with DOS you press any key to restart. With Unix you must press Control-Q.

If you are using a PC to emulate a terminal you might think that it would be convenient to change the stop key to be the <Pause> key. Unfortunately, you can't. The PC <Pause> key makes the DOS screen display pause. That is, it will stop whatever your emulation program is displaying, but it will not send a signal to Unix.

DOS users:

If you are using a PC to emulate a terminal, the <Pause> key on your PC is always handled by DOS.

<Pause> cannot send a signal to Unix.

How Unix Uses return and newline

When you type at the terminal, Unix actually treats the characters as data being read from a file. In other words, the keyboard is considered to be a source of data, just as a file can be a source of data.

Most programs that read data from a file are just as happy to read from the keyboard. That is, you can type in the data as the command executes. Conversely, any command that expects you to type data from the keyboard can also read its data from a prepared file. Obviously, these features allow a great deal of flexibility. This whole topic, redirecting input from one source to another, is important, and we will discuss it later in the book.

The important thing here is that input from the keyboard has to look the same as data from a file. This means that each line that you type has to end with a newline. But how can you do this? You want the Control-J character, but there is no "line feed" key on a terminal. Of course, you could always press Control-J every time you finished typing a line, but this would be a great deal of trouble.

Instead, Unix lets you end a line by pressing the <Return> key. But, as we mentioned above, this sends the return code, not the newline code. So, whenever you send a return, Unix automatically changes it to a newline for you.

In other words, whenever you press <Return>, which is the same as Control-M, Unix changes it to a Control-J. This means that, if you want, you can enter a command by pressing <Return>, Control-M, or Control-J.

Knowing this can come in handy. On occasion, perhaps because of noise on a communication line, a terminal may start acting strangely. Sometimes the <Return> key will not function properly. In such cases, you can enter a command by pressing Control-J. This almost always works. It would do no good to press Control-M—this would be no different from <Return>.

A Unix trick: Try betting someone that you can enter any command they name without touching the <Return> key. Use Control-M. If they complain and say that Control-M is the same as <Return>, offer to avoid either key if they double the bet. Then use Control-J and clean up.

When data is displayed on your terminal, Unix must make sure that at the end of each line the cursor is moved to the beginning of the next line. Now we know that each line of data ends with a `newline`. But the `newline` is really a "line feed"—just like on the teletype. All a `newline` will do is move the cursor down one line.

The `return` character, on the other hand, is really a "carriage return"—again, just like a teletype. A `return` character will send the cursor to the beginning of the *current* line. What is needed is a `return` followed by a `newline`.

So, whenever Unix displays text, it converts each `newline` (end of line character) to a `return` followed by a `newline`. In other words, at the end of each line, Unix issues a "carriage return, line feed." This sends the cursor to the start of the next line.

To summarize, when you press <Return>, Unix converts the `return` to a `newline`. When Unix displays text, it changes the `newline` at the end of each line to a `return` followed by a `newline`.

The Unix Keyboard

As you know, Unix uses the standard keys that are found on most terminals. Some terminals have extra keys, for example, function keys (<F1>, <F2>...) and cursor-control keys (the ones with arrows). In general, Unix does not recognize these keys per se. However, some versions of Unix are designed to run on specific equipment and may use some of these extra keys. For example, PC-based Unix systems sometimes use the function keys that are a part of all PC keyboards.

Nevertheless, to use Unix, all you need are the upper- and lower-case letters, the numerals, the space bar, punctuation, and the Control key.

As a reference, we have summarized the standard Unix keys in Figure 9.1. In the following sections we will discuss the rest of what you need to know about using your keyboard. In particular, we will explain why Figure 9.1 shows the keys in a certain order and why the control characters are written using a ^ (circumflex).

The Order of the Unix Keys in the ASCII Code

In Chapter 3, we explained how Unix uses the ASCII code to represent characters. When Unix sorts data, it uses the order of the characters as they are defined by ASCII.

In Figure 9.1, we have shown all the characters in the order that they appear in the ASCII code. So, for example, the left square bracket, [, comes after the upper-case letter z, and before the backslash, \.

For your convenience, we have included a full summary of the ASCII code in Appendix A.

Names and Nicknames

As you can see from Figure 9.1, some of the characters have more than one name. Actually, there are literally hundreds of different names used for Unix characters. We have listed only the most common names. In each case, we have shown the most important name first.

There are just three names that we want to discuss specifically.

First, you will notice that the exclamation mark, !, is also called "bang." For certain commands or names, you will use the exclamation mark. It is when you read such names out loud that you say "bang."

```
(The Control Characters)
^A ^B ^C ^D ^E ^F ^G ^H ^I ^J ^K ^L ^M
^N ^O ^P ^Q ^R ^S ^T ^U ^V ^W ^X ^Y ^Z

(Escape)
^[ escape, esc (press the <Esc> key)

(Punctuation)
space (press the <space> bar)
! exclamation mark, bang
" double quote, quote, quotation mark
# pound sign, crosshatch
$ dollar sign
% percent sign
& ampersand
' quote, single quote, apostrophe
( left parenthesis
) right parenthesis
* asterisk, star
+ plus sign
, comma
- hyphen, minus, minus sign
. period, dot
/ slash, forward slash

(The Numbers)
0 1 2 3 4 5 6 7 8 9

(More Punctuation)
: colon
; semicolon
< less-than sign, left angled bracket
= equals sign, equal, equals
> greater-than sign, right angled bracket
? question mark
@ at sign

(The Upper-Case Letters)
A B C D E F G H I J K L M N O P Q R S T U V W X Y Z
```

Figure 9.1   *The keys on the standard Unix keyboard.*

```
(More Punctuation)
[ left square bracket
\ backslash
] right square bracket
^ circumflex, caret
_ underscore, underline
` backquote, grave accent
```

```
(The Lower-Case Letters)
a b c d e f g h i j k l m n o p q r s t u v w x y z
```

```
(More Punctuation)
{ left brace bracket, left curly bracket
| vertical bar, vertical line
} right brace bracket, right curly bracket
~ tilde
```

```
(Delete)
^? del (press the <Delete> or <Del> key)
```

Figure 9.1   *continued*

Here is an example. One type of electronic mail address looks like this:

```
uunet!beans!addie
```

If someone asked over the phone for this address, you would say

```
"you-you-net bang beans bang addie"
```

The name "bang" is thought to have originated with people who used keypunch machines to prepare computer cards. On some of these machines, punching the exclamation mark made a loud noise. However, the term "bang" is also used in the American publishing and typesetting industry, so the keypunch explanation may not be true.

The other character that we want to mention, just for interest, is the ampersand, &. In Scandinavia, this character is sometimes referred to as a "Donald Duck." This is because the Danish name for Donald Duck is "Anders And," which sounds like "ampersand."

The Control Keys

As we explained earlier in this chapter, modern terminals trace their ancestry to the old teletype machines. The teletypes had a Control key that was used to send certain control codes.

To this day, virtually all keyboards still have a Control key. It may be <Ctrl>, it may be <Control>, there may even be two of them—but the idea is still the same: by holding it down and pressing another key, you can generate a special signal.

Unix recognizes Control-A through Control-Z as well as a few other combinations. Only a handful of these have standard uses, as we explained earlier.

When we wish to refer to a Control key we have several choices. For instance, you may see Control-C written as <Ctrl-C>, <Control-C>, <Ctrl-c>, or <Control-c>. However, Unix has its own abbreviation, the circumflex, ^, which is used to stand for "Control." So, Control-C would be written ^C.

This is the convention that we will use within this book, and this is what you will see in most Unix documentation. Moreover, when Unix people communicate, especially by electronic mail, using ^ to stand for "Control" makes things much easier. This is why, in Figure 9.1, we have written the control keys as ^A through ^Z.

We should also mention that you do not press <Shift> with these keys. Thus, there is no difference between Control-C and Control-c. But when we write these characters, it is easier to read if we use upper-case letters: compare ^L to ^l.

It is important to understand that when you see something like ^C it is really one character, even though it is written with two symbols. There are times when you will need to use the circumflex on its own and it really is a separate symbol. However, these cases will be clear by context.

The Quote Characters

Notice that Figure 9.1 shows three different quote characters:

the double quote: "
the quote: '
the backquote: `

Take a moment and find these three keys on your keyboard:

The double quote you will recognize with no trouble.
The quote (or single quote) is the same as the apostrophe; on your keyboard, it may look like a single vertical stroke.
The back quote looks like a backward apostrophe.

   Unix is very particular. There are uses for all three of these quotes, and you must take care to type the correct ones. Here is a hint: Sometimes the quote characters are used as single characters, but most of the time they are used in pairs to enclose other characters. When two quotes are used as a pair, they are always the same two quote characters,

```
"like this"

`or like this`

'or like this'
```

You will never use two different quote characters to enclose other characters. Although a backquote on the left paired with a quote on the right can look nice,

```
`it would be wrong'
```

The End of File Character: Control-D

As we mentioned earlier, you produce the end of file character—eof—by pressing ^D. When a program reads data from the keyboard, Unix handles the data as if it were coming from a regular file. With a regular file, Unix knows how much data there is and can signal the program when the end of the file is reached. However, when you type from the keyboard, the data is being created one character at a time. This means that it is up to you to let Unix know when you are finished. You do this by pressing ^D to enter the eof character.

Here is an example. The command

```
cat >filename
```

creates a file named "filename," and copies whatever you type at the keyboard to this file. Since you are creating an entire file, you must end it with the eof character. To do this, you press ^D at the end of the file.

For instance, say that you want to create a short, three-line file named "example." Here is the command you would type, followed by the lines of data you would enter:

```
cat >example<Return>
this is line 1<Return>
this is line 2<Return>
this is line 3<Return>
^D
```

As you can see, it is not necessary to press <Return> after the eof character. Remember that <Return> sends a return, which Unix will change to a newline. There is no need for a newline after an eof character.

Using Control-D Will End Your Work Session

In Chapter 3, we explained that Bourne shell users log out by pressing ^D at the shell prompt:

```
$ ^D
(the shell logs you out...)
```

Now you can understand why: The shell is just a program. It reads what you type and responds to your requests. However, Unix treats your keyboard input as if it is coming from a file. This means that to tell the shell that there is no more input, you press ^D to send the end of file character, eof. Once the shell realizes that there is no more output from the "file" (the keyboard), it does the logical thing and ends the work session.

This is a general convention that you should remember: Most programs that prompt you for input will allow you to quit by pressing ^D.

RULE
———

With programs that prompt you for input, you can quit by pressing ^D at the prompt. This sends the program an eof (end of file) code.

Since the shell reads and interprets commands until it sees an eof character, we can direct the shell to read those commands from a regular file. This is an important service that we refer to as "redirecting standard input." We will cover this topic later in the book.

Now, what about C-shell users? In Chapter 3, we said that if you use the C-shell you log out by entering the logout command.

Actually, the C-shell reads from the keyboard just like the Bourne shell. However, the designers of the C-shell realized that logging out with eof could be a problem. It is all too easy to press ^D by accident.

For example, say you are using a program that requires an eof. It wouldn't be hard at all to press ^D once too often and find yourself logged out. This can be a nuisance, especially if you have to dial the phone to reestablish a connection.

To protect you, the C-shell lets you enter the command

```
set ignoreeof
```

This tells the shell to ignore the eof code—in other words, not to log you out if you press ^D. Rather, you must end the session explicitly by entering the logout command:

```
% logout
(the shell logs you out...)
```

It is a good idea to put the set ignoreeof command in your .login file. This way, the command will be executed automatically each time you log in. With most Unix systems, new users are given a `.login` file that already has this command in it. Thus, it is safe to tell C-shell users that they must use `logout` to log out.

If for some reason you would like to cancel this feature, simply enter the command:

```
unset ignoreeof
```

You can now log out with `^D`.

If you are a Bourne shell user there is no built-in protection. You must take care not to press `^D` too many times. (Perhaps this is the origin of the saying, "Bourne shell users do it carefully.")

The `escape` Character

Take a look at Figure 9.1. Notice the character that comes after `^z`. This character is referred to as `escape`. You produce it by pressing the <Esc> key. On some keyboards the full word is spelled out: <Escape>. This character, `escape`, is the same as `^ [`, Control-Left Square Bracket. If you want, you can press `^ [` instead of the <Esc> key.

Most of the time, you will press <Esc> as a command to a program—say, to change from one menu to another—and you will not actually see the character. However, there will be times when Unix needs to display an `escape`. In such cases, you will probably see `^ [`.

But what exactly is an `escape`? To answer that question we first need to explain where the name comes from.

You will remember from Chapter 8 that some programs can act in more than one distinct manner—each of which is called a mode. For example, the Unix `vi` editor (which we explain later in the book) can either be in command mode or insert mode. In command mode, the characters you type are interpreted as commands; in insert mode the characters are inserted into the file you are editing. Clearly, you need some way to tell the program what your intentions are. In other words, you need some way to specify what mode you want.

Escape Character:
A character that signals a program to change from one mode to another.

An *escape character* is a character that signals a program to change from one mode to another. With `vi`, you press <Esc> to change from insert mode to command mode. When you press <Esc>, you generate an `escape` code that acts as an escape character.

Here is another example. Earlier in this chapter, we explained how you could use the `lnext` control code (usually `^v`) to specify that the next character is to be taken literally. For example, to type `^H` as an actual character, not as a `backspace`, you would type `^v^H` (Control-V, Control-H). When used in this way, `^v` acts as an escape character.

The character that is most often used as an escape character is `escape`, which is where the name comes from.

Sometimes, a program will use `escape` to allow you to cancel what you are doing or to change back to a previous condition. For example, if you are faced with a menu of choices, none of which are appropriate, you might be able to press <Esc> to change back to the previous menu. In this case, we say that you "escape" to the previous menu.

If you are DOS user, you are probably used to using the <Esc>. In Unix, the <Esc> key is employed much less often. Some commercial programs do use it, but for the most part, Unix ignores it. In fact, it is possible that the only time you will press <Esc> is from within `vi`, to change from insert mode to command mode.

DOS users:

In DOS, you use the <Esc> key frequently. With Unix, <Esc> is rarely used, except from within the `vi` editor and the Korn shell.

By the way, other characters besides `escape` are used as escape characters. We have already seen how `^v` (`lnext`) can be an escape character. but `vi` has an even more interesting example. With `vi` you only use `escape` to change from insert mode to command mode. There are actually 12 different ways to change from command mode to insert mode. (As you will see, `vi` is a *very* interesting editor.)

The <Delete> Key

Most keyboards have a <Delete> or <Del> key. On older terminals, the equivalent key is sometimes named <Rubout> or <Rub>. This key generates an unprintable character known as `del`. `del` is the last character in the standard ASCII code and does not have a uniform use.

As the name implies, the key was originally intended to delete something or other. If you are a DOS user you will often use the <Delete> key on you PC to erase characters. However, modern Unix does not use the <Delete> key in this manner.

Some Unix systems use <Delete> to generate the `intr` code—the code that stops (interrupts) a command. Other systems do not use this key at all; they use `^c` for `intr`. If your keyboard has a <Delete> key, you may want to set it to something useful, such as `intr`. You can do this with the `stty` command (explained later in this chapter). If your <Delete> key is not set to `intr`, it is probably undefined.

DOS users:

The <Delete> key is not used to delete characters. The <Delete> key is often used to send the `intr` (stop a program) signal.

Since the `del` character itself is unprintable, Unix usually refers to it a `^?` (Control-Question Mark). Similarly, when you need to specify the name of this key to `stty`, you can use `^?`.

However, you should realize that technically speaking, `^?` is only a representation for `del`. It is not the same as the <Delete> key in the way that `^[` is the same as <Escape> or `^H` is the same as <Backspace>.

For instance, anytime that you need to press the <Escape> key, you can use `^[` instead. Similarly, you can press `^H` instead of <Backspace>. However, if you need to press the <Delete> key, you must use <Delete>—`^?` will not work.

Thus, if the `stty` command tells you that the key that produces the `intr` code is `^?`, this does not mean "Control-Question Mark." It means "whatever key produces the `del` code."

Checking Control Code Keys for Your Terminal:
The `stty` Command

The `stty`—set TTY—command allows you to control a wide variety of terminal settings. (Remember, TTY, which stands for "teletype," is the Unix abbreviation for "terminal.")

There are several tens of these settings, most of which you can safely ignore. They control just about every imaginable characteristic of terminals and communication. Fortunately, Unix uses predetermined defaults that are appropriate most of the time. Most often, you will use the stty command to examine, and perhaps change, the way your terminal specifies control codes.

There are many different versions of Unix. Although we have given the most common key assignments for the control codes, you should check for yourself. Your system may use different defaults. Moreover, there are other, less important control codes that we did not cover here.

In order to see the control code keys used by your terminal, enter the command

```
stty
```

You will see a few lines, one of which looks something like this:

```
erase = ^h; kill = ^u; swtch = ^';
```

The other lines have to do with the other stty settings. For the most part, you can ignore them. If you are interested in seeing everything that stty can possibly display, enter

```
stty -a
```

(The "-a" stands for "all.") You will see even more settings. Here is an example:

```
speed 9600 baud; line = 0;
intr = DEL; quit =^I; erase = ^h; kill = ^u; eof = ^d;
eol = ^'; swtch = ^'
parenb -parodd cs8 -cstopb -hupcl cread -clocal
-loblk -ignbrk brkint ignpar -parmrk -inpck istrip
-inlcr -igncr icrnl -iuclc ixon ixany -ixoff
isig icanon -xcase echo echoe echok -echonl -noflsh
-tostop opost -olcuc onlcr -ocrnl -onocr -onlret
-ofill -ofdel tab3
```

The most important information is what keys your terminal uses to send control codes. In the example above, the settings are those used in most Unix systems.

Notice that the **erase** code is set to ^H, which is the same as the <Backspace> key. Also notice that the **intr** (stop command) code is set to the <Delete> key.

Using the stty Command to Change the Control Code Keys

After you use **stty -a** to display the control code keys for your terminal, you may decide to change them.

Some version of Unix use # for **erase** and @ for **kill**. On such systems, it is usually a good idea to set **erase** to ^H, so you can use <Backspace>. You may also want to set **kill** to ^X, which is convenient and easy to remember. Making these changes will allow you to use # and @ as regular keys.

Another setting to look for is **intr**. Some systems set it to ^C. If your terminal has a <Delete> key, you may prefer using it to ^C.

To change the key for a particular control code, enter **stty**, followed by the name of the code, followed by the name of the key. For example:

```
stty erase ^H
stty kill ^X
stty intr ^?
```

(As we mentioned earlier, Unix uses the name ^? to refer to **del**, the signal sent by the <Delete> key.)

Another handy change is to make the **start** code the same as the **stop** code, ^S. This way ^S acts like a toggle: off-on, off-on. It is also easy to remember that "S" stands for both "stop" and "start."

```
stty start ^S
```

Aside from **stop** and **start**, it is usually a poor idea to set any other pairs of codes to the same character.

When you enter **stty** commands, you cannot simply hold down the Control key and press a letter. Too many of these combinations would be interpreted incorrectly.

Instead **stty** allows you to type an actual ^ character followed by an actual second character. With letters, you can use upper or lower case.

In the previous example, we typed

the ^ character followed by the H character
the ^ character followed by the X character
the ^ character followed by the ? character

Although we typed two characters each time, `stty` converted each pair to a single control character. The ^ and ? combination was, as we mentioned, converted to `del`.

Once you have made some changes, you can use the `stty` command by itself

```
stty
```

to display only those setting that have changed. To display all the key setting, use

```
stty -a
```

After experimenting, you may decide that you want to use `stty` to change the key settings from the defaults on your system. If so, we recommend that you place the appropriate `stty` commands in your `.profile` file (`.login` for C-shell users). That way, these changes will be made automatically each time you log in.

If you want to remind yourself about your choice of control keys, place an `stty -a` command at the end of your `.profile` or `.login` file. This is handy if you use different systems that have their own key settings.

RULE   To learn Unix, place an `stty -a` command at the end of your `.profile` or `.login` file. Every time you log in, you will be reminded of your control code settings.

10
Learning Unix Commands

Introduction

The purpose of this chapter is to show you how to understand and learn Unix commands.

We'll start with a strategy for learning new commands. From there, we will discuss how many commands there are, the two types of commands, and the Unix philosophy.

Finally, we will explain the conventions that are used when Unix commands are described formally.

A Strategy for Learning Unix

Unix is vast, much larger than most people imagine. You can't learn all of Unix; you can't even learn most of Unix.

The best plan is to learn the basics (which we cover in this book) and then teach yourself whatever else you need. Since Unix is constantly evolving and since your needs change from time to time, you will never really stop learning Unix.

Don't be discouraged if it seems like there is too much to learn. Unix is large and complex—it takes months, sometimes years, to become completely proficient.

RULE   Start by learning the basics. Use Unix. As the need arises, teach yourself more.

How Many Unix Commands Are There?

When you start using Unix, much of what you learn is what we might call "Unix theory": what Unix does, what facilities are available, how to use the file system, how to use the editor, how to build tools, and so on. We still have many of these topics left to cover in this book.

However, once you master the basics, most of what you need to know is how to use the commands.

RULE   Keep in mind that most of learning Unix is learning how to use commands.

How many Unix commands are there? The real answer is that nobody knows. At the very least, there are over 500 different commands. For reference, with have compiled a list in Appendix D. You might want to take a moment and scan the list.

How can it be that there are so many commands?

Well, first of all, Unix is a mature operating system. It has been used since the 1970s by a large number of people. There has been plenty of time for commands to have been developed. Moreover, Unix covers a wider variety of tasks than most operating systems, including extensive facilities for software development, text processing, and communications.

For years now, Unix has needed to be streamlined and modernized. However, as we explained in Chapter 1, there is no one organization that controls Unix. Much of the time this works to Unix's advantage, but it also means that there is no one to take charge.

The result is a large, eclectic collection of commands, some of them extremely complex. Even the basic commands have far more options than are necessary to support life. You will find that there are often many ways to perform the same task. Occasionally, there will even be different versions of a command and you can pick the one you like best.

Finally, system managers occasionally add their own commands. For example, some Unix systems have special commands to access a local online help facility.

Two Types of Unix Commands

Unix comes with more built-in commands and programs than any other operating system. There are two types of commands that you will encounter: single-purpose commands and interactive programs.

The bulk of the Unix commands are single-purpose commands, designed to carry out one short task. Examples are the commands to list the names of your files (`ls`), to copy a file (`cp`), and to show the time and date (`date`). When you enter one of these commands at the shell prompt the command executes, terminates, and then returns you to the shell, which then displays another prompt.

Other commands are actually large interactive programs that have their own sets of commands. There are programs to send and receive mail (`mailx`), to display files (`more` or `pg`), to edit text (`vi`), and many others—including an assortment of games.

Typically, to start such a program, you enter the name of the command, such as `mailx`. You then enter the commands that are used for that program. As you work, the program displays its own prompt so that you know what environment you are in. For example, `mailx` displays a question mark.

When you are finished, you enter the "quit" command—whatever it is for that particular program. The program terminates and returns you to the shell. The shell then displays a prompt and waits for a new command.

In order to use a single-purpose command, you need to learn what it does and its various options. In order to use an interactive program, you need to learn its internal commands.

Most of the time, there are so many options or internal commands that you would not want to learn them all. For example, in most versions of Unix, the `ls` command, which is used to list the names of your files, has either 19 or 21 options. On one system, `ls` has 27 options.

The best plan is to learn the most important options and commands. Later, you can learn the other details if you need them.

In this book, we will teach you the essentials of the basic commands and programs. Later in this chapter, we will explain how Unix commands are formally described. In Chapter 11, we will show you how you can learn more about *any* command whenever you need to. Before we do, let's take a moment and discuss some of the important ideas that will help you learn.

The Unix Philosophy

Clearly, there is much to learn and it would be helpful if we could elucidate some underlying principles. Well, we can and here they are:

The most important of these principles form what we like to call the Unix Philosophy. The Unix Philosophy starts with the idea of a collection of well-designed tools.

 Each Unix command should do one thing only, and should do it well.

Think of Unix commands as tools. Once you learn a command, you can add it to your personal toolbox. Instead of having one program that tries to do everything—like a Swiss army knife—Unix gives you a wide selection of single-purpose tools, each of which does one job well. When you need to perform complex tasks, Unix provides ways to combine the tools to suit your needs.

 Unix provides simple tools that can be combined, as you require, to perform complex tasks.

As you start to use Unix commands, you'll find that they are terse. Messages are short and to the point. If there is nothing to say, a command will display nothing.

For example, to check your mail, you enter the `mailx` command. If you have mail, the program will start and you can enter commands to read your messages. However, if you don't have mail, you will see nothing—no message like "you do not have any mail"—just a return to the shell prompt.

Here's another example. The `grep` command looks for a particular string of characters within a set of files. For example, to check for the string "Addie" in a group of several files, you can enter

```
grep Addie file1 file2 file3 file4 file5
```

If `grep` finds the string, you will see an appropriate message. However, if the string is not within those files, you will see nothing—just a return to the shell prompt.

If you use a command incorrectly, you won't get a long error message. All you will see is a short remark or, occasionally, a one- or two-line summary showing you the proper way to enter the command. These summaries are usually prefaced with the word "Usage."

At first, this quietness can be disconcerting, especially if you are used to a computer system that is constantly chattering. However, before long you will find the silence comfortable and appealing.

Moreover, there is a practical reason why Unix commands keep messages to a minimum: Over a slow phone line long messages are irritating, especially if they are unnecessary.

RULE   Unix is terse. Error messages are short. A command with nothing to say will say nothing.

In general, there is a trade-off between how powerful a tool is and how much effort you must put in to learn how to use the tool well. Here is an illustration:

On some computer systems, you delete a file by using a mouse to drag a picture of the file over to a picture of a trash can. With Unix, you need to type `rm` (remove) followed by the name of the file.

Say that you want to erase all the files whose names start with "`temp`" followed by any two characters, along with all the files whose names end with "old". This would be time-consuming and boring with a simplistic system, but with Unix you can use

```
rm temp?? *old
```

Don't worry about the details for now. The idea is that *once you learn how to use it*, a well-designed system can be powerful, useful, easy to use—and a great deal of fun.

This is best expressed as our next Rule for Learning Unix. This rule is probably the most important single sentence in the entire book:

RULE   Unix is difficult to learn but easy to use.

A good analogy is touch typing. Typing is anything but a natural human skill and it takes time to become good at it. But, once you are a good typist, using your computer is much easier.

You will notice this principle if you take a look at the names of the Unix commands. Many of them are short, often without vowels: names like ls (list file names), cp (copy files), and cd (change the working directory). At first, these names are hard to remember, but it doesn't take long before you are glad that they are so short and convenient.

What Unix Commands Look Like: Using Whitespace

Command Line:
When you enter a command, everything you type, up to and including the return.

A Unix command looks like this:

command-name options arguments

In the following sections, we will discuss each part in turn.

When you enter a command, everything that you type, up to and including the return, is called the *command line*. When you type a command, you must separate each part by one or more space or tab characters. These space and tab characters are called *whitespace*. The name comes from terminals that print output. On such terminals, space and tab do indeed produce white space.

Whitespace:
The collective name used to describe the tab *and* space *characters that separate the parts of a command line.*

Usually, we use a single **space** between each word in the command line. However, if you want, you can use any number of **space** or **tab** characters. For example, to enter the command

```
ls -l file1
```

all of the following commands are equivalent:

```
ls<Space>-l<Space>file1
ls<Tab>-l<Tab>file1
ls<Space><Space><Space>-l<Space><Space>file1
ls<Space><Tab>-l<Tab>file1
```

Word:
Part of the command line, a sequence of characters separated by whitespace.

Each sequence of non-whitespace characters is called a *word*. The command

```
ls -l file1
```

has three words: **ls**, **-l**, and **file1**.

As we mentioned in Chapter 3, you can enter more than one command on a line by separating them with semicolons. For example:

```
ls -l file1; who; date
```

Unix treats this exactly as if you had typed each command separately on its own line:

```
ls -l file1
who
date
```

When you enter more than one command on a line, the semicolon acts as a separator. Thus, you do not need whitespace between the commands. However, extra whitespace is ignored and you can include it if you want.

The following command lines are equivalent:

```
ls -l file1;who;date
ls -l file1; who; date
ls -l file1 ;who ;date
ls -l file1 ; who ; date
ls -l file1    ;       who       ;        date
```

Command Line Options

Option:
Part of the command line, a word beginning with a minus sign (-), that controls the operation of the command.

Switch:
Same as option.

Flag:
Same as option.

The first word of every command line is the command name. Following this, there may be a number of *options*. An option is a sequence of characters starting with a minus sign (–) You use options to control the operation of a command. In the command

```
ls -l file1
```

the word –l is an option.

Sometimes options are called *switches* or *flags*. Think of a railway line with various switches. The path that the train takes depends on how the switches are set. Similarly, the way that a command acts depends on which options you use.

Here is an example: You use the ls command to display the names of your files. Normally, all you see are file names. However, if you use the –l option, ls displays the "long" listing—that is, ls shows more information than just the file name.

The character "–" that you type to introduce an option is sometimes called a minus sign and sometimes called a hyphen. But when you talk about using it with options, it is always referred to as "minus."

For instance, if you are explaining to someone how to use the ls command with the –l option, you might say, "If you want to display a long listing, use the minus el option."

A command does not need to have options, but if it does they usually come directly after the command name. For example, it would be wrong to enter

```
ls file1 -l
```

For most commands, options are represented by single letters or numbers. The letters can be upper or lower case, and you must be careful to use the correct case. For example, the ls command has a –r option and a –R option and they are different. Most of the time, however, you will find that options are single lower-case letters.

Here are some examples of options, using the ls command. Normally, ls displays file names in alphabetical order. You can change this order by using certain options. The –t option tells `ls` to sort the file names by creation time; the -r option, to sort in reverse order.

So, to display a list of file names sorted by creation time, you can enter

```
ls -t
```

If you want the same listing in reverse order, enter

```
ls -tr
```

To get a regular listing in reverse order, enter

```
ls -r
```

To get a long listing in reverse order, sorted with respect to creation time, use

```
ls -ltr
```

With almost all commands, you can specify options in any order. Thus, the following examples are equivalent:

```
ls -ltr
ls -lrt
ls -tlr
ls -trl
ls -rtl
ls -rlt
```

Moreover, you can specify options separately or together. Just make sure that each set of options starts with a minus sign. The following commands are equivalent:

```
ls -l -t -r
ls -l -tr
ls -lt -r
ls -ltr
```

Remember, the case of the option is important. With the `ls` command, for example, the -R option is different from the -r option. So,

```
ls -R
```

is different from

```
ls -r
```

You may even use them together:

```
ls -rR
```

If you are a DOS user, here are some important points for you to remember:

••••

DOS users:

To introduce command options, Unix uses a minus sign (-), not a slash (/).

Unix commands have many more options than DOS commands.

Command options may be specified singly or in groups, in any order.

Like DOS, most options are single characters. Be careful to distinguish lower case from upper case.

Unlike DOS, options usually come directly after the name of the command.

Some of the time, the letters representing an option help you remember what the option means. For instance, with the `ls` command, `-l` gives you a "long" listing; `-r` sorts the list in "reverse" order.

However, many options use letters that have nothing to do with what they do. This is because options should be single characters, and it is common to run out of meaningful letters. For instance, with the `ls` command, the `-F` option specifies that the names of certain types of files should be marked in a special way. It is difficult to relate this option to the letter "F." You must simply memorize it.

Furthermore, options names have different effects with different commands. For instance, the `wc` command counts the words, lines, and characters in a file. `wc` has an option, `-l`, which tells it to count only lines. Obviously, this option has nothing to do with the -1 option used with the `ls` command.

RULE
___

To learn Unix, keep in mind that most command options are designated by a single character, usually a lower-case letter.

Unix commands usually have many options.

You will memorize the ones you need by practice. Make a point of using the manual to expand your knowledge by learning new options.

"Zero or More"

You are familiar with the expression "one or more." In Unix we often use a similar expression, *zero or more*. This means that there are none, one, or more than one of something. For instance, we might say, "Each command line contains zero or more options."

Whenever you see "one or more," it means that the quantity being described must be specified—there must be at least one of them. Whenever you see "zero or more," it means that the quantity is optional and does not have to be specified.

Command Line Arguments

Argument:
Part of a command line, specifies information that the command needs to carry out its job.

Parameter:
Same as argument.

Within a command line, after the options, the remaining words are called *arguments* or *parameters*. In the command

```
ls -l file1
```

the word **file1** is an argument. Here are several more examples:

1. `ls -l file1`
2. `ls -l`
3. `ls file1`
4. `ls file1 file2`
5. `ls`

Example 1 has one option (-1) and one argument (file1).

Example 2 has one option (-1) and no arguments.

Example 3 has no options and one argument (file1).

Example 4 has no options and two arguments (file1 and file2).

Example 5 has no options and no arguments.

The purpose of an argument is to specify information that the command needs to carry out its job. The term "argument" is a computer science term, borrowed from mathematics. It is difficult to relate this term to the English word "argument" so it is probably better just to memorize what it means.

Arguments are often optional. If you don't specify them, the command will assume a reasonable default.

The ls command for example, displays the names of all the files you specify as arguments. Example 4, above, displays the names of the two files file1 and file2. If you do not use any arguments, such as in examples 2 or 5 above, ls will, by default, display the names of all your files. The difference between these two examples is that example 2 uses the -1 option, to tell ls to display the "long" listing.

So, with the ls command, if you do not specify any arguments the default is to list all the file names.

Here are three more examples, using the mailx command:

6. mailx

7. mailx harley peter

8. mailx -v harley peter

Example 6 has no options and no arguments. It tells mailx to check to see if you have any messages waiting.

Example 7 has no options and two arguments. It tells mailx that you want to send a message to the userids harley and peter.

Example 8 has one option and two arguments. It is similar to example 7, except that it tells mailx to operate in "verbose" mode. In this mode, mailx displays extra information as the message is being sent.

One last note: Some people use the term "argument" to refer to all of the words after the command name, including the options. If you use the term "argument" in this way, then the command

```
ls -l file
```

would have two arguments, the first of which is the option -1.

The technical distinction as to whether or not options are considered to be arguments is usually clear from context. Most of the time, it's not all that important.

The Formal Description of a Command: Syntax

Syntax:
The formal and precise description of the format of a command.

It is important that there be a mechanism to describe commands. When such a description contains terms that are defined formally and used precisely, we call it the *syntax* of the command. The syntax of a command is its "official" description.

The syntax that we use to describe Unix commands follows five simple rules:

1. Square brackets, [ ] , enclose options and some types of arguments to indicate that they are optional.

2. Anything not in square brackets is obligatory and must be entered as part of the command. This includes the name of the command and some types of arguments.

3. The command name and the options are printed in boldface. This indicates that these words must be typed exactly as they are described.

4. Each argument name is printed in italics. This indicates that you must replace the name by an appropriate value when you enter the command.

5. An argument that is followed by an ellipsis, (...), may be repeated any number of times.

Here are some examples to show how it all works. These examples use the ls command—the command that displays the names of your files. Don't worry about the meanings of the options or arguments. We will discuss them later, in Chapter 21.

The syntax for the **ls** command is

ls [**-abcdfgilmnopqrstuxCFR**] [*name*...]

Notice the following:

The name of the command, **ls**, and the names of the options are in boldface. This shows that they must be typed exactly as shown.

The argument name is in italics. This shows that it must replaced by an appropriate value when the command is entered. (In this case, the argument is the name of a file or the name of a directory of files.)

The name of the command, **ls**, is not in square brackets. This shows that it must be typed as part of the command.

The options and the argument are in square brackets. This shows that they are optional.

The argument name is followed by "..."; this indicates that it may be repeated any number of times (to specify the name of more than one file).

From the syntax of the **ls** command, we see that the following examples are valid:

```
ls
ls -l
ls file1
ls file1 file2 file3 file4
ls -alF file1 file2 file3 file4
```

The following examples are not valid:

```
ls -ael file1   (there is no -e option)
ls file1 -l     (the option must precede the argument)
```

The last example is tricky and shows why you must be precise. If you actually entered the last example, **ls** would consider both **file1** and **-l** to be arguments; **-l** would not be interpreted as an option. The results, as you might imagine, would not be what you intended.

Most of the time, Unix manuals and books use the same syntax that we use here or some reasonable variation. However, when you read documentation that was designed to be displayed on a terminal it will look a little different. After all, most terminals do not have boldface or italics.

System V and BSD: The Two Most Important Types of Unix

As we explained in Chapter 1, there are many versions of Unix. However, when it comes to learning commands, there are two main types of Unix that you need to know about: System V and BSD.

System V:
The version of Unix produced at AT&T.

BSD:
Stands for "Berkeley Software Distribution"; the version of Unix produced at the University of California at Berkeley.

1. *System V* is produced at AT&T. The "V" is the Roman numeral "five." There used to be a System III, although there was never a System I, II or IV.

2. *BSD* stands for "Berkeley Software Distribution" and is produced at the University of California at Berkeley. It is often referred to as *Berkeley Unix*.

Just about every implementation of Unix is based on one of these two variations. Some versions support both System V and BSD. Although System V and BSD have a great deal in common, there are significant differences, especially for programmers.

Hint
••••

DOS users:
The differences between versions of Unix are much more pronounced than the differences between PC-DOS and MS-DOS.

Most of the Unix commands are found in both System V and BSD. However, some commands are different. For example, in System V the command to display a file is named `pg`, because it "pages" through the file, one screenful at a time. In BSD, the command is `more`, because at the end of every screenful of output, it displays the message "more". (Newer versions of System V, however, contain both `pg` and `more`.)

Some of the commands have the same name and function but offer different options. For instance, the System V `ls` command has 21 options; the BSD `ls` command has 19 options. Moreover, only 14 of these options are the same for both versions. Even then, the number of options might vary from one type of System V or BSD to another.

For this reason, it is often impossible to say exactly how many options a command has, or, for that matter, exactly how many different Unix commands there are.

In this book, we will concentrate on System V, the basis for most of the Unix in the world today, especially for PC-based systems. If you are using a BSD-based Unix the book will still help you, it's just that the details for some of the commands will be different.

When we explain a command, we will not attempt to show you every option. Rather, we will describe the options that we have found to be the most useful. If you want an exhaustive explanation of a command, you will need to look it up in the manual that describes your particular system.

11

Where to Find Help

Introduction

Most Unix systems come with a large amount of built-in help: programs that you can access any time you want.

In this chapter, we will explore these help facilities. Not all of these programs are universally available, so we will take care to explain which ones come with the various versions of Unix.

As we explained in Chapter 10, there are two main families of Unix: those that are based on AT&T's System V and those that are based on BSD from U.C. Berkeley. In this book, we are concentrating on System V.

The help commands that we discuss in this chapter are of prime importance. After all, these are the commands that allow you to teach yourself. For this reason, we will, in this chapter, cover both the System V and the BSD commands. As we introduce each command, we will indicate in which system it can be found.

Once you understand how to use these built-in programs, you can teach yourself a great deal of what you need to know. However, there will be times when the assistance of another person will be essential. In the last part of this chapter, we show you how to find experts who will help you when all else fails.

Unix Documentation: The Online Manual

Traditionally, Unix was used in universities and research institutions. Most old-timers learned Unix by working on their own and teaching themselves. When they got stuck, they looked around for someone who knew more than they did.

Manual:
Known as the *manual, the principal online reference manual.*

Basically, there were two types of documentation: a series of tutorial papers and the *manual*. This manual, the original Unix reference, is so important that it is still referred to as *the* manual. In this book, we will call it the "Manual" (with a capital "M").

The Manual has always been stored *online*–that is, it is accessible to users from their terminals. This allows you to look up reference material while you are working. Moreover, having the Manual online makes it easy for the system developers to keep the reference information up to date.

Online:
Accessible to users from their terminals.

Today there are many different Unix publications, but there is still only one main online Manual. When Unix people tell you to "look it up in the Manual," this is the one they are talking about. The information in the Manual represents the "official" description of how something should work.

RULE   The online Manual is the single most important Unix reference.

How important is the Manual? Well, before AT&T had System V and System III, the versions of Unix were called the "Seventh Edition," the "Sixth Edition," and so on. These names came from the edition of the Manual, not from the version of Unix.

The Manual is still the single most important Unix publication. Although some computer companies do develop their own documentation, the Manual forms the basis for most of the essential material. To this day, you can pick up most Unix manuals, look up a command, and read word for word the exact same explanation that you would have seen in the standard Manual of the 1970s.

There are many reasons for this, but it all boils down to one fundamental point: Rewriting the main canon of Unix documentation is a gargantuan job and nobody wants to do it. When a manufacturer or reseller licenses Unix, they also license the Unix documentation.

```
(1)    COMMANDS
(2)    SYSTEM CALLS
(3)    LIBRARY FUNCTIONS
(4)    SPECIAL FILES
(5)    FILE FORMATS
(6)    GAMES
(7)    MISCELLANEOUS INFORMATION
(8)    SYSTEM MAINTENANCE COMMANDS
```

Figure 11.1   *The eight sections of the Unix manual.*

The Format of the Manual

The Manual is organized into eight sections, which are listed in Figure 11.1.

Most of the sections are rather technical and are meant for programmers. Unless you are a programmer, you will probably only need sections 1, 6, and 7.

Section 1 contains a description of each Unix command. Whenever you want, you can look up a command and find out how it works. Section 6 contains a similar description for each of the built-in games.

Section 7 is actually pretty small and most of the topics have to do with text processing. There are, however, two entries of general interest: a summary of the ASCII code, and a brief description of how the Unix file system is organized. We will find this latter description handy when we cover the file system in Chapter 17.

RULE

Section 1 of the online Manual contains a description of each Unix command.

This is the most important section of the Manual.

Page:

As in Manual page or man *page; a specific entry in the Unix online reference manual.*

Each section of the Manual consists of *pages*; each page explains a single topic. For example, section 1 contains a page for the `ls` command, a page for the `who` command, and a page for the `date` command.

If you print these pages you will find that many of them are not short. For example, the description of the Bourne shell (`sh`) is 10 printed pages long; the description of the C-shell (csh) is 27 printed pages. Regardless, the tradition is to refer to each separate entry as a "page." For example, if you ask a Unix expert what to get your mother for Mother's Day, he might say, "Print her a copy of the C-shell Manual page."

The Format of a Manual Page

Each page of the Manual explains one topic. The explanation is organized in a standard manner with certain headings. Take a look at Figure 11.2, which shows a typical Manual page taken from the BSD Manual. This page describes the at command, which allows you to schedule tasks to be done at some future time.

The at Manual page is typical in that it contains the most commonly used headings:

Name
Synopsis
Description
Files
See Also
Diagnostics
Bugs

All pages contain the first three essential headings, Name, Synopsis, and Description. The rest of the headings are used only if needed. Some pages contain other headings that are not listed in Figure 11.2. But, in all cases, the organization should be clear within the context of the discussion.

Let's take a look at each of the headings in our example, starting with Name. Here you will see the name of the command followed by a short, one-line description.

Next comes Synopsis. This shows the syntax of the command. In this case, the syntax is

at *time* [*day*] [*file*]

As you remember from our discussion in Chapter 10, this syntax shows that the at command has no options and three arguments. The first argument, *time*, is obligatory; the other two arguments, *day* and *file*, are optional.

AT(1)   UNIX Programmer's Manual   AT(1)

NAME
    at - execute commands at a later time

SYNOPSIS
    at time [day] [file]

DESCRIPTION
    At squirrels away a copy of the named file (standard input
    default) to be used as input to **sh**(1) (or **csh**(1) if you nor-
    mally use it) at a specified later time. A **cd** command to
    the current directory is inserted at the beginning, followed
    by assignments to all environment variables. When the
    script is run, it uses the user and group ID of the creator
    of the copy file.

    The time is 1 to 4 digits, with an optional following 'A',
    'P', 'N' or 'M' for AM, PM, noon or midnight. One and two
    digit numbers are taken to be hours, three and four digits
    to be hours and minutes. If no letters follow the digits,
    24 hour clock time is understood.

    The optional day is either (1) a month name followed by a
    day number, or (2) a day of the week; if the word 'week'
    follows invocation is moved seven days further off. Names
    of months and days may be recognizably truncated. Examples
    of legitimate commands are

            at 8am jan 24
            at 1530 fr week

    At programs are executed by periodic execution of the com-
    mand **/usr/lib/atrun** from **cron**(8). The granularity of **at**
    depends upon how often **atrun** is executed.

    Standard output or error output is lost unless redirected.

FILES
    /usr/lib/atrun   executor (run by **cron**(8)).

    in /usr/spool/at:
        yy.ddd.hhhh.*   activity for year yy, day dd, hour hhhh
        lasttimedone   last hhhh
        past   activities in progress

SEE ALSO
    calendar(1), pwd(1), sleep(1), cron(8)

DIAGNOSTICS
    Complains about various syntax errors and times out of
    range.

BUGS
    Due to the granularity of the execution of **/usr/lib/atrun**,
    there may be bugs in scheduling things almost exactly 24
    hours into the future.

Revision 1.6 87/02/17   1

Figure 11.2   *A page from the Unix Manual.*

The next heading, Description, introduces the main part of the page. This is the explanation of how the command works, along with how to use any options and arguments. In this case, the description is only fifteen lines, but with many commands, it can be quite long—sometimes many hundreds of lines.

After the description comes the Files heading. Here is a list of all the system files that are used or referenced by the command. Unless you have a particular interest in such files, you can ignore this information.

The next heading, See Also, shows other manual pages that contain related information. In this example, we are advised that we might want to check the following pages:

```
calendar(1)
pwd(1)
sleep(1)
cron(8)
```

These references illustrate a common way to reference a Unix command or term: to follow it with the number of the Manual section in which it is documented.

Within the world of Unix, it is assumed that everybody is aware of the Manual and understands how it is organized into sections. It is common to read remarks like, "to list the names of your files, use the `ls(1)` command." You will need to know that this means that the `ls` command is explained in section 1 of the Manual.

In our example from the sample Manual page, we see references to three pages from section 1 and one page from section 8. Since `calendar`, `pwd`, and `sleep` are in section 1, we can infer that they are commands. Since `cron` is in section 8, it must be a system maintenance command, and probably not of general interest.

Continuing with our example, we come to the Diagnostics heading. Here we find an explanation of what sort of error handling the command provides.

Finally, we reach the last heading, Bugs. As you probably know, a bug is a mistake or shortcoming in a program. All large programs have bugs. (Actually, all large programs have two types of bugs: the ones you know about and the ones you don't know about.)

This part of the Manual page acknowledges that it is important for the user to be aware of the known mistakes and shortcomings of a command. In this example, the Bugs description tells us that the scheduling is not always exact and that we might have problems with events that are almost 24 hours into the future.

A few Unix companies are uncomfortable with admitting that their products have bugs. So some versions of the Manual rename this section, using a euphemism like Limitations. Some companies delete this section completely (which is really not fair).

Accessing the Online Manual: The man Command

To access the Unix online Manual you use the man command. For this reason, the Manual entries are sometimes called "man pages."

Unfortunately, a few Unix companies have removed the Manual from their versions of the operating system. This is usually done on PC-based systems to save disk space. If your system does not have the Manual, the man command will not work. You will have to depend on your printed documentation.

There are three forms of the man command. The most important form has the following syntax:

man [*section number*] *page title...*

This form of the man command displays a specific page at your terminal. For example

```
man date
```

displays the page that describes the date command. If you want to learn more about the man command itself, enter

```
man man
```

man displays information one screenful at a time. After each screenful, man will pause. To continue to the next screenful, press the <Space> bar. Be aware that man displays its output in a form suitable for printing, that is, using 66 lines per printed page. The output you see on your screen will not look as nice as if it had been properly formatted for your terminal.

If you want, you can display pages for more than one command:

```
man date who ls
```

The Manual pages will be displayed one after the other.

With some Unix systems, the output from the `man` command will scroll by so fast that you won't be able to read it on your screen. If this happens to you, there are two things you can do.

First, you can use the `stop` and `start` keys that we discussed in Chapter 9. These keys pause and restart the screen display. With most systems, `stop` (pause) is `^s` and `start` (restart) is `^Q`.

The second alternative is to follow the `man` command with

```
| more
```

For example:

```
man date who ls | more
```

This sends the output of the `man` to the `more` program. As we will learn in Chapter 23, the `more` program will display a file one screenful at a time. If there is more than one screenful of output, the bottom line will display

```
--More--
```

You can then press the <Space> bar to display the next screenful.

If you specify the number of a section before the command name, `man` will search only that section. This will speed things up when you know that you are interested in only one section of the manual.

For example, the name `man` has pages in two different sections. Section 1 (Commands) contains the description of the `man` command. Section 7 (Miscellaneous Information) contains a description of the text formatting features used to produce the `man` pages.

If you enter one of the following commands:

```
man man
man 1 man
```

you will get the description of the `man` command. If you want the text formatting description in section 7, you need to use

```
man 7 man
```

Each section of the Manual has an entry under the name `intro` that contains an introduction. To display the introduction to a section, specify the section number. For example:

```
man 1 intro
man 7 intro
```

If you leave out the section number, `man` assumes section 1. So the commands

```
man intro
man 1 intro
```

are equivalent.

DOS users:

Unlike DOS, Unix has an extensive online manual. Remember to use it.

Quick Information About Commands:
Using `man -f` and `man -k`

Aside from displaying an entire Manual page, the `man` command can also display two types of information about commands. The syntax for these forms of the command is

man -f *page title...*
man -k *keyword...*

These forms of the `man` command are available only with BSD, not with System V.

Sometimes all you want is a quick explanation of what a command does, rather than the entire description. For this, use the -f option. This option displays the one line description that comes under the Name heading. For example, if you enter

```
man -f date
```

you will see

```
date (1)    - print and set the date
```

(Remember, as we explained in Chapter 9, Unix uses the term "print" to mean "display.")

You can specify more than one page title with the -f option. For example,

```
man -f date ls who
```

displays

```
date (1)    - print and set the date
ls (1)      - list contents of directory
ls (8)      - generate a standalone directory listing
who (1)     - who is on the system
```

Notice in this case that we see that `ls` has a page in section 1 (Commands) and a page in section 8 (System Maintenance Commands).

If you wish to perform a particular task and you are not sure of the name of the command, you can use the -k option (again, BSD only). This option searches all the one-line descriptions, including command names, looking for those that contain any of the keywords that you specify.

In order to be as useful as possible, the -k option search is not sensitive to upper or lower case. Moreover, it will match keywords that are part of longer words.

For example, say that you want to figure out what command you would use to connect to another Unix system. You enter

```
man -k connect
```

and you see

```
accept (2)        - accept a connection on a socket
connect (2)       - initiate a connection on a socket
getpeername (2)   - get name of connected peer
listen (2)        - listen for connections on a socket
shutdown (2)      - shut part of full-duplex connection
socketpair (2)    - create a pair of connected sockets
cu (1)            - connect to a remote system
```

Only one of these pages, cu, is in section 1. This would be the best place to start. Use the following command:

```
man 1 cu
```

Quick Information About Commands:
The whatis and apropos Commands

Using the man command with the -f and -k options is handy. man -f is a quick way to find out what a command does, and man -k is a quick way to search for a command name by specifying keywords.

For convenience, there are two commands that will do these jobs directly: whatis and apropos. Their syntax is:

whatis *command-name...*
apropos *keyword...*

Like the -f and -k options, these commands are available only with BSD, not with System V.

The whatis command is exactly the same as man -f. For example, to find out what the date command does, enter

```
whatis date
```

The apropos command is exactly the same as the man -k command. For example, to find the commands that have to do with connecting one system to another, enter

```
apropos connect
```

Of course, each of these commands will accept more than one argument. For example, entering

```
whatis apropos whatis
```

will display

```
apropos (1)     - locate commands by keyword lookup
whatis (1)      - describe what a command is
```

These commands are straightforward. Their main purpose is to save you the trouble of typing the different man options.

Finding the Right Command: The locate Program

As we mentioned above, the whatis and apropos commands are available only with BSD. However, some versions of System V have a program named locate to help you find a command to perform a particular task.

The syntax of the locate command is

```
locate [keyword...]
```

If you specify one or more keywords, locate will list whatever commands are appropriate. For example, to list commands that you can use to print a file, you might enter

```
locate print file
```

If you enter the name of the command by itself

```
locate
```

you will start an interactive program. You can enter any keywords you want and press <Return>. After you see the results, you can enter more keywords and repeat the process until you get what you want. To quit, enter

```
q
```

Generally speaking, `locate` does a better job than `apropos`. However, since `locate` is System V and `apropos` is BSD, you will probably never find both commands on the same system.

Learning How to Use a Command: The `usage` Program

Once you have found a command that you want to use you can display its Manual page by using the `man` command. Some versions of System V have an alternate program, `usage`. The syntax for this command is

`usage` [`-deo`] [*command*]

To display information, specify the command you want along with one of the option. The options display:

```
-d    a description of the command
-e    examples of how to use the command
-o    a description of the command's options
```

For example, to display examples showing how to use the `ls` command, enter

```
usage -e ls
```

If you enter the `usage` command with no arguments

```
usage
```

it will start a menu-driven interactive program. You can ask `usage` to display information about various commands, one after the other. From the menu, you can quit by entering

```
q
```

Online Unix Tutorials: The `starter` Program

Most Unix systems come with built-in tutorial programs. Not all versions of Unix have these programs so you will have to check your particular system.

The newer System V systems have a tutorial program called `starter`. To start this, simply enter the command

```
starter
```

You will see a menu with the following topics:

Basic commands that you should learn first

Unix documents that are important for beginners

Places where you can take Unix courses

Information about your local system

Online teaching aids installed on your system

You can select the topic you want by entering a letter.

When you select a topic, you will be presented with a tutorial, after which you will be returned to the menu. From the menu, you can quit by entering

```
q
```

Online Unix Tutorials: The `learn` Program

As we mentioned, the `starter` program is available only with some System V systems. BSD has a different tutorial system, named `learn`.

The `learn` program has an interesting history. It was originally developed at Bell Labs (the part of AT&T that created Unix) and was then incorporated into BSD. Later, `learn` was dropped by AT&T, which is why you won't find it in System V.

The syntax of the `learn` command is

learn [*subject* [*lesson-number*]]

To start, just enter the command name by itself:

```
learn
```

You will see a list of several tutorials. Choose the tutorial you want and enter its name. You can stop at any time by entering

```
bye
```

The first time you use **learn**, you should ask for instructions. To do this, start the program and then press <Return> by itself, without typing the name of a tutorial. **learn** will display instructions on using the program, as well as a description of each tutorial. Here are typical descriptions:

```
files      - basic file handling commands
editor     - text editor; must know about files first
vi         - screen-oriented text editor;
                       must know files first
morefiles - more on file manipulations and other
                       useful stuff
macros     - "-ms" macros for BTL memos & papers;
                       must know editor first
eqn        - typing mathematics;  must know editor
C          - writing programs in the C language;
                       must know editor first
```

Take a look at the description for the **macros** tutorial. This tutorial deals with text formatting facilities, and we won't go into the details here. But notice the abbreviation "BTL." This stands for "Bell Telephone Labs," the old name for the AT&T research lab. As we pointed out earlier, some parts of Unix have been handed down for years, with little or no change.

If you would like to start **learn** at the beginning of a specific tutorial, specify its name. For example:

```
learn editor
```

When you are ready to stop work, enter

```
bye
```

and **learn** will tell you the current lesson number. You will see a message like

```
To take up where you left off type "learn editor 3.1a".
Bye.
```

To continue where you left off, start with that lesson:

```
learn editor 3.1a
```

Before we leave this section, let's take one more look at the syntax for this command:

```
learn [subject [lesson-number]]
```

Notice that there are square brackets within square brackets. This means that the first argument, *subject*, is optional. If you specify this argument, then the second argument, *lesson-number*, becomes optional.

Finding Out What a Technical Term Means: The `glossary` Command

The `glossary` command will display definitions of common Unix terms and some of the special characters. The syntax for this command is

```
glossary [term]
```

This command is available only with some versions of System V.

Here is an example. To find out what the term "file" means, enter

```
glossary file
```

If you enter the `glossary` command with no arguments

```
glossary
```

it will start a menu-driven interactive program. You will see a menu from which you can select the term for which you want a description. From the menu, you can quit by entering

```
q
```

An Array of Help Systems: The `help` Command

Most systems have a command named `help`. However, the same name is used for a variety of different programs.

On some systems, the `help` command will start a local program that provides special assistance to users at that location. Generally speaking, the only places that provide such services are those that have a large support staff. Usually, this means a university or a large company.

With some versions of System V, there is a built-in `help` command that starts a menu-driven program. This facility ties together the services of the `locate`, `usage`, `starter`, and `glossary` programs. If you have such a `help` program, your system manager can customize it to suit your organization.

Most other systems do not have a general `help` command. However, many systems have a special-purpose `help` that is only for programmers. Here is why.

As part of the Unix software development system, there exists a tool named SCCS—Software Code Control System. Programmers who are working on large software projects use SCCS to keep track of all the different pieces. SCCS comes with its own `help` command. Unfortunately, it only offers help with SCCS commands and messages and offers no general assistance.

If you enter

```
help
```

and your system has a real help system, you should see an easy-to-understand menu. If your system does not have a real help system, your `help` command may start the SCCS help program. In this case, you will see something like

```
msg number or comd name?
```

You are being asked to enter the name of an SCCS command or the number of an SCCS error message. Just press <Return>. The SCCS program will display an error message

```
ERROR:  not found (hel)
```

and terminate.

A Summary of Online Unix Help Programs

As you work with Unix, cultivate the habit of learning. Take a few moments here and there to teach yourself something new. Don't always be in such a rush that you never find the time to check out a new command or option. Continual learning is part of the Unix environment and culture.

Imagine yourself in a large office, filled with terminals. In front of each terminal is a person working with Unix. You walk around looking at all the screens to check on what each person is doing. If the office is well run, you should always find some of the people teaching themselves.

RULE   Continual learning is part of the process of using Unix.

In this chapter, we have covered a variety of online help facilities. These commands, especially `man`, can be your most important tools when it comes to day-to-day learning. Unfortunately, not all help programs are available with every Unix system. To help you understand which programs are likely to come with your system we have prepared a summary. But first, let's take a moment to talk about types of Unix.

We mentioned earlier that the two main types of Unix are System V and BSD. Each of these has several versions. The common versions of System V are V.2, V.3, and V.4. The common versions of BSD are 4.2 and 4.3. All of the BSD commands that we have covered in this chapter are in BSD 4.2 and 4.3. However, the System V commands we described are not in V.2; they are new to System V.3 and System V.4.

This information is summarized in Table 11.1.

More Sources for Help: Help Desks and Experts

There are four main sources of information about Unix. First, there are the printed manuals that come with your system. Second, there are the online help programs that we have just described.

You will always have access to the online programs, but you may not have the system manuals. For example, when you buy a RISC/System 6000 Unix computer from IBM, you will receive only a few rudimentary system administration manuals.

The Unix that comes with these computers, IBM's AIX version 3, contains a comprehensive online help system, called InfoExplorer. InfoExplorer actually contains all the AIX manuals

BSD 4.2, 4.3	System V.2	System V.3, V.4
`man`	`man`	`man`
`whatis`		`locate`
`apropos`		`usage`
`learn`		`starter`
		`glossary`
		`help`

Table 11.1 *The Unix Online Help Programs*

stored on disk. You won't get the regular printed manuals unless you order them separately.

Most systems do come with printed manuals. However, if you are using a large system, your terminal may be a long way from the central site. You will probably not want to run back and forth every time you want to look up something.

This leaves you with two alternative sources of information. You can buy books, like this one, and you can find people to help you.

Most large systems have a gaggle of Unix experts. Your best bet is to see if your site has a permanent help desk. This is likely if you are at a university or a large company. Otherwise, you should do your best to find a few experts and cultivate their acquaintance.

Before you ask questions, there are two Unix traditions that you should understand. First, the Unix documentation has always been inadequate for beginners. It is expected that most neophytes will learn by word of mouth.

Second, it is also expected that before you ask a question you will do everything you can to help yourself. There are many users in this world. Unix experts are in short supply, and they get asked questions all the time.

It is part of the Unix culture to help other people, but it is also traditional for an expert to be annoyed if you ask him a question that is plainly answered in the Manual.

Usenet: The People's Network

If you are at a university, research organization, or Unix-based commercial company, there is a good chance that you can

Usenet:
A loosely administered worldwide network of discussion groups.

access *Usenet*. Usenet is a loosely administered network consisting of thousands of sites.

Essentially, Usenet is a collection of over 800 different discussion groups, called "news groups." There are hundreds of thousands of people, all over the world, who participate. They send "articles" to the groups of their choice via electronic mail.

To access Usenet, you will have to ask around your site to find out the local procedure. Essentially, you will execute a command to "read the news." You can indicate which groups you want to read and which ones you want to ignore. You can follow the discussion in various groups and even submit articles of your own.

Out of the hundreds of news groups, over 200 deal with some aspect of computing. Of these, about twenty are devoted to Unix. There are groups for various types of Unix, as well as groups for people to submit questions and answers.

As you gain proficiency with Unix, you will find the Usenet groups to be a good source of information. If you have a problem that you can't solve, you can submit it to one of the Unix question-and-answer groups. It is not unusual to receive answers from people all over the country.

If you use Usenet, you should be aware that as a self-policing network, it has developed a rich set of customs and guidelines. It is up to you to learn these so that you do not inadvertently cause trouble or annoyance. If you do break a rule, even out of ignorance, you can expect to find your mailbox filled with reminders.

To start using Usenet, you should "subscribe" to the special groups for new users. The articles in this group will teach you a large part of what you need to know.

Then, identify the general-interest Unix groups and start reading. Each month, the coordinators of these groups submit an article that contains a long list of the most frequently asked Unix questions (with the answers). It is considered bad form to ask one of these questions, as they have been answered many times before.

Reading the Manual: Wizards and Gurus

Wizard or Guru:
A Unix expert.

As you use electronic mail and Usenet you will find that there are many people who are willing to take the time to help you. This is so common, that there are even names to describe experts: they are called *wizards* or *gurus*.

DOS users:
Many Unix experts are not familiar with PCs or DOS.
You will have to learn to speak *their* language.

However, as we mentioned earlier, the Unix tradition is that before you ask a question, you must make an honest effort to answer it for yourself. The cardinal sin is to ask a question whose answer is plainly given in the online Manual. Just about everybody has access to this resource, via the `man` command. It is expected that you do not ask a question until you have tried to find the answer using `man`.

12

Exploring Your System

Introduction

Unix systems can be busy systems, especially if you're working on a multiuser computer. In this chapter, we will discuss some of the commands that you can use to display information about your system.

We will start with the system news and move on to finding out what operating system and machine we are using, who is logged in, and what is happening in the invisible Unix universe.

Displaying the System News: The news Command

News:

Files, containing information of general interest, that are accessible to all users via the news *command.*

Unix systems have a built-in command to display files that contain items of interest to the users. The system manager creates these files and places them in a specific directory. Once files are placed in this directory, they are considered to be *news* items and are accessible to all the users.

On most systems, the name of the news directory is /usr/news. In Chapter 17, we will describe directories and this name will make sense.

Here is a typical example of how the news facility is used. Say that your system has a new disk drive and the system manager

147

wants everyone to know that extra storage is now available. He would write a news item and place it in the /usr/news directory. The item would now be available for everyone to read.

As you can see, there will never be any news unless the system manager creates it. If you are using a standalone system, it is unlikely that you would create news for yourself. However, if you are sharing a computer, the news facility is an important way to keep the users informed.

To read the news items that have been stored on your system, use the news command. The syntax is

news [-ans] [*item...*]

news keeps track of which items you have seen by keeping a file named .news_time in your home directory (your principal storage area—home directories—are explained in Chapter 18). By checking when this file was last updated, news can determine when you last read the news. Unless you specifically ask for all news items, news will show only those that you have not already seen.

When you enter the command with no options or parameters, news will display all the items that have been added since the last time you checked the news. So, for example, if you enter

```
news
```

you might see

```
party (root) Tue Jun 19 12:47:13 1990

   There will be a party at Peter's house
   next Tuesday.  At this time, we will be
   giving out free diskettes to all the
   children.  If you want to come, call
   Kevin by Friday at the latest.

new.disk.drive (root) Tue Jun 19 12:44:59 1990

   We now have a new disk drive.
   This brings our total storage capacity
   to 1.1 gigabytes.
```

In this case, there are two items, `party` and `new.disk.drive`. Both items were placed in the news directory by the superuser, logged in as `root`.

Now that you have seen these items, `news` will update your `.news_time` file. This means that if you enter the news command again you will not see anything until the system manager enters new items.

If you want to display all the news items, regardless of whether or not you have already seen them, use the **-a** ("all") option

```
news -a
```

Sometimes you may want to check what news items are available without actually displaying them. The **-s** ("show") option shows you the number of items that you have not yet seen. For example

```
news -s
```

might display

```
2 news items.
```

The **-n** ("names") option shows you the names of all the items you have not yet seen. For example, if you enter

```
news -n
```

you might see

```
news: party.update backup.sched
```

There are two new news items, `party.update` and `backup.sched`. You can display them by entering

```
news
```

Alternatively, you can specify the names of particular items:

```
news party.update
```

Only those items will be displayed:

```
party.update (root) Tue Jun 19 13:09:23 1990

Correction: At the party we will be
giving out balloons, not diskettes.
```

In Chapter 8, we mentioned that every time you log in, Unix automatically executes a startup script for you: `.profile` for the Bourne shell and `.login` for the C-shell. You may want to put a `news -n` or `news -s` command in this file. That way, you will be informed of new items whenever you log in. Some Unix systems do this for you automatically.

RULE Put a `news -n` or `news -s` command in your startup script (`.profile` or `.login`) to keep abreast of what is happening on your system.

Displaying System Information:
The `uname` Command

The `uname` command displays information about the Unix system that you are currently using. This command is handy when you connect to more than one computer and you forget which one you are working on at the time.

The syntax for `uname` is

```
uname [-amnsrv]
```

The `-s` ("system name") option displays the name of the system you are using. This name is specified by the system manager when the system is installed. The `-s` option is the default, so the following two commands are equivalent:

```
uname
uname -s
```

The `-n` ("node name") option displays the name by which your system is known to a network. This option is useful only if your computer is connected to a network.

The other options give information about the operating system and the hardware. The **-r** ("release") option displays the release number of the operating system; the **-v** option displays the version number of this release; and the **-m** option displays the type of computer you are using.

If you want to display all this information, use the **-a** ("all") option:

```
uname -a
```

Here is some typical output:

```
hahn hahn 3.2 2 i386
```

In this case, the system name is **hahn**, which is the same as the node name. The operating system release is 3.2, as we are working with System V.3.2. The version is 2. The machine name is "i386" which indicates that we are using a 386-based PC. (Actually, we are using a 486-based computer, but the operating system considers it to be the same as a 386.)

Displaying Session Information:
The `logname` and `tty` Commands

The **uname** command that we discussed in the last section gives you basic information about your Unix system and computer. To get similar information about your userid and terminal, you use the **logname** and **tty** commands that we mentioned in Chapter 7.

The syntax is simple:

```
logname
tty
```

(The **tty** command does have some options, but they are unimportant for everyday work.)

The **logname** command displays the name of the userid that is currently logged in. For example, if you are logged in as userid **harley** and you enter

```
logname
```

you will see

```
harley
```

This command is handy when you happen upon an abandoned terminal that is still logged in. Use the `logname` command to find out who is using the terminal.

The `tty` command shows you the exact name of your terminal. For example, say that you enter

```
tty
```

You might see

```
/dev/console
```

which means that you are using the console.

What does the name "`/dev/console`" mean? Unix treats all sources of input and output as files. In this case, the console is considered to be a file named `console` within a directory named `dev` ("devices").

Another typical terminal name is `/dev/tty01`. This refers to the file `tty01` within the `dev` directory. We will explore these ideas further in Chapter 17 when we learn more about files.

Displaying Information About Who Is Logged In: The who Command

In Chapter 7, we mentioned the **who** command. This command displays the names of all the userids that are currently logged in. In this section, we will describe the command more formally.

The syntax is

```
who  [-sqHT]
```

The **-s** option displays the userid, the terminal name, and the time that the userid logged in. This is the default. Thus, the following commands are equivalent:

```
who
who -s
```

Here is an example of typical output:

```
harley      console      Jun 19 19:45
peter       tty01        Jun 19 12:32
addie       tty02        Jun 19 13:12
kevin       tty03        Jun 19 12:34
```

The **-H** ("headings") option displays the same information with descriptive headings:

```
NAME        LINE         TIME
harley      console      Jun 19 19:45
peter       tty01        Jun 19 12:32
addie       tty02        Jun 19 13:12
kevin       tty03        Jun 19 12:34
```

The **-q** ("quick") option displays a minimum amount of information: the names of all the userids and the total number of users.

```
harley     peter     addie     kevin
# users=4
```

The final option, **-T**, displays the same information as **-s**, the default, along with one additional item called the "state." The state is shown as a plus sign (+), a minus sign (−), or a question mark (?).

A plus sign means that you can send messages to this terminal. A minus means than you cannot. A question mark means that the line is bad. Here is an example of what you might see:

```
harley      + console     Jun 19 19:45
peter       − tty01       Jun 19 12:32
addie       + tty02       Jun 19 13:12
kevin       + tty03       Jun 19 12:34
```

In this case, the terminal where **peter** is logged in will not accept messages. The other terminals will.

In Chapter 14, we will discuss how you can send messages from one terminal to another. There will be times when you will not want to be interrupted and you will use the **mesg** command (explained in Chapter 13) to prevent your terminal from accepting messages. When you do this, the **who -T** command will display a minus sign to show other users that your terminal is off limits.

Finding Out Who Is Doing What:
The whodo Command

The whodo command does as the name implies: it shows you who is doing what on the system.

The syntax is simple:

```
whodo
```

As you can imagine, this command is used most often by the system manager. For this reason, the whodo program is not stored in one of the directories that contain the bulk of the commands. Rather, it is stored in a directory which holds system maintenance commands. This directory is /etc (pronounced "slash et cetera").

In Chapter 16 we will discuss directories and in Chapter 17 we will show you how to tell Unix which directories contain commands. For now, what you should understand is that when you enter a command Unix looks for the program by the same name. Normally, Unix looks in one of the directories that holds commands. If the command is not in one of these directories, Unix will not be able to find it.

When you are logged in as superuser, Unix will look for commands in the /etc directory. However, when you are logged in as a regular user, Unix will not search this directory as it contains mostly system maintenance programs.

Thus, if you are superuser, you can enter the whodo command as shown above. If you are a regular user, you need to tell Unix that whodo is in the /etc directory. To do this, enter the command as follows:

```
/etc/whodo
```

The data that whodo displays consists of the time, date, and machine name, followed by information on what each userid is doing.

This userid information shows the terminal name, the userid, and the login time. This is followed by a list of all the active processes running from that terminal. For each active process, you will see the terminal name, the processid, the processing time used so far (in minutes and seconds), and the name of the program. (For a discussion on processes, see Chapter 7.)

Here is an example. You enter

```
/etc/whodo
```

and you see

```
Thu Jun 21 12:16:58 1990
hahn

console  root      12:13
    console   416     0:01 sh
    console   430     0:00 eg
    console   431     0:00 utod
    console   432     0:00 whodo
    console   433     0:00 tee

tty01     peter     10:22
    tty01      85     0:00 sh
    tty01     423     0:02 vi

tty02     addie     12:10
    tty02     401     0:01 sh
    tty02     414     0:00 write

tty03     harley    12:37
    tty03      89     0:01 sh
    tty03     198     0:00 write
```

In this case, the whodo program ran on Thursday, June 12, 1990, at 12:16:58 pm. The name of the machine is hahn. There are four userids logged in: root, peter, addie, and harley.

Notice that each userid is running a shell (sh) as well as other programs. For example, peter is running a shell and the vi editor (which we will meet in Chapter 24). This is because all programs must run under the auspices of a shell.

In this case, peter started with a shell, processid 85. This shell was started when peter logged in. When the vi command was entered, the shell started a new process, number 423, and put itself on hold. When peter finishes with vi, process number 423 will end and control will pass back to process number 85, the original shell. This shell will then wait for a new command to be entered.

Displaying Information About Processes:
The ps Command

In Chapter 7, we discussed processes and used the ps command. In this section, we will describe ps more formally.

The ps command displays the status of active processes. The syntax is

```
ps [-adefptu]
```

The simplest form of this command has no options:

```
ps
```

Here is typical output:

```
PID TTY       TIME COMMAND
 89 console  0:01 sh
551 console  0:00 ps
```

In this case, we see that there are two processes: the original shell process (sh) number 89, and the ps command itself, running under the auspices of the shell.

The "PID" column shows the processid. The "TTY" column shows the name of the terminal. The "TIME" column shows all the time used by the process. The time is shown in minutes and seconds. If the time is less than 0.01 seconds, you will see "0:00." This is the case above. The last column, "COMMAND," shows that name of the command that is executing.

If we want more information about each process, we can use the -f ("full listing") option:

```
ps -f
```

The output looks like this:

```
      UID    PID  PPID  C     STIME TTY         TIME COMMAND
harley      89     1  0 11:20:10 console   0:01 -sh
harley     564   563  6 14:15:24 console   0:00 ps -f
```

Here we have several more columns. The only ones we need bother with are "UID," which shows the userid that started the process, and "STIME," which shows the starting time of the process.

If you want to look at all the processes (not just yours) that are executing on the system, use the **-e** ("everything") option:

```
PID TTY         TIME COMMAND
  0 ?          0:01 sched
  1 ?          0:03 init
  2 ?          0:00 vhand
  3 ?          0:01 bdflush
 77 ?          0:22 UEdaemon
 70 ?          0:00 cron
 74 ?          0:00 UEdaemon
 82 ?          0:33 UEdaemon
517 console    0:01 sh
577 console    0:00 ps
523 tty01      0:00 sh
527 tty01      0:00 vi
426 tty02      0:00 getty
248 tty03      0:01 sh
```

To make sense out of this, let's look at the data by TTY name. All the lines with a TTY of "?" refer to daemons. As we explained in Chapter 7, a daemon is a process that executes in the background in order to be available at all times. All the daemons in this example were started automatically so they do not have a TTY name. The three daemons named UEdaemon, by the way, belong to the Norton UnErase facility, part of the Norton Utilities for System V.

The next two processes are running from the console. One is the main shell (processid 517), the other is the **ps** command itself (processid 577).

Following these are two processes from terminal **tty01**. Someone is using the **vi** editor.

The only process for terminal **tty02** is a **getty**. This is a program that waits for a userid to log in. ("**getty**" stands for "get

TTY".) This means that terminal `tty02` is ready for use but, as yet, no one has logged in.

The final line shows that `tty03` has only the main shell running. This means that someone is logged in and, for the moment, is in between commands. The shell, processid 248, is waiting for a command to execute.

Displaying Process Information Concisely

The options that we have used so far with the `ps` display a great deal of information. There are other options that we can use to display only what we want.

Process Group Leader:
A process whose main purpose is to execute other processes.

First, the `-e` option showed us all the processes that were executing on the entire system. Some of these are of little interest because they exist only to run other processes. These are called *process group leaders*. An example would be process 523 in the last example: this is the shell that executed the `vi` command. Another example would be processes 426 and 248, which are just waiting for something to happen.

To display all processes except the process group leaders we use the `-d` option:

```
ps -d
```

If we enter this command just after entering the previous example, we would see

```
PID TTY        TIME COMMAND
  1 ?          0:03 init
  2 ?          0:00 vhand
  3 ?          0:01 bdflush
 77 ?          0:22 UEdaemon
 82 ?          0:33 UEdaemon
577 console    0:00 ps
527 tty01      0:00 vi
```

Notice how using `-d` makes things more understandable by showing only those processes that are actively doing something.

We can summarize things even further by displaying only those processes that are associated with a terminal. To to this we use the `-a` ("all important info") option:

```
ps -a
```

The output from the example above would be

```
PID TTY        TIME COMMAND
577 console   0:00 ps
527 tty01     0:00 vi
```

In most cases, if you want to find out what is going on in the system, the best options to use are **-a** combined with **-f**:

```
ps -af
```

We might call this the "snoop" command. The output looks like this:

```
   UID    PID  PPID  C    STIME TTY        TIME COMMAND
harley    616   615  4 15:33:54 console   0:00 ps -af
 peter    527   523  0 14:04:53 tty01     0:00 vi
review
```

As we can see, the only interesting things happening on the system are **harley** running the **ps** command and **peter** using **vi** to edit a file named **review**.

 RULE   To see what other people are up to, use the **ps -af** command.

If you are using a system with many users, you can specify that you want to look at only some of the information. The -u ("userid") option allows you to narrow your choice to a particular userid. Specify the userid after the option. For example:

```
ps -u peter
ps -fu peter
```

Alternatively, you can use the -t ("TTY") option followed by a terminal name. This will display only those processes executing at that terminal. For example:

```
ps -t tty01
ps -ft tty01
```

Finally, you can use the **-p** option to specify a particular pro-cessid:

```
ps -p 527
ps -fp 527
```

13

Controlling Your System

Introduction

All Unix systems have a set of system administration commands. These commands vary from system to system and are documented in the manuals that come with your system.

However, there are a few standard commands that you can use to directly control your system. In this chapter we will cover those commands. You will learn how to clear your terminal screen and to protect it from disruption; how to change your password and your login userid; and, for PC users, how to manipulate the partitions on your hard disk.

Clearing Your Screen: The `clear` Command

Most versions of Unix have commands to take advantage of particular hardware. If you are running Unix on a PC, there may be commands to program the function keys, use particular character sets, and so on.

Two commands, however, are standard and will be present on most systems.

First, the `clear` command clears the screen of your terminal. The syntax is simple:

```
clear
```

clear will erase the screen if it is possible to do so. To find out how the operation should be done, clear will check the description of your terminal in the **termcap** or **terminfo** database (see Chapter 8).

In Chapter 6, we explained how you can create shell scripts, files of commands to be executed as programs. The clear command is a useful tool for such scripts when you wish to clear the screen of extraneous data.

DOS users:

The Unix clear command works much like the DOS CLS command.

Controlling Access To Your Terminal: The mesg Command

A complementary command is **mesg**, which we mentioned in Chapter 12. While clear erases your screen, mesg helps you preserve it.

From time to time, you may receive messages from someone else. Usually, these message will be sent by the **write** or **wall** commands (which we will discuss in Chapter 14). If you are doing some work where you don't want the screen to be disrupted, you can use the **mesg** command. The syntax is

```
mesg [-ny]
```

The two options stand for "yes" and "no." To deny access to your terminal, use

```
mesg -n
```

If someone now tries to send you a message, they will see

```
Permission denied
```

To restore access to your terminal, use

```
mesg -y
```

If you want to find out which setting is in effect, enter the command with no options:

```
mesg
```

The response will be "is y" or "is no".

If find yourself working within a program, like a word processor or editor, and a message does jumble your screen, there is usually a way to redisplay the data. For example, within the vi editor, you can press ^L to redraw the screen. Check the manual for the software you are using.

Some people choose to leave mesg set to "yes" so as not to be cut off from the outside world. If they are interrupted, they simply redraw the screen.

Setting mesg to "no" blocks communications from regular users only. You will still receive messages from the superuser.

Changing Your Password: The passwd Command

When the system manager adds a new userid to the system he chooses a password for that userid. However, there is no reason for anyone—even the superuser—to know your password. As soon as you start work, you should use the passwd command to create a new, secret password.

Password Aging:
A system that automatically forces users to change their passwords at predetermined intervals.

Some systems have a built-in system called *password aging*. This system forces you to change your password at intervals, such as every 30 days. This is often more trouble than it is worth. If you are the system manager, you may wish to turn off this feature.

The basic form of the password command is used to change your password. The syntax is simple:

```
passwd
```

After you enter the command, you will be asked to type your current password. This is to prevent someone from changing your password if you walk away from your terminal for a moment. (This, by the way, is a bad habit. If you leave your terminal unattended and logged in, anyone can erase all your files, even if they can't change your password.)

Once you have typed your current password, the system will ask for a new one. As you type, the characters will not be echoed, in case anyone is looking over your shoulder. After you press <Return>, you will be asked to retype the password to confirm it.

RULE Don't write down your password or tell it to anyone. If you forget your password, ask the system manager for help.

What password should you choose? Some systems have rules that you must follow. A typical rule is that a password must be at least 6 characters long, of which 2 must be alphabetic and 1 must be a digit or a special character. This is a good rule of thumb, even if it is not enforced on your system.

In any case, use passwords that cannot be guessed. For example, don't use your name, your spouse's name, your birthday, or your initials. A good password would be something like `6ggyyt%`.

Guard your password carefully. A person who has it can wreak havoc with your files. It is usually a good idea not to write down your password. If you forget it, ask the system manager for help. If you suspect that anyone knows your password, change it promptly.

Some older Unix systems have a secret method that allows you to enter a short password. The first time you enter such a password, the system will refuse it and ask for a longer one. However, if you persist, the short password will be accepted after three tries.

Obviously, short passwords are a risk. If your system does allow such passwords and you use one, you do so at your own risk. Just remember, you didn't read about it here.

Managing Passwords

If you are a superuser, there are several forms of the `passwd` command that allow you to control much of the password system. The first form of `passwd` has the syntax

`passwd` *userid*

This allows you to change or eliminate the password for any userid. For example, to set a new password for `peter`, enter

```
passwd peter
```

When you change someone else's password as superuser, you will not be asked to enter the old password. This is because the system manager is allowed to change any password and, in many cases, he may not know the old value.

If you want, you can remove a password by pressing <Return> by itself instead of entering a new password:

```
New Password: <Return>
```

In this case, what you are really doing is specifying a null password. Once you do this, the user will not have to enter a password to log in. On some systems, the login will proceed as soon as the user enters the userid. On other systems, the user will still be prompted for a password, but he can simply press <Return> without entering anything.

If you are using a standalone system there is really no need for you to have passwords and you may want to remove them in this manner.

RULE

If you have a superuser password, be sure not to forget it. If you do, you may have to reinstall the entire system.

Hint

DOS users:

On a multiuser system, passwords are imperative to keep people from causing damage, accidental or otherwise.

Password Attributes:
Values that are used to control the password system, including password aging.

The other forms of the `passwd` command allow you to specify *password attributes*: values that are used to control the password system. Passwords attributes are available only on some systems: in particular, those systems that use a "shadow" file (explained in the next section) for extra security.

The first such form of the `passwd` command allows you to delete a password for a userid. On some systems this will mean that the user will not be prompted for a password when he logs in. On other systems, the user will be forced to enter a new password the next time he tries to log in. If you really want to remove a password permanently, replace it with a null password as in the previous example.

The syntax for deleting a userid's password is:

`passwd -d` [`-f`] [`-x` *maxtime*] [`-n` *mintime*] *userid*

The `-d` option deletes the password. The `-f` ("force") option forces the user to change the password the next time he logs in.

The `-x` ("expires") and `-n` options are followed by numbers that set up automatic password aging. The number after `-x` specifies the maximum number of days for which a password is valid for the specified userid. If this number of days elapses, the user will be automatically prompted to enter a new password. To turn off password aging, enter the number 0.

The number after the `-n` option specifies a minimum number of days that the user must wait before changing a new password.

Here are some examples. To delete the password for userid `peter`, enter

```
passwd -d peter
```

To delete the password for userid `harley`, but force the user to specify a new password the next time he logs in, use

```
passwd -d -f harley
```

(On some systems, `-f` is the default. Even if you omit it the user will still be prompted for a new password.)

To delete the password for userid `kevin`, force the user to specify a new password, require the user to respecify the password every 30 days, and prevent the user from changing a new password until 20 days have elapsed, use

```
passwd -d -f -x 30 -n 20 kevin
```

The next form of the password command allows you to lock someone out of the system. This means that they will not be able to log in until you, as superuser, assign them a password. This is useful to temporarily restrict access for a particular userid without having to actually remove it completely.

The syntax is

passwd -l [**-f**] [**-x** *maxtime*] [**-n** *mintime*] *userid*

The usage is the same as in the previous examples, except you use the **-l** ("lock") option instead of **-d**. For example, to temporarily lock userid **addie** out of the system, use

```
passwd -l addie
```

The final two forms of the **passwd** command are

```
passwd -s
passwd -sa
```

The **-s** ("status") option displays the status of your password. Any user can use this option. For example, if you enter

```
passwd -s
```

you might see

```
peter PS 06/23/90 0 7000
```

The first word is the userid, **peter**. After this comes a 2-character status code. The possibilities are

PS   has a password
LK   locked
NP   no password

Following this code is the date on which the password was last changed, in this case, June 23, 1990. The last two numbers are the minimum number of days required between changes and the maximum number of days the password is valid.

These numbers correspond to the values given with the **-n** and **-x** options described above. They will appear only if your system supports password aging.

If you use the **-a** ("all") option along with **-s**, you will get status information for all the userids in the system. While all userids can use **-s**, only the superuser can use **-sa**.

How Does Unix Keep Track of Passwords?

There is an old system and a new system. In the old system, Unix keeps your userid, password, and some other information in a file named /etc/passwd. (That is, a file named passwd in the directory named etc.)

Shadow File:
A file, used on some Unix systems, that holds encoded passwords and password attributes.

The new system also uses this file. However, the actual password, along with its attributes, is kept in a *shadow file*, named /etc/shadow. Only systems that use shadow files can support password aging.

An interesting thing about Unix is that the /etc/passwd file is not secret. Although only the superuser can modify it, anyone can look at it. However, if there is a shadow file, it is kept secret from everyone except the superuser.

If you would like to look at the /etc/passwd file on your system, use the command

```
more /etc/passwd
```

(As we will learn in Chapter 23, the **more** command will display a file, one screenful at a time. If there is more than one screenful of output, the bottom line will display

```
--More--
```

You can then press the <Space> bar to display the next screenful.)

If you take a look at your /etc/passwd file, you will see that it looks something like this:

```
root:x:0:1:Admin:/:
daemon:x:1:1:Admin:/:
bin:x:2:2:Admin:/bin:
sys:x:3:3:Admin:/usr:
adm:x:4:4:Admin:/usr/adm:
uucp:x:5:5:uucp:/usr/lib/uucp:
nuucp:x:10:10:uucp:/usr/spool/uucppublic:/usr/lib/uucp/uucico
sync:x:67:1:Admin:/:/bin/sync
lp:x:71:2:lp:/usr/spool/lp:
listen:x:72:4:NETWORK:/usr/net/nls:
sysadm:x:0:0:General System
Administration:/usr/admin:/bin/rsh
setup:x:0:0:First Time Setup:/usr/admin:/bin/rsh
powerdown:x:0:0:Power Down Machine:/usr/admin:/bin/rsh
checkfsys:x:0:0:Check Diskette File
System:/usr/admin:/bin/rsh
makefsys:x:0:0:Make Diskette File System:/usr/admin:/bin/rsh
mountfsys:x:0:0:Mount Diskette File
System:/usr/admin:/bin/rsh
umountfsys:x:0:0:Unmount Diskette File
System:/usr/admin:/bin/rsh
harley:x:100:1:Harley Hahn:/usr/harley:/bin/sh
UnErase:NONLOGIN:11:1:UnErase Daemon:/:
peter:x:101:1:Peter Norton:/usr/peter:/bin/sh
kevin:x:102:1:Kevin Goldstein:/usr/kevin:
addie:x:103:1:Addie Breffle:/usr/addie:
```

Each of these entries has the following format:

userid
password
userid number
groupid number
descriptive comment
home directory
name of the shell program

Many of the entries are for system management and we can ignore them. The root userid, which we know well, is always first. At the end are the entries for the various userids used by individual people. Let's take a look at one:

```
peter:x:101:1:Peter Norton:/usr/peter:/bin/sh
```

First, we see that the userid is **peter**. From the descriptive comment in the fifth field, we see that this userid was set up for Peter Norton. This information is put in by the system manager when he adds a new user to the system.

After the userid comes the password. In this example, all the passwords are represented by "**x**". This means that the actual passwords are being kept in the shadow file. In systems without a shadow file, the password would be here. However, it would be encoded.

The encoding uses 13 characters chosen from a 64-character alphabet, including . (period), /, 0 to 9, A to Z, and a to z. Here is a typical example:

```
peter:iI/JsFoOR5sHc:101:1:Peter Norton:/usr/peter:/bin/sh
```

The Unix password encryption is very difficult to break. If you ever think about printing out some encoded passwords and trying to figure out the actual values, don't do it. You'll be wasting your time.

After the password comes the userid number. Within Unix, each userid is known by a number. Although you will rarely care what your number is, it's there if you want to look.

The next field is a groupid number. We won't be dealing with groups until Chapter 16. Briefly, each userid belongs to a group. It is possible to share files within your group without having to give access to everyone on the system. Each group has a groupid—a name. Like userids, each groupid is known internally by a number.

In the last example, **peter** is userid number 101, a member of group number 1.

The next field is the descriptive comment which we already mentioned. Following this is the name of the home directory for the userid. We will meet home directories in Chapter 18. For now, let's say that it is the directory which is set aside for your exclusive use. In this case, the home directory is **peter**, which is within another directory named usr. Thus, the name /usr/peter.

The final part of the /etc/passwd entry gives the name of the shell that will be started when the userid logs in. In this case, peter uses the Bourne shell, so we see /bin/sh. This means that the shell program is stored in a file named sh, within the directory named bin.

Not all entries will have this field specified. In such cases, the shell will be the default shell. On most systems, this is the Bourne shell. On some newer systems, the default is the Korn shell.

Displaying Your Userid and Groupid Numbers: The id Command

Most of the time, you won't care what your userid and groupid numbers are. However, if it does come up, there is an easier way to find them than by displaying the /etc/passwd file. You can use the id command. The syntax is simple:

```
id
```

A example of typical output is

```
uid=101(peter) gid=1(staff)
```

In this case, the userid is peter. This userid is number 101. It belongs to a group named staff that is group number 1.

Changing Your Userid Temporarily: The su Command

From time to time, you may want to change to another userid temporarily without logging out. To do this, you use the su ("substitute userid") command. There are three forms of this command. The syntax is

```
su [-] [userid]
su [-] userid -c "command"
su [-] userid -r "command"
```

In the simplest form, you enter su followed by the name of the userid you wish to switch to. For example, the command

```
su harley
```

requests that the current userid be temporarily changed to har-ley. When you make such a request, you will be prompted for the password for the new userid. If you do not know it, the request will be denied. If you are the superuser, you will not be asked for a password.

When you are finished working under the new userid, you can return to your original userid by pressing ^D (Control-D) to send the eof code.

If, at any time, you wish to confirm what userid you are working under, use the id command. The logname and who am i commands will display the original userid—only the id command always shows the current userid.

RULE	To check what your current userid is, you must use the id command.

If you enter the su command without specifying a userid, su will use root as a default. Thus, the following two commands are equivalent:

```
su
su root
```

This is handy when you are the system manager and you need to enter a few superuser commands. As we mentioned in Chapter 7, it is a good idea to work as superuser only when necessary, in order to avoid causing accidental damage. Using su is a common way to become superuser for just one or two commands.

Here is an example. Say that the system manager is currently logged in as melissa. She wants to enter a command to lock the password for userid mxyzptlk, who is temporarily visiting another dimension. Such a command requires superuser privilege. The sequence of commands that she enters looks like this:

1. `$ su`
2. `Password:`
3. `# passwd -l mxyzptlk`
4. `# ^D`
5. `$`

Here is what happened: At the shell prompt ($), the system manager entered the su command (line 1). Since the default is userid root, this requests a temporary change to superuser. The system prompted for the superuser password (line 2) which she entered.

She then became superuser, as we can see by the # prompt (see Chapter 7). She entered the command to lock the password for mxyzptlk (line 3). At the next prompt, she pressed ^D (line 4) to exit back to her original userid. In line 5, she was back under userid melissa, as we can see from the $ prompt.

Occasionally, you will want to use a different userid under the same environment as that userid. For example, you may want to test something by temporarily changing to userid peter exactly as if peter had logged in. If you put a minus sign (-) just after the command name, the su command will do this for you:

```
su - peter
```

This means that peter's .profile or .login initialization file will be executed just as it is when peter logs in. As always, when you exit by pressing ^D, the environment will revert back to its original context.

As you might imagine, su is often used to execute just one command, usually as superuser. Instead of changing to root, entering the command, and then pressing ^D to exit, you can do it all directly. For this, you use the second or third forms of the su command:

```
su [-] userid -c "command"
su [-] userid -r "command"
```

The -c ("command") option tells su to execute the specified command under the auspices of the specified userid and then return immediately.

For example, to execute the password change that we saw above you can use:

```
su root -c "passwd -l mxyzptlk"
```

Notice that with this form of the su command you must specify the userid. There is no default to root.

The -r ("restricted") option works the same way as -c, except that the command is executed within a restricted shell (see Chapter 6).

14

Communicating With Other Users

Introduction

You may be one of the lucky ones who has a Unix workstation all to yourself. However, if you share a system, you are lucky in another way: Unix provides several ways to communicate with other users and it can be fun to pass messages back and forth.

Basically, there are two ways to communicate with people: you can talk to them directly or you can send them a message. With Unix you have the same two options. In this chapter, you will learn how to "talk" with someone else who is logged in. In Chapter 15, we will explain the mail system, which you can use to send and receive messages.

Communicating with Another User: The write Command

Unix provides a nice way to let you communicate with other users as long as they are logged in at the same time as you. You use the write command to connect your terminal to another terminal. You then type messages back and forth. When you are finished, press the eof key, ^D, to end the command. (The eof key is described in Chapter 9.)

The syntax for the **write** command is

write *userid* [*terminal*]

Simply specify the name of the userid to which you want to connect. For example:

```
write peter
```

As we mentioned in Chapter 7, a userid may be logged in to more than one terminal at the same time. If this is the case with the userid you specify, the **write** command will not know which terminal you want. In this case, you must identify the terminal. For example,

```
write peter tty03
```

If you do not, the **write** command will select one of the terminals for you. However, this may not work out. If the person is not actively working at that particular terminal, you will not get a response.

Preparing to Establish Communication

Before you enter a **write** command, it is a good idea to confirm that the userid you want is logged in. For this, use the **who** command that we discussed in Chapters 7 and 12. As an example, let's say that you are logged in as userid **melissa** and you want to talk to the person whose userid is **randy**. Before you issue the **write** command, you enter

```
who -H
```

and you see:

```
NAME          LINE           TIME
melissa       console        Jun 30  19:45
randy         tty01          Jun 30  12:32
peter         tty02          Jun 29  10:12
peter         tty03          Jun 30  17:34
```

(You will recall that the **-H** option displays the headings.)

In this case, `randy` is logged in so you can go ahead and enter

```
write randy
```

But what if you wanted to talk with the person whose userid is `peter`? Since `peter` is logged in to more than one terminal, you must specify the one you want. If you enter

```
write peter
```

the **write** command will respond with

```
peter is logged on more than one place.
You are connected to "tty02".
Other locations are:
tty03
```

What has happened is that **write** has connected you to the first terminal in the list that `peter` is using. However, as we mentioned above, this may not be the terminal at which the user is actively working. Far better to figure out which terminal you want and specify it directly.

But how do you know which terminal is being used? If we look at the output of the **who** command we will see a clue. We see that `peter` logged in to `tty02` on June 29 at 10:12 pm. Later, the same userid logged in to `tty03` on June 30 at 5:34 pm (remember, Unix uses a 24-hour clock).

However, let's investigate further, using the **ps** command that we discussed in Chapters 7 and 12. As we explained, the **-af** options (the "snoop" command) give you a good way to find out what all the userids are doing:

```
ps -af
```

In this case, you see

```
    UID    PID   PPID  C     STIME TTY       TIME COMMAND
melissa    201   200   7  20:53:18 console  0:00 ps -af
peter      158    92  80  20:00:42 tty03     4:46 vi book
randy      139    91  80  20:52:37 tty01    17:02 mail addie
```

Userid `melissa` is executing a `ps` command, the command you just entered. Userid `randy` is sending mail to userid `addie`. (We will discuss how to do this in Chapter 15.) And userid `peter` is using the `vi` editor to edit a file named `book`.

We know that `peter` is logged in to both `tty02` and `tty03`. We might suspect that terminal `tty03` is where the action is because `peter` has logged in there more recently. The `ps -af` command shows this is the case: Not only do we see that `peter` is active on `tty03`, we also notice that nothing important is occurring on `tty02` as it is not even mentioned. If we want to confirm this, we can ask explicitly by using the `ps` command with the `-t` option:

```
ps -t tty02
```

We see

```
PID TTY        TIME COMMAND
 96 tty02      0:00 sh
```

As we suspected, nothing is happening here. There is just a shell waiting for input.

So, we know that the best command to talk with `peter` at this time is

```
write peter tty03
```

Problems Connecting to Another Terminal

When you enter the `write` command, it will attempt to connect you to the appropriate terminal. Occasionally this will not be possible. For example, say that you want to talk with the user who logs in as userid `kevin`. You enter

```
write kevin
```

However, `kevin` is not logged in (you forgot to check first with the `who` command). You will see

```
kevin is not logged on
```

Even if `kevin` is logged in, you will not be able to establish contact if he has entered the `mesg -n` command (see Chapter 13). This command tells Unix to disallow messages. However, if you are the superuser, Unix will override the prohibition. The superuser can contact anyone at any time.

RULE   The superuser can always send messages to any userid.

When the superuser sends messages, there is no way for him to know if the userid he is contacting has restricted access to its terminal. This means that if you use `mesg -n` and you are subsequently interrupted by someone signaling you, don't be rude: you are dealing with a person who can erase all your files with a single command.

How To Respond When Someone Contacts You

Most of the time, the `write` command will make contact. When it does, it will cause your terminal to beep. This tells you that a connection has been established. At this time, the person you are contacting will see something like this

```
Message from melissa on hahn (console) [ Sat Jun 30
23:50:38 ]...
```

and his terminal will beep as well.

In this case, the notice means that userid `melissa`, logged in at the console on the Unix system named hahn, is trying to make contact. (The system name, hahn in this case, is chosen by the system manager when he installs Unix. This is the same name that is displayed by the uname command—see Chapter 12.)

To complete the connection, you enter your own write command:

```
write melissa
```

If you suspect that the userid is logged in to more than one terminal, specify the one in the notice:

```
write melissa console
```

Otherwise, you may be connected to the wrong terminal. The **write** command is not smart enough to guess that you want to connect to the terminal that contacted you.

Once you enter your **write** command, the person at the other terminal will see a notice telling him that you have connected. You are now ready to talk.

Talking Back and Forth

Once your terminal is connected to another terminal, each line that you and the other person type will be displayed on both screens. As you type, the characters are displayed on your screen. As soon as you press <Return>, the entire line is written to the other terminal.

This means that messages can be passed at the same time, which can be confusing. To avoid a jumble of intermixed words, Unix users follow a convention similar to that used by people who talk over a radio. Only one person at a time types a message. At the end of the message, he types -o-. This stands for "over." This signifies that the other person can now respond.

This is important when you type messages that are more than one line. The other person will not see each line until you press <Return>, and he will have no way of knowing if you are finished until he sees -o-.

At the end of the conversation, one of you types -oo-. This stands for "over and out." You can now press the **intr** key to terminate the **write** command. (The **intr** key aborts a command. On most systems, this key is either <Delete> or ^D. See Chapter 9 for details.)

Here is a sample conversion. Userid **melissa** at the console enters

```
write randy
```

She hears a beep. At the same time, on his terminal, the user logged in as **randy** hears a beep and sees:

```
Message from melissa on hahn (console) [ Sat Jun 30
23:50:38 ]...
```

He enters

```
write melissa
```

This completes the connection. On her terminal, the user who is logged in as melissa sees

```
Message from randy on hahn (tty01) [ Sat Jun 30
23:50:55 ]...
```

She starts the conversation by entering

```
Hi Randy -o-
```

randy enters

```
What's happening? -o-
```

melissa enters

```
I have a riddle for you.
How do you catch a unique rabbit? -o-
```

randy enters

```
I give up. -o-
```

melissa enters

```
You "nique" up on him.
Here's another one:
How do you catch a tame rabbit? -o-
```

randy enters

```
How? -o-
```

melissa enters

```
"Tame" way. -o-
```

After a pause, randy enters

```
I don't get it. -o-
```

melissa enters

```
Don't worry. I'll explain it later.
That's all for now, bye. -oo-
^D
```

Now that **melissa** has pressed **^D** (the **eof** key), the **write** command is terminated.

On **randy**'s terminal, **write** displays **<EOT>** ("end of transmission"). He now presses **^D** and gets back to his work. **melissa**'s terminal displays **<EOT>**, completing the conversation.

Broadcasting a Message to All Users: The **wall** Command

Aside from sending messages to a particular user, you can also send a message to all users. This is convenient when you have something of universal interest to announce. Such messages are typically used to inform users that the system will be going down at a specified time.

The command to use is **wall** ("write to all users"). The syntax is simple:

```
wall
```

If you are not the superuser, you will have to specify that the **wall** command is in the **/etc** directory by using

```
/etc/wall
```

We explained this issue in Chapter 12, when we discussed the **whodo** command, which has the same requirement. Briefly: Since the **wall** command is usually used by the system manager, the program itself is not stored in one of the directories that are readily accessible by regular users. Thus, you have to specify in which directory the program resides. (We will explain directories in Chapter 16.)

Once you enter the command, **wall** will wait for your input. You can type as many lines as you want (although prudence and consideration dictate that you should keep such messages short). When you are finished, press the **eof** key, **^D. wall** will then send your message to every userid that is logged in.

If a userid has set **mesg -n** (see Chapter 13), the terminal will not be interrupted with your message unless you are the super-user. Superuser messages are never blocked.

Here is an example. You are logged in as superuser and you wish to make a system-wide announcement. You enter

```
wall
```

The **wall** command is now waiting for your message. You enter

```
At 3 PM today, the system will be unavailable
for the rest of the day
^D
```

Once you press the **eof** code at the end of the message (**^D**), **wall** sends the message to all users. They see

```
Broadcast message from root (console) on hahn Sun
Jun 1 12:25:26
At 3 PM today, the system will be unavailable
for the rest of the day
```

15

The Unix Mail System

Introduction

Unix provides several ways for you to share information with other users. First, you can send them messages, using the `write` and `wall` commands that we discussed in Chapter 14. Second, you can set up some of your files so that a select group of people have permission to access them. This is a good way to share data.

For most people, though, the most important way to communicate and to share data is via the mail facility. In this chapter, we will introduce you to the various Unix mail programs. We will show you how to use the mail program on your system to send and receive messages.

Mail:
A file of textual information that is sent from one userid to another.

Electronic Mail:
Same as mail.

E-Mail:
Same as mail.

Message:
A specific file of data that is to be mailed.

Where Can You Send Mail? UUCP and the Internet

Mail refers to textual information that you can send from one userid to another. Sometimes mail is called *electronic mail* or *E-mail*. It's all the same. The important idea is that you are sending data from one place to another. A *message* is a particular piece of mail.

The message may be as short as a one-line note; a message might also be a large program that you are sending across the country to someone else. Just about anything that can be expressed using the standard ASCII character set (see Chapter 4) can be sent via the mail.

In principle, you can send mail to anyone on your own system and anyone who uses a computer that is connected to yours. The connection does not need to be direct. You may send mail to another system that connects to yours over the telephone only once a day. Your system will hold the mail and pass it along as soon as it gets a chance.

You can also send mail that will be passed from one site to another until it reaches a final destination. If you have access to a major Unix site, it is altogether possible that, via that site, you can send mail all over the world.

There are a variety of mail systems that are used with Unix. The basic one is called UUCP (each letter is pronounced individually), which stands for "Unix to Unix Copy." UUCP is a family of programs that implements the transfer of files from one Unix computer to another. Many Unix systems use UUCP to transfer mail. The principal UUCP program that handles the mail is called smail.

UUCP:

Unix to Unix Copy; programs that transfer data from one computer to another.

Unix systems using UUCP are connected worldwide. Mail passes from one computer to another, automatically, until it reaches its final destination. The collection of all the computers that can be reached this way is sometimes called the *UUCP network*. Unix people often use the term *UUCP* to refer to this network. For example, someone might ask you, "Is there a way that I can reach you on UUCP?"

UUCP Network:

The collection of all the computers to which mail can be sent via UUCP.

Another important worldwide network is the *Internet*. This is actually a collection of many networks and subnetworks that has its own mail facility, more sophisticated than UUCP. The principal Internet program that handles the mail is called sendmail.

Internet:

A worldwide collection of networks and subnetworks.

The Internet connects most universities and research facilities as well as a good number of government departments and computer-oriented corporations. If you are at a university, you can probably find a way to access the Internet.

The Internet and UUCP handle much of the mail within the country. Considered together, they form the backbone of the Usenet news network that we discussed in Chapter 11.

Gateway:
A connection between two dissimilar networks, often used for delivering mail.

From the Internet, you can also send and mail to other systems, such as MCI Mail, AT&T Mail, and CompuServe. The connection between such networks is called a *gateway*. Gateways provide a means of transferring mail between two different types of networks. From our point of view, fortunately, it is all automatic. All we need to do is make sure that we send the mail to the correct address.

Obtaining Access to Remote Mail

All Unix systems come with built-in mail facilities. With little or no trouble, you should be able to send mail to the other users on your system. Connecting your computer to UUCP or to the Internet is another matter. Most of the software you need should come with your version of Unix. However, hooking things together requires a great deal of expertise and is not for the faint at heart. Unfortunately, managing such connections is beyond the scope of this book.

If you are a beginner and you want outside mail access, the best idea is to dial in to another larger system. As we described in Chapter 2, your computer will emulate a terminal. You can use the larger system as a place to send and receive mail.

Public Access Unix:
A service, possibly costing money, that provides Unix to the public.

To find such a system, ask around your area. If you are associated with a university, you may be able to get an account on one of their Unix machines. Alternatively, many cities have facilities that provide this service, which is often called *public access unix*. You may have to pay for connect time, but if you confine yourself to reading and sending mail the cost won't be much.

On a national level, a nonprofit organization called UUNET Communication Services offers access to UUCP and Usenet (see Chapter 11). UUNET provides service from anywhere in the world. You can reach them at (703) 876-5050. Ask for their free information brochure.

In the Unix mail community the UUNET computer is an important one. It not only acts as one of the principal links in the UUCP network but as a gateway between UUCP and the Internet.

Address:
A description of how to send mail to a particular recipient.

Unix Mail Addresses

When you send mail to someone you have to specify their *address*. An address is a description of how to reach the userid that is to receive the mail. Unlike a regular postal address, a Unix address consists of a single string of characters.

On your own system, a person's address is simply his userid. For example, on our system, we can send mail to Peter by using the address `peter`.

When you send mail outside your own computer, the addresses become more complex. Basically, you will run into two important types of addresses: Internet and UUCP.

Most Internet addresses look like this:

userid@domain

The *domain* is the full name of the destination computer. It is in the form of one or more names separated by periods. Each of these names describes a *subdomain*. Here is an example:

```
alfonso@cs.ucsd.edu
```

An Internet domain usually ends in a short suffix that identifies the type of institution or the country. Some of the common suffixes that you will see within the United States are edu (educational), gov (government), mil (military), and com (commercial).

To understand an Internet address, read from right to left. In the example above, we see that the mail goes to an educational organization which has a computer named `ucsd`. From there, the mail goes to a local computer named `cs` (possibly the Computer Science Department's computer) to a userid named `alfonso`.

With UUCP, you have to know the exact route that you want the mail to take. UUCP addresses are in the form

computer1!computer2!...!userid

—a series of names separated by exclamation marks. You read UUCP addresses from left to right. The mail goes from computer to computer, just as you specify, until it is delivered to the userid on the last computer.

Here is an example:

```
ucsd!sdsu!berick!delbr!eysd!rick
```

In this case, the mail first goes to the computer named `ucsd`. From there it is sent to the computer named `sdsu`, then to the computer named `berick`, then to the computer named `delbr`, then to the computer named `eysd`, and finally, within `eysd`, to the userid named `rick`.

As we mentioned in Chapter 9, the exclamation mark is often pronounced "bang." Thus, if a Unix person were to read you the address in our example—say, over the telephone—he would say "U C S D bang S D S U bang berick bang..." and so on.

For you to be able to send messages to this address, your computer would need to be able to send mail to `ucsd` and all the other computers would have to be connected as described. If any one of these links fails, the mail will be returned to you as being undeliverable.

Internet mail is more sophisticated. All you do is specify the destination and the network software figures out how to route the mail. However, connecting to the Internet is a complex process and is restricted to certain types of organizations. Anyone can use UUCP.

As you might imagine, UUCP addresses can become quite long, especially if you are mailing over a long distance. To simplify matters, you can take advantage of certain UUCP computers that act as well-known switching points.

There are a number of these computers, scattered around the country, and they can directly pass mail to many other computers. Probably the most well known is `uunet`, a computer operated by UUNET Communications Services, the organization that we described earlier.

Many people arrange for their computer to dial `uunet` regularly, to send mail and to check for any mail that is waiting. When you mail to such computers, the UUCP address will be shortened because they are only one connection away from a major connection point.

Let us consider the last example. We had to go through four computers to get to `eysd`. As it happens, `eysd` regularly connects to `uunet`. Thus, if your computer can mail directly to `uunet`, you could use the address

```
uunet!eysd!rick
```

As another example, let's say that you can't reach `uunet` directly, but you can mail to a computer named `herbert` which can reach `uunet`. You could send mail to the address

```
herbert!uunet!eysd!rick
```

If you correspond with many people, you will find that most of the addresses you use will resemble the ones we described here. Occasionally, though, Unix addressing can get complex and you may need to find an expert to help you.

The Mail Programs: `mailx` and `mail`

Earlier we mentioned two programs, `smail` (UUCP) and `sendmail` (Internet). These programs work behind the scenes to send and receive mail from remote systems. However, you never really interact with these programs directly: You use a mail program that is designed to act as a front end for the actual message passing.

There are a number of such programs that you might encounter. In System V, there is a new program and an old program. The old program is named `mail`. This program is included with System V for old time's sake but, in most cases, you will want to use the new program.

The new program is named `mailx`—think of the "`x`" as standing for "extended." Generally speaking, `mailx` can do everything that `mail` can do plus more. In this book, we will assume that you are using `mailx`.

On non-System V systems you may find other programs. BSD (Berkeley Unix) has a program called `Mail` (note the upper-case "`M`"). You may also see `mush` ("mail user's shell"). These programs all provide the same basic service—reading and sending mail—but with different bells and whistles.

The `mailx` program that we describe here is the standard mail program for System V. Like many other Unix programs, `mailx` has far more options, commands, and internal settings than most people need. In this chapter, we will explain the basic facilities that you need for everyday use. As you gain experience with `mailx`, we encourage you to read the documentation that comes with your system to learn the nuances.

If you are using a different mail program, rest assured that it will carry out the same basic functions that we describe here, albeit in a slightly different way.

Sending Mail

The `mailx` command is used to send and to receive mail. There is a different syntax for each use—you might even consider `mailx` as being two separate commands.

To send mail, you use the **mailx** command with the following syntax:

mailx [**-s** *subject*] *userid...*

The most common way to send mail is to use the **mailx** command followed by the userid of the recipient. If you specify more than one recipient, an identical copy of the message will be sent to each of the userids.

Here are some examples:

```
mailx peter
mailx peter harley
mailx peter harley addie randy kevin melissa
```

As we will see in a moment, each message has several lines of information at its beginning. One of these lines shows the subject of the message. When you send a message, you can specify the subject using the **-s** option. If you do not, **mailx** will prompt you for the information. To specify the subject directly, follow the **-s** option with whatever descriptive information you want.

If your description has **space** characters or punctuation, enclose it in single quotes. This will tell the shell to pass the character string to **mailx** exactly as you typed it. If you omit the single quotes, the shell will interpret the **space** characters and punctuation in its own way, which will be incorrect.

Here are several examples:

```
mailx -s test peter
mailx -s 'book signing party' harley peter
mailx -s '*special-note*' peter kevin melissa randy
```

The first message has the subject "test" and will be sent to userid **peter**. The second message has the subject "book signing party" and will be sent to userids **harley** and **peter**. The third message has the subject "*special-note*" and will be sent to four userids, **peter**, **kevin**, **melissa**, and **randy**.

If we had left out the single quotes in the second example,

```
mailx -s book signing party harley peter
```

the shell would have passed all the words after the **-s** to **mailx** as if they were separate entities. **mailx** would interpret this as a message with the subject "book" that should be sent to four different userids, **signing**, **party**, **harley**, and **peter**.

If we had left out the single quotes in the third example,

```
mailx -s *special-note* peter kevin melissa randy
```

the "*" character would have given us trouble. The shell considers this character to have a special meaning (as we will see later in the book) and it would have been interpreted incorrectly.

As we mentioned, if you do not specify the subject, **mailx** will ask you directly. Here is an example. At the shell prompt (**$**), you enter a command to send a message to **peter** and **harley**:

```
$ mailx peter harley
```

Since you did not specify a subject, **mailx** prompts you by displaying "**Subject:**"

```
$ mailx peter harley
Subject:
```

Enter the subject and press <Return>. You do not need to use single quotes since **mailx** is reading your input directly. If you want to specify a blank subject, just press <Return> without typing anything.

In this example, you enter a subject description and the screen looks like this:

```
$ mailx peter harley
Subject: book signing party
```

Input Mode:
In mailx, *a mode in which the characters you type are collected into a message.*

mailx is now ready to accept your message.

Entering a Message

Command Mode:
In mailx, *a mode in which the characters you type are interpreted as commands.*

In Chapter 8, we explained that the technical term *mode* refers to one of several ways in which a program can behave. **mailx**—indeed most mail programs—can operate in two different modes: *input mode* and *command mode*.

When `mailx` is ready to accept a new message as you type it, you are in input mode. Everything that you type will be collected and, when you signal that you are finished, mailed to the proper recipients.

The rest of the time, `mailx` is in command mode. In command mode, there is a whole family of `mailx` commands that you can use. As a general rule, if you are not composing a message, you are in command mode. As we will see in the examples below, the mode you are in is usually clear by context.

In the previous section, we explained that once you enter the `mailx` command and the subject description, `mailx` is ready to accept your message. In other words, you are in input mode. All you need to do is type your message, as many lines as you want.

When you are finished, press <Return> at the end of the last line and then send the `eof` (end of file) code by pressing ^D (Control-D). This tells `mailx` that your message is complete. To confirm this, `mailx` will display "EOT," which stands for "End of Transmission." (The `eof` code is explained in Chapter 9.)

Once you press ^D, `mailx` will consider your message to be ready and will send it off. `mailx` will then terminate and return you to the shell.

In summary, enter the `mailx` command, type your message, and press ^D.

Here is an example of sending a letter, starting from the shell prompt ($).

```
1  $ mailx -s 'book signing party' harley peter
2  Remember that the English book signing party
3  will be at Buckingham Palace next Thursday.
4  -- Kevin
5  EOT
6  $
```

The `mailx` command is entered on line 1. `mailx` goes into input mode, and the message is entered on lines 2 through 4. On line 5, ^D is pressed to signal the end of the message. `mailx` responds by displaying "EOT" and terminating. Line 6 shows the shell prompt. The shell is now waiting for the next command.

If you are entering a message and you decide to cancel it, send the `intr` code. (On most systems, you will press either <Delete>

or ^C—see Chapter 9.) When you send this code, `mailx` will respond by displaying

```
(Interrupt -- one more to kill letter)
```

If you do not really want to stop, just keep typing. If you do want to stop, press `intr` again—`mailx` will display

```
Interrupt
```

and cancel the message. The reason `mailx` makes you press `intr` twice is so that you cannot wipe out your message by accidentally hitting the wrong key.

Being Careful with Addresses

Earlier, we explained that if you specify the subject description on the command line you should put it in single quotes if it contains `space` characters or punctuation. This tells the shell that the string of characters should be passed to the `mailx` program exactly as written. A similar consideration arises when you are using an address that contains punctuation.

There are two circumstances in which this is important. First, Internet addresses have an at sign (@) as part of the address. As we mentioned in Chapter 9, some Unix systems use the @ character as the `kill` code: the signal to cancel the line that you are currently typing.

On most systems, the kill code is signaled by ^X or ^U. However, if your system uses @, you must make sure that the @ in an Internet address is taken literally. To do this, precede the @ by a backslash (\). This tells the shell that the next character should not have a special meaning. For example:

```
mailx alfonso\@cs.ucsd.edu
```

Make sure that you use the backslash, not the regular forward slash (/).

The second instance in which you must make sure that characters are taken literally occurs when you are using UUCP addresses with the C-shell. As you may remember, UUCP addresses consist of a series of names separated by exclamation marks. In a `mailx` command, a UUCP address will look like this:

```
mailx uunet!eysd!rick
```

The trouble is, when you type an exclamation mark as part of the command line, the C-shell (but not the Bourne shell) interprets the character as having a special meaning.

If you are using the C-shell, you will have to make sure that each exclamation mark is preceded by a backslash:

```
mailx uunet\!eysd\!rick
```

This ensures that the entire address is passed to **mailx** correctly.

Reading Your Mail

To read your mail, you will usually use the **mailx** command with no options:

```
mailx
```

There are a few options that you might use on occasion, and we will cover them later.

When you enter the **mailx** command with the name of a userid, **mailx** assumes that you want to send a message. But when you enter the command without a userid, **mailx** assumes that you want to read your mail.

The first thing **mailx** does is check to see if you have any messages waiting. If you do not, mail will display a message showing that there is no mail for your userid. For example:

```
No mail for harley
```

If you do have mail, **mailx** will display a summary of what is waiting for you:

```
mailx version 3.1 Type ? for help.
"/usr/mail/harley": 4 messages 4 new
>N  1 kevin       Sat Jul  7 22:20   14/364   book signing party
 N  2 peter       Sat Jul  7 22:20   14/285   new computer
 N  3 peter       Sun Jul  8 12:17   14/368   re: more money
 N  4 addie       Sun Jul  8 12:20   12/257   party on Friday
?
```

Probably the most important line here is the one that tells you to type a question mark to get help. If you do, you will see a short explanation of 19 of the `mailx` commands that you can use in command mode.

Notice that the `mailx` summary ends in a question mark. This is the prompt. Whenever you see a question mark you can enter a `mailx` command.

In this example, we see that there are four messages waiting to be read. Each message is summarized by a one-line description. At the beginning of each of these lines we see an "`N`." This shows that the messages are new. If you have seen the message summaries before but have not yet looked at the messages, `mailx` will display "`U`," which stands for "old but unread."

The next point of interest is a number that has been assigned by `mailx`. While we are reading the mail, we can use these numbers to refer to specific messages. Following this number is the name of the userid that sent the mail, and the date and time at which the message was sent.

After the time, `mailx` displays the size of the message as the number of lines and the number of characters. For instance, message 1 consists of 14 lines and 364 characters.

Finally, the end of the one-line description shows the subject of the message.

At all times, `mailx` considers one of the messages to be the "current message." This is the one that is marked by a ">" at the left-hand side of the description. In this case, the current message is number 1. To read the current message, just press <Return>. Here is a typical message:

```
Message  1:
From kevin  Sun Jul  8 15:30:07 1990
Received: by hahn (5.61/1.35)
        id AA00369; Sun, 8 Jul 90 15:30:07 -0600
Date: Sun, 8 Jul 90 15:30:07 -0600
From: kevin (Kevin Goldstein)
Message-Id: <9007082030.AA00369@hahn>
To: harley, peter
Subject: book signing party
Status: RO

Remember that the English book signing party
will be at Buckingham Palace next Thursday.
-- Kevin
```

?

At the end of the message, `mailx` displays the prompt (?) to indicate that you can enter a command.

Header:
The first part of a message.

Let's take a closer look at this message. The first part is called the *header*. The header contains standard information. This information may vary according to your system and your circumstances. The header in our example is typical. It consists of the following lines:

The message number

Who the message is from (`kevin`) and when it was sent

Information concerning the reception of the message (in this case, the message was received by the computer named `hahn`)

The date and time that the message was received

More information about the sender

A unique message ID number assigned by the software

The recipients

The subject description

The status

The status may be "R" or "RO". "R" means that you are currently reading the message. "RO" means that you have previously read this message, and it is considered to be old mail.

Notice that some of the time stamps end with numbers like "-0600". This refers to the number of hours difference between the local time and the Greenwich mean time. This allows you to accurately figure out when a message originated if it came from a different time zone.

After the header comes the *body* of the message: the actual text of the message itself. In our example, the body consists of the three lines starting with "Remember that...."

Once the first message has been displayed, `mailx` shows its prompt (?). We can now enter commands. To quit `mailx`, enter the `q` command.

`mailx` Commands

Like many Unix programs, `mailx` has far more commands than you are likely to use. Within command mode—which is all the time, except when you are composing a message—`mailx` recognizes 69 different commands. You can enter the command any time you see the `mailx` prompt: the question mark (**?**).

Realistically, you need to learn only a few basic commands, which we will explain in this chapter. If you are interested in the more esoteric details of `mailx`, see the documentation that came with your system.

`mailx` commands have the form

command-name message-list arguments

This is a strange syntax. As you can see, all three parts of the command are optional, even the command name. We will explain why in a moment. But first, let's take a look at Figures 15.1 and 15.2, which contain summaries of the basic `mailx` commands. Figure 15.1 shows the commands grouped by category. Figure 15.2 is for reference: It shows the same commands in alphabetical order.

Message Lists

Message List:
The specification of one or more messages to be acted upon by a `mailx` *command.*

Messages are the basic entities on which `mailx` commands operate. Each command acts on the *message list* that you specify. `mailx` is nothing if not flexible: There are a number of ways to specify a message list. These are summarized in Figure 15.3.

To help you understand Figure 15.3, Figure 15.4 contains examples using the **p** [print] command, which displays messages. The examples illustrate each type of message list in the order that they are listed in Figure 15.3. When you are entering a `mailx` command, you can specify any type of message list that makes sense for that command.

Reading Messages

The philosophy behind most Unix mail programs, including `mailx`, is that you should read and process your messages one at a time. This involves three steps:

1. Read a message.
2. If you choose, reply to the message.
3. Delete or save the message.

Stopping `mailx`

q	quit `mailx`
x	exit `mailx` neglecting any changes that have been made

Help

?	display a summary of commands
l	list all of the available commands with no explanations

Displaying Messages

\<Return\>	by itself [empty command]: display the next message
p	[print] display the specified messages
to	display the top few lines of the specified messages
si	display the size, in characters, of specified messages

Current Message

=	display the number of the current message
n	go to the next message in the specified message list

Headers

f	[from] display header summary for specified messages
h	display header summaries

Deleting

d	delete specified messages
dp	delete current message; display (print) next message
u	undelete the specified deleted messages

Saving

s	save the specified messages in the specified file
w	[write] same as **s** only do not save the header
c	[copy] same as **s** only do not mark messages as saved
ho	hold specified messages in the mailbox
fi	read messages from the specified file

Replying and Mailing

r	reply to sender and other recipients
R	reply to sender only
m	enter input mode to mail a message to specified userid

Editing

v	edit the specified message using the **vi** editor

Unix commands

!	execute a single Unix command then return to `mailx`
sh	invoke a new shell; to return to `mailx` press `^D (eof)`

Figure 15.1   *A summary of the basic `mailx` commands, grouped by category.*

<Return>	by itself (empty command): display the next message
!	execute a single Unix command, then return to **mailx**
#	comment: useful for **.mailrc** files (explained later)
=	display the number of the current message
?	display a summary of commands
c	same as **s**; do not mark messages as having been saved
d	delete specified messages
dp	delete current message; display (print) next message
f	(from) display header summary for specified messages
fi	read messages from the specified file
h	display header summaries
ho	hold the specified messages in the mailbox
l	list all of the available commands with no explanations
m	enter input mode to mail a message to specified userid
n	go to next message in specified message list
p	(print) display messages
q	quit **mailx**
r	reply to sender and other recipients
R	reply to sender only
s	save the specified messages in the specified file
sh	invoke a new shell; to return to **mailx** press ^D (eof)
si	display the size, in characters, of specified messages
to	display the top few lines of the specified messages
u	undelete the specified deleted messages
v	edit the specified message using the **vi** editor
w	(write) same as **s** only do not save the header
x	exit **mailx** neglecting any changes that have been made

Figure 15.2   *A summary of the basic* **mailx** *commands, in alphabetical order.*

In this section, we will cover the commands you use to read your messages.

The basic command to read messages is **p** [print]. As we explained in Chapter 9, the Unix culture often uses the word "print" to mean "display."

When you start **mailx** to read your mail, the current message is set to 1. If you want, you could read each message in turn by using the commands

. [a period]	the current message
n	message number *n*
n-m	all messages from numbers *n* to *m* inclusive
^ [a circumflex]	the first message that is not deleted
$ [a dollar sign]	the last message
* [an asterisk]	all messages
userid	all messages from the specified userid
/*string*	all messages containing *string* in subject
:d	all deleted messages
:n	all new messages
:o	all old messages
:r	all messages that have already been read
:u	all messages that are still unread

n and *m* are message numbers
userid is the name of a userid
string is a string of characters

Figure 15.3   *A summary of ways to specify* `mailx` *commands.*

p .	(display the current message)
p 3	(display message 3)
p 3-5	(display messages 3 through 5 inclusive)
p ^	(display the first message that is not deleted)
p $	(display the last message)
p *	(display all the messages)
p harley	(display all message from userid `harley`)
p /test	(display all messages with "`test`" in the subject)
p :d	(display all the messages that have been deleted)
p :n	(display all the new messages)
p :o	(display all the old messages)
p :r	(display all the messages that have been read)
p :u	(display all the messages that are unread)

Figure 15.4   *Examples of specifying a message list for* `mailx` *commands.*

```
p 1
p 2
p 3
```

and so on. However, there is an easier way.

When we introduced `mailx` commands, we showed the syntax as

command-name message-list arguments

At the time, we mentioned that all three parts of the command are optional, including the command name. If you do not specify the command name, `mailx` defaults to the `p` command acting on a single message.

Thus, the following commands are equivalent:

```
3
p 3
```

Both will display message number 3.

If you do not specify a message list, `mailx` defaults to the next message. Thus, if the current message is number 3, pressing <Return> without typing a command will display message number 4. In this case, this would be the same as

```
p 4
```

Thus, you can display all your messages, one after another, by pressing <Return> repeatedly. Each time you press <Return>, `mailx` will display the next message. When you have reached the end, `mailx` will display

```
At EOF
```

to indicate that you are at the end of the file. (As we will see later, all mail is kept in a file.)

Replying to a Message

Replying to a message is easy. After you have displayed the message, enter the `r` command with no message list:

```
r
```

`mailx` will assume that you want to reply to the current message (the one you have just read). If you want to reply to a different message, just specify it. For example:

```
r 4
```

Once you enter the `r` command, `mailx` will start the message for you by filling in an appropriate userid and subject. For example, say that you are logged in as userid `harley` and you have just displayed the following message:

```
Message  1:
From kevin  Sun Jul  8 15:30:07 1990
Received: by hahn (5.61/1.35)
        id AA00369; Sun, 8 Jul 90 15:30:07 -0600
Date: Sun, 8 Jul 90 15:30:07 -0600
From: kevin (Kevin Goldstein)
Message-Id: <9007082030.AA00369@hahn>
To: harley, peter
Subject: book signing party
Status: RO

Remember that the English book signing party
will be at Buckingham Palace next Thursday.
-- Kevin

?
```

At the `mailx` prompt (?), you enter

```
r
```

You will see

```
To: peter kevin
Subject: Re: book signing party
```

You are now in insert mode. Type your message. After the last line, press ^D to indicate you are finished. `mailx` will then send the message.

This example shows us two important points: First, when we replied using the `r` command, our response went to the sender of the message (`kevin`) and everyone else who received the message (`peter`). If you want to reply only to the actual sender of the message, use the R (upper-case "R") command. In this case, if we had used

```
R
```

the response would have gone only to kevin.

The second point is that mailx creates the subject for the response by putting "Re:" in front of the old subject. This shows that the new message is a reply.

Deleting a Message

Most of the time, you will probably want to delete your messages. It is a good idea to delete a message right after you have read it. This keeps the old messages from accumulating.

To delete a message, use the d command. If you do not specify a message list, mailx will delete the current message—the one you have just read. For example, if you have just read message number 3, the following two commands are equivalent:

```
d 3
d
```

A related command is dp. This is similar to issuing the d command followed by the p command. The net result is to delete a message and then display the next one. If you usually read and delete your mail, you will find dp useful. Start by pressing <Return> by itself, and read the first message. Then, enter dp repeatedly to delete the previous message and display the next one.

When you delete a message, it is not really gone until you enter the q command to quit. If you want to get a message back, use u [undelete]. For example, suppose you realize that you have mistakenly deleted message number 3. Before you quit, enter

```
u 3
```

The message will be restored.

Be careful—once you enter the q command, all the deleted messages are lost. You cannot restart **mailx** and get back messages from a previous session.

However, if you wish, there is a way to quit without deleting messages. Instead of q use **x** [exit]. This will tell **mailx** to terminate but to ignore any changes that you might have made. The next time you read your mail, it will look exactly the same as in the previous session.

Saving a Message

The alternative to deleting a message is to save it. To do so, use the **s** command. As with other **mailx** commands, if you do not specify a message list, the current message will be assumed. When you use this command, you must specify the name of the file to which the message should be saved. A good choice is the name of the person who sent you the message.

For example, if you have just read a message from userid **kevin**, you might save it by entering

```
s kevin
```

If you wanted to save messages 3, 4, and 5 to the same file, use

```
s 3-5 kevin
```

If you save to a file that does not exist, **mailx** will create it. If the file already exists, **mailx** will append the message to the end of the file. The data already in the file will not be overwritten.

Occasionally, you may want to omit the header and save only the body of the message. To do this, use the **w** [write] command.

Once you save messages, **mailx** considers them to be processed. When you enter the q command to quit, **mailx** will drop all the messages that have been saved so that you don't have to look at them again. If, for some reason, you want to retain these messages as mail, use **x** to quit.

Alternatively, you can save messages with the **c** [copy] command. This operates the same as **s**, except that the messages are not marked as having been processed. When you quit with q, such messages will be retained.

Thus, a typical way to process your mail is to read a message, reply if necessary, and then save or delete the message.

RULE

Reading your mail: As you read each message, decide immediately whether to save or delete it. Do not let old messages accumulate.

Where Messages are Stored

Mailbox:

A file in which incoming messages are kept until they are read.

When someone sends you a message, it is kept in a file called your *mailbox*. Every userid has a mailbox. It is assigned automatically when the userid is created by the system manager. Although you only have one mailbox, `mailx` can separate one message from another by finding the headers.

Each mailbox is actually a file within a directory owned by the `root` userid. (We will discuss files and directories in Chapter 16.) The name of the directory depends on the version of Unix you use. In System V, the standard directory is `/usr/mail`. Within this directory, incoming mail is stored in a file named after the userid. For example, messages for userid `kevin` are stored in the file `/usr/mail/kevin`.

As we will learn in Chapter 18, each userid has a home directory in which to store personal files. Until your mail is read, the messages are kept in the mailbox directory, which is owned by the `root` userid. On a system that keeps track of how much disk space each userid uses, unread mail is not charged to your account.

However, this can cause problems on a multiuser system if people do not empty their mailboxes. To discourage users from using the mail directory as a long-term storage area, `mailx` has a special built-in feature.

Once you read a message, `mailx` will not resave it in your mailbox unless you make a deliberate request. Instead, if you do not delete or save a message, `mailx` will save it for you. The file will be saved on your own home directory (where it is owned by your userid) in a file by the name of `mbox`.

Here is an example. Say that your userid is `addie` and your home directory is `/usr/addie` (this will make sense when we discuss home directories in Chapter 18). You use `mailx` to check you mail. You have five messages. You read only the first four messages. You delete message 1 and save message 2 to a file named `harley`. When you quit `mailx` by using the `q` command, the following will happen:

Message numbers 1 and 2 will be dropped. Messages 3 and 4 will be saved to /usr/addie/mbox—that is, the mbox file in your home directory. If the file does not already exist, mailx will create it. It the file does exist, mailx will append your message—your previous messages will not be lost. Since you have not yet looked at message 5, it will be retained in your mailbox.

If you have read a message and you cannot decide what to do with it, you can request mailx to resave it in your mailbox by using the ho [hold] command. For example, if you enter

```
ho 1-2
```

and then quit, these messages will not be saved in your mbox file. The next time you start mailx they will still be in your mailbox.

Reading Messages from a File

If you have messages stored in a file, you can access them with mailx in the same way as you access your regular mailbox. To do so, use the fi [file] command. Specify the name of the file and mailx will switch to that file. For example, say that you have saved a number of messages in the file named kevin. You are reading your mail and you decide you want to read the mail in this file. Enter

```
fi kevin
```

mailx will switch from your regular mailbox and read the messages in the file kevin. Using the fi command is a good way to access all the messages that were saved for you in your mbox file. Simply enter

```
fi mbox
```

If you know that you want to read messages from an alternate file when you start mailx, you can use the following syntax:

```
mailx -f filename
```

mailx will start by reading from the file you specify rather than your mailbox. For example:

```
mailx -f mbox
```

In a similar manner, you can ask **mailx** to start by reading the messages in someone else's mailbox, by using the syntax

mailx -u [*userid*]

Of course, this only works if you have permission to read the file in which the mailbox resides. (We will discuss file permissions in Chapter 16.) In practice, this means that the superuser can read anyone's mail. For example, to read the mail for userid **peter**, the superuser can enter

```
mailx -u peter
```

This brings up an important point: Do not depend on Unix mail being completely private. Save love letters and personal notes for a more secure environment.

Entering Commands in Input Mode: The Tilde Escapes

As you know, there are many commands that **mailx** will perform when you are in command mode. However, there are times when you will be composing a message in input mode and you need to enter a command.

You can't type the command directly, as it would just become a part of your message. But there is a way to send a command to **mailx** and still remain in input mode.

In Chapter 9, we talked about escape characters. An escape character tells a program to change from one mode to another. While you are in input mode, a~ (tilde) acts as an escape character if you type it as the first character of the line.

Tilde Escape Command:

A **mailx** *command, starting with a tilde (~), that is used in input mode.*

Using the tilde, there are 24 commands that you can enter. Moreover, one of these commands allows you to enter any of the regular **mailx** commands. Figure 15.5 summarizes the most important of these so-called *tilde escape commands*.

As always, the most important command is the one that displays help information. When you enter ~? (remember, all tilde escape commands must be at the beginning of the line), **mailx** will display a long list of each command with short explanations.

~?	display a summary of all the tilde escape commands
~:	enter a regular `mailx` command
~p	[print] display the message being entered
~h	[header] prompt for subject
~t	[to] add userids to the recipient list
~s	specify the subject
~c	add userids to the cc list
~b	add userids to the bcc list
~v	edit the message using the `vi` editor
~!	execute a single Unix command and then return to `mailx`

Figure 15.5 *Summary of tilde escape commands to use within* `mailx` *input mode.*

The ~: command allows you to enter a regular `mailx` command. Simply specify the regular command after the colon. For example, if you are composing a message and you want to remind yourself of what messages are pending, enter

```
~:h
```

to display the list of header summaries.

Once the command has terminated, `mailx` will display

```
(continue)
```

to let you know that you are back in input mode.

As you are composing, you can display the message as it exists so far by using the ~p [print] command. `mailx` will show you the header and the body.

The next tilde escape command helps you access a valuable facility. Within the header, there are four lines that are useful to you. The first line contains the names of the recipients. The second line contains the subject of the message. We have already seen these parts of the header.

There are, however, two more lines that you might use. You can have a third line that specifies one or more userids that should receive copies of the message. This line will appear as "cc:" followed by the userids. For example:

```
Cc: melissa randy
```

When the message is sent, these two userids will get a copy. In a similar manner, you can send secret copies of the message if the header contains a line like this:

```
Bcc: melissa randy
```

("Bcc" stands for "blind copy.")

The difference between Cc: and Bcc: is that the Bcc: line is not sent as part of the message so nobody knows of its existence.

If you use the ~h command, mailx will prompt you, one line at a time, with each of the four header lines: recipients, subject, copies, blind copies. You can change them and add to them as you wish. When you are finished, you will be returned to input mode.

If you want, you can specify each line directly by using ~t [to] for the recipients, ~s for the subject, ~c for the copies, and ~b for the blind copies. After each command, specify the appropriate information.

For example:

```
~t addie
~s new subject description
~c melissa randy
~b harley peter
```

Most of the time, it is easier to use ~h and let mailx prompt you.

Using vi to Edit Messages

Starting with Chapter 25, you will learn how to use the vi editor that comes with Unix. Once you learn vi, you may want to use it to compose and edit messages.

If you are in input mode, you can enter the ~v command. This tells mailx to start vi. If you have already entered part of the message, it will be sent to vi for you to edit. If you have not yet started typing, you can create the whole message from within vi. Once you leave vi, you will return to mailx, in input mode. As always, press ^D to send your message.

Another use for **vi** is to use it to edit a message that you are reading. Enter the **v** command followed by the message list. For example:

```
v 3
```

mailx will start **vi** with that particular message all ready to be edited. This is handy if you want to, say, modify or extract part of the message and save it to a file.

Creating a Message from Command Mode

From command mode, you may decide that you want to create a brand new message. Say that you are reading your mail and you decide to send a message to userid **addie**. You could quit the program and restart using

```
mailx addie
```

However, this would be disruptive to your work.

As a convenience, **mailx** allows you to pause in your reading and create a new message. Use the **m** [mail] command and specify the recipients. For example:

```
m addie
```

mailx will now switch to input mode so you can type the message. If you want, you can enter the **~v** command to use **vi** to create the message. When you press **^D** to show you are finished, **mailx** will send off the message and return you to command mode.

Entering Unix Commands from Within **mailx**

As a convenience, **mailx** allows you to enter Unix commands from within the mail program.

If you are in command mode, you can execute a single Unix command by entering a **!** character followed by the command. For example:

```
!date
```

Once the command is finished, `mailx` will display a ! character of its own and the ? prompt. This shows you that you are back in `mailx` command mode.

On occasion, you may want to enter a series of Unix commands. In this case, you can have `mailx` pause and start a new shell for you. To do this, enter the `sh` command.

You can enter as many Unix commands as you want. When you are finished, you terminate the shell and return to `mailx` by pressing ^D to send the `eof` code (see Chapter 9).

From within `mailx` input mode, you can enter a single Unix command while you are composing a message. Use ~! followed by the command. For example, if you want to see the time, enter

```
!date
```

After the command has finished, `mailx` will display a ! character. This shows you that you are now back in insert mode. You can continue typing your message.

16

Introduction to the Unix File System

Introduction

The heart of any computer system is its data: documents, programs, databases, spreadsheets, and so on. Within Unix, there is a file system that maintains all of the data. The Unix file system plays a much larger role that you would expect, especially if you compare it to other operating systems.

In this part of the book, we will describe the Unix file system. We start by explaining how data is stored as files and organized into directories. Once we have covered the basics, we then show you how files are managed, how directories are organized, and how you can manipulate your data directly to suit your needs.

What Is a File?

In everyday life, a "file" is a collection of papers or documents. A salesman might keep a file of potential customers. An accountant might keep a file of correspondence.

In the computer world, "file" has a more specific meaning: a collection of data that is given a name and stored, usually on a disk or tape. Computer files hold documents, spreadsheets, programs, and so on.

File:

Any source from which data can be read or any target to which data can be written.

Within Unix, the same word, "file," takes on a much broader meaning. A *file* is any source from which data can be read or any target to which data can be written. For example, to print data, you write it to the file that represents the printer. To receive data from the keyboard, you read data from the file that represents the keyboard. Similarly, you display data by writing it to the file that represents the display.

In Unix, all input and output is done using files. As far as we are concerned, Unix makes only minimal distinctions between files that store data on disk and files that represent physical devices.

RULE

The term "file" refers to any source of input or target of output, not only to a repository of data.

This generality is of enormous importance: it means that Unix has a great deal of built-in flexibility. Essentially all input and output facilities can be accessed in a standard manner. For example, when you run a program, you can choose to send its output to the display, the printer, or a disk file, as you see fit.

Just as important, when you write a program, you do not need to concern yourself with where the input will come from and where the output will go. You just design your program to read and write in a standard way. When you run a program, you can choose any input source or output destination you want.

Later in the book we will show you how to specify such choices directly, as you enter commands. If you are a DOS user, you may be familiar with this idea. However, you will find the Unix facilities to be more flexible and much more useful.

Hint

••••

DOS users:
The word "file" is used with far more generality in Unix than in DOS.

The Three Types of Unix Files

Ordinary File:
A file that stores everyday information, such as programs and data.

Regular File:
Same as an ordinary file.

Unix supports three types of files: *ordinary files*, *directories*, and *special files*.

An *ordinary file* is what most people think of when they refer to a "file." Sometimes ordinary files are called *regular files*.

Ordinary files store data. These are the files that you work with most of the time. For instance, when you use a word processor, both the word processing program and your documents are stored as ordinary files.

DOS users:

The type of files that are used with DOS are called "ordinary files" in Unix.

Directory:
A file that contains the information needed to access other files.

Special File:
A file that represents a device.

The next type of file, a *directory*, contains the information used to access other files. We use directories to organize files into convenient groups. In a sense, directories contain other files. Conversely, every file is stored in some directory. To describe a file, you need specify only its name and the name of the directory in which it resides. Two files may have the same name, as long as they reside in different directories.

A directory can contain not only ordinary files and special files, but other directories. This enables you to organize your files into a hierarchical system. Within the bounds of this system, you can arrange your directories using whatever design suits your needs. Moreover, you can modify your storage strategy as conditions change. We will discuss this topic in depth in Chapter 17.

The last type of file, the *special file*, represents a physical device. To read or write to a device, all you need to do is read or write to the special file that represents that device. Unix will take care of the details automatically.

By referring to special files, you can obtain access to any device on the system, including the keyboard and the display (for the console or for any other terminal), a printer, or a plotter. In fact, Unix will allow you to use special files to access a disk drive, a disk partition, the system timer, and even the memory. Moreover, there is a special device, called null, that can be used as an empty source of input or as a place to send unwanted output.

DOS users:

Where DOS uses device names to access devices directly, Unix uses special files.

Since Unix provides such a broad implementation of input and output, you must be careful when you hear the word "file." Sometimes it means an ordinary file; sometimes it means any type of file.

For example, when you read something like

Use the `ls` command to list the names of files in a directory.

the statement refers to any type of file. After all, a directory can contain ordinary files, special files, or other directories.

However, if you read

You can use the `vi` editor to create and modify a file.

you are dealing with ordinary files, as these are the only type that can be edited.

Most of the time, the meaning of the word "file" will be clear from context. In this book, we will make sure to be specific if there is any doubt.

Text Files and Binary Files

Ordinary files can contain just about any type of data. There are two types of ordinary files that you will run into frequently: *text files* and *binary files*.

Text File:
An ordinary file that contains ASCII-coded data.

Text files are ordinary files that contain information in a form that is understandable by people. Text files hold documents, shell scripts, numerical data, and so on. The data in text files is stored using the ASCII code (see Chapter 4), in which each character is represented by a single byte. Since text files are stored using ASCII, you can display or print them.

Binary File:
An ordinary file that contains machine language programs.

Binary files are ordinary files that contain machine language instructions that are meant to be executed. Here is how they fit into the scheme of things:

When you write a program, you use an editor to create instructions in a computer language (C, Pascal, Fortran, or whatever). These instructions are stored in a text file. This makes sense—after all, you need to be able to create and modify the instructions, so they must be stored in a format that you can work with. The instructions that you create are called a *source program.*

Source Program:
A text file that contains a program written in a computer language.

Now a source program is written in a computer language. The name is actually a misnomer because computers cannot understand computer languages. They are for people to use for designing programs. Before you can run your program it must be translated into machine language, which your computer can understand.

Executable Program:
A machine language program, ready to be executed.

This involves several steps, and we won't go into the details here. Suffice it to say that you can run your program once it is translated into machine language. Such a translated program is called an *executable program.*

Like source programs, executable programs are stored in ordinary files which have names. To execute a program, you enter the name of the file that contains the executable program. For example, to execute a program stored in a file named `backup`, you enter

```
backup
```

The shell searches for an ordinary file by that name and runs the executable program stored in that file. If the file does not contain an executable program, the shell will tell you that you have made a mistake.

Most of the commands you enter are really the names of files that contain executable programs. For instance, the `date` command is stored in a file named `date`. (To be completely accurate, we should point out that there are a few commands that are handled directly by the shell. These commands are not stored as separate files.)

As you might imagine, executable programs, which make sense to the computer, do not make sense to people. Like all data stored in ordinary files, executable programs consist of a number of bytes. However, those bytes do not use the ASCII code. If you were to display or print an executable program it would look like gibberish.

As we explained in Chapter 4, data within a computer is stored as bits using the binary system. Thus, we call the files that hold executable programs "binary files."

So, to summarize, there are three kinds of files: ordinary files, directories, and special files. Ordinary files hold data. There are two important types of ordinary files: text files, which hold data that we can understand, and binary files, which hold data that the computer can understand.

What Is Inside of a Directory?

So far, we have talked about directories as if they contain files. This suggests an image of a filing cabinet that contains folders, the folders themselves containing pieces of paper.

However, the image is inaccurate. Directories do not really contain files. Directories contain information that tells Unix where to look for the files. It is as if you opened a filing cabinet and found, not folders, but a list telling you how to find each folder.

Here is how it works:

Inode:
The internal representation of a file, containing all the information Unix needs to access the file.

Index Node:
Same as inode.

Inode Number:
A number that represents the position of an inode within the master table of inodes.

Unix stores descriptive information for every file in the system. This information that describes a particular file is called an *index node* or *inode* (pronounced "eye-node"). Each inode acts as the internal representation of a file.

An inode contains all the information that Unix needs in order to work with a file. This information is summarized in Figure 16.1.

Each inode represents a single file. Unix keeps all the inodes in a special system table. It is this table, then, that contains the information necessary to access all the files in the system.

An inode is referenced by an *inode number*, which represents its position in the table. For instance, inode number 17 refers to the 17th inode.

A directory consists of a number of entries, each of which is 16 bytes long. The first 2 bytes contain an inode number. The

An inode is the internal representation of a file. Each inode contains information describing the following:

- the type of the file
- the size of the file
- where the data is stored
- which userid owns the file
- which userids can use the file
- the last time the file was modified
- the last time the file was accessed
- the last time the inode was modified
- the number of links to the file

Figure 16.1   *The contents of an inode (index node).*

next 14 bytes contain the name of the file. Since each byte holds one character, this means that Unix file names can be up to 14 characters long.

(By the way, the 2-byte inode number is not stored using 2 ASCII characters. Such a scheme would limit Unix to only 100 different numbers: 00 through 99. Instead, the 2 bytes store a number using a numeric format which represents the number as a base 2 value—see Chapter 4. In this way, 2 bytes can represent up to 65,536 different values.)

Figure 16.2 shows a sample directory with a number of entries, each of which contains a file name and its corresponding inode number.

The directory in Figure 16.2 contains 9 entries. The first 2 entries have a special meaning; we will discuss them later, in Chapter 16. The other 7 entries represent files. It may be that some of these files are themselves directories.

So what happens when you tell Unix the name of a file? Unix checks in the appropriate directory, finds the file name, and reads the corresponding inode number. Using this inode number as an index, Unix looks in the inode table and finds the proper inode. Within this inode, Unix finds all the information it needs to access the file. All of this, of course, is done automatically. All you need to do is give Unix a file name.

Inode Number (2 bytes)	File Name (14 bytes)
83	.
13	..
1798	chapter.1
1276	chapter.2
85	example
1268	draft
1798	mcgill
88	notes
2114	abbreviations

Figure 16.2   *An example of entries within a directory.*

Links

When a new file is created, Unix must find a free inode in the inode table and fill in the applicable information. Unix then stores the inode number, along with the file name, as an entry in the appropriate directory.

Of course, this is all done automatically. Say that you create a file named `info`. Unix takes care of all the details. All you will notice is that there is now an entry named `info` in your directory.

Link:
The correspondence between a file name and the inode it represents.

The correspondence between a file name and an inode is called a *link*. It is this link that allows you to specify files by using easy-to-remember names instead of inode numbers. But when you come right down to it, it is the inode number and not the file name that actually identifies the file. The only use Unix has for a file name is to find the directory entry it needs in order to get an inode number.

Once you understand this, you can see that it is possible for different directory entries, with different file names, to contain the same inode number. In other words, you can use more than one file name to refer to the same file.

DOS users:
In Unix, more than one file name can refer to the same file.

Here is an example. Say that you have a file whose inode number is 1798. When you created this file, you specified the name mcgill. Thus, the directory in which this file resides contains the entry

Inode number	File name
1798	mcgill

Now suppose that you want to be able to refer to this file by either of two new names, lil or nancy, in the same directory. You can use the ln (link) command, which we will discuss later, to create two new links to the same inode. Once this is done, the directory will contain the entries

Inode number	File name
1798	mcgill
1798	lil
1798	nancy

You can now refer to the file by any of these three names. Since they all correspond to the same inode number, they all refer to the same file.

Here is a more practical example: You need to share a document, named draft, with a friend. It happens that draft has an inode number of 1268 (although you don't know this, as Unix hides all the details).

You can use the ln command to create a link to the same file in your friend's directory. You can choose the same name or a different name. If you choose the same name there is no ambiguity as the two links are in different directories. In either case, whatever name you choose is entered into your friend's directory, linked to inode number 1268. While you access the file using the old name, your friend can access the file using the alternate name.

Linking a file in this way does not change the file in any way. In particular, if your userid owned the file originally, your userid still owns the file, even though it is now accessible from someone else's directory.

All of this suggests an interesting question: If a file is referenced by more than one directory entry, which is the main link? Which file name is the most important—the name that was specified when the file was created, or the name that was given as the most recent link?

The answer is that Unix treats all links equally. Conceptually, all the file names that refer to a single file have the same priority. In order to control who is allowed to use the file, there are file "permissions" that you can set. We will discuss this topic later.

What Happens When You Remove a File?

As you know, when Unix creates a file it creates a link between the file name and the inode number. To erase a file, Unix needs to break this link. (There is also a certain amount of housekeeping involved in recycling the inode and the storage space, but we will ignore the internal details.)

Remove a file:
To eliminate the link between a file name and an inode.

For this reason, we do not talk about erasing or deleting a file—rather, we *remove* a file. This is because the act of getting rid of a file involves removing its link. Indeed there is no "erase" or "delete" command. We use the `rm` command with ordinary and special files and the `rmdir` command with directories.

Whenever you remove a file, Unix checks to see if there is more than one link to the file. How does it know this? If you glance back at Figure 16.1, you will see that the inode contains a place to note the number of links to the file. Every time you make a link to an existing file, this number is incremented by one.

To remove a file, Unix first decrements the number of links by one. If the new number is zero, Unix knows that there are no more links. The file is then erased. Its directory entry, inode, and storage space are marked as being available for use.

However, if there are any remaining links, the file is not erased. There are other file names that still refer to this file. The file cannot be erased until the last of these links is removed.

Hint
••••

DOS users:
A Unix file is not erased until its last link is removed.

Here is an example: You create a file named `draft` in your directory. You then create a link to this file in another directory using the name `memo`. At this point you have one file with two different names. You can refer to the file as being either in one directory under the name draft, or in the other directory under the name memo.

You now remove the file draft. When you look in your directory, the file named draft is gone. However, the file is not erased. It is still accessible as memo in the other directory. You now remove memo. Unix notices that this is the last link and erases the file. The file, by whatever name, is now gone for good.

RULE	Be careful when removing files. Once a file is erased, it is gone permanently.

By the way, once Unix erases a file there is no way to get it back unless your system operator has installed and properly configured an "unerase" program, like the Norton Utilities for System V. Such programs can intercept your remove requests and store the data in an out-of-the-way place, in case you change your mind.

What Happens When You Copy or Move a File?

Unix allows you to make copies of files and to move them from one place to another.

When Unix copies a file it creates an exact duplicate. This duplicate has its own inode and inode number. The data in the file is duplicated. Once the copy is made it is independent of the original file.

Here is an example: You use the cp (copy) command, which we will explain later, to create a copy of the file draft. The copy is to be called draft.backup. The actual command is

```
cp draft draft.backup
```

You now have two separate files, each with its own name, inode, and directory entry. If you remove the file draft, it will be erased, as long as it does not have any other links. However, this will not affect draft.backup, which is completely independent of the original file.

When you move a file, Unix neither changes nor duplicates the data or the inode. All that happens is that the old directory entry is replaced by a new entry. For example, you use the mv (move) command, which we explain later, to move the file notes to the file information. The actual command is

```
mv notes information
```

Say that the inode number for notes is 88. Before you issue the command, your directory will contain the entry

Inode number	File name
88	notes

After Unix executes the mv command, the directory entry will be

Inode number	File name
88	information

In other words, moving a file within the same directory has the same effect as renaming the file. Indeed, there is no "rename" command.

You can also move a file from one directory to another. You can have the new entry use the same file name or a different one. We will discuss all of this later when we examine the mv command in detail.

The important thing to appreciate is that whenever you move a file, all it does is delete the old directory entry and create a new one. None of this affects any other links to the same file.

Owning a File

If a file can appear in more than one directory, how does Unix control the different links? What if one person creates a file and another person links to it? Unix considers all links to be equal. Does this mean that anybody can link to and control someone else's files?

To handle these and other considerations, Unix requires that each file be *owned* by a userid. To avoid logistical problems, no file may have more than one owner. It is the owner who controls a file, regardless of what links may exist.

Own a file:
To have control over the permissions for a file.

An important point to understand is that users (people) do not own files; userids own files. As we explained in Chapter 7, Unix does not know about users; Unix only knows about userids. Obviously, if you give someone your password, he or she can log in under your userid and have control of all your files.

Hint

••••

DOS users:

Unlike DOS, all Unix files have an owner, a userid that controls the file.

Who Owns the System Files?

As we explained, Unix deals only with userids, not with users. The files created by Harley are not owned by Harley, they are owned by userid `harley`. As a general rule, files are owned by the userid that created them.

RULE

If you use more than one userid, remember that whichever userid creates a file will own it.

However, there are a great many files that are used to run the system and are not created by individual users, for example, the files that hold the Unix commands. Such files are created when you install software, including Unix itself. If you have ever installed Unix you will know that much of the process is devoted to creating files. Moreover, there are also files that need to be created and modified by the system as it goes about its day-to-day work.

As we mentioned earlier, all files must be owned by some userid. Clearly, these system files were not created by a specific person who logged in with his own userid. The question is, Who owns the system files?

If you were to ask someone at random—Plato, for example—he would probably tell you that the reason userids exist at all is because each one represents a real person. Without the idea of an actual user, a userid is meaningless.

However, philosophical imperative notwithstanding, there *are* userids within Unix that do not correspond to real users. The two most common you will see are root and bin. To a lesser extent, you may also see sys, lp, and uucp.

root, of course, is the userid used by the superuser (see Chapter 7). Some of the time, at least, root is used by a real person. In addition, Unix uses root to run certain daemons (see Chapter 7). However, most of the time, root and the other four system userids sit silently, acting as absentee landlords. Their main job is to own the system files.

Most of the system files are owned by root or bin. These files include the executable programs that implement the commands. The name bin stands for "binary"—an appropriate userid to own binary files. There are also a few system files owned by userid sys.

Aside from these userids, lp owns the files that pertain to printing (lp stands for "line printer"), and uucp owns the files involved with the UUCP file transfer facility (see Chapter 15).

Although these userids are important to the functioning of your Unix system, you would never actually use them to log in (except on those few occasions that you use root to become superuser).

RULE

Unix system files are owned by special userids that are not used for everyday work. Do not log in with these userids (except when using root to become superuser).

How File Permissions Are Used

Permission:
The specification of what type of operations can be performed on a file: read, write, or execute.

Unix maintains a set of *permissions* for each file. These permissions are kept in the inode for the file. Each time a userid makes a request to work with a file, Unix checks the file's permissions. If that userid is not supposed to use the file, Unix will disallow the request.

This permission checking is used whenever you enter a command that manipulates files or whenever you execute a program that needs to work with files on your behalf

DOS users:
You can control who is allowed to access your files by setting file permissions.

Read Permission:
Permission to read a file, or to read file names in a directory.

Write Permission:
Permission to modify a file, or to create or remove directory entries.

Execute Permission:
Permission to execute a file, or to fully access a directory.

Unix recognizes three types of permissions, each of which may be either allowed or not allowed. They are *read permission*, *write permission*, and *execute permission*. The role played by these permissions depends on the type of file being accessed.

With a regular file or a special file, the permissions are straightforward: Read permission allows a userid to read the file. Write permission allows a userid to modify the file. Execute permission allows a userid to execute the file.

Of course, it makes no sense to set execute permission for a file unless it can, in fact, be executed. In practice, this means that only programs (binary files) and shell scripts have execute permission. To avoid mistakes, it is a good idea to avoid setting execute permission unless the file really is a program or a shell script.

RULE

Do not set execute permission for an ordinary file unless it is executable.

Conversely, you cannot execute a file unless your userid has execute permission. A common mistake is to create a shell script and then forget to set the execute permission. Even though you created the file, you will not be able to execute it until the proper permission is set.

RULE

Whenever you create a shell script, remember to give yourself execute permission.

These three permissions work hand in hand in a logical manner. For example, if you want to change a file you will need both read and write permission. If you want to execute a program or shell script, you will need both read and execute permission. This only makes sense: the shell cannot execute a file on your behalf if you do not have permission to read it.

With directories, the story is somewhat different. Read permission allows a userid to access the information in the directory. For example, with read permission you can display the contents of a directory. Write permission allows a userid to create and remove files in the directory. Execute permission allows a userid to access the files.

Execute permission acts as a lock on the directory. Without this permission, a userid may be able to look at the names of files but it cannot use those files in any way. Nor can it ask for any information about those files except the name. If one of those files is itself a directory, it too is locked.

RULE   To keep other users from fiddling with one of your directories, restrict the execute permission.

For example, say that your userid has read permission but not execute permission for a particular directory. You can use the `ls` command to display the file names, but you cannot display any other information, such as the size of the files. Nor can you change to the directory (explained later) or use the directory in any way.

Figure 16.3 summarizes the three types of permissions and how they affect each type of file.

Groups

Group:
A collection of userids that share file permissions.

Unix maintains various permissions for each file. These permissions allow you to control who may or may not access your files. In order to understand how the system works we first need to understand the idea of *groups*.

As we explained in Chapter 1, Unix was developed at Bell Labs, a part of AT&T. At the time, Unix was used for software development and text processing by people who worked in groups. The developers of Unix found that it was important to allow the people in a work group to share files without having

Unix File Permissions	Unix File Permissions

Ordinary File

Read:	file can be read
Write:	file can be modified
Execute:	file can be executed

Directory

Read:	file names only can be read
Write:	entries can be created or removed
Execute:	full access

Special File

Read:	file can be read
Write:	file can be modified
Execute:	file can be executed

Figure 16.3   *Summary of Unix file permissions.*

to open those files to everybody on the system. They devised a scheme that is still in use today.

Groupid:
The name of a group.

Each userid in a Unix system belongs to a group. Each group is known by a *groupid* (pronounced "group-eye-dee")—a name, similar to a userid. The groupid can be anything reasonable, even the name of an existing userid. The system manager can create any groups he wants. When it is time to register a new user, he not only assigns a userid, he assigns a groupid. That is, he tells the system to what group the new userid belongs.

A typical system will have the following groups:

```
root
bin
system
mail
daemon
uucp
adm
other
```

On our system, these are the groupids that were set up automatically when we installed Unix. Your system may vary slightly, but the idea is the same: there are a number of groupids used only by the system (root, bin, system, mail, daemon, and uucp), a group for administrative userids (adm), and a group for all other userids (other).

The intention is that most new userids will be put into the other group. If your system is sufficiently large, you can—as system manager—create any groups you want. For instance, you might supplement other with three groupids named sales, accounting, and managers. This would allow a more natural distribution of your userids. More to the point, it would allow your users to share files directly with the people they work with.

RULE	To learn Unix, keep in mind that there is no need to create extra groups if you do not have a compelling reason.

In Chapter 13, we explained that a master list of all userids is kept in the file /etc/passwd. There is a similar file, named /etc/group, for all the groupids. If you want to display this file and see all the groups on your system, use the command

```
more /etc/group
```

(As we will learn in Chapter 23, the more command will display a file, one screenful at a time. If there is more than one screenful of output, the bottom line will display:

```
--More--
```

You can then press the ace bar to display the next screenful.)

If you want to display your current userid and groupid, you can use the id command that we described in Chapter 13.

How Unix Organizes File Permissions

Unix allocates three sets of permissions for each file: one for the owner of the file, one for the owner's group, and one for everybody on the system. You can tell Unix what permissions you want for your userid, for any userids in your group, and for everyone else.

For example, say that you have just created a new file. You may decide that you or anyone else in your group should be able to read or modify the file. Everyone else on the system should be able to read the file but nothing else. In this case, you would make sure that you and your group have read and write permissions, and that everyone else has only read permission.

The files that hold the Unix commands typically have read and execute permissions for everyone. Nobody has write permission. This means that all users can execute commands but that nobody can modify the actual programs and shell scripts, accidentally or otherwise.

When you create a file, Unix usually assigns the following permissions:

your userid:	read, write
your groupid:	read
everyone else:	read

This means that, by default, everyone can read your files. It also means that, by default, your files cannot be executed. As we mentioned earlier, when you create a new shell script you will have to give yourself execute permission before you can run the script.

If you want to change permissions, you can use the chmod command that we will discuss in Chapter 20. If you want to display the permissions for a file, you can use the -1 (long) option with the 1s command. We will discuss this in detail in Chapter 21.

17

The Tree-Structured
File System

Introduction

In Chapter 16, we explained how directories can be used to organize files. As you remember, directories can contain not only files, but other directories. This allows you to create a hierarchy.

In this chapter, we will discuss directories in detail. You will learn how the Unix file system is organized and how to structure your own directories to suit your needs.

Subdirectories and Parent Directories

Subdirectory:
A directory that lies within another directory.

Parent Directory:
With respect to a subdirectory, the directory that contains the subdirectory.

In Chapter 16, we explained that directories do not really contain files; they hold entries that contain the information that Unix needs to find the files. However, Unix is pretty good about hiding all those details from us. Most of the time, it is convenient to treat directories as if they actually contain files.

As you know, directories can contain all three types of files: ordinary files, special files, and other directories. A *subdirectory* is a directory that is contained in another directory. The directory that contains the subdirectory is called the *parent directory*.

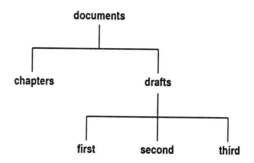

Figure 17.1 *An example of directories and subdirectories.*

Since directories are themselves files, they are named in the same way as ordinary files. The name can be up to 14 characters, including lower-case letters, upper-case letters, numerals, and certain punctuation. We will discuss the rules for naming files later in the chapter. For now, let's just say that when naming directories it is a good idea to confine yourself to lower-case letters only.

Here is an example: You have a directory named `documents`. Within this directory are two more directories, `drafts` and `chapters`. Within the `draft` directory are three more directories, `first`, `second` and `third`. This family of directories is illustrated in Figure 17.1.

In this example, `chapters` and `drafts` are subdirectories of `documents`; `first`, `second` and `third` are subdirectories of `drafts`. With respect to `chapters` and `drafts`, `documents` is the parent directory; with respect to `first`, `second` and `third`, `drafts` is the parent directory.

Organizing with Subdirectories

The importance of subdirectories is that they enable you to group your files into categories and subcategories. You can create your directories so that they reflect the natural organization of the data you are using.

RULE Create directories so that the structure of the tree reflects the natural organization of your data.

Here is an example. You are setting up a Unix system for the Santa Barbara Surf and Chicken Soup Corporation. It is your job to plan the directory structure.

You will need a file for service records and a file for payroll data. You will also need two files for each of your salespeople: one file for customer information, the other for sales orders. Similarly, you need two files for each of your repair people: one file for keeping track of the stock, the other for repair orders.

You have two salespeople, Bill and Cynthia, and three repair people, Carol, Julie, and Matt.

What you must do is come up with a plan for directories that will make it easy to work with all the files. If you reread the last few paragraphs, you can see that even a small company can start to look complex when you are planning a computer system. However, if you can design the right directory system, everything will fall into place.

Take a look at Figure 17.2. It shows a directory structure that implements the requirements we just described.

The directory structure starts with a directory called `surf`, which represents the name of the company. This directory has three subdirectories `admin`, `sales`, and `repairs`.

The first subdirectory, `admin`, holds the two administrative files, `payroll` and `service`.

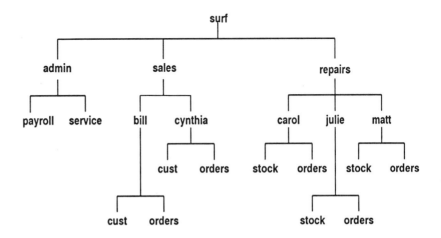

Figure 17.2 *An example of a directory structure.*

The `sales` subdirectory has two subdirectories of its own, `bill` and `cynthia`, one for each salesperson. Each of these directories contains the requisite files, `customers` and `orders`.

Likewise, the `repairs` directory contains one subdirectory for each repair person, `carol`, `julie` and `matt`. Each of these directories contains the two files needed for repairs, `stock` and `orders`.

Notice that there are five directories that contain a file named `orders`. However, since each of these files lies in a different directory there is no ambiguity.

By now, it should be clear how the simple idea of a directory containing other directories can lead to large, robust structures. Moreover, many designs that are difficult to describe in words are easy to understand when they are expressed as hierarchies.

Guidelines for Organizing a Directory System

You will find that there are many ways to design a directory structure. For example, in Figure 17.2, we could have placed the administrative files, `payroll` and `service`, directly in the main directory, `surf`. Or we could have collected the subdirectories `sales` and `repairs` together in their own directory, say `employees`.

Of course, some designs are better than others. To help you, here are two design guidelines:

RULE	When designing a directory structure:

1. Try to use each directory to hold either files or subdirectories, but not both.
2. Keep your subdirectories to within three levels of your main directory.

It may not be possible to follow these guidelines all of the time, but keep them in mind.

Unix doesn't care if you mix files and subdirectories or if you create deep, complex structures. But it is not hard to create a structure so complex that you will have trouble managing it. These two rules will go a long way toward helping you keep things simple and easy to understand.

The Tree-Structured File System

The entire Unix file system is organized along the lines that we have described in the previous two sections. There is one main directory. Within this directory are subdirectories. In these sub-directories are other subdirectories, and so on.

If we draw a diagram of such a system, we see a treelike organization with the subdirectories forming branches. (Actually, the tree is upside down.) We can even consider the files to be leaves. For this reason, we refer to this type of organization as a *tree-structured file system*.

Figure 17.3 shows the principal directories of a typical Unix file system and how they are related. Your system may differ somewhat, but the general idea will be the same. If you consider such a system as forming a tree, you will see that there is one main directory from which the tree branches. We call this directory the *root directory*.

Now you can see why the most powerful userid, the one used to log in as superuser, is called `root`. It is named after the most important directory in the file system.

Tree-Structured File System:
A hierarchical system of directories, based on a single root directory, in which all directories except the root directory are subdirectories.

Root Directory:
The directory that, directly or indirectly, contains all the other directories in the file system.

A Closer Look at the Unix Directory System

The tree structure in Figure 17.3 shows some of the more important directories in a Unix system. Let's take a quick tour. As we do, bear in mind that not all Unix systems are the same. Moreover, we have included only the most important directories—there will be others in your system.

Starting from the top, we see the root directory. Within the root directory are seven subdirectories. They are used as follows:

`bin`: The name stands for "binary." This directory contains executable programs, including many of the Unix commands. However, the name is a misnomer as not all of the files are binary files (executable programs); some are text files that contain shell scripts.

`dev`: The name stands for "device." This directory contains all the special files (see Chapter 16). The name of each file is usually an abbreviation that stands for the device. For example, the file `hd00` represents hard disk 0, partition 0.

`etc`: The name of this directory is usually pronounced "et cetera." The `etc` directory contains the programs, shell

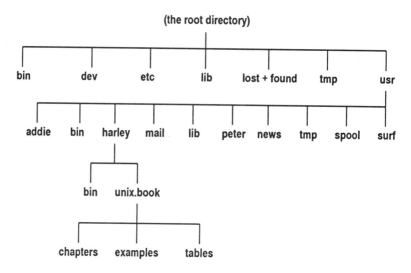

Figure 17.3 *The directory structure of a typical Unix system.*

scripts, and data files used for system administration. It is not uncommon for a system manager to have to modify a file in this directory.

lib: The name stands for "library." This directory holds collections of standard programs and tools that are available for general use. When you install software, the installation program will often copy files into this directory.

lost+found: The name is straightforward. Notice that the plus sign is a valid character within a name. Normally, this directory is empty. Occasionally, Unix will run into some data that may need to be salvaged–say, while a file system is being repaired. Unix will place such data in a file and store it in the "lost and found" directory. Later, the system manager can examine the data and discard or keep it as he sees fit.

tmp: The name of this directory is usually pronounced "temp," even though the "e" is left out of the name. You will often see Unix names that omit vowels. Remember, Unix was developed to be used over slow communication lines. Omitting a letter here and there went a long way toward making things faster.

RULE The directory name tmp is pronounced "temp."

As the name implies, `tmp` is a directory in which programs can create temporary files: a temporary storage area. The `tmp` directory is cleared automatically every time you restart Unix. If you have a program that requires temporary files, you can place them in this directory, knowing that once you are finished the space will be recycled.

`usr`: Again, we have a directory name in which the letter "e" has been left out. Regardless, this directory is almost always referred to as the "user" directory. Its chief use is to contain other subdirectories.

RULE   The directory name `usr` is pronounced "user."

The `bin`, `lib`, and `tmp` subdirectories act as supplements to the directories of the same name that we just described. For instance, some Unix commands reside in files in the main `bin` directory, others reside in the `bin` directory under `usr`.

The `mail` subdirectory contains mail that has been received but not yet read. (The Unix mail system is described in Chapter 15.) If you look in this directory, you will see that each userid has its own file to act as a personal mailbox.

The `news` subdirectory holds news items that have been created by the system manager (see Chapter 12).

The `spool` subdirectory is used to hold text files that are waiting to be printed. When you print a file, it is first sent to this directory, where it is stored until the printer is free. Once the file is printed, it is erased from the holding area. The name "spool" is from an old acronym that stands for "simultaneous peripheral operations off-line."

Aside from these system subdirectories, the `usr` directory contains one subdirectory for each user of the system. In our example, there are four such subdirectories: `addie`, `harley`, `peter`, and `surf`. These represent four userids—three for users named Addie, Harley and Peter, and one (`surf`) for the example that we described earlier.

These subdirectories act as the main directory for their users. Each user is free to create any files and subdirectories he wants within his own area of the tree. In the example in Figure 17.3, userid `harley` has created two subdirectories, `bin` and `unix.book`. The `unix.book` directory contains three of its own subdirectories, `chapters`, `examples` and `tables`.

The name `bin` is a fairly common one. Most people create such a subdirectory to hold their personal programs and shell scripts. As we mentioned earlier, the name reminds us that some of the items in the directory are binary files. However, you may want to think of this directory as a bin into which you throw all your programs and scripts.

Earlier in this chapter, we discussed an example in which we developed a tree structure based on a directory named `surf` (see Figure 17.2). In Figure 17.3 we can see that this directory is situated within the `usr` directory.

If you imagine the structure in Figure 17.2 grafted onto the `surf` directory in Figure 17.3, you will appreciate how different parts of the tree are isolated from one another. The people who use the subdirectories under `surf` can spend all of their time in this part of the tree—as far as they are concerned, `surf` is their "root directory."

Similarly, Addie can create as many subdirectories as she wants under the `addie` directory, just as if she had her own personal file system.

••••

DOS users:

Unlike DOS, Unix maintains a number of directories for its own purposes.

How Files and Directories are Named

In Chapter 16, we explained how directory entries are 16 bytes long. Of these 16 bytes, 2 of them contain an inode number. The other 14 bytes are used to store the file name. As you remember, each byte can hold one character—thus, a file name can be up to 14 characters long.

Within commands, Unix will let you specify longer names, but it will ignore all but the first 14 characters. Thus, you must be careful if you are creating a file with a long name. Unix will use only the first 14 characters of the file name without warning you that the excess characters have been omitted.

If you are used to DOS, you are coming from a world in which you cannot use a file name longer than 8 characters with an optional 3-character extension. Usually, you will find that 14 characters are more than enough. At times, however, you might think that even longer file names would be nice. But it is a great deal of trouble to type long names, and most of the time it isn't be worth the bother.

The Unix policy for naming files (including directories) is a liberal one: you can use any characters you want except / (the slash). However, there are some characters that are best avoided:

```
space
tab
backspace
?   @   #   $   ^   &   (   )   `   [   ]   |   ;   '   =   <   >
```

The punctuation characters are used for various purposes in Unix and using them in file names is begging for unexpected problems.

Another habit to avoid is using a + [plus sign], - [minus sign], or . [period] as the first character of a file name. (Although, as we will see later, there are times when you will want to start file names with a period).

Remember also, that Unix distinguishes between upper and lower case. Thus, `info` and `Info` are considered to be two different names.

The best guideline to follow is to keep things simple:

RULE	When naming files, confine yourself to using lower-case letters and the period.

You will do better to take a few moments to choose an appropriate name than to use punctuation or upper-case letters. Choose names that are meaningful, easy to remember, and easy to type. For example, `invoice`, `summary` and `chapter.1` are much better names than `doc-A`, `doc-B`, and `doc-C`.

If you are a DOS user, you are used to following the file name with an extension. You separate the two components with a period, for example, AUTOEXEC.BAT. Unix file names can have a period, but it is treated as just another character and it counts as part of the actual name. Unix does not use extensions per se. For example, `autoexec.bat` and `AUTOEXEC.BAT` are two different, valid Unix names. However, there is no significance that the names end in a period followed by three letters.

DOS users:
Unix file names can be up to 14 characters long and do not use extensions.

Path Names

Path:
The series of file names that shows which directories must be traversed in order to reach a particular file.

Path Name:
The exact specification of a path.

To specify a file name, it is sometimes necessary to describe its location in the directory tree. To do so, we start at the root directory and list in turn each directory that we would need to traverse, ending with the name of the file itself. The route that we take through the tree is called a *path*. The description of the path is called a *path name*. A path name shows the location of a file and provides the directions for reaching it.

To form a path name, we list each directory in turn, ending with the name of the file. We separate each part of the path name with a / (slash).

Here is an example. Say that we have an ordinary file named `tree`, in a directory named `examples`. The directory `examples` is in a subdirectory named `usr`, which is in the root directory. The path is

root directory-usr-harley-examples-tree

We specify the path name as follows:

/usr/harley/examples/tree

The initial / indicates that we are starting from the root directory (which does not have a formal name).

Hint

DOS users:
The parts of a Unix path name are separated by slashes, not backslashes.

The Working Directory: Full and Relative Path Names

Working Directory:
A designated directory that acts as a base for the specification of path names.

As you might imagine, path names can be long and it is all too easy to make typing mistakes. As a convenience, Unix recognizes one directory as your *working directory*. When you specify a path name, you can do so relative to your working directory. As we will see in Chapter 18, you can change your working directory whenever you want, by using the cd (change directory) command.

Here is the rule that Unix follows: If a path name begins with a / (slash), the path starts from the root directory. If the path name does not start with a /, the path starts from your working directory.

Full Path Name:
A path name, beginning with a / [slash], that starts from the root directory.

A path name that starts from the root directory is called a *full path name* or *absolute path name*. A path name that starts from your working directory is called a *relative path name*.

The path name that we used in the last section

Absolute Path Name:
Same as a full path name.

```
/usr/harley/examples/tree
```

is an example of a full path name. If your working directory happened to be **/usr/harley**, you could specify the same path by using the relative path name:

Relative Path Name:
A path name, not beginning with a / [slash], that starts from the working directory.

```
examples/tree
```

Since this path name does not begin with a /, Unix knows to start from your working directory. If your working directory were **/usr/harley/examples**, you would only have to specify the name of the file. The relative path name would be

```
tree
```

If your working directory were the root directory, the relative path name would be almost as long as the full path name:

```
usr/harley/examples/tree
```

To specify the root directory itself, just use

```
/
```

We can express the relationship between the two types of path names as an equation:

RULE

The Fundamental Equation of Directory Names:
Full Path Name = Working Directory + Relative Path Name

Whenever you specify the name of a file, you must always give Unix enough information to find the file. Although you can always specify a full path name, it is much easier to set your working directory so that you can use relative path names as much as possible.

The Unix concept of a working directory is similar to the DOS current directory. The main difference is that DOS keeps track of a separate current directory for each disk. Unix uses one working directory for each userid that is logged in.

DOS users:

The Unix working directory is similar to a DOS current directory.

18

Navigating Within the Directory Tree

Introduction

In the last chapter we discussed the Unix tree-structured file system. We explained how, using directories and subdirectories, Unix maintains a large, hierarchical directory structure.

We now turn our attention to the commands you need to navigate this structure. We start with your home directory: the base from which you operate.

Changing Your Working Directory: The `cd` and `pwd` Commands

Home Directory:
Your present directory upon log in.

Each time the system manager sets up a new userid, Unix assigns it a *home directory*. This is the directory that will serve as your home base. Whenever you log in, Unix automatically sets your working directory to be your home directory.

RULE	Think of your home directory as your base within the overall directory tree.

Your home directory is usually a subdirectory under /usr with the same name as your userid. Your home directory is the "root" of your personal part of the tree. For example, the home directory of userid `harley` is /usr/harley; the home directory of userid `addie` is /usr/addie.

It is customary for Unix people to pronounce `usr` as "user," even though the "e" is omitted. Thus, you might say, "My home directory is slash user slash harley."

DOS users:

Rather than store files anywhere on the disk, each Unix user has his own home directory, within which he can build his own tree structure.

You can change your working directory at any time by using the `cd` (change directory) command. The syntax is

cd [*directory*]

Unix will change your working directory to whatever directory you specify. If you do not specify a directory

cd

Unix will change to your home directory. This is a good way to jump back to your home base when you are in some far distant part of the tree.

If you want to display the current name of your working directory, use the `pwd` (print working directory) command. Remember, as we pointed out in Chapter 9, Unix often uses the word "print" to mean "display." The syntax for the `pwd` command is simple:

pwd

Moving Around the Directory Tree Using Full Path Names

Earlier, we described the directory system as a tree structure branching out from the root directory. As you work with Unix, it is handy to imagine yourself sitting in the tree. Your current location is your working directory.

Thus, you might say "I am in this directory" or "I am moving to that directory." The effect of the cd command is to move you instantly from one part of the tree to another. Remember, if you are ever unsure as to your whereabouts, use the pwd command to display your current location.

Here are some examples to show how it works:

You log in using userid harley. Unix starts you off by placing you in your home directory. To check this, you enter

```
pwd
```

as your first command. You see

```
/usr/harley
```

You decide to change to the root directory. You enter

```
cd /
```

followed by the pwd command, which confirms that you are in the root directory by displaying

```
/
```

(Remember, a path name that begins with a / is a full path name. This tells Unix that the path starts from the root directory. Thus, a single / refers to the root directory itself.)

From the root directory, you decide to change to several more directories. After each change, you enter the pwd command to confirm your location.

First, you change to the directory in which the special files are kept:

```
cd /dev
```

Next, you change to the directory where the incoming mail is stored:

```
cd /usr/mail
```

Next, you change to someone else's home directory:

```
cd /usr/peter
```

Finally, you decide to return to your home directory. One way to do this is to specify the name of the directory:

```
cd /usr/harley
```

However, an easier way is to enter the **cd** command with no arguments. As a default, Unix will move you to your home directory.

```
cd
```

To check, you enter the **pwd** command, which displays

```
/usr/harley
```

to confirm that you are indeed back where you started.

Knowing Where You Are in the Tree

If you are a DOS user, you are used to being able to set the DOS prompt to display your current directory. Every time DOS finishes a command you will see just where you are in the directory tree.

Unfortunately, there is no easy way to set the Unix shell prompt in this manner. If you want to find out where you are, you need to use the **pwd** command. However, this is not as much of a problem as you might imagine, for two reasons:

First, DOS maintains a default device as well as a current directory. Thus, you have to remember more than your location in the tree; you also need to remember which tree you are in—that is, whether you are on the A: drive, the B: drive, the C: drive, or whatever.

Mount (a device):
To connect a directory structure, stored on a device, to the main tree structure.

Unlike DOS, Unix maintains a single directory structure. There is only one tree and you are always in it. If you ever do access another disk, its directory structure will be grafted onto the main tree at a specific point. This is called *mounting* a device.

DOS users:
Unlike DOS, there is no easy way to make the Unix shell prompt display the name of the working directory. Use `pwd`. to see where you are.

DOS users:
While DOS maintains separate directory systems for each device, Unix uses one large tree structure.

Indeed, most Unix systems maintain the `/usr` part of the tree as a separate file system on its own device. These systems use two disk partitions or two separate disks: one for the "root" system and one for the "user" system. Each time Unix starts, the "user" system is automatically mounted. Its directory structure is grafted onto the main tree at the `/usr` directory. Unix makes sure that the details are transparent to users. To you, the whole thing looks like one large tree structure.

On larger systems, this is how more storage space is added. The system manager installs a new disk and creates a file system on it. He then tells Unix to automatically mount that file system at a particular directory. The new space is now available as part of the main tree.

There is also another reason why, coming from DOS, you will not get lost in the Unix directory tree: With DOS you are more than just a user, you are also the system manager. In order to maintain your system you need to change all over the place, from one device to another, and from one directory to another.

With Unix, you will usually confine yourself to a small area of the tree: the part under your home directory. Most people have no trouble navigating within this limited space. After all, you create the directory structure yourself. Unless you are the system manager, you need to maintain only your own data, not all the programs on the system.

DOS users:

Unix users tend to stay in the part of the tree defined by their home directory.

Moving Around the Directory Tree Using Relative Path Names

In our previous examples, we used the **cd** command with full path names to move from one directory to another. However, most of the time you will be in your own small part of the tree, and it is much easier to use relative path names. Here are some examples:

Say that you are logged in as userid **harley**. Your home directory is **/usr/harley**. Under this directory, you have created your own small subtree, as shown in Figure 18.1. When you log in, Unix sets your working directory to your home directory. You enter

```
pwd
```

and you see

```
/usr/harley
```

You want to move to the **bin** directory. You could enter

```
cd /usr/harley/bin
```

but since you are already in **/usr/harley** you can use a relative path name:

```
cd bin
```

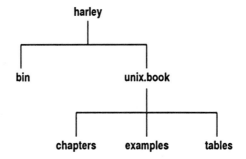

Figure 18.1 *An example of one user's directory structure.*

Since the path name does not begin with a /, Unix starts from your working directory. You check with the **pwd** command and see

```
/usr/harley/bin
```

You now want to move to the **tables** directory within the **unix.book** directory. First, you move back to your home directory by entering the **cd** command with no arguments:

```
cd
```

Next, you change to the **tables** directory by using a relative path name:

```
cd unix.book/tables
```

To check, you enter the **pwd** command. You see

```
/usr/harley/unix.book/tables
```

Alternatively, you could have moved to this directory in two steps. Starting from **/usr/harley**, you could have used

```
cd unix.book
cd tables
```

Navigating the Unix directory is like life: Whether you move by small steps or by large leaps, your final resting place is still the same.

Two Special Directory Names: . and ..

In Chapter 16, we explained how a directory contains one entry for each file. Each entry consists of 16 bytes: a 2-byte inode number and a 14-byte file name.

When you create a directory, Unix always puts in two entries. One has the file name .. [two periods in a row]; the other has the file name . [a single period]. (Remember, as we explained in Chapter 17, a . is a valid character in a file name.)

Figure 18.2 shows the directory entries that we looked at in Chapter 16. Notice that . and .. are the first two entries in the directory.

These strange directory entries are initialized as follows: The inode number of the .. entry is set to point to the parent directory. The inode number of the . entry is set to the same directory in which it resides. In our example, the inode number of the parent directory is 13; the inode number of the directory itself is 83.

Of course, Unix hides all of these details. But what it means to you is that, at any time, you can use . to refer to your working directory, and .. to refer to the parent of your working directory.

Here are some examples. You are logged in as userid `harley` and your working directory is currently set to

```
/usr/harley/unix.book/tables
```

Inode number (2 bytes)	File name (14 bytes)
83	.
13	..
1798	chapter.1
1276	chapter.2
85	example
1268	draft
1798	mcgill
88	notes
2114	abbreviations

Figure 18.2   *An example of entries within a directory.*

You want to use the **cd** command to move up one level to the **unix.book** directory. You could use a full path name:

```
cd /usr/harley/unix.book
```

Or you could first change to your home directory (**/usr/harley**) and then change to the unix.book directory:

```
cd
cd unix.book
```

However, the easiest way is to move directly to the parent directory. Starting from **/usr/harley/unix.book/tables** you enter

```
cd ..
```

To check, you enter the **pwd** command and you see

```
/usr/harley/unix.book
```

After working awhile, you decide to move up one more level, to your home directory. Again you enter

```
cd ..
```

You are now in **/usr/harley**. You enter the same command again. You are now in **/usr**. You enter the same command again. This time you are in **/**, the root directory.

What happens if you try to change to **..** from the root directory? When the root directory is first created, Unix sets both the **..** and **.** entries to point to the same place, the root directory itself. That way, if you try to move to the "parent" you will stay where you are: in the root directory at the top of the tree.

It is sometimes useful to use **..** more than once in the same path name to move up more than one level. For example, say that your working directory is currently set to

```
/usr/harley/unix.book/tables
```

You can move to the root directory all at once by entering

```
cd ../../../..
```

Here is another shortcut. As you may remember, in Chapter 3 we explained that you can enter more than one command at a time as long as you separate them with semicolons. In this particular case, you can use a cd command with no arguments to change to your home directory, followed by another cd command to move up two levels to the root directory:

```
cd; cd ../..
```

The advantage of this strategy is that it will work from anywhere in the tree.

Another technique is to move up one level and then down to a different directory. For example, say that you are in your home directory:

```
/usr/harley
```

You want to move to the home directory for userid **addie**. Enter

```
cd ../addie
```

As you can see, the .. directory entry is especially important. The . entry is less useful. However, there will be the odd time when you may be required to specify a directory name. On such occasions, you can substitute . for the name of your working directory. For instance, you can use

```
./info
```

to refer to a file named **info** in your working directory.

19

Maintaining Your Directories

Introduction

Now that you know about the Unix tree-structured file system, it is time to start creating directories. In this chapter we will explain how you can build and maintain your own tree structure. You will learn all the commands you need to make, remove, rename, move, and copy your directories.

Making Directories: The mkdir Command

To make a directory, use the mkdir command. The syntax is

mkdir [-m *mode*] [-p] *directory*...

Most of the time, you will use this command without options. All you do is specify the path name of the directory you want to make and Unix takes care of the rest. The argument *directory* can be a full path name or a relative path name. If you like, you can make more than one directory by specifying more than one path name.

Here is an example. You want to make the directory
/usr/harley/examples/chart. You enter

```
mkdir /usr/harley/examples/chart
```

If your working directory happens to be **/usr/harley/examples**,
you can use a relative path name. In this case, all you need is

```
mkdir chart
```

Since the path name does not start with a /, Unix assumes that
you want to start from the working directory.

To make more than one directory, specify more than one
name:

```
mkdir chart graph data
```

In order to make a directory, you must have proper permission. That is, your userid must have write permission within
the parent directory. If you do not, **mkdir** will display a message like

```
mkdir: "/usr/harley/examples/chart": permission denied
```

If you try to make a directory that already exists, you will see a
message like

```
mkdir: Failed to make directory "chart"; File exists
```

Notice that the directory is referred to as a "file." After all, as we
explained in Chapter 16, directories are files.

Occasionally, you may want to make a directory whose parent directory does not already exist. For example, say that you
want to make the directory **/usr/harley/big/files**, but the
parent directory, **/usr/harley/big**, does not exist. When you
enter the command

```
mkdir /usr/harley/big/files
```

mkdir will display

```
mkdir: "/usr/harley/big/files": No such file or directory
```

You could enter two `mkdir` commands, first making the parent directory and then making the subdirectory:

```
mkdir /usr/harley/big
mkdir /usr/harley/big/files
```

A faster way is to use the **-p** (parent) option. This tells `mkdir` to make all the necessary parent directories if they do not exist. Thus, the command

```
mkdir -p /usr/harley/big/files
```

will successfully make the directory. If the **big** directory does not already exist, `mkdir` will create it.

File Modes

The second `mkdir` option is -m, which stands for "mode." A *file mode* specifies what permissions you want a file to have. As you will see in a moment, the -m option allows you to tell `mkdir` what permission you want to assign to the new directory.

In our discussion in Chapter 16, we explained how Unix provides three different types of permissions: read, write, and execute. Each permission is either granted or denied. For instance, you might assign read and write permission, but not execute permission.

Each file has three sets of permissions: one for the owner, one for the owner's group, and one for all the other userids in the system. For example, you might set up a file as follows:

The owner (your userid) has read, write, and execute permission.

The userids in your group have read and execute permission.

All others have no permission at all.

We can summarize such permissions by building a simple table for each file. In this example, the table would look like this:

	Read	*Write*	*Execute*
Owner	yes	yes	yes
Group	yes	no	yes
Others	no	no	no

In order to specify such information for a command, you enter a 3-digit file mode. Each digit is one of the numbers 0 through 7. Here is how it works:

Consider the various permissions as having the following values:

```
Read     = 4
Write    = 2
Execute  = 1
```

For each of the three categories—owner, group, others—decide which of the permissions you want to assign. Add the corresponding values to create one digit for each category.

For instance, in our example, we wanted the owner to have read, write, and execute permissions. The numeric value for this is $4 + 2 + 1 = 7$.

The group should have only read and execute permissions. The value for this is $4 + 1 = 5$.

All the other userids should have no permission. The value is 0.

The file mode is simply these three numbers: 750.

Now, let's take another look at the syntax for the mkdir command:

mkdir [-m *mode*] [-p] *directory*

As you can see, you have the option of using -m and a file mode to specify the permissions for the new directory. For example, if we want to create a directory named **examples** with the permissions described above, we would enter

```
mkdir -m 750 examples
```

If you do not specify a file mode (which will be most of the time), Unix will use the default file mode, 755. This translates into full permission for the owner, and read and execute permission for the group and all others. That is, by default, everyone else can use, but not modify, your directories.

If you want to keep all your work completely private, use file mode 700 (remembering, of course, that nothing is ever private from the superuser).

RULE	No matter how you set your file permissions, the superuser will always be able to read and modify your files.

Later, in Chapter 20, we will explain how to change a file mode for an existing file, and how to set the default file mode value.

A Closer Look at File Modes

At first, the 3-digit file mode may be confusing, but with a little practice the numbers become easy to understand. As we explained, each digit is the sum of one or more of

>   4   (read permission)
>   2   (write permission)
> and   1   (execute permission)

Observe that there are only eight different combinations, 0 through 7. These are shown in Table 19.1. Whenever you need help creating or decoding a file mode, just refer to this table.

For example, say that you want a file mode to give the owner read and execute permissions, and give the group and all others read permission only. Checking the table, we see that read and

	Read	Write	Execute
0	-	-	-
1	-	-	1
2	-	2	-
3	-	2	1
4	4	-	-
5	4	-	1
6	4	2	-
7	4	2	1

Table 19.1 *The eight different permission values for file modes.*

execute permissions correspond to 5 (4+1). Read permission by itself corresponds to 1. Thus, you use the file mode 511.

Conversely, say that you see a file mode 640. Checking the chart, we see that 6 corresponds read and write permissions (4+2); 4 corresponds to read permission only. Thus 640 stands for the owner having read and write permissions, the group having read permission, and all others having no permissions.

Removing Directories: The `rmdir` Command

To remove a directory, use the `rmdir` command. The syntax is

rmdir [**-ps**] *directory*...

Removing a directory is straightforward: you specify the path name of a directory. If certain conditions are met, `mkdir` removes the directory. To remove more than one directory, specify more than one path name.

For example, to remove a directory named **/usr/harley/test**, enter

```
rmdir /usr/harley/test
```

As with all path names, you can use a name relative to your working directory. For instance, say that your working directory is **/usr/harley**. Instead of the previous command, you could use

```
rmdir test
```

If you want to remove more than one directory, specify more than one path name:

```
rmdir test data chart
```

The conditions that must be met in order to remove a directory are sensible:

First, the directory must be empty. This is for your own protection. If you try to remove a nonempty directory, the `mkdir` command will display an error message and refuse to carry out the command. For example, say that the directory named `test` contains some files. If you try to remove `test` you will see

```
rmdir: test: directory not empty
```

If you do want to remove a nonempty directory, you have two choices:

Empty the directory and then remove it. Use `rmdir` to remove subdirectories and `rm` (see Chapter 22) to remove files.

Use the `rm` command with the `-r` option (also discussed in Chapter 22) to force the removal of the directory.

The second condition that must be met before `rmdir` will remove a directory is that you must have write and execute permission for the *parent* directory.

You need execute permission to provide access, so `rmdir` can search the parent directory to find the entry to be removed. Then, you need write permission to make the actual modification to the parent directory. (For an explanation of how file permissions work with directories, see Chapter 16.)

Interestingly enough, the permissions for the directory that you want to remove are irrelevant: they control only those files that lie within that directory.

You cannot remove your working directory. After all, you must have a working directory at all times. That is, you must always be somewhere in the tree. If you were allowed to remove your working directory, where would you be?

The conditions for removing a directory are summarized as follows:

RULES

In order to remove a directory using `rmdir`, the following conditions must hold:

1. The directory must be empty.

2. Your userid must have write and execute permission for the parent directory.

3. The directory cannot be your working directory.

A Quick Way to Prune Your Directory Tree

On occasion, you may need to prune large portions of your part of the directory tree. At such times, it is inconvenient to have to remove each directory separately. By using the -p (parent) option, you can have rmdir remove the directory and empty parent directories.

Here is an example. Say that your home directory is /usr/harley. At one time, you created a subdirectory named files. Within files, you created several other subdirectories, one of which was documents. Within documents, you again created several subdirectories, one of which was backups.

As it happens, you do not need these directories anymore and you have cleared them of files. You want to remove them. You could use one command for each directory:

```
rmdir /usr/harley/files/documents/backups
rmdir /usr/harley/files/documents
rmdir /usr/harley/files
```

However, by using the -p option, you can do it all at once:

```
rmdir -p /usr/harley/files/documents/backups
```

rmdir will remove each directory by starting with the last one and then processing each parent in turn. The command will stop when all the directories have been removed or when a directory is found that cannot be removed. Once the directories are removed, rmdir will display an appropriate message. In this case, for example, you will see

```
rmdir: /usr/harley/files/documents/backups:
/usr/harley not removed; directory not empty
```

Only the directories backups and documents were removed.

To make things easier, it is usually a good idea to change to a directory close to the ones you want to remove before you use the rmdir command. In this case, you could change to the home directory (/usr/harley) and use a relative path name:

```
cd; rmdir -p files/documents/backups
```

(Remember, you can enter more than one command on the same line, as long as you separate the commands with semi-colons.)

In this case, `rmdir` is able to remove all the directories that you specified. You will see

```
rmdir: files/documents/backups: whole path removed
```

If you wish to suppress the messages that are displayed with the `-p` option, you can use the `-s` (suppress) option:

```
rmdir -ps files/documents/backups
```

This option is handy when you use `rmdir` within a shell script, and you do not want to see messages every time you run the script. Without the `-p` option, the `-s` option has no effect.

Renaming Directories: The `mv` Command

To rename a directory, you use the `mv` command. As we explained in Chapter 16, renaming is considered a "move" operation because the process involves moving links from one directory entry to another.

As we will see in Chapter 22, the `mv` command is used to rename or to move ordinary files. However, with directories you can use `mv` only to rename. The syntax for directories is straightforward:

`mv` *old-directory-name new-directory-name*

You specify two path names. The first describes a directory that must already exist. The second path name is the new name. The `mv` command will rename the first directory using the new name.

Here is an example: Within the directory **/usr/harley** lies a subdirectory named **current**. You wish to rename it to **obsolete**. Use the command

```
mv /usr/harley/current /usr/harley/obsolete
```

As a shortcut, you can make sure that the working directory is first set to /usr/harley and then enter the command using relative path names. For example, if /usr/harley is your home directory, you can use

```
cd; mv current obsolete
```

In order to rename a directory, you need both write and execute permission for the parent directory. (For a discussion of how file permissions apply to directories, see Chapter 16.)

Moving Directories: The mvdir Command

A moment's thought will show you that moving a directory can have profound consequences. After all, any directory may have subdirectories, those subdirectories may themselves have subdirectories, and so on. Moving a directory is nothing less than moving a whole limb of the tree structure from one location to another.

For this reason, there is no easy way for regular users to move a directory. You will have to create the new directory structure, move all the files from the old directories to the new ones, and then remove the old directories.

The mvdir command will do this all at once, but its use is reserved for the system manager. To use mvdir, you will have to log in as root or temporarily switch to superuser by using the su command (see Chapter 13).

The syntax for mvdir is

mvdir *directory-source directory-destination*

You specify two path names. The first is the name of the original directory, which must already exist. The second describes the directory to which you want to move.

If the destination directory already exists, mvdir will move the source directory to be a subdirectory of the destination.

If the destination directory does not exist, mvdir will create it and use it as a replacement for the source directory.

Here is an example: Within your home directory, you have a tree structure involving multiple subdirectories. One subdirectory, accounts, has its own subdirectory, summaries. A second

subdirectory, january, has two of its own subdirectories, pay-
ables and receivables. It looks like this:

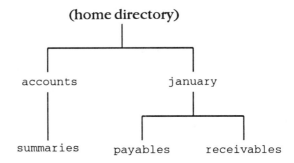

Assume that your working directory is your home directory.
You enter the command

```
mvdir january accounts/summaries
```

Since the destination directory (summaries) already exists,
mvdir moves the january subtree under the destination. The
result looks like this:

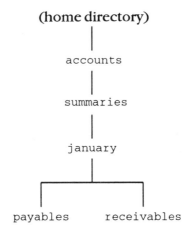

Now, consider starting with the same situation except that instead of the previous command, you enter

```
mvdir january accounts/reports
```

In this case, the destination directory (`reports`) does not exist. `mvdir` creates it, and then uses it to replace the source directory. The result is

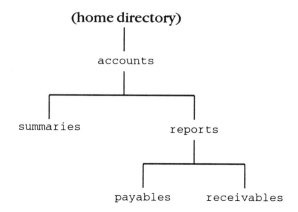

To summarize: If you move to an existing directory, that directory becomes the parent of the source directory. If you move to a directory that does not already exist, it will be created and used to replace the source directory. (Now you can see why this command is reserved for the system manager.)

An interesting point: We mentioned earlier that some commands are shell scripts, rather than executable programs. `mvdir` is one of these commands. It is stored as a text file in `/etc` (the system administration directory). You can look at the script by using the following command:

```
more /etc/mvdir
```

(As we will learn in Chapter 23, the `more` command will display a file, one screenful at a time. If there is more than one screenful of output, the bottom line will display

```
--More--
```

You can then press the <Space> bar to display the next screenful.)

Copying Directories: The `copy` Command

Although you cannot move directories without being super-user, you can copy the contents of one directory to another.

The command you use is copy. As we will see in Chapter 22, this command is also used to copy groups of ordinary files. The syntax for copying directories (showing only the most important options) is

copy [-alrv] *directory-source directory-destination*

You specify two path names. The copy command copies the contents of the source directory to the destination directory. The source directory must already exist. If the destination does not already exist, copy will create it.

Here is an example. To copy the contents of the directory /usr/harley/documents to the directory /usr/harley/backups, enter

```
copy /usr/harley/documents /usr/harley/backups
```

If /usr/harley is the working directory, you can use relative path names:

```
copy documents backups
```

In either case, if the directory backups does not already exist, copy will create it.

The four options allow you to control the copying process in important ways. The most useful is the -v (verbose) option. This tells copy to display messages as it executes, showing each file that is being copied.

The -a (ask) option tells copy to ask your permission before each copy operation. If you enter any input that begins with a y (for "yes"), the copy will be performed. If you enter anything else, including a simple <Return>, the copy will not be performed. Using this option, you can control which files you want copied and which files you want to ignore.

Here is an example: The directory documents contains three files, letter, memo, and summary. You want to copy the files letter and summary to the backups directory. You want to ignore the file memo. Enter the command

```
copy -a documents backups
```

As `copy` processes each file you will be asked if you want to copy it. First, you will see

```
copy file documents/letter?
```

Enter

```
y
```

and the copy will take place. Next, you will see

```
copy file documents/memo?
```

Press <Return> by itself. The copy will not take place. Next, you will see

```
copy file documents/summary?
```

Enter

```
y
```

and the copy will take place.

The net result is that you have copied only the `letter` and `summary` files.

Note: When responding to the prompt, anything that starts with a y means "yes," for example, `y`, `ye`, `yes` or even `yellow`. For your protection, anything else means "no," for example, <Return> by itself, `n`, `no`, `hello`, or even `Y` or `Yes` (because the upper-case `Y` is a completely different character from the lower-case `y`).

The next option, `-r` (recursive), tells `copy` to process any subdirectories that it may find. This allows you to copy a complete tree structure from one location to another.

For example, say that the `documents` directory had subdirectories under it, some of which had their own subdirectories. To copy all of these directories, along with their contents, to the directory `backups`, enter

```
copy -r documents backups
```

If you combine the -a option with the -r option, copy will ask your permission to examine each subdirectory as it is encountered.

The final option, -1 (link), is used only occasionally. This option tells copy to make links rather than create all new files. (For a discussion of making links compared to making copies, see Chapter 16.)

Here is an example. The directory documents has three files. You enter

```
copy documents backups
```

You now have six separate files, three in documents and three in backups. However, if instead you enter:

```
copy -1 documents backups
```

you end up with only three separate files. Each file in backup is linked to the corresponding file in documents.

The -1 option is handy when you want to duplicate a large tree structure. If you make a copy of the entire structure, it will require a great deal of disk space. By making a copy of the links, you use only minimal space.

A Summary Of Directory Commands: Unix Compared to DOS

For reference, here is a table showing the directory commands that we have discussed. Beside each command is the DOS command that is most similar.

Hint
••••

DOS users:
Summary of Unix Directory Commands

	Unix Command	DOS Command
change working directory	cd	CHDIR, CD
display working directory	pwd	CHDIR, CD
make directory	mkdir	MKDIR, MD
remove directory	rmdir	RMDIR, RD
rename directory	mv	–
move directory	mvdir	–
copy directory	copy	XCOPY

20

Creating Ordinary Files

Introduction

In Chapter 16, we explained that there are three types of files: ordinary files, which hold your data and programs; special files, which represent physical devices; and directories, which organize other files into groups.

In the last few chapters, we discussed directories—how you create, organize, and maintain them. Special files, on the other hand, are set up and maintained by the system. That leaves ordinary files, which will form the bulk of your directory tree.

In the next three chapters, we will cover the commands you need to work with ordinary files. We start, in this chapter, with a discussion of how files are created.

How Files Are Created

There are several ways in which files are created. The most common occurrence is that a file is created automatically. For instance, a program that you are using may create a file on your behalf: your word processor creates a document, your spreadsheet program creates a spreadsheet, and so on.

Other files are created by Unix for some administrative function: these are the files that the system manager manages. Finally, when you install software, including the operating system itself, many files are created as part of the installation process.

A second way to create files is to initiate the process directly. You can do this in several ways: First, you can use the `vi` editor to make and edit a new file. Second, you can use the `cat` command to copy a small amount of data directly from the keyboard to a file. Finally, you can use the `touch` command to create a brand new, empty file.

The `vi` editor is a powerful program with many features and commands. We will defer a discussion of `vi` until Part IV of the book, where we will cover the topic in depth. The other two commands, `cat` and `touch`, will be explained later in this chapter. But first, let's take a moment to discuss how permissions are assigned when you create a file.

How File Permissions Are Assigned

When you create a file, Unix assigns file permissions automatically. As we explained in Chapters 16 and 19, file permissions are described by a file mode: a 3-digit number. Each digit in a file mode has a value from 0 to 7. The 3 digits represent permissions for the owner, the owner's group, and all other users.

For example, a file mode of 644 signifies a permission of "6" for the owner of the file, a permission of "4" for userids within the owner's group, and a permission of "4" for all other userids on the system.

To interpret a file mode digit, use Table 19.1 (on page 259). By using the table, we see that 644 represents read and write permission for the owner, read permission for the owner's group, and read permission for all other userids. (For a longer discussion of file modes, see Chapter 19.)

Generally speaking, you will create ordinary files and directories. An ordinary file can have one of two purposes. Either it will hold data, or it will hold a program or shell script to be executed.

If a file is to hold data, it will be considered for read and write permissions. This corresponds to a file mode value of 6. If a file is to be executable, it will be considered for read, write, and execute permissions. This corresponds to a file mode value of 7. Directories are also considered for full permissions.

Thus, a data file with full permissions will have a file mode of 666. An executable file or directory with full permissions will have a file mode of 777.

Whenever Unix creates a file or directory, the permissions are determined as follows: Starting with either 666 or 777, whichever is appropriate, Unix subtracts a 3-digit number called a *user file-creation mode mask*: this value represents the permissions that are to be withheld.

The user file-creation mode mask is usually referred to as a *file-creation mask*, or more simply, a *mask*. (Think of how a Halloween mask covers part of your face.) Unix maintains a file-creation mask for each userid that is logged in.

In most Unix systems, the default file-creation mask is 022. By checking with Table 19.1 (page 259), we see that this means that, by default, Unix withholds the following permissions:

User File-Creation Mode Mask:
Same as file-creation mask.

File-Creation Mask:
A 3-digit number that represents the permissions for a file.

Mask:
Same as file-creation mask.

owner:	none	(0)
group:	write	(2)
others:	write	(2)

RULE The default file-creation mask used by Unix is 022. This withholds the following permissions:

owner:	none	(0)
group:	write	(2)
others:	write	(2)

Let us consider the two possible types of file creation and see how it all works.

In the first case, Unix is creating a file that will hold data. Starting with the full permissions for such a file, 666, Unix subtracts the value of the file-creation mask, 022. This results in permissions of 644:

owner:	read, write	(6)
group:	read	(4)
others:	read	(4)

The other possibility is that Unix is creating a directory or a file that will be executable. Starting with 777, Unix subtracts the same file-creation mask, 022, resulting in permissions of 755:

owner:	read, write, execute	(7)
group:	read, execute	(5)
others:	read, execute	(5)

Thus, the default file mode is 644 for data files and 755 for directories and executable files.

RULE   When you create data files, the default file mode assigned by Unix is 644. This represents the following permissions:

owner:	read, write	(6)
group:	read	(4)
others:	read	(4)

Whenever you create an ordinary file directly, Unix assumes that it will contain data and assigns a default file mode of 644. If the file contains a shell script, you will need to change the file mode to include execute permission before you can run the script. You do this using the chmod command (discussed later in the chapter).

Controlling Your File-Creation Mask

The default user file-creation mask, 022, was chosen because it yields the permissions that make the most sense for most users. However, if you want full control, you can specify your own file-creation mask directly. Once you do, the new value will be used until you log off.

The command to specify your user file-creation mask is umask. If you decide to use this command, you may want to put it in your initialization file so that it takes effect every time you log in.

(Initialization files are discussed in Chapter 8. An initialization file is kept in your home directory and is executed automatically each time you log in. If you use the Bourne shell, your initialization commands go into your .profile file; if you use the C-shell, your commands go into your .login file.)

The syntax for the umask command is

umask [*nnn*]

You specify a 3-digit number that represents the permissions that are to be withheld. If you enter the command with no argument, umask will display the current file-creation mask. (Note: On some systems, you will see 4 digits. The leftmost digit is used for an esoteric feature that we can ignore: the standard mask consists of the rightmost 3 digits.)

Here is an example of how you might use umask. To determine your default file-creation mask, you enter

umask

with no arguments. You see

022

This means that, as things stand now, all new files will be created without the following permissions:

owner:	none	(0)
group:	write	(2)
others:	write	(2)

You decide that you want all your files, including directories, to be completely private. Thus, you want to withhold all permissions from your group and from all other userids:

owner:	none	(0)
group:	read, write, execute	(7)
others:	read, write, execute	(7)

You enter

umask 077

Any new files you create will be off-limits to everyone else except the superuser. There is nothing you can do to hide files from the superuser.

RULE

To create files with permissions that afford the maximum privacy, use the command **umask 077**.

For the rest of your work session, Unix will create your new files with a file mode of 600, for ordinary files,

owner:	read, write	(6)
group:	none	(0)
others:	none	(0)

or 700, for directories

owner:	read, write, execute	(7)
group:	none	(0)
others:	none	(0)

If you want these values to be permanent, use the **vi** editor to put the **umask** command in your initialization file.

Changing a File Mode: The chmod Command

To change the permissions for one of your own ordinary files or directories, use the **chmod** command. The syntax is

chmod *nnn file...*

You specify a 3-digit file mode and the names of one or more files. **chmod** will change the file permissions for those files.

The only userids that can use **chmod** to change file permissions are the owner of a file and the superuser. Using **chmod** does not depend on file permissions, only on ownership. This allows you to control all of your files, even those for which you may not have full permissions.

Here is an example of how to use **chmod**. You have a file named **secret.stuff** that was created with the default file-creation mask of 022. This means its file mode is 644:

owner:	read, write	(6)
group:	read	(4)
others:	read	(4)

You want to change the permissions so that no one but you can access the file. Enter

```
chmod 600 secret.stuff
```

The file mode is now 600:

owner:	read, write	(6)
group:	none	(0)
others:	none	(0)

Next, you have three files, **peace**, **love**, and **happiness**, that you want everyone to be able to share. You enter

```
chmod 666 peace love happiness
```

Each of these files now has a file mode of 666:

owner:	read, write	(6)
group:	read, write	(6)
others:	read, write	(6)

Changing a File's Owner or Group: The chown and chgrp Commands

If you own a file, you can change its owner or group. Once you transfer ownership to another userid, you lose the associated privileges: being able to change permissions and being able to change the owner and group. As you might expect, the super-user can change the ownership and group for any file.

To change a file's owner, use the **chown** command. To change a file's group, use the **chgrp** command. The syntax for these commands is similar:

```
chown userid file...
chgrp groupid file...
```

You specify a userid or groupid, respectively, and one or more files. Here are some examples:

You have created a file named **tasks**. You now want to transfer ownership to userid **kevin**. Enter

```
chown kevin tasks
```

You have three files, `peace`, `love`, and `happiness` for which you want the groupid to be `world`. Enter

```
chgrp world peace love happiness
```

When you work with files that are linked, changing the owner or group affects all the links simultaneously. After all, as we explained in Chapter 16, Unix considers all links to be equal.

Here is an example: You are logged in as userid `harley` and you create a file named `timetable` within your home directory, `/usr/harley`. You then create a link to this file. The link is named `schedule` and is within the directory `/usr/peter/notes`. You create the link by using the `ln` command (which we will cover in Chapter 22):

```
ln /usr/harley/timetable /usr/peter/notes/schedule
```

(In order to create this link, you will need write permission for the target directory.)

You now have the same file linked to two different names in two different directories. As far as Unix is concerned, each link has the same value. However, the ownership and groupid have not been changed. Both links are still owned by userid `harley`.

You now decide to pass ownership of the file to userid `peter`. Since both links are equal, either of these commands will do the job:

```
chown peter /usr/harley/timetable
chown peter /usr/peter/notes/schedule
```

The file is now owned by `peter`.

Creating Empty Files: The `touch` Command

The most important way to create a file directly is to use the `vi` editor that we will discuss in Part IV. However, there are two commands that you can use to create a simple file quickly: `touch` and `cat`.

As we explained in Chapter 16, Unix represents each file internally by an inode. The number of the inode, along with the file name, is stored in the directory entry for the file. Within the inode, Unix stores the information needed to maintain the file.

This information was shown in Figure 16.1 (on page 219). As the figure shows, the inode contains the last time that the file was modified (written or created) and accessed (read).

The `touch` command was designed to allow you to change these values. For instance, if you are selling a software product, you can use the `touch` command to ensure that all the files on the distribution diskettes have the same date and time stamp.

The two things about `touch` that make it useful for creating files are

1. By default, `touch` uses the current date and time.
2. If the file does not already exist, `touch` will create it.

This means that you can use `touch` to create an empty file, stamped with the current date and time.

RULE   To create an empty file, use the `touch` command.

    DOS users:
Unlike DOS, Unix will allow you to create empty files.

The syntax for this command is

touch [-acm] [*mmddhhmm*[*yy*]] *file...*

Most of the time, you will use `touch` with no options. You specify the name of one or more ordinary files and `touch` will create them. The access and modification times will be the current date and time. The file will be empty (0 bytes). The permissions will be set according to the current value of the file-creation mask.

For example, to create two files, **names** and **addresses**, in your working directory, enter

```
touch names addresses
```

That's all there is to it. If a file already exists, the touch command will change its access and modification times. For instance, to use the current time as the access time and modification time for an existing file old.data, enter

```
touch old.data
```

If you want to update only the access time, use the -a (access time only) option:

```
touch -a old.data
```

If you want to update only the modification time, use the -m (modification time only) option:

```
touch -m old.data
```

If you need to specify a date and time, you can do so using the format *mmddhhmm*. The first 2 characters represent the month; the second 2 characters represent the day; the next 2 characters represent the hour; the final 2 characters represent the minutes. When you specify the hour, remember that Unix uses a 24-hour clock.

If you want to specify the year, you can add two extra characters to the end of the date. These characters must be between 70 (1970) and 99 (1999).

Here is an example: To change the access time of the file birthday to December 21, 10:30 am, use

```
touch -a 12211030 birthday
```

If the file does not already exist, Unix will create it.

If you do not want touch to create files that do not already exist, use the -c (do not create) option:

```
touch -c backup
```

This example updates the access and modification times of the file backup to the current date and time. However, if backup does not already exist, it will not be created.

Creating Short Files: The `cat` Command

We will discuss the `cat` command in detail later, in Chapter 23. For now, we will explain how you can use `cat` to create a short file with a minimum of fuss.

The `cat` command will copy data from the keyboard to a text file. The syntax is

```
cat >file
```

If the file does not already exist, `cat` will create it. If the file does exist, it will be replaced.

The greater-than sign (>) tells Unix that the output of the command is to be written to the file that you specify. This is called "redirecting standard output" and will be discussed later in the book.

After you enter the command, `cat` will read whatever you type at the keyboard. Enter as many lines as you want. When you are finished, press the `eof` character, ^D (see Chapter 9). `cat` will take all the data you have entered and write it to the file. If you change your mind in the middle of entering the data, press the `intr` key for your terminal (probably ^C or <Delete>) to cancel the command.

RULE
——

To create a short text file, use the command:
   `cat >file`

DOS users:
Creating a short Unix file by using `cat >file` is similar to creating a DOS file with COPY CON: *FILENAME.EXT*

Here is an example of how to use `cat` in this manner: You want to create a file named `friends` in your working directory. You enter:

```
cat >friends
```

The `cat` command is now waiting for your input. You enter several lines, ending with the `eof` character:

```
Harley
Peter
Kevin
Eileen
Addie
Scott
^D
```

`cat` now writes these lines to the file `friends`. If the file did not already exist, it will be created. You now have a file with six lines.

If you need to add lines to the end of an existing text file, you can use a variation of the `cat` command. By using two greater-than signs (`>>`), you specify that if the file already exists, `cat` is to append the data to the end of the file, rather than replace it. The syntax is:

```
cat >>file
```

Continuing with our example, say that you want to add two more lines to your `friends` file. You enter

```
cat >>friends
Randy
Melissa
^D
```

Once you send the `eof` signal by pressing `^D`, `cat` appends the new lines to the end of the file. You now have a file with 8 lines.

 RULE   To add a few lines to the end of a short text file, use the command `cat >>`*file*

Using `cat` in this way is quick, but it has a disadvantage: if you make a mistake you need to start all over again. You will find that for small files, especially short shell scripts, `cat` is useful. However, for most work, you will need to use the `vi` editor.

21

Displaying Information About Your Files

Introduction

In this chapter we will show you how to display information about your files. We will meet one of the most important commands in the world of Unix: the ls command.

We will start by discussing how you can use this command to list the names of your files. From there, we will explore some of the many options that ls offers and how you can use them to keep track of your files and directories.

Displaying Information About Files: The ls and lc Commands

Overall, the single most useful Unix command is the one that displays information about our files: ls. The ls (list) command is robust, having 21 options, most of which you can ignore. The syntax for ls, showing only the most important options, is

ls [-adlrtxCFR] [*file*...]

The ls command displays information about the files whose names you specify. If you specify the name of a directory, ls displays information about the files in that directory. If you do not specify a file name, ls displays information about the files in your working directory.

Without options, ls displays file names, one per line. Thus, to display the names of all the files in your working directory, enter

```
ls
```

Here is some sample output:

```
backups
bin
documents
setup
treeinfo.ncd
```

In this case, there are 5 files (some of which may be directories).

Notice that the names are displayed in alphabetical order. As a general rule, ls automatically sorts all output by file name.

DOS users:
Unlike the DIR command, ls displays file names in alphabetical order.

If you want to display the output sorted in reverse order, use the -r (reverse) option:

```
ls -r
```

Our sample output looks like this:

```
treeinfo.ncd
setup
documents
bin
backups
```

You can use the -r option with any of the other options.

To display the file names in columns, rather than one name per line, use the `-C` (column) option. Notice that the `C` is upper case. Here is an example that lists the files in the `documents` directory:

```
ls -C documents
```

The output is

```
address     chapter.3   invoice       memo    summary
chapter.1   chapter.4   letter        names
chapter.2   chapter.5   master.list   order
```

If you have a long directory, it is often easier to read a listing displayed in this way.

Some Unix systems have an `lc` command. This command works much like `ls`, except that it automatically displays file names in columns. That is, `lc` is the same as `ls -C`.

DOS users:

The `ls -C` and `lc` commands are analogous to the DOS DIR /W command.

Why have two commands that differ but are so similar? The answer is that `ls` is the original command. `lc` was added later to some versions of Unix, as a matter of convenience: listing in columns is a common request and it is much easier to type "`lc`" than "`ls -C`". If your system has an `lc` command, the following two examples have the same effect:

```
ls -C
lc
```

The next two commands are also equivalent. They both use columns to display the names of the files in the `documents` directory:

```
ls -C documents
lc documents
```

If you want to display file names in columns, use the `lc` command. Otherwise, use the `ls` command.

When you use `ls -C` or `lc` to display file names in columns, the output is sorted vertically. If you want to display file names in columns, but sort from left to right, use the **-x** (across) option. The following two examples, which use **-x**, are equivalent:

```
ls -xC documents
lc -x documents
```

The output looks like this:

```
address     chapter.1   chapter.2   chapter.3   chapter.4
chapter.5   invoice     letter      master.list memo
names       order       summary
```

Sometimes, it is helpful to know what types of files you have. The **-F** (function) command will tell you which files are directories and which files are executable. Directories are marked with a / (slash), the character used with path names. Files that have execute permission are marked with an * (asterisk). Here is an example. You enter

```
ls -F
```

and you see

```
backups/
bin/
documents/
setup*
treeinfo.ncd
```

In this case, there are three directories, **backups**, **bin**, and **documents**, and two ordinary files, **setup** and **treeinfo.ncd**. Of the two ordinary files, only **setup** is executable.

Displaying the Names of Hidden Files: The `ls -a` Command

The `-a` option for the `ls` command controls the listing of so-called hidden files. Normally, `ls` will display all file names except those that begin with . (a period)—for example, `.profile`. As a convention, we use such file names for initialization or control files that we do not want to look at every time we list a directory. Usually, these files are used only in the home directory.

If you use the `-a` (all files) option, `ls` will display the names of all the files, even those that begin with a period. For example, if you enter

```
ls -a
```

you would see output like this:

```
.
..
.exrc
.lastlogin
.news_time
.nortonrc
.profile
backups
bin
documents
setup
treeinfo.ncd
```

The first two files are the . and .. files that we discussed in Chapter 18. They represent the directory itself and the parent directory, respectively. The next five files are names that would normally not be displayed without the `-a` option.

The files `.lastlogin` and `.news_time` are not found on all systems. These files are actually empty. Unix keeps them around just to be able to look at the date and time that they were last modified.

When you log in, Unix can tell you the time of your previous login by checking the modification time of your `.lastlogin` file. Unix then updates the time to reflect the new login. Similarly, Unix uses the modification time of the `.news_time` file to

Program	Initialization File	Executes
Bourne shell	.profile	after login (for sh users)
C-shell	.login	after login (for csh users)
C-shell	.cshrc	whenever a csh is started
mailx	.mailrc	when mail program starts
vi editor	.exrc	when editor starts

Table 21.1   *Standard initialization files.*

keep track of which news items you have already seen (see Chapter 12).

The other files whose names begin with a period are initialization files. These are files that contain commands to be executed automatically each time a particular programs starts.

We have already seen some examples, such as the .profile file that contains initialization commands for the Bourne shell (see Chapter 8). Table 21.1 lists the most commonly used initialization files and what programs use them. The .nortonrc file contains initialization commands for the Norton Utilities for System V. They are kept in the home directory and contain commands for a particular program. Each time the program starts, it searches the home directory for its initialization file. If the file is found, the program executes the commands. (By the way, the letters "rc" stand for "run commands.")

Displaying More Information About Files: The ls –l Command

To display more information about each file, use the ls command with the -l (long) option. Here is an example that will display a long listing for each file in the working directory:

```
ls -l
```

The output from this particular command is useful—you will find yourself using ls -l repeatedly. Here is some sample output:

```
total 10
drwxr-xr-x    2 harley    other         96 Aug 21 09:34 backups
drwxrwxrwx    2 harley    other        176 Aug 21 08:48 bin
drwxr-xr-x    5 harley    other        240 Aug 21 19:37 documents
-rwxr-xr--    1 harley    other        581 Jan 22  1990 setup
-rw-r--r--    1 harley    other         91 Aug 21 08:48 treeinfo.ncd
```

Block:

A unit of disk storage, 512 bytes.

The first line tells you the amount of storage used by these files. The storage is measured in *blocks*, one block being 512 bytes. The rest of the lines show information about the files, one file per line. Here is what all the information means, reading from right to left:

On the far right is the file name. To its left is the time and date that the file was last modified. (Remember, Unix uses a 24-hour clock.) If the file has a modification date over six months old or in the future, the year is displayed instead of the time. In this example, the file `setup` was last modified over six months ago.

(You might ask: Can a file have a modification date in the future? The answer is, yes, if you have set the date yourself with the `touch` command—see Chapter 20.)

To the left of the modification date is the size of the file, in bytes. If the file is a directory, the size indicates how many bytes the directory itself uses. The size does not say anything about the size of the files contained in the directory.

To the left of the file size are the groupid and userid associated with the file. In our example, all the files are owned by userid `harley` and are associated with the group `others`.

To the left of the userid is a number. If the file is an ordinary file or a special file, this number shows how many links there are to this entry. In our example, `setup` and `treeinfo.ncd` are ordinary files, each with 1 link.

If the file is a directory, this number represents the number of entries in the directory that, in turn, point to other directories.

As we explained in Chapter 18, all directories contain two entries . and .. that point to the directory itself and to the parent directory, respectively. In our example, we have three directories: `backups`, `bin`, and `documents`. `backups` and `bin` have a value of 2 to the left of the owner; `documents` has a value of 5. Each directory contains 2 entries that point to directories:

. and ..—documents also contains 3 subdirectories, which is why it shows a value of 5.

Thus, we can say that the number to the left of the owner shows us the following information:

ordinary and special files: number of links

directories: number of subdirectories + 2 (for . and ..)

Finally, the 10 characters at the left-hand side of the listing give us information as to the type of file and its permissions.

Block Device:

A device, such as a disk, that handles data in chunks.

Character Device:

A device, such as a keyboard, that handles data one character at a time.

The leftmost character represents the type of file. Directories have a "**d**"; ordinary files have a "**-**" (minus sign); and special files have either a "**b**" or a "**c**", standing for *block device* and *character device*, respectively. A block device, such as a disk, handles data in chunks; a character device, such as the keyboard, handles data one byte at a time. Most of the time, you will see special files only in the /dev directory.

The 9 characters to the right describe the permissions associated with the file. (Permissions are described in Chapters 16 and 20.) These 9 characters should be interpreted as three sets of 3 characters. From left to right, these sets show the permissions for the owner, for the group, and for all others.

Within each set of 3 characters, the permissions are shown in the order read, write, execute. If the permission is granted, there will be an "**r**", a "**w**", or an "**x**" respectively; if the permission is not granted, there will be a "**-**" (minus sign).

Consider the following example, taken from the listing for the file **setup** in our example:

```
-rwxr-xr--
```

To understand what this means, let us separate the first character and the three sets of permission characters:

```
-   rwx   r-x   r--
```

We can categorize the information as follows:

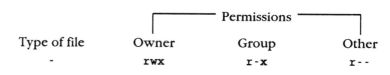

	Permissions		
Type of file	Owner	Group	Other
-	rwx	r-x	r--

We see that `setup` is an ordinary file. The owner has read, write, and execute permissions. The group has read and execute permissions. All other userids have only read permission.

As you can see, the `ls -l` command shows you a great deal of information about a file. As a final, complete example, let us take a last look at the information for the file `documents`.

```
drwxr-xr-x   5 harley    other        240 Aug 21 19:37 documents
```

This file is a directory with the following permissions:

owner:	read, write, execute
group:	read, execute
others:	read, execute

`documents` has 3 subdirectories (5-2). The file is owned by userid `harley` and is associated with the group `other`. The file is 240 bytes long and was last modified on August 21 of this year, at 7:37 pm.

Displaying Information Sorted by Time:
The `ls -t` Command

Normally, file names are displayed alphabetically or in reverse alphabetical order (with the `-r` option). If you want to display file names sorted by modification time, use the `-t` (time) option.

With `-t`, file names are displayed from newest to oldest. If you want to display the oldest first, use both the `-t` and `-r` options.

Most of the time, the `-t` option is used with the `-l` option so you can see the actual time and date. Here are some examples.

First, to display a long listing of all the files in your working directory, sorted by time, from newest to oldest, enter

```
ls -lt
```

The following is typical output:

```
total 10
drwxr-xr-x   5 harley    other        240 Aug 21 19:37 documents
drwxr-xr-x   2 harley    other         96 Aug 21 09:34 backups
drwxrwxrwx   2 harley    other        176 Aug 21 08:48 bin
-rw-r--r--   1 harley    other         91 Aug 21 08:48 treeinfo.ncd
-rwxr-xr--   1 harley    other        581 Jan 22  1990 setup
```

To display the same information sorted from oldest to newest modification time, enter

```
ls -lrt
```

Using the same sample working directory, the output would look like this:

```
total 10
-rwxr-xr--   1 harley    other      581 Jan 22  1990 setup
-rw-r--r--   1 harley    other       91 Aug 21 08:48 treeinfo.ncd
drwxrwxrwx   2 harley    other      176 Aug 21 08:48 bin
drwxr-xr-x   2 harley    other       96 Aug 21 09:34 backups
drwxr-xr-x   5 harley    other      240 Aug 21 19:37 documents
```

Displaying Information About Subdirectories:
The `ls -R` Command

The `-R` (recursive) option adds to the information that the `ls` command displays. With this option, `ls` displays information about the contents of every subdirectory it encounters.

In other words, `ls -R` will show you information about a complete subtree. If you want to see a long listing, use `ls -lR`. If you want to see whether a file is a directory or is executable, use `ls -FR`.

Here is an example: Your working directory is set to your home directory. To take a look at all your files and subdirectories, enter

```
ls -R
```

Here is an example of the type of output you might see. Remember, a single period (`.`) refers to the working directory.

```
backups
bin
documents
setup
treeinfo.ncd

./backups:
letter
memo
summary
```

```
./bin:
dos
modem
stop
unix

./documents:
chapter.1
chapter.2
chapter.3

./documents/chapter.1:
introduction
test
examples

./documents/chapter.2:
introduction
test
examples

./documents/chapter.3:
introduction
test
examples
```

Displaying Information About a Directory: The `ls -d` Command

If you enter the `ls` command and specify the name of a directory, `ls` will display information about the contents of that directory. For instance, say that `documents` is a subdirectory of your working directory. If you enter

```
ls -l documents
```

you will see information about the files contained in `documents`. For example:

```
total 6
drwxr-xr-x   2 harley   other       32 Aug 21 22:31 chapter.1
drwxr-xr-x   2 harley   other       32 Aug 21 22:31 chapter.2
drwxr-xr-x   2 harley   other       32 Aug 21 22:31 chapter.3
```

But what if you want information about **documents** itself? Use the **-d** (directory) option. For example:

```
ls -dl documents
```

This tells **ls** that you want information about the directory, not about its contents:

```
drwxr-xr-x   5 harley    other        272 Aug 21 22:31 documents
```

A Summary of the Important Options
Used with the **ls** Command

The **ls** command displays file names, in alphabetical order, and information about those files. If you do not specify the name of a file or directory, **ls** will display information about your working directory. If you do not specify any options, **ls** will display file names only. Without the **-a** option, **ls** will display only those file names that do not start with a period.

The **ls** command has many options. Table 21.2 lists the most important ones.

Option	Meaning
-a	display all file names
-d	display data about a directory entry
-l	display a long listing
-r	display in reverse order
-t	display in order of modification time
-x	display names sorted horizontally
-C	display names in columns (if your system has an **lc** command, it has the same effect as **ls -C**)
-F	show which files are directories/executable
-R	display information about all subdirectories

Table 21.2 *Summary of options for the **ls** command.*

22
Maintaining Ordinary Files

Introduction

In Chapter 20, we discussed how ordinary files—those containing programs and data—are created. These are the files that you will work with most of the time. In the last chapter, we showed how to use the `ls` command to display information about your files and directories.

In this chapter, we continue our discussion by considering the day-to-day commands that you will use to maintain your files.

What Are Regular Expressions?

One of the fundamental concepts of Unix is that, wherever it makes sense, you should be able to specify a group of items instead of a single item.

For example, say that you are using the `ls` command to display information about your files. The following command displays information about a file, named **standards**, in your working directory:

```
ls -l standards
```

To enter this command, you had to specify the name of a single file. You should also be able to specify a whole group of files. For instance, the following command displays information about all the files whose names begin with the characters "st":

```
ls -l st*
```

Regular Expression:
A compact way of specifying all character strings that match a particular pattern.

The tool we use to express such specifications is called a *regular expression*. The name "regular expression" is taken from a branch of theoretical computer science. In Unix, a regular expression is a compact way of specifying all the character strings that match a particular pattern. In the example above, "st*" is a regular expression.

Regular expressions are used throughout Unix, with many different commands. For instance, the file commands allow you to use a regular expression to specify a group of file names; the vi editor allows you to use a regular expression to define patterns of characters that are to be modified; the egrep program will find all the lines in a text file that contain a particular pattern.

Unfortunately, most of the Unix commands were developed at different times by different people. As a result, the rules for forming regular expressions are not exactly the same for every program. For instance, the vi editor will accept regular expressions that are far more complex than the ones we use for file names.

However, the basic concepts do carry over from one command to another. In this chapter, we will explain how to use regular expressions to specify file names. You can use these types of patterns in all the commands that deal with files and directories.

DOS users:

Unix regular expressions can be used to specify file names, like DOS wildcards. Regular expressions are much more powerful than DOS wildcards.

Regular Expressions: Using ? and * to Match Characters

The idea of a regular expression is to represent a pattern. Within a regular expression, letters and numbers stand for themselves, while the characters

```
?    *    [    ]    -    !
```

have special meanings.

The question mark, ?, stands for any one character. For example, the regular expression ch?? would match the letters "ch", followed by any two characters.

How would you use this? When you use a regular expression as a file name, Unix looks in your directory and finds the names of all the files that match the expression. Unix then substitutes all these file names for the regular expression.

For instance, say that your working directory contains the following files: ch01, ch02, ch11, ch123, and ch. If you enter the command

```
ls -l ch??
```

it would be the same as entering

```
ls -l ch01 ch02 ch11
```

Notice that ch?? does not match ch123 or ch.

Here is a more complex example. The regular expression

```
?a??bc???1
```

specifies any one character, followed by the letter "a", followed by any two characters, followed by the letters "bc", followed by any three characters, followed by the digit "1". Here are some names that this regular expression would match:

```
XaXXbcXXX1      manobcpqr1      7a65bc4321
```

The **?** represents any single character. If you want to match more than one character, use ***** (the asterisk). The ***** matches zero or more characters of any type.

We first met the expression "zero or more" in Chapter 10. At the time we said that a Unix command has zero or more options. Similarly, each ***** in a regular expression matches zero or more characters. That is, it will match no characters, one character, or more than one character.

For example, to display information about all the files in your working directory whose names start with the letters "ch", use

```
ls -l ch*
```

The regular expression **ch*** will match all the names from our first example: **ch01**, **ch02**, **ch11**, **ch123**, and **ch**.

You can use a ***** at any position in the pattern to represent zero or more characters. For example, to match a character string that starts with "**st**", followed by zero or more characters, followed by the single character "**e**", use

```
st*e
```

Such a pattern would match file names like

```
store    ste    stampede    st1234567890e
```

The ***** character is more powerful than you might realize. For example,

```
*
```

by itself will match any character string. As a convenience, when you use ***** at the beginning of a file name, the pattern will not match names that begin with a period. Thus, the command:

```
rm *
```

will remove all of your files, except those whose names begin with a period. (We will discuss the **rm** command later in this chapter.) As we explained in Chapter 21, files whose names begin with a period, such as **.profile**, are used for automatic initializations. You would not want to remove such files accidentally.

To continue, the regular expression

```
a*
```

will match any character string that begins with "**a**". The expression

```
*a
```

will match any character string that ends with "**a**". For example, to list the names of all of your files that end with "**old**", use:

```
ls *old
```

You can use both ***** and **?** in the same regular expression. For example, to list the names of all files that begin with an "**a**", followed by zero or more characters, followed by "**old**", followed by any two characters, use

```
ls a*old??
```

This command will list files with names like

```
a123old11     alanoldxx     aXXXXXXXold01
```

By itself, **?** will match exactly one character; ***** will match zero or more characters. Sometimes, you will want to match one or more characters. In such cases, use a **?** followed by a *****. For example, the command

```
ls data?*
```

will list the names

```
data1     data1.bak     data1xyz     data1.old.copy
```

but not the names

```
data      dat
```

Regular Expressions: Using [,], -, and ! to Define a Set

So far, we have seen how to use ? and * to match any character. However, sometimes you want to match a specific character, one that is a member of a particular set. To do this, enclose the set of characters in square brackets and use the whole thing as part of the pattern. The entire set, square brackets included, represents one character.

Here is an example. Using your working directory, you want to display the names of all the files whose names begin with "example." followed by "a", "b", "c", "d", or "e". That is example.a, example.b, example.c, example.d, or example.e.

Enter

```
ls example.[abcde]
```

Here is another example. You want to list the names of all files that start with either the letter "a" or the letter "A". Use

```
ls [aA]*
```

In this case, the [aA] specifies one character, either "a" or "A". The * specifies zero or more characters. This command would display file names such as

```
a    A    animal    Animal    axyz
```

You can also use numbers within square brackets. For example, the command

```
ls chapter.[0123456789][0123456789]
```

displays files names that end with exactly two digits. The two sets of characters in square brackets each represent a single character. This command displays names such as

```
chapter.01    chapter.10    chapter.57
```

As a convenience, you can use a - (minus sign) to stand for a range of consecutive letters or numbers. For instance, you can shorten the last command to

```
ls chapter.[0-9][0-9]
```

And you can shorten the first command in this section to

```
ls example.[a-e]
```

Directly following a set of characters in square brackets, we can use a * to indicate zero or more members of the set. For example, to display file names starting with **chapter** and followed by zero or more numbers, enter

```
ls chapter[0-9]*
```

This will match names like

```
chapter     chapter0     chapter15     chapter999999
```

You can also use more than one range within the same set. The command

```
ls example.[a-zA-Z]
```

displays names that end in either a lower-case or an upper-case letter.

Finally, you can use ! (an exclamation mark) just after the left square bracket to indicate that you want to match any character that is *not* in the set. For example, the command

```
ls record[!0-9]
```

will display file names that end in any single character that is not a number. This command will display names like

```
recordA     records     record.     recordx
```

but not

```
record0     record5     record9
```

> Within a regular expression, letters and numbers represent themselves. A few characters have special meanings. They are as follows:
>
> | ? | match any single character |
> |---|---|
> | * | match zero or more characters |
> | [ ] | match one of the enclosed characters |
> | [!] | match any character that is not enclosed |
> | [ ]* | match zero or more of the enclosed characters |
> | [!]* | match zero or more nonenclosed characters |
>
> Inside [ ], you can use - (minus sign) to indicate a range of single letters or digits.

Figure 22.1 *Summary of characters used to match file names.*

A Summary of the Characters Used with Regular Expressions

A regular expression is a compact way of specifying character strings that match a particular pattern. When you use a regular expression as the name of a file, Unix will search your directory and substitute all the file names it finds that match the pattern. Figure 22.1 summarizes regular expressions.

DOS users:

Within a regular expression, the ? works the same way as within a DOS wildcard; however, the * works differently.

Removing Files: The rm Command

As we explained in Chapter 16, in Unix you do not "erase" or "delete" files; rather, you remove them. What you are actually doing is removing the link between the file name and its corresponding inode. If there is only one link to the file, removing it will erase it. However, if it happens that the file has more than one link, Unix will wait until the last link is gone before removing the file.

To remove a file, you use the rm command. The syntax is

```
rm [-fi] file...
```

The rm command removes the directory entries for the files you specify. If an entry was the last link for the file, rm erases the file. Most of the time this is the case, so that rm acts like an "erase" command.

Here are some examples. To remove the file named **data** in your working directory, enter

```
rm data
```

To remove the file named **test** from a directory named **data**, and a file named **extra** from a directory named **backup**, use

```
rm data/test backup/extra
```

One of the most useful ways to use rm is to specify file names using a regular expression. For instance, to remove all the files whose names end with ".bak" from your working directory, enter

```
rm *.bak
```

Removing all the files from your working directory is easy:

```
rm *
```

As we mentioned earlier, when you use a regular expression to match file names, a * at the beginning will not match files whose names begin with a period. Thus, initialization files, such as .profile, are safe from accidental erasure.

Whenever you use a regular expression to specify the files you want to remove, it is a good idea to check which files will be matched before you remove them. For example, say that you have three old files that you don't need any more: old.addresses, old.phone, and old.names. You decide to remove them by entering

```
rm old.*
```

However, just to be sure, you first use the ls command to check exactly which files will be matched:

```
ls old.*
```

You see:

```
old.addresses
old.friends
old.names
old.phone
```

There is an extra file, **old.friends**, that you forgot. If you had entered the **rm** command without checking first with **ls**, you would have removed all four files. Since **rm** does not display a message telling you how many files have been removed, you would have been unaware of the extra file. Even if you did find out, it would have been too late: once a file is removed, it's gone for good (unless there is another link to it).

RULE   There is no way to get back a file that has been removed.

RULE   Before using a regular expression with the **rm** (remove) command, use the same regular expression with the **ls** command to check exactly which file names are matched.

Aside from checking first with **ls**, there is another way to guard against accidental catastrophe: use the **-i** (interactive) option. This tells **rm** to ask your permission before removing each file.

For example, if you enter

```
rm -i old.*
```

you will be asked, file by file, for permission to perform the removal. The queries work exactly the same way as when you use the **rmdir** command with the **-a** (ask) option (see Chapter 19). **rm** will display the name of each file in turn, followed by a question mark. For example:

```
old.addresses: ?
```

If you enter anything that begins with a lower-case "**y**" (for yes), the file will be removed. If you enter anything else, including pressing <Return> by itself, the file will not be removed. With our example, you will be asked, one at a time, if you want to remove the files matched by `old.*`. You can enter

```
y
```

for each one until you get to

```
old.friends: ?
```

Realizing that this is a file that you don't want to remove, you can skip it by pressing <Return>.

RULE

To learn Unix, keep in mind that whenever you use a regular expression with the rm (remove) command, use the `-i` (interactive) option so you can approve the removal of each file.

If you try to remove a file for which you do not have the proper ownership, you will see the message

```
Permission denied
```

Even if you do own a file, you cannot remove it unless you have write permission for both the file and for the directory in which it resides. If you do not have write permission for the file, rm will display the file name and its file mode, and then ask you if you really want to remove it.

For example, say that you own a file named `old.data` for which you have removed the write permission. You enter

```
rm old.data
```

You will see

```
old.data: 500 mode ?
```

You are being told that the file mode is 500. If you still want to remove the file, enter anything that begins with a "**y**". If you do not want to remove the file, enter anything else.

If you try to remove a file which resides in a directory for which you do not have write permission, **rm** will refuse to remove the file. Even if you own a file and have full permissions for it, you cannot remove it if you do not have the permission to modify its directory.

On rare occasions, you may wish to forgo the warnings and remove files for which you do not have write permission. If you use the **-f** (force) option, **rm** will not bother to show you the file mode and ask your permission. Be sure to use this option sparingly, and with the greatest of care. However, even the **-f** option will not let you remove a file if you do not have write permission for its directory.

Removing Files from Subdirectories: The **rm -r** Command

By itself, the **rm** command operates only in the directory you specify or, if you do not specify a directory, in your working directory. Thus, the command

```
rm documents/*
```

will remove all the files in the **documents** directory. The command

```
rm *
```

will remove all the files in your working directory.

By using the **-r** (recursive) option, you can have **rm** remove files in every subdirectory it encounters. In other words, **rm -r** will remove an entire portion of a directory tree. This option works like the **-R** option we used with the **ls** command in Chapter 21. Note, however, that the **rm** command uses a lower-case **r**, while the **ls** command uses an upper-case **R**.

Here is an example of how this option works. You want to remove all the files and subdirectories under the directory **/usr/harley/documents**. You enter

```
rm -r /usr/harley/documents
```

This command will also remove the documents directory itself. If you want to remove all the files and subdirectories but leave the documents directory intact, use:

```
rm -r /usr/harley/documents/*
```

Sometimes it is easier to change working directories first:

```
cd /usr/harley/documents
rm -r *
```

This last command, rm -r *, is powerful. It will wipe out whole parts of a directory tree before you have time to realize what is happening. Be careful.

Here is an example of how you could accidentally cause a catastrophe. Your home directory has several subdirectories that hold old backups. All these subdirectories have names that end with .bak, such as jan.bak, feb.bak, and so on.

You decide to remove all these directories by moving to your home directory:

```
cd
```

and using the command

```
rm -r *.bak
```

However, you make a mistake and enter

```
rm -r * bak
```

Notice what has happened: you have accidentally omitted to type the period after the * character. The rm command assumes that you have specified two arguments, just as if you had entered

```
rm -r *
rm -r bak
```

The result? You have accidentally removed all your files—and once they are removed, there is no way to get them back.

If you are the system manager, you must be extra careful, because the superuser can remove any file or directory on the system. Imagine what would happen if the system manager logged in as superuser and entered the command

```
rm -r /* bak
```

Even worse, imagine the system manager entered

```
rm -fr /* bak
```

(The -f [force] option will remove all files, regardless of their permissions.)

One way to guard against this problem is to make sure that you never use the -r option without the -i option. This forces rm to ask you before removing each file. If you accidentally enter

```
rm -ir * bak
```

you will notice your mistake as soon as rm asks you for permission to remove the first file. You can then abort the command by pressing the intr key (see Chapter 9).

Renaming and Moving Files: The mv Command

To move or rename a file, you use the mv command. The syntax is

mv [-f] *source... destination*

You specify a source and a destination. The source may be one or more ordinary or special files. The destination may be any type of file, including a directory. The mv command will move the source to the destination.

The mv command actually performs three different functions: rename, move and rename, and move without rename. The effect of the mv command depends on what you choose for a source and what you choose for a destination.

Here is how the *rename* function works: If you specify a source file and a destination file that lie in the same directory, mv

will rename the file. For example, to rename the file
/usr/harley/data/new to **/usr/harley/data/old**, enter

```
mv /usr/harley/data/new /usr/harley/data/old
```

If you want, you can shorten the **mv** command by first changing
the working directory:

```
cd /usr/harley/data
mv new old
```

As this last command illustrates, to rename a file in your working directory, simply move it from one name to another.

Any time you move a file you must be careful. If the destination file already exists, it will be replaced; and once a file is
replaced, it is gone for good. In the last example, if the file **old**
had existed, it would have been wiped out by the **mv** command.

The **mv** command can also be used to *move and rename*: If you
specify a source file and a destination file that lie in different directories, **mv** will move and rename the file. For example, say that you
want to move the file **new**, in the directory **/usr/harley/data**, to
the file **old** in the directory **/usr/harley/backups**. Enter

```
mv /usr/harley/data/new /usr/harley/backups/old
```

Again, we can simplify the **mv** command by first changing to an
appropriate directory:

```
cd /usr/harley
mv data/new backups/old
```

And, if it happened that **/usr/harley** was your home directory,
you can use a shorter **cd** command:

```
cd
mv data/new backups/old
```

(Recall that the **cd** command with no arguments moves you to
your home directory.) To make things easier still, we can enter
more than one command on the same line (remembering to
separate the commands with semicolons):

```
cd; mv data/new backups/old
```

The *move without rename* function works as follows: If you specify one or more source files and a destination directory, mv will move the files to the directory, keeping the same file names. For example, say that your working directory has two subdirectories, **data** and **backups**. To move a file named **info** from the **data** directory to the **backups** directory, use

```
mv data/info backups
```

Because you did not specify a new file name, mv will not rename the file. In other words, the previous command has the same effect as

```
mv data/info backups/info
```

When the destination is a directory, you can specify more than one source file. The mv command will move the source files to the directory.

For example, you want to move the files **info1**, **info2**, and **info3** from the **data** directory to the **backups** directory. Enter

```
mv data/info1 data/info2 data/info3 backups
```

In this case, you could use a regular expression to specify the source files:

```
mv data/info[123] backups
```

In summary, the mv command performs three functions. Here is the syntax for each function, along with an example:

1. Rename:

    mv *old-name new-name*
    ```
    mv new old
    ```

2. Move and rename:

    mv *source-file destination-file*
    ```
    mv data/new backups/old
    ```

3. Move without rename:

mv *source-file... destination-directory*
```
mv data/info[123] backups
```

Like the **rm** command, **mv** will ask you for your approval before moving to a destination that does not have write permission. **mv** will display the name of the file and the file mode, and ask for confirmation. To confirm the move, enter any response that begins with a "**y**". To cancel the move, enter anything else.

To tell **mv** to perform all such moves without asking for your approval, use **-f** option.

The details work the same way as with the **rm** command, explained earlier in this chapter. See that section for examples.

Copying Files: The cp Command

To copy one or more files, use the **cp** command. To copy a single file, the syntax is

cp *source-file destination-file*

To copy one or more files to a specified directory, the syntax is

cp *source-file... destination-directory*

Here are some examples: Within the file **/usr/harley/docs**, you have a file named **orders**. You want to make a copy named **backup** and put it in the directory **/usr/harley/archives**. Enter

```
cp /usr/harley/docs/orders /usr/harley/archives/backup
```

You can simplify the command by first changing the working directory to **/usr/harley**:

```
cd /usr/harley
cp docs/orders archives/backup
```

Even easier, if **/usr/harley** is the home directory, you can use

```
cd; cp docs/orders archives/backups
```

Here is another example: Within your working directory, you want to make a copy of the file **data** and call it **extra**. Enter

```
cp data extra
```

To copy one or more files to a different directory, use the second form of the **cp** command. Specify one or more source names and a single destination directory. All the copies will have the same names as the source files.

For example, within the **docs** directory, you have a file named **orders**. You want to make a copy, also named **orders**, in the **backups** directory. Enter

```
cp docs/orders backups
```

As another example, you have several files in the **pals** directory: **addie**, **harley**, **kevin**, **scott**. You want to make copies of these files and store them in the **backups** directory. Use

```
cp pals/addie pals/harley pals/kevin pals/scott backups
```

If these four files happen to be the only files in the **pals** directory, the previous command can be simplified by using a regular expression:

```
cp pals/* backups
```

This command copies all the files in the **pals** directory.

Copying Files Using The copy Command

In Chapter 19, we explained how you can use the **copy** command to copy directories and even whole directory trees. We can also use **copy** for the straightforward copying of one or more files.

When you copy files, there is only one difference between using **copy** and using **cp**: **copy** has a few important options that are not available with **cp**. (The **copy** command was developed after **cp**, to serve as a more powerful copying utility.)

Most of the time, you will use **cp** because it is easier to type "cp" than "copy"; the only time you will use **copy** is when you want to use one of the options.

When you use `copy` to copy files, the syntax is the same as `cp` but with options. To copy a single file, the syntax is

`copy` [`-anv`] *source-file destination-file*

To copy one or more files to a specified directory, the syntax is

`copy` [`-anv`] *source-file... destination-directory*

Without options, `copy` works the same as `cp`—indeed, all the examples we discussed in the previous section, using `cp`, will work with `copy`. Thus, in this section we will concentrate on the options.

The `-a` (ask) option tells `copy` to ask your permission for each file that is to be moved. This option works the same way as the `-i` (interactive) option that we used with `rm`.

Before a file is copied, its name will be displayed, followed by a question mark. To proceed with the copy, enter anything that begins with a "y" (for "yes"). If you enter anything else, including just pressing the <Return> key, the file will not be copied.

For example, if you want to copy all of the files from the `docs` directory to the `backups` directory, you can use either of these commands:

```
cp docs/* backups
copy docs/* backups
```

However, if you wanted to copy only some of the files, you can use

```
copy -a docs/* backups
```

This asks `copy` to display the name of each file and ask your permission before making the copy. For instance, you might see

```
copy file docs/addresses?
```

This message asks you whether or not to copy the file named **addresses**. If you want to, enter

```
y
```

If not, just press <Return> without typing anything.

For a more detailed discussion of the -a option, see the section describing the copy command in Chapter 19.

As you can see, the -a option acts as a safety feature. You can check each file before you copy it. Remember, if you copy onto an existing file it will be lost.

The -n (new) option provides a related service. It tells copy to proceed only if the destination file is new. If the file already exists, copy will not replace it.

For example, say that you try to copy the file **addresses** from the **docs** directory to the **backups** directory. However, a file by the same name already exists in the **backups** directory. If you use the -n option

```
copy -n docs/addresses backups
```

you will see

```
copy: cannot overwrite backups/addresses
```

With the -v (verbose) option, copy will display messages as it works, showing exactly which files are being copied. For example, say that the **pals** directory has four files: **addie**, **harley**, **kevin** and **scott**. You want to copy these files to the **backups** directory and keep track of what is happening. You enter

```
copy -v pals/* backups
```

As copy executes, you will see these messages:

```
copy file pals/addie
copy file pals/harley
copy file pals/kevin
copy file pals/scott
```

As you can see, all four files were copied successfully.

RULE To copy a file: if you want to use an option

-a (ask)
-n (new)
-v (verbose)

use the copy command; otherwise, use the cp command.

Creating Links: The `ln` Command

We discussed links in detail in Chapter 16. At the time, we explained how Unix uses links to associate the name of a file with the file itself.

Within a directory, Unix stores one entry for each file. The entry consists of a 14-byte file name and a 2-byte number that points to an inode. The inode—which contains all the information that Unix needs to work with a file—is the internal representation of that file.

The connection between the file name and the inode is called a link. That is, a link is what allows Unix to find a file based on a name that you specify.

The `ln` command is much like the `cp` command. The only real difference is that where `cp` makes a duplicate of the file, `ln` creates a new link to the original file. After you copy a file, you will have two different file names that each point to their own separate file. After you link a file, you will have two different file names that point to the same file.

Unix considers all links to the same file to be equal, even if they are in different directories. If a file is linked to more than one name, it does not matter which name you use; the results are the same.

When would you create a link to an existing file? Not often. First, there may be an occasion when it is convenient for a file to be known by two different names. For instance, two users may want to access the same file, each within their own home directory. Second, if you have very large files, it may take too much space to make duplicates. If you need to access the data from more than one part of the tree, you may want to have multiple links pointing to a single file.

Whenever you use multiple links, it is important that you coordinate file access. You do not want two users or two programs trying to change the same file at the same time.

To create a link, use the `ln` command. The syntax is

`ln [-f]` *existing-file new-file-name*

You specify the name of a file that already exists and a new name. The `ln` command will create a link under the new name. You can link only ordinary and special files, not directories.

If the new file name is the name of a directory, `ln` will create a link in that directory under the same name as the existing file.

Here is an example: In the directory **/usr/harley**, there is a file named **secret.stuff**. You want to create a link to that file, using the identical name, in the directory **/usr/peter/safe.place**. Enter

```
ln /usr/harley/secret.stuff /usr/peter/safe.place
```

This command will create a link named

```
/usr/peter/safe.place/secret.stuff
```

that points to the existing file.

If the name used for the new link was previously being used for a file, this file will be lost. In the example above, if there had already been a file named **secret.stuff** in the **safe.place** directory, this file would have been lost when the new link was created. The situation is like copying a file onto an existing file.

Another example: You want to create a link using the same file and the same directories as the last example. However, this time you want to create the link under a different file name, **x**. Enter

```
ln /usr/harley/secret.stuff /usr/peter/safe.place/x
```

This command will create an identical link, except that it will be named

```
/usr/peter/safe.place/x
```

As with all file commands, you can use wild cards with **ln**. Here is an example. The following command creates links to all the existing files in your working directory. The links will be in the **extra** directory (which you must have created already):

```
ln * extra
```

If you try to create a link that does not have the requisite write permission, **ln** will ask for confirmation before proceeding. For instance, you enter the command

```
ln docs/letter backups/invoice
```

to create a link named invoice in the backups directory. However, the file invoice already exists and has a file mode of 444—you have read permission only. Because you do not have the write permission you need to replace the file, ln will display the following message:

```
ln: backups/invoice: 444 mode?
```

If you enter anything that begins with a "y" (for "yes"), ln will create the link. If you enter anything else, including pressing <Return> by itself, ln will not create the link.

If you want ln to create all such links automatically without asking for confirmation, use the -f (force) option:

```
ln -f docs/letter backups/invoice
```

As you may recall, both the rm and ln commands have a -f option that works in the same way. For more details, see the section of this chapter that describes rm.

23

Working with Text Files

Introduction

In Chapter 16, we discussed the three types of files: directories, which you use to organize your files; special files, which represent physical devices; and ordinary files.

There are two types of ordinary files: binary files, which contain executable programs, and text files, which contain shell scripts and data. Text files contain information stored as ASCII characters (see Chapter 4) and are the only type of file whose contents you can manipulate directly.

From day to day you will, by far, devote more time to text files than to any other type of file. Unix has a rich set of programs for manipulating text files. These commands are the basic essential tools that you must master.

In Part IV of this book, we will cover the most important of these tools, the vi editor. In this chapter, we will explore the smaller utility programs: commands to classify, analyze, display, and combine your text files.

Determining the Type of a File:
The `file` Command

Unix provides a command that will look at a file and tell you what type it is. The command is `file`. The syntax is

file [-f *input-file*] *file...*

You specify the name of one or more files and `file` will tell you the type of each.

The `file` command goes far beyond distinguishing between directories, special files, and ordinary files; `file` performs a series of tests in an attempt to classify each file you specify. Most of the time it does pretty well.

Here is an example. You enter

```
file /bin
```

The output is

```
/bin:   directory
```

As we explained in Chapter 17, **/bin** is a system directory that holds many of the Unix commands. The next example classifies one of these command files, the one that holds the **ls** command. Enter

```
file /bin/ls
```

You will see

```
/bin/ls:   iAPX 386 executable
```

The output tells us that **/bin/ls** holds an executable program for a 386-based computer. ("iAPX 386" is Intel's official name for the 386 processor.)

How does `file` do it? First, it decides whether or not the file in question looks like ASCII text. If it does, `file` examines the first 512 bytes of the file. If the file contains a program, `file` will try to guess the language. If the file contains a shell script, `file` will categorize it as "commands text." Otherwise, `file` calls the file "ascii text."

Here are some examples using ASCII files. The first file is a C program, the second file is a shell script, and the third file is plain ASCII data. The commands are

```
file /usr/harley/programs/calculate.c
file /lib/norton/demos/menu.sh
file /etc/passwd
```

The output from these commands is

```
/usr/harley/programs/calculate.c:  c program text
/usr/norton/demos/menu.sh:  commands text
/etc/passwd:  ascii text
```

If you try to classify a file that you do not have permission to read, for example,

```
file /etc/shadow
```

you will see

```
/etc/shadow:  cannot open for reading
```

Magic Number:
*A numeric value,
that identifies the
file type.*

But what if the file does not contain ASCII text? Such a file could hold just about anything. In this case, **file** looks at the beginning of the file for a special identification marker called a *magic number*. Next, **file** checks the file **/etc/magic**, which contains a reference list of all the magic numbers and what they mean. If the magic number is found in the reference list, **file** will display the appropriate description. If a file is not ASCII text, and it does not begin with a valid magic number, **file** will classify it as "data."

Here are some examples that classify nontext files. Each of these files is identified by a magic number. The commands are:

```
file /dev
file /dev/hd00
file /dev/console
file /bin/file
```

The first file is a directory; the next two files are special files for the first hard disk partition and for the console, respectively; the last file holds the program that implements the `file` command itself.

The output from these commands is

```
/dev:  directory
/dev/hd00:  block special (0/0)
/dev/console:  character special (5/0)
/bin/file:  iAPX 386 executable
```

Where do magic numbers come from? They are part of the format of nontext files. Magic numbers are placed at the beginning of each nontext file that is created. For instance, every time you create a directory, the `mkdir` command puts the magic number that means "directory" at the beginning of the file that holds the directory.

Major Number:

A numeric value that indicates the type of device a file represents.

Notice that when `file` describes a special file the output shows two numbers, separated by a slash. The first number is called the *major number*; the second is called the *minor number*. The major number indicates the device type, such as a disk or a terminal. The minor number indicates a specific device.

Minor Number:

A numeric value that indicates which device of a particular type a file represents.

You will see major and minor device numbers when you examine a special file using the `ls -l` command (see Chapter 21). These numbers are displayed instead of the file size. For example, if you enter

```
ls -l /dev/hd00 /dev/console
```

you will see

```
brw-------   1 root     sys      0, 0 Mar 28 11:19 /dev/hd00
crw--w--w-   4 harley   other    5, 0 Aug 25 23:30 /dev/console
```

The `file` command has one important option, `-f` (input file). You use this option when you have a list of files that you want to classify. Instead of entering a long list of `file` commands, you can tell `file` to classify all the files whose names appear in the list.

For example, you have a text file, **names**, in your working directory, which contains the following file names:

```
/bin
/bin/ls
/dev
/dev/console
/dev/hd00
/etc/passwd
/etc/shadow
/lib/norton/demos/menu.sh
/usr/bin/help
/usr/bin/mailx
/usr/harley/bin/modem
/usr/harley/programs/calculate.c
```

You enter

```
file -f names
```

The **file** command will read every file name and classify it. The output is

```
/bin:  directory
/bin/ls:  iAPX 386 executable
/dev:  directory
/dev/console:  character special (5/0)
/dev/hd00:  block special (0/0)
/etc/passwd:  ascii text
/etc/shadow:  cannot open for reading
/lib/norton/demos/menu.sh:  commands text
/usr/bin/help:  commands text
/usr/bin/mailx:  iAPX 386 executable
/usr/harley/bin/modem:  commands text
/usr/harley/programs/calculate.c:  c program text
```

Counting Characters, Words, and Lines: The wc Command

The **wc** command will read a file and tell you how many lines, words, and characters it contains. The name "wc" stands for "word count," which is something of a misnomer, as the command also counts characters and lines.

The syntax for the **wc** command is

wc [-clw] [*file...*]

Most of the time, you enter this command with the name of a file. wc displays the number of lines, words, and characters, in that order, followed by the name of the file.

For example, you have a file named document in your working directory. You enter

```
wc document
```

The output is

```
11      38      215 document
```

In this case, the file has 11 lines, 38 words, and 215 characters. For the purposes of this command, "words" are strings of characters separated by a space, tab, or newline (see Chapter 9).

You can specify one or two of the options to restrict the counting: -c (characters), -1 (lines), -w (words). If you specify options, wc will count only what you specify.

For example, say that you are interested only in the word count. Use

```
wc -w document
```

You will see

```
38 document
```

To count words and lines, use

```
wc -lw document
```

You will see

```
11      38 document
```

By default, wc counts lines, words, and characters. Thus, the following two commands are equivalent:

```
wc document
wc -clw document
```

As with many file commands, you can specify more than one file name. You can also use a regular expression. When you specify more than one file, wc will count each one and then give you the overall totals.

Here is an example. In your working directory, you have three files, names, addresses, and phone. To count the lines, words, and characters in these files, enter

```
wc names addresses phone
```

The output looks like this:

```
 6     10     60 names
17     37    153 addresses
16     28    111 phone
39     75    324 total
```

If these were the only three files in your working directory, you could use a regular expression

```
wc *
```

to specify the counting of all files.

The wc command is a tool that can be combined with other tools. Later in the book, we will explain how to combine tools by using the output of one command as the input to another. For now, here is one such example that uses wc.

Say that you want to find out how many files are contained in a directory named backups. By itself, the ls command does not give you this information. But ls will display the names of the files, one name per line. You can find out how many files are in the backups directory by counting the number of lines of output from the command

```
ls backups
```

An easy way to do this is to enter

```
ls backups | wc -l
```

In this case, there are 5 files, so the output is

The "|" (vertical bar) indicates that the output from ls is to be sent to wc. In this example, we used wc with the -l option as we were interested in counting lines only.

Here is another example: You want to find out how many userids there are on the system. As we explained in Chapter 13, the master list of userids is kept in the file /etc/passwd. Within this file, there is one userid per line. To find out how many userids are on the system, all you need to do is count the number of lines in the file:

```
wc -l /etc/passwd
```

On our system, the output of this command is:

```
22
```

Thus, there are 22 userids.

Two Programs to Display a File: more and pg

There are two commands that you can use to display a text file. The pg command was developed at AT&T; the more command was developed at Berkeley.

These commands perform pretty much the same function—however, the details are different. Both more and pg display information, one screenful at a time. If there is more than one screenful, you will see a prompt. When you are finished reading the current screenful, you press a key and see the next one. You continue, one screenful after another, until you have read the entire file.

As you are reading a file, there are commands that you can use: for example, to search for a particular string of characters. If you need help, you can display a list of commands. You can also enter a regular Unix command or start a new shell from within the program.

Unfortunately, although both more and pg perform the same task, they have different prompts and commands. The best idea is to try both programs and choose one. One advantage of pg is that, unlike more, it is easy to back up and display information that has already passed. However, both programs are adequate: the choice is simply a matter of personal preference.

In the next two sections, we will take a close look at more and pg. As we do, it will be helpful for you to have a text file ready to display. If you do not have one available, use the following commands which will create a text file named temp in your home directory.

First, change to your home directory:

```
cd
```

Next, enter the following command:

```
ls -l /dev | nl > temp
```

Here is what happens. The ls command produces a long listing of all the files in the /dev directory. This should be long enough to take several screenfuls to display.

The | (vertical bar) sends the output of the ls command to the nl command. This command will put a line number onto the front of each line. When you display the file, the line numbers will help you see where you are.

Finally, the > (greater-than sign) indicates that the output of nl is to be written to the file named temp.

To check on the temp file, enter the command

```
wc -l temp
```

This should confirm that temp exists by displaying how many lines it has. You are now ready to practice using more and pg.

Displaying the Contents of a Text File Using the more Command

The more command is one of two programs that is used to display files; the other command is pg. more has a number of options, but they are not of general interest. Most of the time, you will start more with the following simple syntax:

more *file*...

You specify one or more files—more displays them one at a time.

As you read this section, follow along at your own terminal. We will be displaying a text file named `temp` that we created in the section that introduced the `more` and `pg` commands. You can use this file or any file that you happen to have.

To display the file named `temp`, enter

```
more temp
```

If the entire file can be displayed at once, `more` will do so and the command will end.

In this case, however, the file is longer, so `more` displays one screenful of data, followed by a line similar to

```
--More--(15%)
```

This is the prompt. You can now enter commands. The prompt tells you two things: first, there is more data to display; second, you are 15% of the way through the file. (By the way, this prompt, the word "`--More--`" followed by a percentage, is where the name of the command comes from.)

When you enter the single-character commands you do not have to press <Return>. For example, to display a summary of the possible commands, press either h (the lower-case letter "h", for "help") or ? (a question mark). You will see a short description of each command.

In this section, we will discuss the most important commands. Figure 23.1 gives a summary.

At any time, you can press ^L (Ctrl-L) to redraw the current screen. Pressing ^L will not change your position in the file. For instance, after you display the help summary, you can press ^L to redisplay what you were looking at.

In order to display data, you can press either the <Space> bar or <Return>. <Space> will display the next screenful; <Return> will display the next line. Thus, you can page through a file, one screenful at a time, by pressing <Space> repeatedly. You can display one line at a time by pressing <Return> repeatedly.

If you want to quit before the entire file is displayed, press q. The `more` command will terminate and you will be back at the shell prompt. Alternatively, you can abort the program by pressing the `intr` key (probably <Delete> or ^C—see Chapter 9).

As you display the file, the prompt will show you what percentage of the file has been displayed. If you want to know what

h	display command summary
?	display command summary
^L	redraw current screen
\<Space\>	display next screenful
\<Return\>	display next line
q	quit
=	display line number
/reg-exp	search for pattern
!command	execute Unix command

Figure 23.1 *Summary of* more *commands.*

line you are looking at, press = (the equal sign). more will display the line number of the last line that was displayed.

Occasionally, you may want to search for a particular pattern. Type a / (slash), followed by a regular expression (see Chapter 22) that describes the pattern, and then press \<Return\>.

Starting from the current line, more will look for the first line that contains the pattern. If such a line is found, more will display the message

```
..skipping
```

followed by a new screenful of data, starting two lines before the place where the pattern was found. For example, you enter

```
/tty01
```

Starting from the current line, more will find the first line that contains "tty01". more will display a new screenful of data, starting two lines before the line containing "tty01".

If you search for a pattern that cannot be found between the current line and the end of the file, more will display

```
Pattern not found
```

Your position in the file will not change.

Finally, you can put more on hold temporarily and enter a Unix command by prefacing the command with ! (an exclamation mark). The ! acts as an escape character (see Chapter 9).

For example, say that you are displaying a file and you need to know what time it is. Enter

```
!date
```

The **date** command will execute, showing you the time and date. When it is finished, you will be back at the **more** prompt. To redisplay the data you were looking at before you entered the Unix command, press ^L.

If you want to enter a number of Unix commands, enter the **sh** command to start a new copy of the shell:

```
!sh
```

(If you use the C-shell, enter !csh.) You can now enter as many Unix commands as you want. When you wish to return to **more**, press ^D (the **eof** key) to end the shell. You will find yourself back at the **more** prompt. Again, you can restore your screen by pressing ^L.

This idea, putting a program on hold temporarily to execute other commands, is discussed in Chapter 3, in the section entitled "Wheels Within Wheels."

Displaying the Contents of a Text File Using the pg Command

The **pg** command is one of two programs that is used to display files; the other command is **more**. **pg** has a number of options but only one is of general interest. Most of the time, you will start **pg** with the following syntax:

pg [-n] *file...*

You specify one or more files; **pg** displays them one at a time.

As you read this section, follow along at your own terminal. We will be displaying a text file named **temp** that we created in the section that introduced the **more** and **pg** commands. You can use this file or any file that you happen to have.

To display the file named **temp**, enter

```
pg temp
```

If the entire file can be displayed at once, pg will do so. At the end of the file you will see

```
(EOF):
```

Press <Return> to end the command.

In this case, however, the file is longer, so pg displays one screenful of data, followed by a single colon:

```
:
```

This is the prompt. You can now enter commands.

Unlike the more command, pg requires you to press <Return> each time you enter a command. If you find this bothersome, you can start pg with the -n (newline) option:

```
pg -n temp
```

With this option, you will not have to press <Return> with most of the single-character commands. As with more, simply pressing a single key will be enough.

To display a summary of the possible commands, enter the h (help) command. In this section, we will discuss the most important commands. Figure 23.2 gives a summary.

At any time, you can enter the ^L (Ctrl-L) command to redraw the current screen. Entering ^L will not change your position in the file. For instance, after you display the help summary, you can enter ^L to redisplay what you were looking at.

In order to display data, you can either press <Return> or use the d (down) or 1 (line) commands. <Return> will display the next screenful; the d command will display the next half screenful; the 1 command will display the next line.

Thus, you can page through a file, one screenful at a time, by pressing <Return> repeatedly. If you start pg with the -n option, you can also press <Space> repeatedly.

You can page through a half screenful at a time by entering d repeatedly. You can display one line at a time by entering 1 repeatedly.

If you want to go backward in the file, use the - (minus sign) command to display the previous screenful. Thus, you can go forward by pressing <Return> and backward by pressing

h	display command summary
^L	redraw current screen
<Return>	display next screenful
-	display previous screenful
d	display half screenful
l	display next line
$	display last screenful
q	quit
/reg-exp	search for pattern
?reg-exp	search backward
!command	execute Unix command

Unless you start **pg** with the -n option, you need to press <Return> after every command.

If you do start **pg** with the -n option, you can also use

<Space>	display next screenful

Figure 23.2   *Summary of* **pg** *Commands*

–<Return>. If you start **pg** with the -n option, you can go forward by pressing <Space>

To skip to the end of the file, enter the $ command. This will display the last screenful of the file.

If you want to quit before the entire file is displayed, enter the q command. The **pg** program will terminate and you will be back at the shell prompt. Alternatively, you can abort the program by pressing the **intr** key (probably <Delete> or ^c—see Chapter 9).

Occasionally, you may want to search for a particular pattern. Type a / (slash), followed by a regular expression (see Chapter 22) that describes the pattern, and then press <Return>.

Starting from the current line, **pg** will look for the first line that contains the pattern. If such a line is found, **pg** will display a new screenful of data, starting with the first line that contains the pattern. Unlike **more**, **pg** does not display the two lines before the place where the pattern was found.

Here is an example. You enter

```
/tty01
```

Starting from the current line, pg will display a new screenful of data, starting with the first line that contains "tty01".

If you search for a pattern that cannot be found between the current line and the end of the file, pg will display

```
Pattern not found:
```

Your position in the file will not change.

If you want to search backward, use a ? instead of a /. For example:

```
?tty01
```

pg will search backward, starting from the current line, for the first line that contains the pattern. When the pattern is found, pg will display a full screenful of data, starting with the line containing the pattern.

Finally, you can put pg on hold temporarily and enter a Unix command by prefacing the command with ! (an exclamation mark). The ! acts as an escape character (see Chapter 9).

For example, say that you are displaying a file and you need to know what time it is. Enter

```
!date
```

The date command will execute, showing you the time and date. When it is finished, you will be back at the pg prompt. To redisplay the data you were looking at before you entered the Unix command, enter the ^L command.

If you want to enter a number of Unix commands, enter the sh command to start a new copy of the shell:

```
!sh
```

(If you use the C-shell, enter !csh.) You can now enter as many Unix commands as you want. When you wish to return to pg, press ^D (the eof key) to end the shell. You will find yourself back at the `pg` prompt. Again, you can restore your screen by entering the `^L` command.

Displaying the Last Part of a File: The `tail` Command

The `tail` command will display the last part of a file. The syntax is

`tail` [[+-]*number*[lbc]] [-f] [*file*]

At first glance, the syntax seems formidable. However, it is not as complex as it seems.

Most of the time, you will enter the command with just the name of a file. For example, say that your working directory has a file named `temp`. To display the last part of this file, enter

```
tail temp
```

Without any options, `tail` will display the last 10 lines of a file. You can specify a starting point by preceding the name of the file with + or - (a plus sign or a minus sign) and a number. If you use + and a number, `tail` will start that many lines from the beginning of the file. If you use - and a number, `tail` will start that many lines from the end of the file.

Thus, to display the file `temp`, starting 5 lines from the end, enter

```
tail -5 temp
```

To display the same file, starting 20 lines from the beginning of the file, enter

```
tail +20 temp
```

If you specify a starting point, you must use either + or -; you cannot use a number by itself.

As we mentioned, when you enter the `tail` command without options, it displays the last 10 lines of the file. Thus, the following two commands are equivalent:

```
tail temp
tail -10 temp
```

You can tell `temp` to measure the starting place differently by following the number with a single letter. A "`c`" means to count characters; a "`b`" means to count blocks (one block is 512 bytes); and an "`l`", the default, means to count lines.

Thus, to display the file `temp`, starting 243 characters from the beginning of the file, enter

```
tail +234c temp
```

To display the same file, starting 3 blocks from the end of the file, enter

```
tail -3b temp
```

Since the default is to count in lines, the following three commands are equivalent:

```
tail temp
tail -10 temp
tail -10l temp
```

One of the important uses of `tail` is to keep track of an ongoing process that is adding data to a file. You can do so by using the `-f` (follow) option.

With `-f`, the `tail` command will not terminate after displaying its data. The command will wait, constantly checking the file. Whenever new data is written to the file, `tail` will display the data on your screen. To stop the command, press the `intr` key (probably <Delete> or `^c`—see Chapter 9).

Here is an example. You want to monitor a program that, from time to time, adds data to the end of a file named `log`. Enter

```
tail -f log
```

`tail` will display the last 10 lines of this file and then wait. Every time a line is written to `log`, `tail` will display the line on your screen. To stop the command, press the `intr` key.

Combining and Copying Files: The `cat` Command

We have mentioned that Unix supplies many tools and that being good with Unix means developing the skill to combine those tools skillfully. One of the most useful tools is the `cat` command.

This command copies data from an input source to an output target. Usually, you will use `cat` to copy files. If you specify more than one file, `cat` will join them together into one large file. If the output target is a file that already exists, it will be replaced.

Many people think that the name "`cat`" comes from the word "concatenate." More properly, the name is derived from the archaic word "catenate," which means to join in a chain. (As all classically educated computer scientists know, "catena" is the Latin word for chain.)

The syntax of the `cat` command is as follows:

```
cat [-s] [file...]
```

By default, `cat` copies from the keyboard to the display. (More precisely, `cat` copies from "standard input" to "standard output." We will meet these terms later in the book, at which time we will discuss them thoroughly.)

If you enter `cat` with no arguments, it will copy what you type at the keyboard to the display. To see how this works, enter

```
cat
```

The command is now waiting for your input. Enter a line of input:

```
This is a line of data.
```

As soon as you press <Return>, `cat` will copy the line. Since the data is to be copied to the display, you will see a duplicate of what you just typed:

```
This is a line of data.
This is a line of data.
```

Keep typing, one line after another. Each time you press <Return>, `cat` copies the line to the display.

When you are finished, tell cat that there is no more input by pressing the eof key (see Chapter 9):

```
^D
```

cat will terminate and you will be at the shell prompt.

Used in this way, cat is of limited usefulness. However, if we redirect the output from the display to a file, we can copy directly from the keyboard to a file. As we saw in Chapter 20, this is an easy way to create a small file quickly.

Say that you want to create a file named info in your working directory. Enter

```
cat >info
```

Again, cat waits for you to enter data and signal when you are through by pressing ^D:

```
This is line 1.
This is line 2.
This is line 3.
^D
```

This time, though, the data is copied to the file named info. If info does not already exist, cat will create it. If the file already exists, it will be replaced—any data already in the file will be lost.

If you want to add data onto the end of a file, use >> instead of >:

```
cat >>info
```

In this case, the data will be appended to the end of info. No existing data will be lost. Again, if info does not already exist, cat will create it.

An Interesting Experiment Using cat

Here is an interesting experiment you can try. You and a friend both log in to the system, using different terminals. Have your friend create a file named cattest in his home directory:

```
touch cattest
```

As an example, if his home directory is /usr/peter, the file's full path name will be /usr/peter/cattest.

From your terminal, enter the tail command with the -f (follow) option to monitor the file:

```
tail -f /usr/peter/cattest
```

Now, have your friend add data to the file. At his terminal, he will enter

```
cat >>cattest
```

As he types, each line of data will be copied to the file and, courtesy of the tail -f command, displayed on your terminal.

To finish, he presses the eof key, ^D, to end his cat command. You press the intr key (probably <Delete> or ^c) to end your tail command.

Using cat to Catenate Files

As we mentioned, the main use of cat is to combine files. Let's take another look at the syntax of the cat command:

```
cat [-s] [file...]
```

You can specify one or more files. cat will combine them and write them to the output target—by default, the display.

For example, if you enter

```
cat names addresses phone
```

cat will display the files named names, addresses and phone, one right after the other. This is a fast way to display files. However, unless the files are short, the output will go by so fast that you will not have time to read it. To prevent this problem, run the output of the cat command through either the more or pg commands:

```
cat names addresses phone | more
cat names addresses phone | pg
```

(The |, vertical bar, specifies that the output of one command is to be used as the input to the next command. We will discuss this later in the book.)

However, if all you want to do is display these three files, it would be easier to use **more** and **pg** directly:

```
more names addresses phone
pg names addresses phone
```

Similarly, using **cat** with the name of a single file seems like a fast way to display the file. For example,

```
cat names
```

However, this only works well when the file is small. If the file is larger than the size of your screen, all but the last part of your data will scroll past so fast that you won't be able to read it.

Although many people use **cat** to display files, it is a bad habit. It is much better to use either **more** or **pg**:

```
more names
pg names
```

RULE

Get into the habit of displaying files with **more** or **pg**, rather than with **cat**.

Hint
••••

DOS users:

Displaying a file with **cat** is like using the DOS TYPE command.

Displaying a file with **more** or **pg** is like using TYPE | MORE.

When you combine files, you will usually want to save the output rather than display it. In such cases, specify that the output is to be redirected to a file. For example, the following command combines the output of the three files we mentioned above, and writes it to the file **bigfile**:

```
cat names addresses phone >bigfile
```

If `bigfile` does not already exist, `cat` will create it. If `bigfile` already exists, it will be replaced and its data will be lost.

If you want to append data to the end of a file, use `>>` instead of `>`:

```
cat names addresses phone >>verybigfile
```

Be sure to keep these two techniques straight—it is a common mistake to use `cat` in the wrong way and wipe out a great deal of data.

Here is an example: A person has a large file named `info` in his working directory. He also has several smaller files, `info1`, `info2`, and `info3`. He decides to append all the data in these smaller files to the large file, after which he will remove the smaller files. He plans to enter

```
cat info info1 info2 info3 >info
rm info1 info2 info3
```

He thinks that `cat` will combine the four input files and write the output to `info`.

What you must appreciate is that `cat` will not start reading until it has set up its output file. In this case, `cat` will start by clearing out the `info` file. Before he knows it, the original contents of `info`, the main file, are gone for good. And by removing the three smaller files, our hapless guffin has deleted what little data he had left.

Fortunately, most modern versions of `cat` will check file names for you. If you try to direct the output to one of the input files, you will see a message like

```
cat: input/output files 'info' identical
```

However, don't count on this. In certain circumstances `cat` will not be able to catch the mistake for you. Remember, when you redirect output to a file you *always* lose the original contents of the file.

In this case, the correct way to use `cat` would be to combine the data in the three small files and then append it to the single large file:

```
cat info1 info2 info3 >>info
```

By using >>, we ensure that no data will be lost.

Whenever you combine files, **cat** will display an error message if one of the input files does not already exist. In our example, if the file **info2** did not exist, you would see

```
cat: cannot open info2
```

However, **cat** would continue with the rest of the command.

If you do not want to see such messages, you can use the **-s** (silent) option:

```
cat -s info1 info2 info3 >>info
```

This may come in handy when you are using **cat** in a shell script. If you anticipate that there will be times when an input file will not exist, you may decide to silence the error message.

24

Text Processing with Unix

Introduction

Most of the work you do with files will be with text files. In the past few chapters, you learned how to create and maintain your files. The commands we covered—copy, remove, and so on—manipulate entire files. In this part of the book you will start to work with the information inside your text files.

We will spend most of our time discussing **vi**, the built-in editor program. However, before we start, let's take a guided tour of the other text processing facilities and see how much Unix has to offer.

Text Processing with Unix

As we mentioned in Chapter 1, Unix was originally developed by a small group of people at AT&T Bell Labs. They wanted an operating system that would let them manage and share their files. At the time, they had two important needs: the need to write computer programs and the need to create documents. From the beginning, Unix has always offered superior tools in these two areas.

Today, Unix includes a large variety of text processing tools. With larger computers, these tools are included as part of the system. With PCs, Unix is usually broken into several parts, one of which contains the bulk of the text processing programs. For PC Unix systems, AT&T calls the collection of these tools the Documenter's Workbench. You may have to purchase this product separately.

The Editors

Editor:
A program used to create and modify text files.

An *editor* is a program that you use to create and modify text files. Unix comes with several editors. To understand the choices, you need to appreciate the conditions under which they were developed.

When Unix was first developed, it was used with terminals that printed on paper, one line at a time. (This is why the Unix tradition is to use the term "print" as a synonym for "display"; think of `pwd`, the "print working directory" command.)

By today's standards, these old terminals were limited. They could only print lines of text, one after another. They could not backspace and erase, or go back and replace lines that had already printed. The first Unix editors were developed to work with these terminals and had to respect their limitations.

Line Editor:
An editor that works with groups of lines.

For example, it was far too slow to reprint large chunks of a file every time you made a change. Nor was it possible to use cursor keys to move to a particular place in the file and make a change. The early Unix editors, called *line editors*, were designed to work with lines of data. As you worked with a file, each line of data was numbered. You could, for example, enter a command to print lines 3 through 7; or you could delete line 27; or you could move lines 3, 4, and 5 to line 13.

The first line editor was named `ed` (most of the early Unix commands are either two or three letters). The name `ed` is pronounced as two separate letters, "ee-dee." `ed` is a sturdy, functional line editor that is still useful today. Indeed, the EDLIN editor that comes with DOS can be thought of as a less-powerful version of `ed`.

Within a few years, a more powerful line editor, `ex` ("extended editor"), was developed at the Computer Science Department of the University of California at Berkeley. `ex` was far

Screen Editor:
An editor that uses the whole screen to work with more than one line at a time.

more comprehensive and complex than ed. As you will see, we routinely use parts of ex in our day-to-day editing.

With the advent of modern terminals, there arose a need for editors that could take advantage of a screen and its characteristics. Such programs are called *screen editors*.

Imagine you want to read a file. With a line editor, you would have to enter command after command to display one set of lines after another. With a screen editor, you can press a key and scroll through the file, one screenful at a time.

The programmers at Berkeley developed a powerful screen editor, which they called vi, for "visual editor." Like ed, the names ex and vi are pronounced as two separate letters: "ee-ex" and "vee-eye."

vi and ex are actually different faces of the same program. If you start the program with the vi command, it acts like a screen editor; if you start the program with the ex command, it acts like a line editor.

One nice thing about editing with vi is that you have the best of both worlds. Most of the time you use the vi screen-oriented commands, but you can enter an ex line-oriented command whenever you want. Thus, to learn how to use vi effectively, you also need to learn how to use some ex commands.

Associated with the Unix editors are a number of related programs. First, there are the restricted versions of each of the editors. As you may remember, in Chapter 6 we described rsh, a version of the Bourne shell (sh) that offers a limited range of capabilities. Similarly, each Unix editor has a restricted version, suitable for beginners. These programs are designed to offer a limited set of commands for environments in which ease of use or security is an issue.

The restricted version of ed is called red; the restricted version of ex is called edit; the restricted version of vi is called vedit.

Aside from the restricted editors, there is a special version of vi called view. This program is similar to vi except that it will not let you make permanent changes to the file you are editing. You use view when you want to use vi to read, but not change, a file.

Out of all the editors, vi is, by far, the most important. It is the single most important tool in your Unix toolbox. No matter what version of Unix you use, you will have vi, even if your system is a PC that does not include the text processing package.

Some Unix systems have another editor named `emacs`. `emacs` is distributed by the Free Software Foundation that we mentioned in Chapter 1. Choosing between `vi` and `emacs` is a matter of personal preference; both editors are in widespread use.

However, even if `emacs` is available on your system, `vi` is still the standard Unix editor. Learn `vi` first.

The Text Formatters

If you use a word processor you are used to being able to move around the screen at will, arranging things to look just how you want them. However, the early Unix systems could not support such software. The first word processors operated on dedicated machines; word processing became widespread only with the advent of personal computers.

The text processing software that was developed for Unix was based on line editors. This is how it works:

You use an editor to create a file that holds the text of a document. Within the file, you embed instructions that indicate how the document is to be formatted. For instance, you specify where each new paragraph is to start, if you want single or double spacing, which words should be in boldface or underlined, and so on.

Text Formatter:
A program that reads a text file containing embedded commands and creates a formatted document using those commands.

In order to produce a finished product, you run your file through a *text formatter* program. This program reads your document and outputs a finished product according to your specifications. The output of a text formatter is suitable for printing. If you want to make changes, you modify the original file, reformat, and reprint.

One of the original text formatters was named `roff`, which stood for "run off." Later, this program was replaced by a newer version named `nroff` ("new `roff`"). This is the text formatter that is in general use in Unix systems today. Along with `nroff`, which generates output for a printer, there is also `troff`, which generates output for a typesetter. The name "`nroff`" is pronounced "en-roff"; the name "`troff`" is pronounced "tee-roff."

Here is an example of some simple `nroff` input:

```
.po 10
.ll 50
All of these sentences will be formatted together
into one
paragraph and right justified.
nroff commands all start with a period
and are placed on a line by themselves.
The first command sets the page
offset to 10 characters.
The next command sets the line length
to 50 characters.
This is the first paragraph.
The next command indicates a break, the end
of the paragraph.  The command following it
leaves a space (empty line) between the paragraphs.
.br
.sp
.in 5
Here is the second paragraph.  This paragraph is
indented 5 spaces.
```

If these lines were stored in a file called document, you could format them by entering

```
nroff document
```

The output would look like this:

```
All of these sentences will be formatted  together
into  one  paragraph  and  right justified.  nroff
commands all start with a period and are placed on
a  line by themselves.  The first command sets the
page offset to 10 characters.   The  next  command
sets  the  line  length to 50 characters.  This is
the first paragraph.  The next command indicates a
break,  the  end  of  the paragraph.  The command
following it leaves a space (empty  line)  between
the paragraphs.

     Here is the second paragraph.  This paragraph
is indented 5 spaces.
```

Macro:
A single text formatting command that executes or that issues one or more other commands.

This example is a simple one. There are many `nroff` commands, and they can take a long time to master.

To make text formatting easier, `nroff` allows you to define *macros.* A macro is a text formatting command that is defined in terms of one or more `nroff` commands. One macro can stand for many commands. When your data is processed, `nroff` will replace your macros by the equivalent commands.

Unix systems come with several built-in macro packages, set up to make it easy to prepare various types of documents. You put the macros in your text, just like regular `nroff` commands.

The basic set of macros is called mm, which stands for "memorandum macros." There is an mm command that you can use to process files that use these macros. The mm command is actually an easy way to start `nroff` with the appropriate options. There is also a command mmt, which uses `troff` to process a file.

To help with the definition and maintenance of macros, there is a command `macref` that reads a file and makes a cross-reference of all the macros contained in the file. Another command, `checkmm`, reads your file and makes sure that all the mm macros have been used correctly.

Preprocessor:
A program that reads a data file and processes certain commands before the file is sent to a final processing program.

To augment `nroff` and `troff`, there are several *preprocessors.* These are programs that read your data before you submit it to `nroff` or `troff`. Each preprocessor recognizes commands of its own that it translates into valid `nroff` or `troff` instructions.

The standard preprocessors that come with Unix are as follows. For typesetting with `troff`:

eqn	to format equations and mathematical text
grap	to create graphs
pic	to draw pictures and shapes
tbl	to lay out tables

For regular printing with `nroff`:

neqn	to format equations and mathematical text
tbl	to lay out tables

One preprocessor command can generate many `nroff` or `troff` instructions. For example, the following short file instructs `pic` to draw a circle:

```
.PS
circle
.PE
```

When you run this file through **pic**, it generates the following output for **troff**:

```
... 0 -0.25 0.5 0.25
... 0.000i 0.500i 0.500i 0.000i
.nr 00 \n(.u
.nf
.PS 0.500i 0.500i
.br
\v'0.250i'\D'c0.500i'
.sp -1
.sp 1+0.500i
.PE
.if \n(00 .fi
```

If you send this output through **troff** to the proper typesetter, you will see a circle.

The final text formatting command reads a file full of **nroff**, **troff**, and preprocessor commands and outputs only the text. That is, this command strips out all text formatting commands. Appropriately enough, this command is named **deroff**.

Automated Text Processing

Unix contains several programs that allow you to process text automatically. You prepare a file of commands, called a script. You then instruct one of the automated text processing programs to follow your script as it reads a text file. The result is that your text file is edited and processed according to your predefined instructions.

The three programs in this category are **sed**, **awk**, and **nawk**.

The name "**sed**" stands for "stream editor." The image is one of a stream of data being processed automatically, according to your instructions. **sed** is a noninteractive text editor that can perform all of the basic editing functions.

For example, you can write a **sed** script to change all the occurrences of the word "UNIX" to "Unix". You can then use this script to edit any file you want, automatically.

As you might guess, a script with one simple change requires only a single command. However, it is not uncommon to build long sed scripts to perform a large number of editing tasks.

The sed program performs straightforward editing chores. The awk program, on the other hand, implements a rich programming language, including variables and control flow constructs. The nawk program is a newer, more powerful version of awk. The purpose of these programs is to make it easy to specify and to perform common tasks that involve information retrieval and text manipulation.

awk and nawk work by reading and processing a text file according to a script. They check the file for specified patterns and then perform operations on those lines that contain the patterns.

Although this may not sound like much, awk and nawk programs can be extremely complex and powerful. A few of the common uses of these tools:

- Read a file of data and produce a report with totals, subtotals, and so on.
- Validate that the data in a file follows a particular format.
- Transform the data from one program into the form expected by another program.

One of the most valuable features of awk and nawk is their ability to work with both numeric and textual data.

The name awk, by the way, is an acronym representing the last names of the three computer scientists who developed the program: Al Aho, Peter Weinberger and Brian Kernighan.

Proofreading a Document

Unix has several programs to help you proofread documents. First, the spell program will help you find misspelled words. You specify one or more file names. spell checks all the words in those files against a master list of words. spell will output the words from your file that are not in the master list. spell has been programmed to recognize and ignore nroff and troff commands.

Wherever possible, spell will match words by recognizing valid prefixes and suffixes (such as "ing" at the end of a verb).

You can create your own list of words to augment the standard master list. If you wish, you can use an option that tells spell to use British rather than American spellings.

When you format a file with nroff or troff, you have the option of using automatic hyphenation. If you do, you can use the hyphen command to list all the hyphenated words from the formatted document. This allows you to check your final document for mistakes before you print it.

Another way in which you can proofread is to compare successive versions of a document by using the diffmk command.

When you need to change a document, copy the document and edit the copy. After you finish, you can use diffmk to compare the two versions of the document. diffmk will show you the most recent version, along with a list of those lines that have been changed.

The output of diffmk is designed to be processed by nroff. The resulting output will show you the revised document with certain markings: a vertical bar (|) will indicate each line that has been modified; an asterisk (*) will indicate each place where lines have been deleted.

Altering a Document

The next two commands, cut and paste, take files apart and put them together. The cut command extracts selected portions from each line in a file. These portions may be in the same place in each line (say, columns 3-12), or may be parts of the line that are separated by delimiters (say, commas).

cut is useful, not only with documents, but with extracting information that was generated in a standard format by another program. For example, you can start with a long directory listing and extract only the modification date and the name of the file.

The paste command combines lines from one or more files into columns. Think of paste as being the counterpart to cat. Where cat combines files horizontally, paste will treat each file as a column and combine them vertically. To reorder columns in a table you can combine the use of cut and paste.

To modify parts of a file, you can use the tr and newform commands. The tr (translate) command substitutes or deletes selected characters in your file. For example, you can use tr to change all lower-case letters to upper-case.

The `newform` command reformats lines according to your specifications. `newform` works with spacing, `tab` characters and line lengths. You can, for example, replace `tab` characters with `space`'s or remove a fixed number of characters from the beginning or the end of each line.

Preparing a Document for Printing

There are two commands, `nl` and `pr`, that are useful for preparing documents for printing. The `nl` command numbers each line according to your specifications. You can control the size and increment of the line numbers and instruct `nl` to respect headers and footers.

The `pr` command provides a variety of different formatting facilities. Typically, `pr` will read a document, divide it into pages, and insert page numbers along with the modification time of the file. By using options, you have a large degree of control over the output. You can define headers or footers, specify the size of the pages, request double spacing, expand `tab` characters, insert line numbers, print multiple files in columns, and on and on.

Creating an Index

There are several Unix commands that help you prepare an index for a document. The `subj` command looks at a document and produces a list of keywords that are suitable for indexing. The `ndx` command uses this list, along with your formatted document, to create an index.

Although no indexing program is perfect, `subj` uses some sophisticated techniques. It looks for proper nouns and modifier-noun sequences. In addition, `subj` pays attention to the words you use in abstracts, headings, introductory paragraphs, and topic sentences (the first sentence of each paragraph).

After building a preliminary list of keywords, `subj` examines your document in increments of two sentences, in an attempt to tie together relevant keywords.

The `subj` command works well with documents that use text formatting commands and macros. `subj` is programmed to understand how such commands are normally used—this allows it to identify cues that are missing from conventional text.

Once you have used `subj` to create a file of keywords, you use `ndx` to create an index. `ndx` reads the keyword file and searches for the keywords within your formatted document. As it works, `ndx` focuses on the root of each word; thus, different cases and tenses are not a problem. The output of `ndx` is an index, suitable for printing.

Permuted Index:
An index consisting of keywords within their immediate contexts.

Aside from being able to create a regular index, Unix has a command that will make a *permuted index*. A permuted index is a catalog of keywords taken in their immediate contexts, similar to a concordance. The words on each line are moved and rotated within the index entry so that the keyword is in the middle: thus, the name "permuted." The lines that make up a permuted index are presented in alphabetical order by keyword.

The command that helps you create a permuted index is `ptx`. You take the output of `ptx` and format it with `nroff` or `troff`, using a special set of macros called `mptx`.

Figure 24.1 shows part of a permuted index based on some of the subject matter in this chapter. The page numbers are imaginary. Where the words in a line have been rotated, the beginning of each entry is marked by a slash.

Permuted indexes are often used in Unix manuals to make it easy to find a command. With a permuted index you can look up either the name of the command or its description.

```
            red: restricted version of    ed . . . . . . . . . . . . . . . . . . 5
       standard text editor; superset of  ed /ex: newer,  . . . . . . . . 7
           line-oriented text editor      ed: /older   . . . . . . . . . . . 5
            for casual or novice users    edit: variant of ex  . . . . . . 6
         ed: older line-oriented text     editor . . . . . . . . . . . . . . . 5
                     vi: screen           editor; based on ex  . . . . . . 7
       ed /ex: newer, standard text       editor; superset of   . . . . . . 7
            vi: screen editor, based on   ex . . . . . . . . . . . . . . . . . . 8
       novice users /edit: variant of     ex for casual or  . . . . . . . . 7
            text editor; superset of ed   ex: newer, standard  . . . . . 7
```

Figure 24.1 *Part of a permuted index.*

A Summary of Unix Text Processing Commands

For reference, here is a summary of the text processing commands that we discussed in this chapter:

Editing

ed	older standard line-oriented text editor
ex	newer, standard text editor; superset of **ed**
vi	screen-oriented editor, based on **ex**
red	restricted version of **ed**
edit	variant of **ex** for casual or novice users
vedit	same as **vi** with defaults set for beginners
view	same as **vi** in read-only mode

Text Formatting

checkmm	check the usage of **mm** macros within a document
deroff	remove **nroff**, **troff**, **tbl**, and **eqn** constructs
eqn	format mathematical text, output suitable for **troff**
grap	preprocessor for **pic**, for typesetting graphs
macref	display cross-reference of macros in **nroff**, **troff** docs
mm	format **nroff** documents that use the **mm** macros
mmt	format **troff** documents that use the **mm** macros
neqn	format mathematical text, output suitable for **nroff**
nroff	text processor, output suitable for printing
pic	format simple figures, output suitable for **troff**
tbl	format tables, output suitable for **nroff** or **troff**
troff	text processor, output suitable for typesetting

Automated Text Processing

awk	pattern scanning and processing language
nawk	new **awk**: pattern scanning and processing language
sed	perform a script of editing commands upon a file

Proofreading a Document

diffmk	mark differences between files, suitable for **nroff**
hyphen	find all the hyphenated words in a document
spell	check text, display words that may be spelled wrong

Altering a Document

cut	cut out selected fields of each line in a file
newform	reformat text changing tabs, spaces, or line length
paste	concatenate lines from one file or several files
tr	translate or delete selected characters in text

Preparing a Document for Printing

nl	add line numbers to text
pr	format text, suitable for printing

Preparing an Index

ndx	create a subject-page index for a document
ptx	make permuted index, output suitable for **nroff**, **troff**
subj	examine document, display subjects suitable for index

25

The vi Editor:
The Basics

Introduction

By far, the most important part of Unix that you must learn is the vi editor. This is the program that you will use to create your own text files, including shell scripts.

The vi editor is powerful and complex. In this chapter, we will introduce you to vi and cover the most important aspects of getting started. The next three chapters cover the day-to-day details.

Learning vi

RULE	vi is easy to use but difficult to learn.

What does this mean? Once you learn vi you will like it. However, there are a great many commands and, at the beginning, you may feel overwhelmed. Moreover, vi provides a peculiar working environment to which you will have to accustom yourself. vi is different from any other editor or word processor, so even if you are an experienced computer user, it may take you a while to get up to speed.

You will find that most tasks can be performed in more than one way. Indeed, there are often five or six ways to do something. The art of using vi is to feel so comfortable with all the commands that you can instantly choose the best one, no matter what the situation.

Of course, this will take a while and you must practice. With vi, this means that you must go out of your way to add new commands to your repertoire. It is possible to get by with only a few commands; however, to do so would be a mistake. It is not until you have a good many commands at your fingertips that you will be able to appreciate the power and ease of vi. Fortunately, vi commands are simple so it will not take you too long to become proficient.

Here is how you should learn vi: Read the next few chapters slowly. As you read, try each new command at your terminal. Do not expect to memorize all the commands right away. Just make sure that you use each command at least once.

After you finish this chapter, start using vi with only a few commands. Every few days, force yourself to learn a few new commands. We strongly recommend that you continue learning and practicing until you are familiar with almost all the commands.

If you are a DOS user, you may or may not know how to use EDLIN, the editor that comes with DOS. With DOS, many people use other editors instead of EDLIN.

With Unix, you need to learn vi. Even if your system has emacs (see Chapter 24), you should still learn vi. It is the only editor that you can depend on finding with every Unix system.

DOS users:

The vi editor is much more powerful than EDLIN. You need to learn vi.

Starting vi

To start vi, use the vi command. There are several options but only two of general interest. The syntax is vi [-rR] [*file...*]

Current File:

In vi, the text file that you are currently editing.

where *file* is the name of the file you want to edit. If you want, you can specify more than one name. vi will start with the first file and you can switch to the others whenever you want. At any time, the file that you are editing is called the *current file*.

If the current file does not exist, vi will create a new file with the name you specify. If you do not specify a file name, vi will let you work with an unnamed current file. You can give the file a name when you save it.

Most of the time you will start vi with no options and with one file name. For example, to edit a file named document in your working directory, enter

```
vi document
```

Editing Buffer:

In vi, a working copy of the current file.

As you edit, vi does not actually work with the current file; rather, vi makes a copy of the file and stores it in a work area called the *editing buffer*. vi works only with the editing buffer, not with the original file. Before you stop vi, you can save your work. At this time, vi will copy the contents of the editing buffer to the file. On the other hand, you can choose not to save your work. vi will discard the editing buffer, and your original file will be left untouched.

The vi command has two important options. The first is -r (recover). You use this when you have been interrupted in the middle of an editing session without having a chance to save your work. This may happen, for example, if the power fails or if your telephone line drops.

In such a case, there is a good chance that vi will be able to save part or all of your work. When you log in again, you may have mail waiting for you telling you that vi has saved your work. A typical message looks like this:

```
A copy of an editor buffer of your file "doc"
was saved when the editor was killed.
This buffer can be retrieved using the "recover"
command of the editor.
An easy way to do this is to give the command "vi -r doc".
This works for "edit" and "ex" also.
```

Enter the vi command with the -r option and no file name:

```
vi -r
```

vi will display a list of all the files that were saved:

```
/usr/preserve/harley
On Sat Sep 01 at 17:58 saved 128 lines of file "doc"
```

If you see your file, you can recover it by starting **vi** with the -r option and specifying the name of the file.

For example, say that you are working with a file named doc and someone turns off the power to the computer. When you log in again, you can recover your work by entering

```
vi -r doc
```

The **-r** option will recover only files that were being edited when **vi** was interrupted. This option will not work if you stop **vi** yourself without saving the file. Nor will it work if you save the file but then erase it accidentally with an rm, a cp or an mv command.

The second option, -R (read-only), allows you to use **vi** to look at, but not change, an existing file. Use this option when you want to examine an important file and guard against accidentally changing it. (Alternatively, you can use the more or pg commands to display the file.)

As a convenience, you can use the **view** command to examine a file without being able to change it. Some people find it easier to type "**view**" than "**vi -R**". Thus, the following two commands are equivalent:

```
vi -R important.file
view important.file
```

How vi Uses the Screen

The bottom line of the screen is called the *command line*. **vi** uses the command line to display messages and commands. The rest of the screen is used to display the editing buffer. **vi** will display as many lines as possible.

Of course, the number of lines depends on the size of your screen. If you are using the console on a PC, the screen has 25 lines. vi will display up to 24 lines of the editing buffer at a time. The 25th line is the command line.

When you start vi, it will display the first 24 lines of the file. As you work, there are many commands that you can use to display any part of the file that you want.

At times, your editing buffer may not contain enough lines to fill up the screen—for instance, if you are editing a file that has only 10 lines. It would be confusing if vi left these lines blank. After all, your file might actually contain blank lines. Instead, vi marks each unused screen line with a tilde (~).

So, if you are editing a file with only 10 lines, vi will display them on the top 10 lines of the screen. Below will be 14 empty lines, each marked with a tilde. As you add more lines, they will take up more and more of the screen and the tildes will disappear.

vi continually updates the information on the screen, so what you see is what you have. However, some terminals have characteristics that make it difficult to erase lines in the middle of the screen. With such terminals, there will be times when vi may have trouble erasing lines from the screen after you have deleted them from the editing buffer. When this happens, vi will mark the lines with an at sign (@). If you want vi to redraw the screen and get rid of these lines, press ^R (Ctrl-R). (The "R" stands for "redraw.")

In a more general sense, you can have vi redraw the entire screen, not just deleted lines, by pressing ^L (look). This is handy when someone sends you a message while you are editing, or when you are using a noisy phone line that generates spurious characters.

As you type, it is possible to put control characters into the editing buffer. For example, you may want to insert the character ^B into a file. vi will display this character just as you see it here, a circumflex followed by an upper-case letter. Even though the symbols take up two spaces on the screen, they still count for a single character.

To aid you in formatting your text, vi has built-in tab settings. vi assumes that these settings occur at every eight places across the line. If you like, you can change the positions to suit your needs.

When you press the <Tab> key, you are really sending the tab character, which is the same as ^I. (In fact, you can press ^I instead of the <Tab> key.) However, when you enter a `tab` character, `vi` does not display it as "`^I`". Rather, `vi` displays enough `space` characters to bring the cursor to the next tab setting. This is handy for indenting paragraphs or making tables. Remember, even though the `tab` character is displayed as one or more `space` characters, it still counts as a single character.

The Two Modes

As we explained in Chapter 8, a "mode" refers to a particular way in which a program can work. In Chapter 15, we saw that the mail program, `mailx`, operates in one of two modes, command mode or input mode.

Like `mailx`, `vi` too can work in one or two modes: *command mode* and *insert mode*. In command mode, you can use any of the `vi` or `ex` commands. In insert mode, you can add data to the editing buffer.

Although it is the `vi` program that is in one mode or another, we often speak as if the user is in a particular mode. For example, we might say that in order to type over existing text, you must be in insert mode.

`vi` commands can be used only when you are in command mode. Most commands consist of one or two characters. For example, the command to delete a line is `dd`. To use a command all you do is type the characters. Except for a few commands, you do not press <Return>. For example, to delete a line, simply press the "d" key twice.

`vi` does not echo commands. If you type `dd` to delete a line, you will not see "`dd`" on the screen. All that will happen is that a line of text will disappear. At first, this may seem a bit confusing, but it won't take you long to get used to it.

If you make a mistake and type a bad command, `vi` will beep at you. There are no error messages for `vi` commands. However, if you make a mistake entering an `ex` command, `vi` will display an error message on the command line.

`vi` automatically starts in command mode. From command mode, you can change to insert mode whenever you want to add to the editing buffer. There are 11 different `vi` commands that you can use to change to insert mode.

While you are in insert mode, everything that you type will be added to the editing buffer. As you type, `vi` will update the

Command Mode:

In `vi`, *a mode in which the characters you type are interpreted as commands.*

Insert Mode:

In `vi`, *a mode in which the characters you type are inserted into the editing buffer.*

screen. At all times, what you see on the screen is what you have. When you are finished adding to the editing buffer, you can switch back to command mode by pressing the <Esc> key. (By the way, this will probably be the only case in which you will use the <Esc> key with a Unix command.)

Entering ex Commands

As we mentioned in Chapter 24, vi and ex are actually different faces of the same program. This means that while you are working with vi you can use ex commands whenever you want. To enter an ex command, you must already be in command mode.

To enter the ex command, type a colon (:) followed by the command, and then press <Return>. For example, the command to substitute the string Harley for the string Peter is s/Peter/Harley/. To enter this command from vi you would type

```
:s/Peter/Harley/<Return>
```

We mentioned earlier that vi commands are short and simple, and that vi does not echo them. ex commands, however, are more complicated, and you really have to see what you are doing as you type. For this reason, vi will echo ex commands on the command line (the bottom line of the screen).

As soon as you type the colon, vi displays it on the command line. As you type the rest of the command, vi echoes it on the same line. If you make a mistake, you can correct it with <Backspace> before you press <Return>. Alternatively, you can press the kill key and retype the entire command. If you decide not to enter the ex command after all, press the intr key.

(The kill and intr keys are discussed in Chapter 9. The kill key cancels the line you are typing; the intr key cancels a command. For most terminals, kill will be ^U or ^X and intr will be <Delete> or ^C. You can find out what keys your terminal uses by entering the stty -a command.)

As we describe commands, we will make sure to put a colon in front of all ex commands, so you can distinguish them from vi commands. For example, we will refer to the substitute command that we used above as the :s command. Whenever you see a command that begins with a colon, remember that vi will echo it on the command line as you type and that you must press <Return> when you are finished.

On rare occasions, you may want to change from **vi** to **ex** so that you can enter a sequence of **ex** commands. To make the switch, type Q. This is a **vi** command that changes to **ex**. To switch back to **vi**, use the :**vi** command. This is an **ex** command that changes to **vi**.

ex differs from **vi** in that you enter one command at a time. **ex** will display a colon as a prompt after each command. Since **ex** displays the colon, you do not need to type it yourself in front of each command. Once you have changed to **ex**, you cannot use any **vi** commands until you change back to **vi**.

If you are using **vi** and, all of a sudden, things are strange, and you keep seeing a colon displayed on the command line, don't worry. The problem is that somehow you have accidentally changed to **ex**. Perhaps you typed a "Q" inadvertently while you were in command mode. In any event, all you need to do is enter the :**vi** command and change back to **vi**.

As a reference, we will end each section that deals with **vi** with a summary. The summary will show the commands that we have just covered in that section.

To start, here is a summary of the commands that we have just discussed:

Q   change from **vi** to **ex**
:vi   change from **ex** to **vi**

Saving Your Work and Stopping vi

There are several ways to stop **vi**. Most of the time, you will use the **vi** command **zz**. (Notice that these are upper-case letters.) Since **zz** is a **vi** command, you do not press <Return> after typing the two letters. As soon as you press the second "z", **vi** will copy the editing buffer to the current file and then stop. You will return to the shell.

Here is an example. You start **vi** by entering

```
vi document
```

vi copies the file **document** to the editing buffer. You make some changes and additions, and then type

```
ZZ
```

vi copies the editing buffer to the file `document` and then returns you to the shell.

You might wonder why so fundamental a command is named "zz". There are two reasons: First, "Z" is the last letter of the alphabet and zz is always the last command that you use in an editing session. Second, remember that the command takes effect as you soon as you type the second letter. You do not need to press <Return>. Thus, it is important to choose a name that will not be typed by accident.

Aside from zz, which is a vi command, there are several ex commands that will stop vi. We will describe the most useful ones.

The first command, :x (exit), is almost the same as zz. The only difference is that if you want, you can specify that the editing buffer is to be copied to a different file. Simply type the name of the file after :x.

For example, say that you start vi with the command

```
vi document
```

and end with

```
:x
```

This has the same effect as if you had used zz. The editing buffer is copied to the file named `document` and you are returned to the shell.

However, if you end the session with

```
:x newfile
```

the editing buffer is copied to a file named `newfile`. If this file does not already exist, vi will create it.

If you want to copy the contents of the editing buffer to a file without stopping vi, use the :w (write) command. You can use this command any time you want to save your work without having to stop vi. As with :x, you can specify a different file name if you want.

For example, the command

```
:w
```

will copy the editing buffer to the current file, `document`, but will not stop `vi`. The command

```
:w newfile
```

will copy the editing buffer to the file `newfile`.

In order to protect you from mistakes, the `:w` command will not copy to a file that already exists, as this would replace the file. In such a case, you can override the protection mechanism by putting a `!` (exclamation mark) character after the `:w`.

For example, if the file `newfile` exists, `vi` will not let you use the command

```
:w newfile
```

However, if you really want to replace `newfile`, you can use

```
:w! newfile
```

As you will see, typing a `!` character at the end of a command name is used with several `vi` commands in order to override some sort of automatic checking.

If you want to stop `vi` without saving the contents of the editing buffer, use the `:q` (quit) command. Again, to protect you from mistakes, `vi` will not carry out the command if you have changed the editing buffer but have not yet saved your work. To override this check, use `:q!`. Be careful, `:q!` will stop `vi` no matter what the situation. If you haven't already saved your work, it will be lost.

Here is a summary of the commands in this section. In all cases, the file name is optional. If you do not specify the file name, `vi` will copy to the current file.

zz	save editing buffer to current file and stop
:x [*file*]	save editing buffer and stop
:w [*file*]	save editing buffer; do not stop
:q [*file*]	stop without saving editing buffer
:w! [*file*]	same as :w but override check
:q! [*file*]	same as :q but override check

Editing More Than One File at a Time

When you start **vi** by using the **vi** command, you can specify the name of more than one file. **vi** allows you to edit each file in turn. Before you move on from one file to the next, you must make sure to save the editing buffer.

When you start **vi**, the first file becomes the current file. At any time, you can move on to the next file by using the :n (next) command. To make sure that you do not accidentally lose data, **vi** will not execute the :n command if you have not saved changes to the editing buffer. If you want to override this check, you can use :n!.

If you forget the name of the current file, use either the ^G or :f commands. **vi** will display the name of the file and other information. The only difference between these two commands is that, since ^G is a **vi** command, it is faster to use because you do not have to type a colon or press <Return>.

You can change the name of the current file by specifying a new file name with the :f command. For example, to change the name of the current file to **newname**, enter

```
:f newname
```

This command does not affect the original file at all. It just means that whenever you use a command that saves the editing buffer to the current file, the data will be copied into this new file.

If you want to see the names of all the files in the argument list, use the :args command. The current file will be enclosed in square brackets. For example, say that you start **vi** by entering

```
vi doc1 doc2 doc3 doc4
```

and that **doc3** is the current file. If you enter

```
:args
```

you will see

```
doc1   doc2   [doc3]   doc4
```

If you want to start editing again at the beginning of the file list, use the :rew (rewind) command. This command resets you from the current file to the first file in the list. For instance, if you are working with the files in the previous example and you enter

```
:rew
:args
```

you will see:

```
[doc1]   doc2   doc3   doc4
```

As with other commands that affect the current file, vi will not execute the :rew command if you have not saved changes to the current file. To override this check, use :rew!.

If you want to edit a file that is not in the argument list, you have two choices: First, you can use the :n (new) command to specify a new list of files. This list replaces the argument list.

Second, you can use the :e (edit new file) command with the name of a single file. This command will change the file you are editing—the current file—but it will not change the argument list. You can return to these files whenever you want by using the :rew command.

As with other commands that change the contents of the editing buffer, you can use a ! character to override the automatic checking.

Here is a summary of the commands from this section:

:n	edit next file in argument list
^G	display name of current file
:f	display or change name of current file
:args	display argument list
:rew	edit first file in argument list
:n [*file...*]	edit new file; change argument list
:e [*file*]	edit new file; same argument list
:rew!	same as :rew but override check
:n!	same as :n but override check
:e!	same as :e but override check

26

The vi Editor: Displaying Files and Moving the Cursor

Introduction

The vi editor uses the full screen to display as many lines of the current file as possible. However, unless your file is small, you will not be able to see all of the lines at once.

vi has many commands to move from one part of the current file to another. These commands involve moving the cursor to the place that you want to display or modify. In this chapter, we will discuss how vi uses the cursor and how you can control its position.

The Importance of the Cursor

Current Line:
With vi, the line on which the cursor is positioned.

As you know, the cursor is the symbol that marks your position on the screen. On most terminals, the cursor is a blinking underscore character. Within vi, the line on which the cursor lies is called the *current line*.

As you edit with vi, the cursor marks the position at which you can modify the editing buffer. For example, if you want to add a word to a sentence, you must first move the cursor to the position at which you want to add the word. You then change to insert mode and add the word.

Although it is the cursor that moves and that has a particular position, we often speak as if the user is occupying that position. For instance, we may say that in order to delete a word, you move to the beginning of the word and use the **dw** command.

vi makes sure that the cursor is always somewhere on the screen. For example, if you move 100 lines further into the editing buffer from your current position, **vi** will automatically update the screen to keep the cursor on the screen. Thus, you can display any part of the editing buffer by moving to that position.

vi has many different ways to move the cursor. This gives you a great deal of control over your work. With a single short command you can move backward, forward, left, and right. You can move to the next word, the previous word, the next paragraph, the previous section, and so on.

The cursor commands are simple and easy to use. In the next few sections, we will show you how these commands work. As you read, we recommend that you experiment with the commands on your terminal. To do so, you will need a file to edit. If you do not have one, use the file that holds the system password information, **/etc/passwd** (see Chapter 13).

To prepare for practicing, start **vi** as follows:

```
vi -R /etc/passwd
```

The **-R** (read-only) option ensures that you won't accidentally make changes to this very important file. Alternatively, you can start **vi** using the **view** command, which works the same as **vi -R**:

```
view /etc/passwd
```

Once you are editing **/etc/passwd** you need to make the file longer so as to have many lines with which to practice. To do this, enter the following **ex** command. It has the effect of copying the entire editing buffer to line 1, effectively doubling the size of the file:

```
:%co1
```

Enter this command several times. Each time, you will double the number of lines. After each command, you can press ^G to check how many lines you have.

Moving in Big Jumps

vi displays the editing buffer by starting with the first line at the top of the screen. Thus, it is convenient to refer to moving toward the end of the editing buffer as moving "down" or "forward." Similarly, moving toward the beginning of the editing buffer can be thought of as moving "up" or "backward."

vi has four commands that are named in this way:

^F	move one screenful down (forward)
^B	move one screenful up (backward)
^D	move a half screenful down
^U	move a half screenful up

Try these commands. They are the ones to use when you want to page through the editing buffer in large or medium jumps.

Moving Using Line Numbers

vi gives each line of the editing buffer an internal number. You can move to any line by telling vi to go to that line number. Of course, to do this, you need to see the line numbers. You can tell vi to display line numbers by using the **ex** command

```
:set number
```

Enter this command now. (Remember, since this is an **ex** command you must press <Return>.) You will see line numbers along the left side of the screen. Move up and down using ^B and ^F. Notice how the line numbers show you where you are in the file. When you want vi to stop displaying line numbers, enter

```
:set nonumber
```

Most of the time it is convenient to see line numbers. For this reason, many people routinely use :set number. Our suggestion is that you always display line numbers, at least while you are learning.

In Chapter 28, you will learn how to specify that certain commands are executed automatically every time you start `vi`. At that time, you can arrange to have the `:set number` command become a part of your regular initialization routine.

It is important to realize that the line numbers that `vi` displays are not really a part of the editing buffer; `vi` simply displays them for your convenience. The line numbers always run consecutively from 1 through the last line in the file. When you insert or delete lines, `vi` automatically updates the line numbers that are affected by the change. For example, if you insert new lines after line 10, all the lines from 11 to the end of the editing buffer are renumbered to make room.

To go to a particular line in the file, type the line number followed by `G` (goto). Notice that the "G" is upper-case.

Here is an example. To go to line 50, type

```
50G
```

To go to the beginning of the file (line 1), type

```
1G
```

`vi` recognizes the `$` (dollar sign) character as standing for the last line in the editing buffer. This means that you can refer to the last line even if you don't know its number. For example, to go to the last line in the editing buffer, type

```
$G
```

As a convenience, `vi` lets you use

```
G<Return>
```

as a synonym for `$G`. You will find this to be an easy way to go to the end of the editing buffer.

With some commands, you can use 0 (zero) as a line number. In such cases, "0" is used to mean "before line 1." For example, in order to copy a line to the beginning of the editing buffer, you would copy to line 0.

Here is a summary of the commands in this section:

*number*G   go to line with specified number
G<Return>   go to the last line

Searching for a Pattern

To go to a line that contains a particular pattern, type / (slash) followed by the pattern, and then press <Return>. As you type, vi echoes the / and the pattern on the command line (just like when you enter an **ex** command). If necessary, you can make corrections to the pattern before you press <Return>. To do so, use <Backspace> or the **kill** key. To cancel the entire command, use the **intr** key.

Here is an example. To go to the next line that contains the pattern "uucp", enter

```
/uucp
```

When you use / to search for a pattern, vi starts from the current line and moves forward (down) in the editing buffer. If vi reaches the end of the editing buffer without finding the pattern, the search will wrap around to the beginning of the editing buffer and continue with line 1. If vi gets all the way around the editing buffer and reaches the current line without having found the pattern, you will see the message

```
pattern not found
```

If you want to search backward (up) instead of forward, use a ? (question mark) instead of a /. In this case, if the pattern is not found between the current line and line 1, vi will wrap around to the bottom of the file and continue searching backward. For example:

```
?uucp
```

You will find that it is often handy to search repeatedly for the same pattern. For example, suppose you search for the pattern "uucp", but the line that vi finds is not the one you want. You will have to look for the next line that contains the pattern. To repeat the previous / or ? command, type n (next). If you want to repeat the last command but in the reverse direction, type N.

For example, say that you search backward for the pattern "uucp":

?uucp

You can press n repeatedly to continue the search in the same direction (in this case, backward). Take a few moments now and experiment with forward and backward searches and with the n and N commands.

If you enter a / or ? by itself, vi will continue the search in the direction you specify. For example, say that you search forward for the pattern "uucp" by entering

/uucp

If you enter

/<Return>

vi will repeat the command. If you enter

?<Return>

vi will search backward for the same pattern.

Make sure that you understand the difference between /<Return> and ?<Return>, and n and N. The /<Return> and ?<Return> commands always search forward and backward respectively. The direction that n and N search depends on the previous command.

There may be times when you want to find a particular pattern and then immediately move up or down from there. You can do so by appending a + (plus sign) or - (minus sign), followed by a number, to the end of the command. In this case, you need to end the pattern with a / or ?. The general syntax looks like this (where *n* stands for a number):

/pattern/+*n*
/pattern/-*n*
?pattern?+*n*
?pattern?-*n*

For example, to go to the 5th line past the next occurrence of the pattern "uucp", enter

```
/uucp/+5
```

To go to the 3rd line before the previous occurrence of "uucp", enter

```
?uucp?-3
```

Here is a summary of the commands in this section. Take a moment to make sure that you understand how each command works. Within this summary

pattern	represents a regular expression (see next section)
n	represents a number

Here is the summary:

/pattern	search forward: go to next line with *pattern*
?pattern	search backward: go to next line with *pattern*
/	search forward for previous pattern
?	search backward for previous pattern
n	same direction: repeat last / or ? command
N	reverse direction: repeat last / or ? command
/pattern/+n	search forward: go to *n*th line after *pattern*
/pattern/-n	search forward: go to *n*th line before *pattern*
?pattern?+n	search backward: go to *n*th line after *pattern*
?pattern?-n	search backward: go to *n*th line before *pattern*

Using Regular Expressions with vi

In Chapter 22, we explained how you can use regular expressions to represent patterns that match file names. With vi, you can use regular expressions to specify search patterns.

When you use regular expressions with vi, most of the rules are the same as we covered in Chapter 22. However, there are some differences. Moreover, vi will support more complex expressions than what you can use with file names.

In this section, we will discuss how you form regular expressions to use with vi. Before you read this section, you should be familiar with regular expressions and what they do. You may want to take a moment and review the appropriate sections of Chapter 22.

Whenever you use the / or ? commands you need to specify a search pattern. To make the search more flexible, vi allows you to use a regular expression according to the following rules.

The . (period) character matches any single character except a newline. (As you may remember from Chapter 9, a newline marks the end of each line.)

Here is an example: To search for the next occurrence of a, followed by any character, followed by c, enter

```
/a.c
```

Here are some examples of character strings that would be found by this command:

```
abc   aBc   ahc   a%c
```

As we explained in Chapter 22, when we specify file names we use a ? to represent any single character; when we use vi we use a . (period). Why is that?

With file names, the . character has a special meaning so ? is used. With vi, the ? character has a special meaning (it's the backward search command) so a . is used.

The * (asterisk) character works the same with file names and with vi: it matches zero or more occurrences of the preceding character. For example, to search for a character string consisting of a, followed by zero or more occurrences of b, followed by c, enter

```
/ab*c
```

Here are examples of strings that this command would find:

```
ac   abc   abbbbbc   aSAMPLEc
```

The ^ (circumflex) character matches the beginning of a line. The $ character matches the end of a line. For example, to search for the word sample you would enter

```
/sample
```

However, to search for `sample` but only at the beginning of a line, enter

```
/^sample
```

To search for `sample` at the end of a line, enter

```
/sample$
```

To search for a line that contains only the character string `sample`, enter

```
/^sample$
```

Think of ^ and $ as being invisible characters at the beginning and the end of every line.

Analogously, the two characters \< (backslash, less-than sign) match the beginning of a word. The two characters \> (backslash, greater-than sign) match the end of a word. For example, to search for the next word that begins with `sa`, enter

```
/\<sa
```

Here are some character strings that this command would find

```
sa   sample   samABBCDEple
```

To search for the next word that ends with `ple`, use

```
/ple\>
```

Here are some character strings that this command would find:

```
ple   sample   people
```

To search for the word `sample`, enter

```
/<sample/>
```

This command would find `sample` but not `Xsample`. The command

```
/sample
```

on the other hand, would find both. Think of \< and \> as being invisible characters at the beginning and end of every word. A "word" is defined as a group of consecutive upper- or lower-case letters, numbers, or underscore characters.

You might be wondering why **vi** uses two characters, \< and \>, rather than a simple < and >. The reason is that you might use the < and > characters in your text, and you may want to search for a string like **<extra comment>**. To do so, you can use a command like

```
/<extra comment>
```

When you use \< and \> to indicate the beginning and end of words, the \ indicates that the next character has a special meaning and is not to be taken literally.

To move on: you can use the [and] (left and right square bracket) characters to enclose a set of characters. Such a pattern will match any one member of the set. For example, to search for either **sample** or **Sample**, enter

```
/[sS]ample
```

Within [and] you can use the - (minus sign) character to indicate a range of letters or numbers. For example, to search for the next lower-case letter, use

```
/[a-z]
```

To search for a string consisting of one lower-case letter followed by zero or more upper-case letters, enter

```
/[a-z][A-Z]*
```

Notice that the * character refers only to the preceding character, the one matched by **[A-Z]**. This last example would match the following strings:

```
xZZZZZZ  tEST  alfredEneuman  xX
```

If you want to match this pattern, but only as a complete word, you can use

```
/\<[a-z][A-Z]*\>
```

Of the four character strings above, this last command would match only

```
xZZZZZZ   tEST   xX
```

Sometimes, you want to match a character that does not belong to a particular set. In this case, put a ^ immediately after the [character. (As you may remember, when we use regular expressions to match file names, we use a ! character in this way.) For example, to search for the next word that starts with any character except x, y, or z, enter

```
/\<[^xyz]
```

If you want to match a character that has a special meaning, you must precede it with a \ (backslash) character. For example, to search for the string my.addie, enter

```
/my\.addie
```

Sometimes it can get tricky and you have to think carefully. For example, to search for zero or more lower-case letters, followed by a * character, followed by zero or more numbers, enter

```
/[a-z]\*[0-9]*
```

The first * is taken literally as a character; the second * means "zero or more."

You will have to remember that the < and > characters have special meanings only when preceded by a \ character. The same goes for \(and \) —the parentheses characters—as we will see later. For example, to search for 99<100, enter

```
/90<100
```

To search for (99), enter

```
/(99)
```

Within a regular expression, letters and numbers represent themselves. A few characters have special meanings:

.	match any single character except a `newline`
*	match zero or more of the preceding characters
^	match the beginning of a line
$	match the end of a line
\<	match the beginning of a word
\>	match the end of a word
[ ]	match one of the enclosed characters
[^]	match any character that is not enclosed

Inside [ ], you can use - (minus sign) to indicate a range of single letters or digits.

A \ (backspace) character indicates that the following character is to be taken literally, except

```
\<    \>    \(    \)
```

Figure 26.1   *Using regular expressions with* vi *to match patterns.*

However, to search for [words in square brackets], enter

```
/\[words in square brackets\]
```

At first, this sounds confusing, but it won't take long for you to get used to it.

Figure 26.1 summarizes the rules that we covered in this section. The special characters have meaning only when used within regular expressions to match a pattern.

Moving in Medium Jumps

There are three vi commands that move the cursor to the beginning of the top, middle, and bottom lines of the screen, respectively. These commands are

H	move cursor to top line of screen
M	move cursor to middle line of screen
L	move cursor to bottom line of screen

The names of these commands stand for "high," "middle," and "low."

There are also commands to move the cursor in terms of paragraphs, sentences, and words:

{	move cursor forward to beginning of paragraph
}	move cursor backward to beginning of paragraph
(	move cursor forward to beginning of sentence
)	move cursor backward to end of sentence
w	move cursor forward to beginning of next word
e	move cursor forward to last character in word
b	move cursor backward to beginning of word

The names of the last three commands stand for "word," "end of word," and "backward," respectively. When interpreting these commands, vi uses the following definitions:

"Paragraphs" are separated by blank lines.

A "sentence" ends in a period, a question mark, or an exclamation mark, followed by two space characters or a newline character.

A "word" ends with any character that is not a letter, a number, or an underscore.

Take a moment now to try these commands. Make sure that you understand how they work. In particular, remember the e (end of word) command. It will come in handy when you want to add letters to the end of a word.

You may have noticed that the w, e, and b commands stop at every punctuation character. If this is inconvenient, you can use the W, E, and B commands. They work the same way except they use a different definition of what ends a word: with W, E, and B, a "word" ends with a space character or a newline character. Think of the upper-case letters as standing for bigger words:

W	same as w; ignore punctuation
E	same as e; ignore punctuation
B	same as b; ignore punctuation

Moving in Small Jumps

vi has a few commands that are well suited to moving within a small area.

The o (zero) command moves the cursor to the beginning of the current line. The ^ (circumflex) command moves the cursor to the first character in the current line that is not a space character or tab character. The ^ command is handy when you are working with lines that are indented. If the current line does not start with a space or tab, these two commands are equivalent.

The $ (dollar sign) command moves the cursor to the end of the current line.

If you want to move to a particular column in the current line, use the | (vertical bar) command. Type the column number followed by a |. (Think of the | character as referring to a column, straight up and down.)

Here is an example. To move to column 25 of the current line, enter

```
25|
```

You can also move forward within the current line to the next occurrence of a particular character. Use the f (find) command. Type f followed by the character you want to find. For example, to go to the next question mark on the current line, use

```
f?
```

The f command will search only up to the end of the current line. If the f command cannot find the character, vi will beep to indicate an error.

The F command is similar to the f command; however, F searches backward on the current line.

The t and T commands are similar to f and F, except that they leave the cursor one position before the character (in the direction of the search).

For example, say that the current line is

```
abcdefghijklm+nopqrstuvwxyz
```

and the cursor is at the + character (between m and n). Here are the effects of several commands:

fx	move cursor right to **x**
Fc	move cursor left to **c**
tx	move cursor right to **w**
Tc	move cursor left to **d**

vi remembers the last f, F, t, or T command. You can type ; (semicolon) to repeat the command. You can type , (comma) to repeat the command in the opposite direction. This is analogous to using n and N to repeat the / and ? search commands.

Here is a summary of the commands in this section. Take a moment now to make sure that you understand how each command works. Within this summary

char	represents any character
n	represents a number

Here is the summary:

0	move cursor to beginning of current line
^	move cursor to first non-**space**/**tab** in current line
$	move cursor to end of current line
n|	move cursor to *n*th column of current line
f*char*	move cursor right to next occurrence of *char*
F*char*	move cursor left to next occurrence of *char*
t*char*	move cursor right to position before *char*
T*char*	move cursor left to position before *char*
;	same direction; repeat last f, F, t, T command
,	reverse direction; repeat last f, F, t, T command

Moving in Very Small Jumps

vi has a variety of commands that you can use to move the cursor very short distances. The + (plus sign) command moves down to the beginning of the next line. The - (minus sign) command moves up to the beginning of the previous line.

Both - and + position the cursor at the first character of the line that is not a **space** or **tab**. This makes it easy to work with indented lines. If you are using indented lines and you want to move the cursor to the absolute beginning of the current line, before any leading space or tab characters, use the 0 (zero) command.

The + and - commands are particularly easy to use with a PC because there are <+> and <-> keys on the right side of the numeric keypad. As a convenience, you can press the <Return> key to mean the same thing as the <+> key. In other words, you can press <Return> repeatedly to move through the editing buffer one line at a time.

To move the cursor one position at a time, use the cursor control keys. These are the four keys with arrows. We will call them <Up>, <Down>, <Left>, and <Right>. When you press one of these keys, vi will move the cursor one position in the direction of the arrow.

When you use <Up> or <Down>, vi will move the cursor to the same column in the line above or below. If the line is not long enough, vi will move the cursor to the end of the line. For example, if you are at column 32 of the current line, <Up> will move you to column 32 of the line above. If this line is less than 32 characters long, the cursor will be at the end of the line.

As a convenience, there are two alternate ways to specify each of these four cursor movements. These are shown in Figure 26.2. Think of ^P as meaning "previous position"; think of ^N as meaning "next position."

You might wonder why the letters h, j, k, and l were chosen as alternate ways to move the cursor left, right, up, and down. The reason is that when vi was first developed, most terminals did not have separate cursor control keys. The terminal that was used by the programmers at Berkeley happened to use ^H, ^J, ^K, and ^L to move the cursor. These keys had arrows printed on the keytops. Thus, it was convenient to design vi to use h for <Left>, j for <Right>, and so on.

There is no need for you to learn three different ways to move the cursor. Try the different keys on your terminal and select the set that you like best. If you are using a terminal where the cursor control keys are easy to access, you may want to use them. If you are a touch typist, you will probably want to use the h, j, k, and l keys so you won't have to take your fingers off the keyboard.

<Right>	j	<Space>	
<Left>	h	<Backspace>	
<Up>	k	^P	
<Down>	l	^N	

Figure 26.2 vi *commands to move the cursor one position at a time.*

Here is a summary of the commands in this section. Take a moment now to make sure you understand how each key works.

–	move cursor to first non-**space/tab** of previous line
+	move cursor to first non-**space/tab** of next line
<Return>	same as +
<Right>	move cursor one position right
<Left>	move cursor one position left
<Up>	move cursor one position up
<Down>	move cursor one position down
<Space>	same as <Right>
<Backspace>	same as <Left>
^P	same as <Up>
^N	same as <Down>
l	same as <Right>
h	same as <Left>
k	same as <Up>
j	same as <Down>

Changing the Screen Position of the Current Line

As we mentioned in Chapter 25, you can tell **vi** to redraw the screen by pressing ^L (look). By using the **z** command, you can tell **vi** to redraw the screen with the current line at a particular position:

z<Return>	redraw screen: current line at the top
z.	redraw screen: current line in the middle
z-	redraw screen: current line at the bottom

Notice that you press <Return> only with the first form of the **z** command.

Here is a common way to use the **z** command: You want to display a particular line at the top of the screen. Move the cursor to that line, press **z**, and then press <Return>.

If you want, you can tell **vi** to redraw the screen with a specific line at the top, middle, or bottom. Simply type the line number in front of the **z**. For example, the following commands will redraw the screen with line number 132 at the top, middle, and bottom, respectively:

```
132z<Return>
132z.
132z-
```

You can also put a search command (/ or ?) in front of a **z** command. The pattern can search for any regular expression. The **z** command will find the line and then redraw the screen so that the line is in the specified position.

Here are two examples: The first command searches forward for the first line that begins with the string **sample** and redraws the screen with that line in the middle:

```
/^sample/z.
```

The second command does the same thing, only it searches backward:

```
?^sample?z.
```

There are two important points to notice. First, you must type a second / or ? after the pattern, to separate it from the **z** character; second, as soon as you type the / or ?, **vi** will start to echo whatever you type on the command line. With these commands, you will have to press <Return> to enter the command, even with the **z.** and **z-** commands.

Here is a summary of the commands in this section. Take a moment to make sure you understand how each command works. Within the summary

| *n* | represents a line number |
| *pattern* | represents a regular expression |

Here is the summary:

z<Return>	redraw screen: current line at top
z.	redraw screen: current line in middle
z-	redraw screen: current line at bottom
*n***z<Return>**	redraw screen: specified line at top
*n***z.**	redraw screen: specified line in middle
*n***z-**	redraw screen: specified line at bottom
/pattern/z<Return>	redraw screen: line with pattern at top
/pattern/z-<Return>	redraw screen: line with pattern in middle
/pattern/z-<Return>	redraw screen: line with pattern at bottom
?pattern?z<Return>	redraw screen: line with pattern at top
?pattern?z.<Return>	redraw screen: line with pattern in middle
?pattern?z-<Return>	redraw screen: line with pattern at bottom

Returning and Marking

Absolute move command:
With vi, *a command that moves the cursor to a specific line.*

A command that moves the cursor to a specific line is called an *absolute move command*. So far, we have covered three absolute move commands: G, /, and ?, and their variations.

Whenever you use one of these commands, vi makes a note of the cursor position before the move. This allows you to use one of several commands to return quickly to the line from which you moved.

To move the cursor to the position it had just before the last absolute move command, type `` (two backquote characters). For example, say that you are editing a long document and you suddenly remember that you want to change something in the first line. Use 1G to move the cursor to line 1. After you have made the change, type `` to return to your previous position.

The `` command will return you to the exact position on the line from which you moved. If you want to return to the beginning of that line, type '' (two single quotes). The '' returns you to the first non-space, non-tab character in the line.

For example, say that current line is

```
This is the current line.
```

and the cursor is at the "c" in current. You enter

```
/sample
```

to move to the next line that contains the character string `sam-ple`. Now, if you type `` ` `` (two backquotes) you will return to the "c" in `current`; if you type `' '` (two single quotes) you will return to the "T" in `This`.

The `` ` `` and `' '` are handy but they do have a limitation: they will return you only to the most recent place from which you used an absolute move command. There will be times when you want to mark a place in the editing buffer and return to that place at your convenience. To do this, use the `m` (mark) command.

When you mark a place in the editing buffer, you give the place a name. The name must be one lower-case letter, any letter from `a` to `z`. Thus, you can mark up to 26 places (although you will rarely need more than one or two). To mark a place, move the cursor to that place and type `m` followed by the name. For example, to mark a place using the name `a`, type `ma`.

When you mark a place, `vi` does not display anything special on the screen. You have to remember where you placed the mark. So think of the `m` command as letting you place up to 26 invisible marks in the editing buffer.

To move the cursor to a place you have marked, type `` ` `` (a backquote) followed by the name. For instance, to move the cursor to the position that you marked with `ma`, type `` `a ``.

If you use a `'` (single quote) instead of a `` ` `` (backquote), `vi` will move the cursor to the first non-space, non-tab character on the line. This is analogous to the distinction between `` ` `` and `' '`.

For example, say that the current line is

```
This is the current line.
```

and the cursor is at the "c" in `current`. You type `ma` to mark the place with the name `a`. Anytime later, you can type

```
`a
```

to move to the "c" in `current`. If you type

```
'a
```

you will move to the "T" in `This`.

Once you place a mark, it persists until you make a new one with the same name. In addition, all marks are lost when you stop vi or change to a new file. That is, vi does not save marks when it saves a file.

Since these commands—`` `` '' ` ` '—move the cursor to a specific line, they are absolute move commands.

Here is a summary of the commands in this section. Take a moment now to make sure you understand how each one works. Within this summary

lchar	represents any single lower-case character
absolute move command	refers to one of the following commands: G / ? `` `` '' ` ` '

Here is the summary:

`` ``	move cursor to place of last absolute move command
''	same as `` `` but move to first non-**space**/**tab** on line
m*lchar*	mark place in editing buffer with specified name
` *lchar*	move cursor to specified place
' *lchar*	same as ` but move to first non-**space**/**tab** on line

Repeating vi Commands

There are two ways that you can execute vi commands repeatedly. First, you can precede most vi commands with a number. This executes the command that number of times. For example, the command w moves the cursor forward to the beginning of the next word. The command 5w moves forward 5 words.

Similarly, the (command moves backward to the beginning of a sentence. The command 10(moves backward 10 sentences.

If you are using a PC with a numeric keypad, you can use the keypad to type a number followed by a + or - character. This is a particularly easy way to move down or up a specific number of lines. For instance, to move up 10 lines, type 10-.

You can place a number in front of any commands for which it would make sense to do so. For example, you cannot put a number in front of the `` `` command, and a number in front of a G or z command is taken as a line number, not a repeat factor.

The second way to repeat a vi command works for those commands that are one character long. Most terminals are designed so that if you hold down a key, it sends the signal for that character repeatedly. You can take advantage of this feature to repeat most of the cursor movement commands. For example, you can hold down the <b> key to move backward, word by word. Or you can hold down a cursor control key to move in a particular direction.

The two ways to repeat commands are simple, but you must build the habit of using them. For instance, it is better to type 5b or to hold down the <b> key than to press <Left> many times.

Just as important, you should teach yourself to move the cursor as efficiently as you can. When you have to move to a new position, try to make a large jump first to get near the new place; then, use small jumps to zero in.

For example, say that you are near the bottom left-hand corner of the screen and you want to move to a word near the top right-hand corner. It would be slow to press the <Up> and <Right> keys many times. Rather, type H$ to move to the end of the top line. Next, use b to back up to the word that you want.

Take a few moments now to practice the commands that you have learned in this chapter. If you find yourself constantly depending on the cursor control keys, it is a good indication that you should take some time to practice the other commands.

27

The vi Editor: Modifying Text Files

Introduction

In the previous two chapters, we showed you how to start and stop vi and how to display your file by moving the cursor. In this chapter, you will learn how to add to and modify the information in the editing buffer. By the time you finish this chapter, you will be able to create and modify your own text files.

Preparing for This Chapter

In order to create your own text files, you start vi and enter insert mode. You then insert text into the editing buffer. As the need arises, you change back and forth from insert mode to command mode. When you are finished, you save the editing buffer into a file. If the file does not exist, Unix will create it for you.

As you read this chapter, you will need to practice the commands to insert and modify text. To do this, start vi with a file name of temp. You can use this file as a temporary work file. If you happen to have an existing file named temp, use a different name.

Before you go on to the next section, log in and enter this command:

```
vi temp
```

As soon as **vi** starts, enter the following **ex** command to display line numbers:

```
:set number
```

This will make it easier for you to keep track of the contents of your editing buffer.

As we explain each command, try it out to make sure that you understand how it works. When you are finished, you can stop **vi** and either save the file (by using **ZZ**) or discard the file (by using **:q!**).

Undoing and Repeating

vi has a particularly useful feature: at any time, you can reverse the effect of the last command that modified the contents of the editing buffer. To do this, use the u (undo) command.

For example, say that you have mistakenly deleted the first 1,000 lines of the editing buffer. Simply type u and they will reappear.

Take care: The u command only undoes the last command to modify the editing buffer. If you make a bad mistake, make sure that you type u immediately. Do not get all excited and accidentally enter another command that modifies the editing buffer.

Since the u command itself changes the editing buffer, a second u will undo the effects of the first one. For instance, say that you delete 1,000 lines and then type u to recover them. If you type u again, they will disappear; type u again and they reappear; and so on.

A similar command, U (upper-case "U"), will reverse all the modifications to the current line that have taken place since you last moved the cursor to that line. For example, say that you move the cursor to line 22 and then make all sorts of changes to that line. If you type U, **vi** will restore line 22 to what it looked like before the changes.

Be careful: The U command only undoes changes to the current line. If you make changes to line 22 and then move the cursor to line 23, you will not be able to restore line 22. Thus, if you accidentally ruin the current line, make sure that you type u before you move the cursor.

The u command undoes the last command that modified the editing buffer. The . (period) command does the opposite: it repeats the last command that modified the editing buffer.

For example, after you use the dw command to delete a word (explained later in this chapter), you can type . to delete another word. On occasion, you will find it useful to press . repeatedly to execute a command over and over. You can type a number before the . to repeat the command that many times. For instance, to repeat the last command that changed the editing buffer, type

To repeat this command 10 times, type

```
10.
```

Here is a summary of the commands in this section. Take a few moments to make sure you understand how each one works.

u	undo last command that modified the editing buffer
U	restore current line
	repeat last command that modified the editing buffer

Inserting Text into the Editing Buffer

There are twelve vi commands that you can use to enter insert mode. In this section, you will learn six commands that you can use to insert text anywhere in the editing buffer. The other six commands are used to replace text that is already in the editing buffer.

Think of being in insert mode as having an opening into the editing buffer. Everything you type is inserted into this opening. All the characters to the right are moved over to make room; nothing is lost. If you create new lines, vi automatically renumbers all the following lines. As you type, vi constantly updates the screen, so what you see is what you have.

When you want to change from insert mode back to command mode, press the <Esc> key. If you are already in command mode and you press <Esc>, `vi` will beep at you.

Occasionally, you may forget whether you are in command mode or insert mode, especially if you are a beginner. Most of the time, there is no way of telling which mode you are in by looking at the screen. If this happens, press <Esc> until your terminal beeps. You will be in command mode.

At first, this may happen frequently and you will curse the designers of `vi`: "Why couldn't they display something on the command line to tell me when I am in insert mode?" Don't worry. Once you get used to `vi`, you will know what mode you are in without even thinking about it. Remember, `vi` is easy to use, not easy to learn!

The commands in this section differ only as to where they open the editing buffer. Once you are in insert mode, the commands are all the same.

The `i` (insert) command opens the editing buffer directly before the position of the cursor. The `a` (append) command opens the editing buffer directly after the position of the cursor.

For example, say that the current line is

```
This is the current line.
```

and the cursor is positioned under the "h" in "`the`". If you use the `i` command to change to insert mode, everything that you type will be inserted between the "`t`" and the "`h`". If you use the `a` command to change to insert mode, everything you type will be inserted between the "`h`" and the "`e`".

The `I` (upper-case "I") command opens the editing buffer before the first non-`space`, non-`tab` character in the line. The `A` (upper-case "A") opens the editing buffer after the last character of the line.

For example, say that the current line is

```
This is the current line.
```

If you use `I` to change to insert mode, everything you type will be inserted before the "`T`" in "`This`". If you use the `A` command to change to insert mode, everything you type will be inserted after the `.` (period) at the end of the line.

The o (open) command opens a whole new line above the current line. The o (upper-case "O") command opens a whole new line below the current line.

For example, say that the current line is line 57. If you use the o command to change to insert mode, vi will create an empty line below line 57. Everything you type will be inserted into this line. All the lines below will be renumbered. The new line will be number 58.

If the current line is line 57 and you use the o command to change to insert mode, the new line will be created above the current line rather than below it. The new line will be number 57, and all the lines below will be renumbered. The original line will now be number 58.

You might ask, Why are there so many ways to change to insert mode? Couldn't we get by with just one such command, say the i command?

The answer is that, most of the time, you *could* get by with just the i command. However, it would mean that you would have to move the cursor frequently, in order to position it in just the right place. Moreover, without the a and A commands, it would be difficult to insert text at the end of a line.

When you start work with a new file, vi automatically places the cursor at the beginning of an empty line 1. To begin, type i to change to insert mode. Type as much as you want. When you are finished or when you want to stop to make a change, press <Esc> to change to command mode.

As with other vi commands, you can execute the insertion commands repeatedly by preceding them with a number. vi will repeat the insertion as many times as you specify.

For example, if you type

```
5iaddie<Esc>
```

it is the same as if you had typed

```
addieaddieaddieaddieaddie<Esc>
```

Thus, an easy way to insert 25 periods is to type

```
25i.<Esc>
```

Here is a particular combination of commands that is so handy you should memorize it outright. Whenever you want to add the letter "s" to a word, move the cursor anywhere in the word and type

```
eas<Esc>
```

The **e** command moves the cursor to the last letter in the word. The **a** command puts you in insert mode following this letter. The **s** inserts the "s" character. Pressing <Esc> changes back to command mode.

Here is a summary of the commands in this section. Take a few moments and make sure you understand how each command works.

i	change to insert mode; insert before cursor position
I	change to insert mode; insert at beginning of current line
a	change to insert mode; insert after cursor position
A	change to insert mode; insert at end of current line
o	change to insert mode; open new line below current line
O	change to insert mode; open new line above current line

Correcting Mistakes in Insert Mode

If you are typing in insert mode, you can make corrections while you are typing by using the following commands:

<Backspace>	erase last character
^W	erase last word
kill	erase to beginning of insertion on current line

(The **kill** key is usually ^U or ^X—see Chapter 9.)

Here is an example: Say you want to insert

```
I love you
```

but you accidentally type

```
I love me
```

Before you change back to command mode by pressing <Esc>, you can correct the last word by pressing ^W and then typing "you". So the whole thing looks like:

```
I love me^Wyou
```

Here is an important point: When you type in insert mode, vi makes room for the characters and shows them on the screen. However, nothing is actually inserted into the editing buffer until you press <Esc>.

When you correct mistakes, vi moves the cursor to the left but does not erase the characters from the screen; it looks as if they are still there. Don't worry, the characters really are erased—they will disappear when you press <Esc>. This may take a little while to get used to, especially if you have used a word processor that clears the screen as you press <Backspace>.

As you may have noticed, the rules for correcting mistakes in insert mode are the same as the ones you use when you type an ex command or a search pattern (after the / or ?).

Inserting Characters That Have Special Meanings

Occasionally, you may want to insert a character that has a special meaning, such as a control character. If so, type ^v before the special character. The ^v acts as an escape character—it tells vi to insert the next character literally and not to interpret it in a special way. This is the way to insert characters such as ^W, newline, or erase. To insert ^W, type

```
^V^W
```

To insert the newline character, type

```
^V<Return>
```

To insert the erase character, type

```
^V<Backspace>
```

vi displays control characters using the same notation that we use here: a ^ (circumflex) followed by an upper-case letter. Even though you see two characters, each control character takes up only one byte of the editing buffer.

When you insert a `newline`, it is displayed as `^M`, the "carriage return" character; when you insert an `erase`, it is displayed as `^H` (see Chapter 9).

Replacing Text

There are several commands that you can use to replace text that is already in the editing buffer. These are the commands to use when you need to make changes.

The simplest of these commands is `r` (replace). This command allows you to replace exactly one character. Whatever character you type after the `r` replaces the character at the current cursor position.

For example, say that you mistype the word `cat` as `cqt`. Move the cursor to the letter "q" and type

```
ra
```

`vi` will replace the "q" with an "a".

The `r` command is a quick way to replace a single character without having to stay in insert mode. All the other commands in this section stay in insert mode.

The `R` (upper-case "R") command allows you to replace characters by typing over them. Position the cursor to where you want to start the replacement and type

```
R
```

You are now in insert mode. Whatever you type replaces what is on the screen.

For example, say that you want to change the line

```
This is a bad line.
```

by replacing everything from the "b" to the end of the line. You move to the "b" and type

```
Rgood line.<Esc>
```

The result is that the line now looks like this:

```
This is a good line.
```

The **s** (substitute) command is similar to the **r** command in that it replaces exactly one character. However, the **s** command changes to insert mode so you can insert as many characters as you want.

For example, say that the current line reads

```
You have a cat of $956.
```

You want to change the word "**cat**" to "**credit**". Move the cursor to the "**a**" in "**cat**" and type **s**. You are now in insert mode; everything you type will replace the single character "**a**". In this case, you type **redi** and press <Esc>. The whole thing looks like this:

```
sredi<Esc>
```

As soon as you type the **s** command, **vi** erases the character that will be replaced and displays a **$** (dollar sign) character as a marker. This is to remind you that you are in the middle of a replacement. The **$** has nothing to do with the **$** command.

If you want to replace an entire line, move the cursor to that line and type **s** (an upper-case "S"). **vi** will erase the line and change to insert mode. Whatever you type replaces the line.

Sometimes you may want to replace a particular object: a sentence, a word, or a paragraph. To do this, use the **c** (change) command. Type **c**, followed by the command to move the cursor over the characters that you want to replace.

For example, to replace a word, move the cursor to the beginning of the word and type

```
cw
```

to replace a sentence, move to the beginning of the sentence and type

```
c)
```

and so on.

When you use a c command, **vi** will change to insert mode and display a $ character to mark the end of the text that will be replaced. Type whatever you want, and then press <Esc>.

The c command is powerful. You can combine it with any cursor movement command that does not use the <Ctrl> key or one of the cursor control (arrow) keys. Here are some examples. Make sure that you take a moment to understand how each example works:

w	replace 4 words
c4W	replace 4 words separated by **space** characters
c (	replace back to beginning of previous sentence
c4b	replace back to beginning of 4th previous word
c}	replace to beginning of paragraph

As we mentioned, you cannot use the c command with ^w, <Up>, and so on. However, you can use <Space>, <Return>, and h, j, k, and l.

The c (upper-case "C") command will replace all the characters from the position of the cursor to the end of the line. The cc command will replace the entire line. (That is, cc is the same as s.) These commands are not followed by a cursor movement command.

As with other **vi** commands, you can execute the replace commands repeatedly by preceding them with a number. Here are some examples. Notice the subtle distinction between 4r and 4s.

4s	replace 4 characters
4r	replace 1 character with 4 copies of the insertion
4cw	replace 4 words (same as c4w)
4S	replace 4 lines

Here is a summary of the commands in this section. Take a moment now to make sure you understand how each one works. Within the summary

move	represents any cursor movement command that does not use the <Ctrl> or cursor control (arrow) keys

Here is the summary:

r	replace exactly 1 character
R	replace by typing over
s	replace 1 character by insertion
S	replace current line by insertion
c*move*	replace from cursor to *move* by insertion
c	replace from cursor to end of current line by insertion
cc	same as S

All of these commands, except r, stay in insert mode.

Changing the Case of Letters

The ~ (tilde) command changes the case of a letter and then moves the cursor one position to the right. If a letter is upper-case, the ~ command changes the letter to lower-case; if a letter is lower-case, it is changed to upper-case. The reason the ~ command moves the cursor is to make it easy to change consecutive letters.

Here is an example. Say that the current line is

```
tHIS is the current line.
```

and the cursor position is at the "t" in "tHIS". If you type a single

the "t" will change from lower-case to upper-case and the cursor will move one position to the right. The line will look like this:

```
THIS is the current line.
```

If you press ~ three more times, three more characters will change case; the current line will look like this:

```
This is the current line.
```

The cursor will be at the **space** between "This" and "is".

Unfortunately, you cannot precede the ~ command with a number to change the case of a group of letters. (This is probably an oversight on the part of the designers of vi.) However, since the ~ command does move the cursor to the right, you can press the ~ key repeatedly to change consecutive letters.

If you press ~ when the cursor is pointing to a character that is not a letter, vi will leave the character unchanged but the cursor will still move to the right. Thus, if you want to convert a long group of letters from one case to another, move the cursor to the beginning of the group and hold down the ~ key. Even if some of the characters are not letters, there will not be a problem.

Forming and Breaking Lines

When you type in insert mode, there are two ways that you can control the position of the right-hand margin. First, you can press <Return> whenever you want to start a new line. This is similar to the carriage return on a typewriter. Pressing <Return> inserts a `newline` into the editing buffer at that point, and vi assumes that all lines end with a `newline`.

If you type a great deal, it is inconvenient to have to put in your own `newline` characters. Instead, you can have vi do it for you automatically, whenever the cursor nears the right side of the screen.

To do this, you use an `ex` command. Type `:set wm=` followed by the distance from the right-hand margin of the screen at which you want the automatic line breaking to take place. (The "wm" stands for "wrap margin.")

For example, if you want vi to insert a `newline` whenever you move within 10 positions of the right-hand margin, enter

```
:set wm=10
```

If you want a line as long as possible, use

```
:set wm=1
```

It is usually a good idea to keep the margin value from being too small, to allow some room for small changes. As a rule of thumb, set wm to a value of 6 or larger. To turn off the automatic margin control, enter

```
:set wm=0
```

If you do not set **wm** and you type without pressing <Return>, you will end up creating one very long line. If you type a line that is longer than the width of the screen, **vi** will display the line using more than one screen line. However, **vi** still considers it to be one long line.

You will find it awkward to work with lines that do not fit on one screen line. You should avoid creating such lines by pressing <Return> as you insert or by setting the **wm** control.

However, you may occasionally find yourself with extra long lines. At such times, you will need a way to break a line into two.

To do this, all you have to do is insert a **newline** character where you want to break the line. For example, say that the current line is

```
This line is much too long and should be broken into two lines.
```

You decide to break the line between the "**and**" and the "**should**".

Move the cursor to the **space** between the "**d**" of "**and**" and the "**s**" of "**should**". Then, type

```
r<Return>
```

This replaces the **space** with a **newline**, effectively breaking the line. The text now looks like this:

```
This line is much too long and
should be broken into two lines.
```

Sometimes you will want to perform the opposite operation: to join two short lines into one long one. This is even easier. Move the cursor to anywhere in the first line and type **J** (join)—an upper-case "J". **vi** will automatically delete the **newline** at the end of the first line, effectively joining it to the second line. If you want to join a number of lines, type that number before the **J**.

For example, to join 5 lines, type

```
5J
```

When vi joins lines, it automatically inserts space characters in appropriate places. For example, vi will put a space between the last word of one line and the first word of the next line. If the end of the first line was the end of a sentence, vi will insert two space characters.

If you are typing large documents, you will find it time consuming to line up the margins and to readjust them every time you make changes. In this case, you should use one of the text formatting programs (nroff and troff—see Chapter 24) to process your documents.

Here is a summary of the commands in this section. Take a few moments now to make sure you understand how each one works. Within this summary

n	represents a number

Here is the summary:

:set wm=*n*	set automatic margin *n* positions from right
J	join lines

Deleting Text

There are four commands that delete text from the editing buffer. The **x** command deletes one character at the position of the cursor. (Think of typing "x" on a typewriter to cross out a mistake.) For example, say that the current line is

```
This is the curQrent line.
```

and you want to delete the "Q". Move the cursor to the "Q" and type

```
x
```

The "Q" will be deleted. The line will look like this:

```
This is the current line.
```

You can type a number before the **x** to delete that many characters, starting from the cursor and moving right. For example, to delete 5 characters, type

```
5x
```

Another way to delete consecutive characters is to move the cursor to the first character and either press x repeatedly or hold down the x key.

The x (upper-case "X") command deletes one character to the left of the cursor. For example, say that the current line is

```
0123456789
```

and the cursor is at the "6". If you type x, you will delete the "6". If you type x you will delete the "5".

You can type a number before an x command to delete that many characters, moving left from the position of the cursor. For example, if the current line is

```
0123456789
```

and the cursor is at the "6", the command 3x will delete "345".

Aside from x, there is a more powerful command, the d (delete) command. The d command works much like the c (change) command. You type d, followed by a cursor movement command, and vi deletes from the cursor to where the cursor would be after being moved.

For example, to delete from the cursor position to the end of a word, type

```
dw
```

to delete 5 words, type

```
d5w
```

to delete backward to the beginning of the third previous sentence, type

```
d3(
```

and so on. As with the c command, you can use any cursor movement command that does not use the <Ctrl> key or the cursor control (arrow) keys. A particularly useful combination is

```
dG
```

which deletes from the cursor to the end of the editing buffer.
To delete the current line, type

```
dd
```

To delete from the position of the cursor to the end of the
current line, type

```
D
```

These two commands are analogous to the cc and c commands.
Here is a summary of the commands in this section. Take a
moment now to make sure you understand how each one
works. Within the summary

move   represents a cursor movement command that does
                   not use the <Ctrl> key or cursor control (arrow) keys

Here is the summary:

x   delete character at position of cursor
X   delete character to left of cursor
d*move*   delete from cursor to *move*
dd   delete current line
D   delete from cursor to end of line

Remember, to undo any of these commands, use the u (undo)
command.

Recovering Deletions Using the Delete Buffers

Delete Buffer:

With vi, *one of 9
temporary storage
areas, numbered* 1
through 9, *used to
hold the 9 most
recent deletions
that involved a
line, a sentence, or
anything longer.*

vi maintains 9 storage areas called *delete buffers*. These buffers
are designated by the numbers 1 through 9. The delete buffers
hold the last 9 deletions that involved a line, sentence, or anything longer. (In other words, these buffers are not updated
when you delete words or characters.)

Buffer 1 holds the most recent such deletion, buffer 2 holds
the next most recent deletion, and so on. At any time, you can
recover these deletions by using the p (put) and P commands.

To recover the text in a delete buffer, type a " (double quote) character, followed by the number of the delete buffer you want, followed by p or P. Notice that this is one double quote character, not two single quotes.

Here is an example. To recover the 3rd last deletion, type

```
"3P
```

The p and P commands both insert the contents of the specified delete buffer. The only difference is that p places the insertion to the right of the cursor; P places the insertion to the left of the cursor. If the insertion is a full line or more, p opens a new line above the current line; P opens a new line below the current line.

As we explained earlier, you can use the u (undo) command to undo a deletion. However, the u command only undoes the last change to the editing buffer. What if you delete a line and you do not realize that you want it back until after you have deleted another line? In this case, it is too late to use the u command. Since you have performed a second deletion, the original one is in delete buffer 2.

Move the cursor to where you want to insert and type

```
"2P
```

You can use the . (period) command to execute the p and P commands repeatedly. Usually, the . command repeats the last command that changed the editing buffer. However, as a special case, when you use . to repeat a command that uses a delete buffer, vi automatically increases the number of the buffer by 1.

For example, say you want to recover a deletion, but you are not sure which delete buffer holds the text you want. Move the cursor to where you want to insert and type

```
"1P
```

The contents of delete buffer 1 will be restored. If this was not the right delete buffer, type

```
u
```

to undo the P command. Then type

to repeat the P command. vi will automatically change the buffer number to 2. The contents of delete buffer 2 will be restored, just as if you had typed:

```
"2P
```

If this is not the right delete buffer, type

```
u.
```

again. Keep going until you find the delete buffer you want.
    Remember this pattern,

```
"1Pu.u.u.u.
```

It will come in handy.
    The contents of the delete buffers are lost when you stop vi, but not when you start editing another file. However, it is not a good idea to use the delete buffers to move text between files. Use the named buffers (see the next section).

Moving Text Using the Named Buffers

Named Buffer:
With vi, *one of 26 temporary storage areas, named* a *through* z, *available to the user to hold text.*

vi has a set of storage areas that you can use to hold text temporarily. These storage areas are designated by the letters of the alphabet, a through z, and are called the *named buffers*.
    vi has a number of commands to move text back and forth between a named buffer and the editing buffer. You can copy text into a named buffer and then insert the text anywhere in the editing buffer.
    To copy text from the editing buffer into a named buffer, you use the y ("yank"), Y, and yy commands. These commands do not modify the editing buffer; they merely copy from it.
    Using the y command is similar to using the c and d commands. You follow the y with a cursor movement command. vi copies from the current position of the cursor up to the position to which the command would move the cursor. You precede a y command with a " (double quote) and the name of the buffer to which you want to copy.

For example, to copy 5 words to the **a** buffer, type

```
"ay5w
```

To copy 4 sentences to the **b** buffer, type

```
"by4)
```

To copy 10 characters to the **c** buffer, type

```
"cy10<Space>
```

As with the **c** and **d** commands, you cannot use a cursor movement command that involves the <Ctrl> key or a cursor control (arrow) key.

The **Y** and **yy** commands both copy an entire line to the named buffer you specify. For example, to copy the current line to the **d** buffer, type either

```
"dY
```

or

```
"dyy
```

(Note: There is a subtle inconsistency here. The **y**, **c**, and **d** commands behave similarly, as do the **yy**, **cc**, and **dd** commands. However, the **Y** command copies the entire current line, while the **c** and **D** commands process only from the cursor to the end of the line. Thus, **Y** is the same as **yy**, while **c** and **D** are not the same as **cc** and **dd**.)

You can repeat the **y**, **Y** and **yy** commands by typing a number in front of them. For instance, to copy 10 lines to the **e** buffer, type

```
"e10yy
```

Once you have copied text into a named buffer, you can insert the text in the editing buffer by using the **p** and **P** commands. Use these commands in the same way as when you are working with delete buffers (see the previous section).

For example, to copy text from the e buffer to the editing buffer, type

```
"ep
```

or

```
"eP
```

The p and P commands do not change the named buffer; they merely copy from it. Thus, you can copy from the same named buffer over and over.

There is one more way to put text into a named buffer. If you precede a delete command with a double quote and the name of a buffer, whatever is deleted will be copied to the buffer. This works with all three delete commands: d, dd, and D.

For example, to delete 10 words, you would type

```
d10w
```

If you type

```
"fd10w
```

the words are deleted, but they are saved in the f buffer. This would be the same as if you had typed the following two commands in succession:

```
"fy10w
d10w
```

When you copy text to a named buffer, the text replaces whatever was in the buffer. Sometimes, it is convenient to add on to the end of the buffer, rather than to replace the contents. To do this, specify the buffer name as an upper-case letter instead of a lower-case letter.

For example, if you type

```
"gy10w
```

you will replace the contents of the g buffer with the 10 words that are copied. The command

```
"Gy10w
```

adds the 10 words on to the end of the g buffer.

Here is how this might come in handy: Suppose you are writing a Unix book and you want certain lines to be repeated as part of a summary.

Go through the editing buffer and find the lines. For the first line, copy it to a named buffer, say h, by typing

```
"hyy
```

For each subsequent line, add it to the end of the buffer by using

```
"Hyy
```

Once you have gathered all the lines, move the cursor to where they are to be inserted, and type

```
"hp
```

Text stored in named buffers is lost when you stop vi, but not when you start editing another file. Thus, an important use of named buffers is to pass text between files. Copy the text into a named buffer and switch files. Since the named buffer is unchanged, you can insert the text into the new editing buffer.

Recovering the Last Deletion Using the Unnamed Buffer

Unnamed Buffer:
With vi, *a temporary storage area used to hold the most recent deletion.*

There is one more storage area that you need to understand. It does not have a particular name so it is called the *unnamed buffer*.

As you know, vi uses the delete buffers to save your 9 most recent deletions. However, these are only deletions that are at least as long as a sentence or a line. vi uses the unnamed buffer to save your most recent deletion, no matter what size it is. For instance, if you type

```
10dd
```

to delete 10 lines, vi will save the lines in both the unnamed buffer and in delete buffer 1. But if you type

```
10x
```

to delete 10 characters, `vi` will save the characters only in the unnamed buffer; delete buffer 1 will remain unchanged.

If you use the `p` and `P` commands without specifying a specific buffer, they will use the unnamed buffer. Do not use a double quote; simply type

```
p
```

or

```
P
```

For example, say that you want to move a sentence from one paragraph to another. Move the cursor to the beginning of the sentence and type

```
d)
```

to delete the sentence. Then, move the cursor to where you want the sentence and type

```
P
```

Remember, `vi` will replace the contents of the unnamed buffer the next time you delete anything; if you want to save some text, put it in a named buffer.

Here are two ways to use the `p` command with the unnamed buffer that are so handy, you should memorize them outright: To swap two adjacent characters, type

```
xp
```

and to swap two consecutive lines, type

```
ddp
```

Here are some examples. Say that the current line is

```
This is the current lnie.
```

You want to change "lnie" to "line". Move the cursor to the "n" in "lnie", and type

xp

The **x** command deletes the "n" character and puts it in the unnamed buffer. The **p** command copies the contents of the unnamed buffer back to the editing buffer. However, immediately after the deletion, the cursor is at the "i", so the "n" is inserted to the right of the "i". The net effect is to swap the two characters.

Typing

ddp

works analogously. The **dd** command deletes the current line, and the **p** command copies it back from the unnamed buffer to the editing buffer. The line is copied below the new current line. The net effect is to swap the two lines.

The contents of the unnamed buffer are lost when you stop **vi** but not when you start editing another file. However, if you want to move text between files, it is better to use a named buffer.

You might wonder, is the unnamed buffer the same place that **vi** keeps the last deletion for use by the **u** command? The answer is no: the **u** command undoes the last deletion or insertion; the unnamed buffer holds only the last deletion. The unnamed buffer is not changed when you perform an insertion.

Here is a summary of the commands to use the buffers. Take a moment to make sure you understand how each command works. Within the summary

move	represents any cursor movement that does not use either the <Ctrl> key or a cursor control (arrow) key
buf	represents the name of a delete buffer (1 through 9) or a named buffer (a through z)
BUF	represents the upper-case name of a named buffer (A through Z)

Here is the summary:

p	copy from unnamed buffer; insert after cursor
P	copy from unnamed buffer; insert before cursor
"bufp	same as p but use specified buffer
"bufP	same as P but use specified buffer
y*move*	copy to unnamed buffer from cursor position to *move*
yy	copy one line to unnamed buffer
Y	same as yy
"bufymove	same as y*move* but use specified buffer
"bufyy	same as yy but use specified buffer
"bufY	same as Y but use specified buffer
"BUFymove	same as y*move* but add onto specified buffer
"BUFyy	same as yy but add onto specified buffer
"BUFY	same as Y but add onto specified buffer
"bufdmove	same as d but save in specified buffer
"bufdd	same as dd but save in specified buffer
"bufD	same as D but save in specified buffer
"BUFdmove	same as d but save onto end of specified buffer
"BUFdd	same as dd but save onto end of specified buffer
"BUFD	same as D but save onto end of specified buffer

28

The vi Editor:
The Rest of What You
Need to Know

Introduction

This is the last of the chapters describing the vi editor. In this chapter we will teach you the rest of what you need to know, including using the shell from vi, how to use the important ex commands, and how to set up your working environment.

Setting and Displaying Options

Option:

In vi, a value that you can set to specify how you want vi to behave.

Switch Option:

In vi, an option that is either on or off.

String Option:

In vi, an option that has the value of a string of letters or numbers.

An *option* is a value that you can set to specify how you want vi to behave. Each option controls one facet of vi's behavior. When you start vi, it automatically assigns each option a default value. If it suits you, you can change the value of any option to be different from the default.

There are two types of options: *switch options* and *string options*. A switch option is either on or off, like a light switch. When you start vi, some of the switch options are set on, others are set off.

An example of a switch option is the number option that we met in Chapter 26. When the number option is on, vi displays a line number in front of each line. When the number option is off, vi does not display a line number.

A string option has the value of a string of letters or numbers. An example of a string option is the **wm** option that we used in Chapter 27. The value of **wm** is a number that specifies the position for automatic margin control.

To display the current value of an option or to set an option, you use the **ex :set** command. To display a list of all the options and their current values, enter

```
:set all
```

To display a list of those options whose values have been changed from their default, enter

```
:set
```

To display the current value of a particular option, enter

```
:set name ?
```

where *name* is the name of the option. For example, to display the current value of the **wm** option, enter

```
:set wm ?
```

To turn on a switch option, enter

```
:set name
```

where *name* is the name of the switch option. To turn off a switch option, enter

```
:set noname
```

For example, to turn on the **number** option, enter

```
:set number
```

To turn off the **number** option, enter

```
:set nonumber
```

Notice that you do not put a space between the no and the name of the option. To set a string option to a particular value, enter

```
:set name=value
```

where *name* is the name of the string option, and *value* is the value that you want the option to have. For example, to set the wm option to the value 10, enter

```
:set wm=10
```

Notice that you do not put a space on either side of the = character.

The Different Options

vi has many different options. Here is a description of the most important ones. For a full list, see the Unix manual for your system, under the section that describes the vi command.

Some options have a full name and an abbreviation. vi displays the full name, but when you set the option, you can refer to it by the abbreviation.

autowrite
abbreviation: aw
type: switch
default: off
effect: automatically write the contents of the editing buffer
                 to the current file whenever you use a command
                 that might change the current file

ignorecase
abbreviation: ic
type: switch
default: off
effect: do not distinguish between upper- and lower-case
                 when matching regular expressions

`list`

abbreviation:	none
type:	switch
default:	off
effect:	display invisible characters: `tab` is displayed as `^I` (upper-case "I"); each `newline` is marked by `$`

`mesg`

abbreviation:	none
type:	switch
default:	on
effect:	turning off this switch prevents messages from being sent to your terminal while you are using `vi`; this is like taking your telephone off the hook

`number`

abbreviation:	nu
type:	switch
default:	off
effect:	display each line with its line number; this is a useful option to keep on all the time

`report`

abbreviation:	none
type:	switch
default:	5
effect:	display a message whenever a command modifies more than the specified number of lines

`warn`

abbreviation:	none
type:	switch
default:	on
effect:	if the editing buffer has not been saved, display a warning message every time a `:!` shell command is executed

window

abbreviation:	none
type:	string
default:	varies
effect:	display the specified number of lines on the screen; the default varies with the type of terminal:

console of PC or workstation:	full screen
fast terminal (over 1,200 bps):	full screen
medium terminal (1,200 bps):	16 lines
slow terminal (300 bps):	8 lines

wrapmargin

abbreviation:	**wm**
type:	string
default:	0 (**zero**)
effect:	during insert mode, automatically break a line into two (by inserting a **newline**), this many characters from the right end of the line; to turn off this option, specify a value of 0 (the default)

wrapscan

abbreviation:	**ws**
type:	switch
default:	on
effect:	if a forward search reaches the end of the editing buffer, wrap around to the beginning and continue searching; similarly, if a backward search reaches the beginning of the editing buffer, wrap around to the end

writeany

abbreviation:	**wa**
type:	switch
default:	off
effect:	allow any type of write command to replace an existing file; for example, when this option is on, the **:w** command will replace an existing file and **:w!** is not necessary.

Using Unix Commands from Within `vi`

There are several `ex` and `vi` commands that you can use to execute Unix commands from `vi`. This obviates having to stop `vi` every time you want to use a Unix command.

To execute one Unix command, enter

`:!`*command*

where *command* is a Unix command. For example, to find out the time without stopping `vi`, enter

`:!date`

To repeat the last such command, enter

`:!!`

If you want to execute a number of Unix commands, you can pause in `vi` and start a new copy of the shell. To do this, enter

`:!sh`

You can now enter as many Unix commands as you want. When you are finished, press `^D` (the `eof` key). Unix will stop the shell and restart `vi`.

You can execute a Unix command and insert the output into the editing buffer by using a form of the `:re` (read) command. (We will cover this command later in this chapter.) Enter

`:`*line*`re !`*command*

where *line* is the line number at which you want the insertion to take place, and *command* is a Unix command. If you do not specify a line number, `vi` will insert at the current line.

For example, to insert the output of the `date` command into the editing buffer at the current line, enter

`:re !date`

So far, all the commands in this section have been `ex` commands. There are two `vi` commands that you can use to have a

Unix command act on part of the editing buffer. vi will replace the part of the editing buffer that was processed with the output of the command. For example, you can insert a table of data and then have Unix sort it for you.

The first way to use this facility is to enter

```
:!move  command
```

where *move* is a cursor movement command and *command* is a Unix command. As with the c, d and y commands, the cursor movement command cannot use the <Ctrl> key of the cursor control (arrow) keys.

vi will execute the Unix command on part of the editing buffer, starting from the position of the cursor, up to where the cursor movement command would move the cursor.

Here is an example. You want to count the number of characters in a group of 4 sentences and insert that number into the editing buffer. First, make a copy of the 4 sentences. Next, position the cursor at the beginning of the first sentence. Then, enter

```
:!4)wc -w
```

The output of the wc -w command (the number of characters) will replace the sentences. (This is why you execute the Unix command on a copy of the sentences.)

Here is what happens as you type this command. As soon as you have finished typing the cursor movement part of the command—in this case, 4)—vi will display a ! on the command line. As you type the actual Unix command, vi will echo it on the command line, after the ! character.

As you enter the command, you can correct what is being echoed by using <Backspace> (to erase one character), ^w (to erase a word), and kill (to erase the line). The kill character is usually ^x or ^u.

To cancel the command before you press <Return>, use the intr key (usually <Delete> or ^c).

Finally, if after pressing <Return> you are not satisfied with the results of the command, you can always undo it by using the u command.

Aside from following a ! character with a cursor movement command, there is an alternate way to have a Unix command act on part of the editing buffer. You can use this method when the part of the editing buffer consists of a number of consecutive lines. Enter

n!!*command*

where *n* is the number of lines, starting with the current line, and *command* is the Unix command. After you type the second ! character, vi will display a ! on the command line. Then, as you type the Unix command, vi will echo it.

Here is an example. You want to sort 10 lines to put them in alphabetical order. You can use the sort command (which we will cover later in the book).

First, move the cursor to the first line. Next, enter

```
10!!sort
```

The sort command will sort the 10 lines. vi will replace the lines with the output of the sort command. The net effect is that the 10 lines are sorted in place as you watch.

In some cases, it is possible to get the same effect with the variation of the ! command that uses a cursor movement. The last example, for instance, is equivalent to

```
!10jsort
```

(Remember, the command 10j moves the cursor down 10 lines.)

Here is a summary of the commands in this section. Take a moment to make sure that you understand each one. Within this summary

command	represents a Unix command
move	represents any cursor movement that does not use either the <CTRL> key or a cursor control (arrow) key
line	represents a line number
n	represents a number

Here is the summary:

`:!`*command*	execute the specified Unix command
`:!!`	repeat previous Unix command
`:!sh`	pause vi and start a new copy of the shell
`:`*line*`re!` *command*	insert Unix command output at specified line
`:re!` *command*	insert Unix command output at current line
`!`*move command*	execute Unix command from cursor to *move*
n`!`*command*	execute Unix command on *n* lines

Specifying Line Numbers for ex Commands

We have already covered a number of useful ex commands. There are a few more commands that you should know because they perform tasks that cannot be done easily by vi commands.

The reason is that ex was developed as a line editor. Its commands work particularly well with groups of lines. When vi was developed, there was no need to duplicate all these commands. Thus, when vi needs to work with groups of lines, it passes the ball to ex.

Many ex commands require that you specify one or two line numbers as part of the command. In this section, we will show you how this works.

When you use an ex command, you put the line numbers on which the command is to act before the name of the command. For example, to use the `:d` command on line 10, you would enter

```
:10d
```

(The `:d` command, which deletes whole lines, is explained later in the chapter.)

When you want a command to act on a range of numbers, you specify the first and last number of the range, separated by a comma. For instance, to use the `:d` command on lines 10 through 15 inclusive, enter

```
:10,15d
```

The most straightforward way to specify a line number is to use an actual number, as in the previous two examples. The question is, how do you know the numbers of the lines?

There are two ways. First, you can set the number option to on, using

```
:set number
```

vi will display a line number in front of each line. Many people prefer to keep this option on all the time.

Second, to find out the number of the current line, you can use the :nu (number) command:

```
:nu
```

vi will display the current line along with its number. For example:

```
100  this is the text of what is on the current line
```

Alternatively, you can use the ^G and :f commands that we described in Chapter 25. These commands display the name of the file, whether or not it has been modified, the line number, the total number of lines, and the percentage of lines up to and including the current line. For example:

```
:"doc" [Modified] line 100 of 200 --50%--
```

In this case, we are on line 100, which is halfway through the file.

There are some ex commands that can act on one line. If you use one of these commands without specifying a line, the command will use the current line. For example, to use the :d command on the current line, enter

```
:d
```

Aside from actual numbers, there are several abbreviations that you can use to specify line numbers:

. (period)	the current line
$ (dollar sign)	the last line in the editing buffer
% (percent sign)	the entire editing buffer

Here are some examples that use the :d command on different ranges of lines. To the right of each example we have indicated which lines are specified:

:d	current line
:.d	current line
:$d	last line in editing buffer
:%d	entire editing buffer
:1,$d	lines 1 through last line (same as %)
:1,.d	lines 1 through current line
:.,$d	current line through last line

You can also specify a line by using one of the search or goto commands. In the following, *mark* represents the name of a marker set by the m command.

/	search forward for a pattern
?	search backward for a pattern
''	go to position of previous absolute move command
'*mark*	go to marker

These commands are explained in Chapter 26. The last two commands are two quotes and one quote, respectively.

Each one of these commands can take the place of a line number. If you use a / or ? command, you must use a second / or ? at the end of the pattern.

Here are some examples. To have the :d command act on the next line that contains the string sample, enter

```
:/sample/d
```

To search backward for the characters "begin", and search forward for the characters "end", and have the :d command act on this range of lines, enter

```
:?begin?,/end/d
```

The '' (two quotes) and ' (one quote) commands are often useful when you need to specify a range of lines. For example, say that you use the command

```
:100G
```

to go to line 100. You then decide to have the :d command act on the range of lines between 100 (the current line) and the line you came from. Enter

```
:.,''d
```

As another example, say that you have used the m command to mark a line with a marker named **a**:

```
:ma
```

Later, you want to use the :d command on all the lines from line 50 to the marker **a**. Enter

```
:50,'ad
```

   Aside from what we have already covered, there is one more way to specify line numbers. Say that *n* represents a number. You can refer to a line that is *n* lines before a particular line by using -*n*. Similarly, +*n* *refers to n* lines after a particular line.
   For example, to have the :d command act on the line following the next occurrence of "**sample**", enter

```
:/sample/+1d
```

Here is an example that uses :d on a range of lines. The range starts 2 lines before the last occurrence of "**begin**" and ends 3 lines after the next occurrence of "**end**":

```
:?begin?-2,/end/+3d
```

If you use -*n* and +*n* by themselves, they refer to before and after the current line. For example, here are two equivalent ways of using the :d command, ranging from 4 lines before the current line to 5 lines after the current line (a total of 10 lines):

```
:.-4,.+5d
:-4,+5d
```

   Here is a summary of the ways to specify line numbers for **ex** commands. Take a moment now and make sure that you understand how it all works. Within this summary

pattern	represents a regular expression describing a pattern
mark	represents the name of a marker set by an **m** command
n	represents a number

Here is the summary:

.	current line
$	last line in editing buffer
/*pattern*/	search forward; next line containing *pattern*
?*pattern*?	search backward; next line containing *pattern*
' '	line of previous absolute move command
'*mark*	line containing *mark*

To indicate a line before or after a specific line:

| -*n* | *n* lines before |
| +*n* | *n* lines after |

If you do not specify a line, most **ex** commands use the current line.

Writing and Reading Using ex

In Chapter 25, we explained how to use the :w and :w! commands to write from the editing buffer to a file. By themselves, these commands copy the entire editing buffer to a file. If you want, you can copy a line or a range of lines by identifying the lines directly.

For example, to copy lines 50 through 120 to the file doc, enter

```
:50,120w doc
```

When you use the :w or :w! commands, whatever you write replaces the file to which it is being written. If you want to add to a file, rather than replace it, use

```
:w>>
```

vi will copy the saved text to the end of the file.

For example, to copy lines 50 to 120 to the end of the file doc, enter

```
:50,120w>> doc
```

You can copy text from a file into the editing buffer by using the :re (read) command. Enter

:linere file

where *line* is a line number and *file* is the name of a file. For example, to copy the contents of the file doc to the end of the editing buffer, enter

```
:$re doc
```

To copy the same text to the beginning of the editing buffer, enter

```
:0re doc
```

To insert the text after line 45, use

```
:45re doc
```

To insert after the current line, use

```
:re doc
```

An alternate form of the :re command lets you copy the output of a Unix command into the editing buffer. Enter

:linere! command

where *line* is a line number and *command* is a Unix command.

Here is an example. You want to make a long listing of your files by using the ls -l command (see Chapter 21). You want to insert this listing into your editing buffer, after line 150. Enter

```
:150re! ls -l
```

Here is a summary of the commands in this section. Take a moment to make sure that you understand each one. Within this summary

file	represents the name of a file
line	represents a line number
command	represents a Unix command

If you do not specify a line number, vi will use the current line. Here is the summary:

:*line*w *file*	copy specified line to *file*
:*line*,*line*w *file*	copy specified range of lines to *file*
:w>>	same as :w but add to end of the file
:*line*re *file*	insert contents of *file* after *line*
:*line*re! *command*	insert output of Unix command after *line*

Deleting, Copying, and Moving Using ex

You can use ex commands to delete, copy, and move groups of lines. Although it is possible to do this with vi commands, the ex commands are more convenient when you are working with lines.

To delete one or more lines, use the :d command. vi will delete whatever lines you specify. For example, to delete line 100, enter

```
:100d
```

To delete from the current line to the next line containing the characters "sample", enter

```
:.,/sample/d
```

To delete the entire editing buffer, use

```
:%d
```

To copy one or more lines, use the :co (copy) command. It looks like this:

```
:line,linecotarget  :linecotarget
```

Here *line* is a line number and *target* is the number of the line after which you want to insert the copied lines. For example, to copy lines 5 to 10 and insert them after line 25, enter

```
:5,10co25
```

To search backward and copy the first line with the string **sample** to the beginning of the editing buffer, enter

```
:?sample?co0
```

To move a line or group of lines, use the :m (move) command. This command has the same form as the :co command:

```
:linemtarget
:line,linemtarget
```

The difference between the two commands is that :m deletes the original lines and then inserts them somewhere else. The :co command does not delete the original lines.

Here are some examples. To move lines 15 through 20 and insert them after line 25, enter

```
:15,20m25
```

To move the last line of text to the beginning of the editing buffer, enter

```
:$m0
```

If you make a mistake, you can undo the effects of a :d, :co, or :m command by using the u command.

Here is a summary of the commands in this section. Take a moment to make sure you understand each one. Within this summary

line	represents a line number
target	represents a line number after which the insertion is to take place

Here is the summary:

:*line*d	delete specified line
:*line*,*line*d	delete specified range
:*line*co*target*	copy specified line; insert after *target*
:*line*,*line*co*target*	copy specified range; insert after *target*
:*line*m*target*	move specified line; insert after *target*
:*line*,*line*m*target*	move specified range; insert after *target*

Substituting Over a Range of Lines

There are two **ex** commands that will search for patterns and perform substitutions. The **:s** (substitute) command will search over a specified range, and the **:g** (global) command will search over the entire editing buffer. Both these commands search forward.

To use the **:s** command, you must tell it what pattern to search for and what to substitute. The pattern can be any regular expression. The command looks like this:

:s/*pattern*/*replace*/

Here *pattern* is the regular expression for which you want to search, and *replace* is the string of characters that should take the place of *pattern*.

Here is an example. To replace "**SAMPLE**" by "**sample**", enter

:s/SAMPLE/sample/

Here is a more complicated example. You want to search for a word that begins with either "h" or "H", and replace the entire word by "**xxx**". Enter

:s/\<[Hh].*\>/xxx/

In this example

\<	matches the beginning of a word
[Hh]	matches either "h" or "H"
.*	matches zero or more of any character except a newline
\>	matches the end of a word

If you want to delete something, you can search for it and re-place it by nothing. For example, to delete any digit, enter

```
:s/[0-9]//
```

By itself, the `:s` command will search the current line. If you want to search a different line or a range of lines, you can spec-ify the line numbers in front of the command.

   For example, the following command replaces "`sample`" by "`(sample)`" on line 100:

```
:100s/sample/(sample)/
```

The following command inserts 5 `space` characters at the begin-nings of lines 100 through 105. (Remember, the `^` character matches the beginning of a line.)

```
:100,105s/^/     /
```

In this form, the `:s` command will match and replace the first occurrence of the pattern on each line you specify. Sometimes you want to substitute all the occurrences on the line. To do this, put a `g` (global) at the end of the command. Here is an example. To replace every occurrence on the current line of "`sample`" by "`Sample`", enter

```
:s/sample/Sample/g
```

(Note: Do not confuse a `g` at the end of a command with the `:g` command, which is explained below.) This next example searches for all the occurrences of "`bad`", from the current line to the last line in the editing buffer, and replaces them with "`good`":

```
:.,$s/bad/good/g
```

The `g` ending is particularly useful when you have discovered that you have misspelled a word many times throughout the editing buffer. For example, the following command changes every occurrence of "`mispell`" to "`misspell`". (Remember, % specifies the entire editing buffer.)

```
:%s/mispell/misspell/g
```

There is one other way to modify a :s command. If you put c (confirm) at the end of the command, vi will ask you for permission before it makes each substitution.

For example, say that you want to search each line from 100 to 150. Many of these lines contain the string "bad". You want to replace the first occurrence of "bad" with "good" on some, but not all of these lines. Enter

```
:100,150s/bad/good/c
```

For each pattern that is matched, vi will display the line and show you where the pattern is. For example:

```
This is a bad line.
             ^ ^ ^
```

If you enter

```
y
```

(for "yes"), vi will make the replacement. If you enter anything else, such as simply pressing <Return>, vi will not make the replacement.

You can add both g and c, in any order, to the end of a :s command. For example, you want to search lines 100 through 150 and, subject to your confirmation, replace every occurrence of "bad" with "good". Enter

```
:100,150s/bad/good/cg
```

Here is a summary of how to use the :s command. Take a moment and make sure that you understand the different forms. Within the summary

line	represents a line number
pattern	represents a regular expression
replace	represents the characters to substitute for *pattern*

Here is the summary:

:s/*pattern*/*replace*/	substitute on current line
:*lines*/*pattern*/*replace*/	substitute on specified line
:*line*,*lines*/*pattern*/*replace*/	substitute over specified range

To replace all occurrences on the specified lines, put a g at the end of the command. To have vi ask you for confirmation before making a substitution, put a c at the end of the command.

Executing Commands Over a Range of Lines

The :g (global) command lets you search over a specified range of lines and select each line on which a particular pattern occurs. You can then execute an ex command on each of these lines.

The :g command looks like this:

:*line*,*line*g/*pattern*/*excom*

Here *line* is a line number, *pattern* is a regular expression, and *excom* is one or more ex commands. You can specify any ex command except another :g command.

If you specify more than one ex command, you must separate them with a | (vertical bar) character. If you find it easier to read, you can put space characters between the commands.

Here is an example. You want to replace each character "5" with the word "five" on every line, from lines 100 to 150, that has the word "number" in it. Enter

```
:100,150g/number/ s/5/five/g
```

Here is the same command, except that two substitutions are performed on each line: "5" is replaced by "five", and "6" is replaced by "six".

```
:100,150g/number/ s/5/five/g | s/6/six/g
```

Most ex commands will act on the current line if you do not specify any line numbers. The :g command—like the :w and :w! commands—will act on the entire editing buffer. For example, the following command replaces "5" by "five" on every line in the editing buffer that contains "number":

```
:g/number/ s/5/five/g
```

You will often find that the string you use for the :g command is the string you want to replace in a subsequent :s command. For your convenience, vi will consider that each unspecified search pattern has the value of the last pattern that was matched.

For example, throughout the entire editing buffer, you want to substitute each occurrence of "Peter" with "Harley". Here are three ways to do it:

```
:%s/Peter/Harley/g
:g/Peter/ s/Peter/Harley/g
:g/Peter/ s//Harley/g
```

In the last command, the search pattern for the :s command is not specified, so vi uses the last pattern that was matched. In this case, it is "Peter" from the :g command.

Sometimes, you will want a command to act on each line that does not contain a particular pattern. In such cases, use the :g! command. This command works exactly like :g except that it selects those lines that do not contain the specified pattern.

For example, to change "bad" to "good" everywhere in the editing buffer, except on those lines that do not contain the word "okay", enter

```
:g!/okay/ s/bad/good/g
```

Here is a summary of the :g and :g! commands. Take a moment to make sure you understand the different forms. Within the summary

pattern	represents a regular expression
excom	represents one or more **ex** commands, but not another :g or :g! command

If you specify more than one **ex** command, you must separate them with a | (vertical bar) character. You can put **space** characters between multiple **ex** commands to make them easier to read.

:g/*pattern*/*excom*	execute *excom* on lines containing *pattern*
:*line*,*lineg*/*pattern*/*excom*	same as :g over specified range
:g!/*pattern*/*excom*	execute *excom* on lines not containing *pattern*
:*line*,*lineg*!/*pattern*/*excom*	same as :g! over specified range

Note: You can undo all the effects of a :g command with a u (undo) command.

Matching and Substituting Complex Patterns

When you enter the :s and :g commands, you use a regular expression to specify the search pattern. In Chapter 26, you learned how regular expressions are used with vi. In this section, we will explain a few more ways to match patterns and to specify replacement text. These capabilities extend the power of the :s and :g commands.

When you specify the replacement text in an :s command, only two characters have special meaning: the ~ (tilde) and the & (ampersand). All other characters are taken literally. For example, consider the following command:

```
:s/^/^/
```

The first ^ character is in the search pattern, so it matches the beginning of the line. The second ^ character is in the replacement text, so it literally means "^". The effect of this command is to insert a "^" character at the beginning of the current line.

Within replacement text ~ (tilde) means the replacement from the previous :s command, and & (ampersand) means the characters that were matched by the :s command. This may seem complicated but a few examples will explain it all.

Say that you are typing a long dissertation in which the names "Felix" and "Felix the Cat" are used frequently. To make the job easier, you type F each time you want Felix, and c each time you want Felix the Cat. When you are finished, you can use the :s command to replace all the words consisting of F or c.

The following command replaces all the F words:

```
:%s/\<F\>/Felix/g
```

(Remember, % refers to the entire editing buffer.) Notice that we use \< and \> to make sure that we replace only whole words. Otherwise, we would accidentally replace all the F characters that were part of a word, such as RTFM.

When we make the next substitution—the one to replace the c words—we can use a ~ character to stand for the last replacement text, in this case, **Felix**:

```
:%s/\<C\>/~ the Cat/g
```

Here is an example that shows how to use an & character to stand for the pattern that was matched by the :s command. Say that you want to put parentheses around all the words that start with an upper-case letter. To match such a word, we would use

```
\<[A-Z].*\>
```

In other words, the beginning of a word, followed by any letter from A to Z, followed by zero or more occurrences of any letter, followed by the end of the word.

Here is the :s command to put parentheses around each such word in the editing buffer:

```
:s\<[A-Z].*\>/(&)/
```

See how easy it is when & stands for the pattern that has just been matched.

Sometimes you want to refer to only part of the pattern that has just been matched. In that case, you can divide the pattern into parts when you specify it. In the replacement text, you can refer to the first part as \1, the second part as \2, and so on. To divide a search pattern into parts, enclose each part in \(and \).

Here is an example. You want to search for all the strings that consist of one upper-case letter followed by a single digit—such as A5 or B9—and then reverse the two characters. The way to do it is to divide the search pattern into two parts. Part 1 will be the letter; Part 2 will be the number. You can then replace the pattern with Part 2 followed by Part 1. Here is the command:

```
:%s/\([A-Z]\)\([0-9]\)/\2\1/g
```

This sort of thing can become complicated. Here is another example using a command that would give most people nightmares. Read it slowly.

You want to search for any words that contain a hyphen and remove the hyphen. Before we start, let us recall that the - character has a special meaning within regular expressions. To use a - character literally, we must precede it with a \ (backslash):

```
\-
```

First, we cannot use a simple command such as

```
:%s/\-//g
```

to replace all the hyphens by nothing. Remember, we want to replace only - characters within words. We do not want to replace - characters that are used, say, as minus signs within arithmetic expressions. Let us assume that a nonhyphenated word consists of

the beginning of a word:	\<
followed by an upper- or lower-case letter:	[A-Za-z]
followed by zero or more lower-case letters:	[a-z]*
followed by the end of a word:	\>

Putting these components together into a regular expression, we get

```
\<[A-Za-z][a-z]*\>
```

We are interested in words that do have hyphens. Such words contain

the beginning of a word:	\<
followed by an upper- or lower-case letter:	[A-Za-z]
followed by zero or more lower-case letters:	[a-z]*
followed by a hyphen:	\-
followed by a lower-case letter:	[a-z]
followed by zero or more lower-case letters:	[a-z]*
followed by the end of a word:	\>

Putting these components together into a regular expression, we get

```
\<[A-Za-z][a-z]*\-[a-z][a-z]*\>
```

(One thing about regular expressions: they may seem complicated, but they are much better than regular English for describing patterns.)

To use this regular expression within an appropriate :s command, all we need to do is define two parts within the pattern:

Part 1: the letters before the hyphen
Part 2: the letters after the hyphen

The hyphen itself will not be inside a part. All we have to do is replace

Part 1, followed by a hyphen, followed by Part 2

with

Part 1 followed by Part 2

The following command does it all

```
:%s/\(\<[A-Za-z][a-z]*\)\-\([a-z][a-z]*\)\>/\1\2/g
```

We can analyze this command as follows:

ex command:	:
process all lines in editing buffer:	%
substitute:	s
start of search pattern:	/
beginning of Part 1:	\(
beginning of a word:	\<
one upper- or lower-case character:	[A-Za-z]
zero or more lower-case characters:	[a-z]*
end of Part 1:	\)
hyphen:	\-
beginning of Part 2:	\(
one lower-case character:	[a-z]
zero or more lower-case characters:	[a-z]*

end of Part 2:	\)
end of a word:	\>
end of search pattern, start of replacement:	/
Part 1:	\1
Part 2:	\2
end of replacement:	/
substitute all occurrences on a line:	g

Yes, it looks awful, but it works.

Most of the time, you will not need commands like this. But if someone gives you a file containing 10,000 words with superfluous hyphens, you will be glad that vi is so powerful.

Changing the Case of Character Strings

You can use the :s command to convert strings to upper or lower case. You do this by using the characters \u, \l, \U, \L, and \E in the replacement string.

The characters \u and \l cause the next character in the replacement string to be converted to upper or lower case, respectively. If the character is not a letter it is left unchanged.

For example, to convert the first character of every word that begins with a, b, or c to upper case, enter

```
:%s/\<[abc]/\u&/g
```

In this command

\<	matches the beginning of a word
[abc]	matches a or b or c
&	stands for the pattern that was just matched

By putting \u before the & character, we specify that the first character of the pattern that was just matched is to be converted to upper case.

The characters \U and \L cause all subsequent letters to be converted to upper or lower case, respectively. This continues until either the end of the string is reached or \E (end) is encountered.

Here is an example that converts the first word of every line to upper case. To start, a word can be defined as

the beginning of a word: \<
followed by any character not a `newline`:   .
followed by zero or more characters not a `newline`:   *
followed by the end of a word: \>

Putting these components together into a regular expression, we get

```
\<.*\>
```

The command we want is

```
:s/\<.*\>/\U&/
```

The `\U` means that all the following characters are to be converted to upper case. In this command, `\U` affects `&`, the pattern that has just been matched.

Here is an example that uses `\E`. This command searches for all the words `Unixsystem` or `unixsystem` and changes them to `UNIXsystem`.

The search pattern is divided into two parts: Part 1 will be the pattern `[Uu]nix`, Part 2 will be `system`. The conversion to upper case will be turned on for Part 1 and turned off for Part 2. The command is

```
:%s/\([Uu]nix\)\(system\)/\U\1\E\2/g
```

We can analyze this command as follows:

ex command:	:
process all the lines in editing buffer:	%
substitute:	s
start of search pattern:	/
beginning of Part 1:	\(
"U" or "u" followed by "nix":	[Uu]nix
end of Part 1:	\)
beginning of Part 2:	\(
"system":	system
end of Part 2:	\)
end of search pattern, start of replacement:	/
start: convert to upper case:	\U

Part 1:	\1
end: convert to upper case:	\E
Part 2:	\2
end of replacement:	/
substitute all occurrences on a line:	g

Using an Editing Script

Editing Script:
A text file that contains **ex** *commands.*

As you can see, it is not difficult to come up with complex **ex** commands to carry out specialized tasks. Occasionally, you will want to perform a series of such commands repeatedly. In such cases, it is frustrating and time consuming to enter the commands over and over.

Instead, you can create a file that contains these commands. Whenever you want, you can have **vi** read the file and execute the **ex** commands, just as if you had entered them from your terminal. Such a file is called an *editing script*. (We discussed the idea of scripts in Chapter 6.)

You can use **vi** to create an editing script. Insert each command, just as you want it to execute, and then save the file. You do not need to put a **:** in front of each command. When you want to execute the script, use the **:so** (source) command. Enter

```
:so
```

followed by the name of the file that holds the script. For example, to execute the commands in the file named **ex.commands**, enter

```
:so ex.commands
```

Here is an example of how you might use an editing script. You have several files in which you want to change the digits **0** through **9** to the words **zero** through **nine**. Create a file with these commands:

```
%s/0/zero/g
%s/1/one/g
%s/2/two/g
%s/3/three/g
%s/4/four/g
```

```
%s/5/five/g
%s/6/six/g
%s/7/seven/g
%s/8/eight/g
%s/9/nine/g
```

If you save this file under the name **number**, you can execute the commands by entering

```
:so number
```

Abbreviations

There will be times when you find yourself typing a long word or phrase over and over. In such cases, you can use the :ab command to set up an abbreviation. Whenever you type the abbreviation as a whole word, **vi** will automatically replace the abbreviation with what you want.

To set up an abbreviation, enter

```
:ab
```

followed by the short form, followed by the long form. For example, to abbreviate **Mxyzptlk** as **m**, enter

```
:ab m Mxyzptlk
```

The abbreviation does not have to resemble the long form it represents. For instance, you could use **m** as an abbreviation for

```
Sincerely yours,
```

vi ignores an abbreviation if you use it within a word. **vi** recognizes only those abbreviations that are preceded and followed by a **space**, **newline**, or punctuation character. Thus, if **m** is an abbreviation, the sequences

```
m<Space>
```

or

```
m<Return>
```

will be substituted; but both **m** characters in

```
marshmallow
```

will be ignored.

If you ever want to type an abbreviation as a word and you do not want it substituted, type **^v** before the character that follows the abbreviation. For example, if **m** is an abbreviation and you really want an "m" by itself, you can type

```
m^V<Space>
```

At any time, you can display a list of all the current abbreviations by entering

```
:ab
```

Abbreviations are lost when you stop **vi** but not when you start editing a new file.

If you want to cancel an abbreviation, use the **:una** (unabbreviate) command, followed by the abbreviation you want to cancel. For example, to cancel the abbreviation **m**, enter

```
:una m
```

Here is a summary of the **:ab** command. Take a moment now to make sure you understand how it works. Within this summary

short	represents the abbreviation
long	represents the string to be substituted

Here is the summary:

:ab *short long*	set *short* as an abbreviation for *long*
:ab	display current abbreviations
:uab *short*	cancel abbreviation *short*

Setting Up Your **vi** Working Environment Automatically

Every time **vi** starts, it looks for a file named **.exrc** in your home directory. If such a file exists, **vi** will execute each line in the file as an **ex** command. You can use an `.exrc` file to set up your working environment automatically. The name "exrc" stands for "**ex** run commands."

Another way to explain what happens is to say that if the file `.exrc` exists in your home directory, **vi** will perform the command

`:so` *home-directory*`/.exrc`

where *home-directory* is the path name of your home directory.

The great thing about the `.exrc` file is that you can use it to set up things exactly the way you want them. This is the place to put the `:set` and `:ab` commands that you use all the time. You can also put in Unix commands by using the `:!` command.

Within the `.exrc` file, any lines that begin with a **"** (double quote) character are ignored. Thus, you can put in descriptive comments. This is especially useful if you are using complicated commands. In addition, **space** and **tab** characters at the beginning of a line are ignored, so you can use indentations to make the file easier to read.

Here is a sample `.exrc` file:

```
" set the options
    set wm=5
    set number
    set window=10
" set abbreviations
    ab m Mxyzptlk
    ab sy Sincerely yours,
" display the date and time
    !date
```

If an `.exrc` file contains a bad command, **vi** will stop executing the file at that command. Although **vi** will start, the rest of the commands in the `.exrc` file will not be processed. **vi** will usually display an error message, but sometimes it will go by so fast that you miss it. Make sure that you test a new `.exrc` file carefully to make sure that all the commands execute properly.

One drawback to the `.exrc` file is that it is executed every time you start **vi**. You cannot use this file to set up an environment that you use occasionally. For example, there may be some option settings and abbreviations that you use when you are editing reports, but not otherwise. You don't want to put these commands in your `.exrc` file where they will be executed each time you use `vi`.

The solution is to put these commands in a separate file and access them with a `:so` (source) command. For example, you might put a set of commands in a file named `reports`. Whenever you edit a report, you can set up your environment by entering

```
:so reports
```

Although the `.exrc` file must be in your home directory, the `:so` command will look in any directory that you specify. For example:

```
:so /usr/harley/ex.scripts/reports
```

29

More About Entering Commands

Introduction

In Chapter 3, we explained how to enter commands. At the time, you learned three basic rules:

- To enter a command, you type the command and press <Return>.
- To type more than one command on the same line, separate commands with semicolons.
- You can type as fast as you want. The shell saves your input and processes the characters in the order they were received.

In this chapter, you will learn more about entering commands: how to type characters that have a special meaning, and the various ways in which you can combine commands in the same line.

As you read this chapter, you will find it helpful to try these new techniques for yourself. For this reason, we will start by describing two commands that are not only useful in their own right, but are especially good for experimenting.

Displaying a Set of Arguments:
The echo Command

You will remember that a command has three parts: the name, the options, and the arguments. In the command

```
ls -lF myfile yourfile
```

the command name is ls, the options are -lF, and the arguments are myfile and yourfile.

The echo command is straightforward: it reads and then outputs its arguments. For example, if you enter

```
echo hi there
```

you will see

```
hi there
```

There are two important uses for echo: First, you can place echo commands in shell scripts to send messages as the script executes. (Remember, a shell script is a set of Unix commands stored in a text file. When you execute the script, the shell processes the commands just as if you had entered them from your terminal.)

Within a shell script, you can use the echo command to display error messages or other information. Here are two typical echo commands:

```
echo The file you want cannot be found.
echo Data is processed, starting report generation.
```

The second important use for echo is to experiment: you can specify various types of arguments and see how they are interpreted by the shell. That is what we will be doing in this chapter.

The syntax of the echo command is

echo [-n] [*argument...*]

where *argument* is any argument you want. If you have more than one argument, use a space to separate them.

The action of echo is to write its arguments, separated by space characters and ending with a newline. That is, echo displays what you give it, and then returns the cursor to the beginning of the next line.

Although we won't use it in this chapter, the -n (no newline) option is useful in shell scripts. This option tells echo to refrain from writing a newline at the end of its output. The cursor will be left at the end of the line, just past the last character that was displayed. This is convenient when your shell script asks a question. For example:

```
echo -n Do you want to continue?
```

Displaying Large Characters:
The banner Command

The banner command is similar to the echo command in that they both display their arguments. banner, however, uses large characters. The output of this command is suitable for printing, if you need to make signs or banners.

The syntax of the banner command is

banner *argument...*

You can specify more than one argument. banner will display each one separately. Here is an example:

```
banner Yertle the Turtle
```

The output is

```
#       #
#    #   ######  #####   #####  #      ######
 # #     #       #    #  #   #  #      #
  #      #####   #    #  #   #  #      #####
  #      #       #####   #   #  #      #
  #      #       #   #   #   #  #      #
  #      ######  #    #  #      ######  ######

 #####   #    #  ######
     #   #    #  #
     #   ######  #####
     #   #    #  #
     #   #    #  #
     #   #    #  ######

#######
     #   #    #  #####   #####   #      ######
     #   #    #  #   #   #   #   #      #
     #   #    #  #   #   #   #   #      #####
     #   #    #  #####   #   #   #      #
     #   #    #  #   #   #   #   #      #
     #     ####  #   #   #      ######  ######
```

The number of characters that you can specify for each argument varies from system to system: with PC-based systems, each argument can be up to 10 characters long. banner will ignore any extra characters.

The type of characters we have shown here is an example of what is displayed by System V implementations of banner. BSD-based systems draw much larger characters, oriented sideways. Such banners look particularly nice when you print them on continuous computer paper. (For a discussion of System V and BSD Unix, see Chapter 10.)

Using echo and banner to See How the Shell Processes Arguments

When you enter a command line, the shell reads the name of the command, the options, and the arguments. One of the first things the shell does is examine the arguments. If necessary, the shell changes the arguments before passing them to the command.

For instance, say that you enter

```
ls -lF myfile yourfile
```

The shell executes the `ls` program and passes to it the options `-lF` and the arguments `myfile` and `yourfile`. If you enter

```
ls -lF *file
```

the shell first changes the argument before it is passed to the `ls` program. In this case, the argument `*file` is replaced by the names of all the files in the working directory that are matched by the regular expression "`*file`" (see Chapter 22)—that is, all the file names that end with the four characters "`file`".

Every time you enter a command, the shell examines the arguments for characters that have special meaning, like the "`*`". There will be times that you want to specify that such characters are not to be changed by the shell. For instance, you may want to use an argument `*file` in which the "`*`" is just an asterisk character, not part of a regular expression.

Quote:
Tells the shell to take one or more characters literally and not endow them special meaning.

In a sense, you need to be able to protect such characters from being changed by the shell. To do this, you *quote* the characters. This is a way of specifying to the shell that certain characters are to be taken literally and not endowed with special meaning.

In the next few sections, we will examine the three ways that you can quote characters in a command. As you read, you will probably want to test the examples for yourself. In order to do so, you can use either the `echo` or `banner` commands. The importance of these commands is that they display their arguments after they have been processed by the shell.

For example, say that you want to compare the effect of specifying an argument in each of these ways:

```
*file    "*file"    '*file'
```

All you have to do is use each argument in an `echo` command:

```
echo *file
echo "*file"
echo '*file'
```

and see what happens. The `echo` command will display its arguments just as it receives them. You will be able to see how, if at all, the shell has processed each argument.

If you decide that you need a little variety, you can use the **banner** command:

```
banner  *file
banner  "*file"
banner  '*file'
```

and the output will be in large letters.

In the following sections we will use `echo`, but feel free to try **banner** whenever you want.

Quoting with a Backslash

There are a group of characters that are interpreted by the shell in special ways. If you want one of these characters to be taken literally, you must quote it; otherwise, the shell will interpret the characters according to their special characteristics.

The characters that have special meaning are

```
;    &    (   )    |    ^    <    >
newline    space    tab
$    #    '    "    `    \    @
*    ?    [   ]    -    !
```

With the C-shell, the following characters are also special:

```
%    {   }    ~
```

There are three ways to quote a character. The simplest way is to precede the character with a \ (backslash). The shell recognizes a \ as meaning that the following character is to be taken literally.

For example, say that you enter:

```
echo  *
```

As you know, the shell will change the * into the names of all the files in your working directory (see Chapter 22). Say that you have three files in your working directory: `document`, `myfile`, and `yourfile`. The shell changes the previous command to

```
echo document myfile yourfile
```

Since the job of `echo` is to display its arguments, the result of this command is

```
document myfile yourfile
```

However, if you quote the * character:

```
echo \*
```

it is taken literally and has no special meaning. The output is

```
*
```

You can use the backslash to quote any character, including another backslash. Here is a second example. Normally, a semicolon separates more than one command on the same command line. For example:

```
echo line 1; echo line 2
```

produces

```
line 1
line 2
```

However, if you quote the semicolon, it loses its special meaning. The output of

```
echo line1\; echo line 2
```

is

```
line1; echo line 2
```

Here is another example. If you enter

```
echo Hello; date
```

you will see the output from two commands:

```
Hello
Mon Sep 10 20:10:59 PDT 1990
```

However, if you quote the semicolon

```
echo Hello\; date
```

you will see

```
Hello; date
```

If you want to use a \ character literally, use two \\'s in a row. For example, the output of

```
echo Here is the \\ character.
```

is

```
Here is the \ character.
```

One last example. In Chapter 8, we explained how the shell maintains variables that contain strings of characters. At the time, we described the variable $TERM, which contains the name of the type of terminal you are using. Another important variable is $HOME. When you log in, the shell initializes $HOME with the name of your home directory.

At any time, you can display the name of your home directory by entering

```
echo $HOME
```

Typical output would be

```
/usr/harley
```

However, if you quote the $ it loses its special value. The command

```
echo \$HOME
```

produces

```
$HOME
```

If you quote a character that has no special meaning, the quoting has no effect. Thus, the following two commands are equivalent:

```
echo Hello
echo \H\e\l\l\o
```

In both cases, the output is

```
Hello
```

Continuing Commands Onto More Than One Line

An important use of the backslash is to quote a `newline` in order to continue a command onto more than one line. To do this, type \ just before you press the <Return> key. For example:

```
echo line1\<Return>
```

The resulting `newline` loses its meaning as an end-of-line marker. As far as the shell is concerned, you have not yet entered a real `newline` and the command is not yet complete.

You can use this when you need to enter a complex command that is difficult to type as one long line. Simply break the command into several shorter lines. As you type, end all but the last line with \<Return>. This tells the shell that the command is to be continued onto the next line. After the last line, press <Return> as usual. The command will now be executed just as if you had entered it in one long line.

Here is an example. If you type

```
echo 0123456789<Return>
```

you will see

```
0123456789
```

Say that you want to split this command onto two lines. After the "5", type \<Return>:

```
echo 012345\<Return>
```

You can now enter the rest of the command:

```
6789<Return>
```

Since the `newline` at the end of the first line has been quoted, it loses its meaning. The shell ignores it and joins the two lines as if the command had been typed as one long line.

As you know, the shell displays a prompt when it is ready to accept a command. The prompt for the Bourne shell is $; the prompt for the C-shell is %; the prompt for the superuser is #.

Whenever you end a line with \<Return>, the Bourne shell displays a special prompt, > (greater-than sign). This tells you that the next line you type will be appended onto the end of the last line. This prompt is called the *secondary prompt*. In this context, the regular prompt ($ or #) is called the *primary prompt*.

Here is an example. The shell displays the primary prompt:

```
$
```

You type the first part of a command:

```
echo 012345\<Return>
```

The shell displays the secondary prompt:

```
>
```

You type the rest of the command:

```
6789<Return>
```

The shell puts together the two parts of the command, just as if you had entered

```
echo 0123456789
```

Secondary Prompt:
In the Bourne shell, a prompt (the > character) indicating that the current line is a continuation of the previous line.

Primary Prompt:
In the Bourne shell, the same as the regular shell prompt ($ for regular users, # for the superuser).

all on one line. On the screen, the whole thing looks like this:

```
$ echo 012345\
> 6789
```

And the output is

```
0123456789
```

The C-shell does not have a secondary prompt. When you con-tinue a command onto more the one line, there is no prompt after the first line. Our last example would look like this:

```
% echo 012345\
6789
```

There is one difference though. With the Bourne shell, a quoted **newline** is removed from the command. With the C-shell, a quoted **newline** is changed to a **space**. Thus, the output of the previous command is

```
012345 6789
```

Quoting with Single Quotes

There will be times when you will want to quote more than one character in a command. For example:

```
echo Do you want \$100 \(today\)\?
```

For convenience, you can enclose more than one character within a pair of single quotes. This is the same as if each charac-ter were quoted by a \. The last example, for instance, can be entered as

```
echo Do you want '$100 (today)?'
```

or

```
echo 'Do you want $100 (today)?'
```

This last command is the same as

```
echo \D\o\ \y\o\u\ \w\a\n\t\ \$\1\0\0\ \(\t\o\d\a\y\)\?
```

Remember, quoting has no effect with a character that does not have a special meaning.

Within a string of characters that is quoted with single quotes, a \ character has no special meaning. For example, the output of

```
echo 'Here is a \ character.'
```

is

```
Here is a \ character.
```

With the Bourne shell, placing a `newline` inside of single quotes acts much like quoting the `newline` with a \ character. If you enter a quote and then press <Return> before entering the second quote, the shell will continue the command onto the following line. For instance:

```
$ echo 'This command consists
> of two lines.'
```

There is one difference, though, compared to using a \ character. When the shell sees a `newline` inside of quotes, it inserts an actual `newline` into the command line. Thus, the output of the previous command is

```
This command consists
of two lines.
```

When you quote a `newline` with a \ character, the shell removes it. The output of

```
$ echo This command does not consist \
> of two lines.
```

is

```
This command does not consist of two lines.
```

What happens when you quote a **newline** character?

	Bourne Shell	*C-Shell*
\\<Return>:	continues line	continues line replaced by **space**
'<Return>':	continues line replaced by **newline**	not allowed
"<Return>":	continues line replaced by **newline**	not allowed

Figure 29.1 *Quoting a* **newline***.*

With the C-shell, single quotes cannot be continued onto more than one line. If you enter a line like

```
% echo 'This command consists
```

you will see an error message:

```
Unmatched '.
```

telling you that a single quote was left unmatched. If you want to continue a line with the C-shell, you must use \\<Return>.

For reference, Figure 29.1 summarizes how each of the two shells handles a quoted **newline**. Notice that, in this context, single quotes work the same as double quotes (which are explained in the next section).

Quoting with Double Quotes

The **"** (double quote) character can be used in place of the **'** (single quote), with one difference: when you quote an argument with **"** characters, the **$** (dollar sign) and **è** (backquote) characters retain their special meanings.

Earlier, we mentioned that certain names, when preceded by a **$**, are given a value by the shell. We used the example $HOME, which has the value of the name of your home directory.

You can see the difference between double and single quotes by entering the following two commands:

```
echo 'My home directory is $HOME.'
echo "My home directory is $HOME."
```

In the first command, all the characters are quoted. The $ has no special meaning and the output is

```
My home directory is $HOME.
```

In the second command, the $ retains its special meaning as it is quoted within double quotes. The output will display the name of your home directory:

```
My home directory is /usr/harley.
```

Aside from the $ character, the only other character that retains its meaning within double quotes is ` (the backquote). As we will see in the next section, the ` character is not a real quote character and is used only occasionally.

Overall, we suggest the following guideline:

RULE

As a habit, use \ (backslash) or a pair of ' (single quote) characters for quoting arguments. Use " (double quote) characters only when you specifically want to preserve the meaning of $ (dollar sign) or ` (backquote).

Command Substitution Using Backquotes

Command Substitution:
In a command line, a command enclosed in ` (backquote) characters. (The enclosed command is executed and replaced by its output before the entire command line is processed.)

The ` (backquote) character looks like a quoting character but it is not. It is used to specify *command substitution*. Here is how it works:

Within a command line, you can enclose a command in backquotes. The shell will execute this command and then replace it by its output. Only then is the original command line processed.

Here is an example. You enter

```
echo The time is `date`.
```

Before the `echo` command is processed, the shell will execute the `date` command and replace it with its output. As an intermediate step, the `echo` command becomes

```
echo The time is Tue Sep 11 10:51:14 PDT 1990.
```

The overall output of the `echo` command looks like this:

```
The time is Tue Sep 11 10:51:14 PDT 1990.
```

As we mentioned above, quoting with double quotes preserves the special value of backquotes. Quoting with a backslash or with single quotes causes the backquotes to be taken literally.

For example, the two commands

```
echo 'The date *today* is `date`.'
echo The date \*today\* is \`date\`.
```

both produce the following output:

```
The date *today* is `date`.
```

Within double quotes

```
echo "The date *today* is `date`."
```

the special value of the backquotes is preserved and the command substitution takes place. The output looks like this:

```
The date *today* is Tue Sep 11 10:58:17 PDT 1990.
```

Command substitution is often used within shell scripts. Here are several commands that you might put in a shell script to display general information.

```
echo The time is `date`.
echo Your userid is `logname`.
echo Your working directory is `pwd`.
echo This directory has `ls | wc -l` files.
```

The output of these commands looks like this:

```
The time is Tue Sep 11 11:04:54 PDT 1990.
Your userid is harley.
Your working directory is /usr/harley.
This directory has 10 files.
```

Note: The last command sends the output of the `ls` command (the names of the files in the working directory) to the `wc` command to be counted. We will discuss such constructions in Chapter 30.

Entering Background Commands

In Chapter 7, we discussed processes and the `ps` (process status) command. Later, in Chapter 12, we discussed the `ps` command in more detail. As we explained, whenever you enter a command, the shell starts a process to execute that command. The process is known by an identification number called a processid.

In most cases, all the input and output are associated with your terminal. The process reads from your keyboard and writes to your display; this allows the program to be interactive.

Under certain conditions, you may want a program to run by itself. For instance, say that you enter a command that reads a large file, sorts it, and writes the output to another file. It may take a long time for the sort to complete, and there is no reason to tie up your terminal while you wait.

Foreground:
Describes a process that, while executing, reads from and writes to the terminal.

Background:
Describes a process that executes on its own, without input from the terminal.

When a process uses your terminal for input and output, we say that it executes in the *foreground*. When a process runs on its own, not reading from the terminal, we say that it executes in the *background*. Since background processes cannot read from the terminal, they cannot be interactive. The sorting example we just mentioned would be a good process to run in the background.

Whenever you enter a command in the regular manner, the command runs in the foreground. However, if you end the command with an `&` (ampersand) character, the command runs in the background.

Here is an example. The following command will sort a file named `bigfile`, and write the sorted output to a file named `sorted.file`:

```
sort bigfile >sorted.file
```

(You will meet the `sort` command in Chapter 31. You will learn how to redirect output to a file in Chapter 30.)

If you enter this command as is, it will run in the foreground. As the process executes, your terminal will be tied up waiting for the `sort` program to finish. To run the program in the background, add an `&` to the end of the command:

```
sort bigfile >sorted.file &
```

The shell will start the `sort` program in the background. Once it starts, which takes only a moment, the shell will display a new prompt. You can now enter another command.

Terminating Background Processes: The `kill` Command

To specify that a command should run in the background, you add an `&` character to the end of the command. In the previous section, we used the example

```
sort bigfile >sorted.file &
```

to run the `sort` program as a background process.

With a regular foreground process, you can stop the program by pressing the `intr` key. (Usually, this is <Delete> or `^D`; see Chapter 9.) With a background process you do not have direct control—once the process starts, it is off and running by itself. However, you can stop a background process if you know its identification number, the processid.

Whenever you enter a background command, the shell will display its processid. For instance, if you enter the previous `sort` command you might see

```
223
```

This means that the shell has started the command as a background process and has assigned it processid `223`. If you forget a particular processid, you can display it using the `ps` (process status) command that we covered in Chapters 7 and 12.

In order to stop a background process, you use the `kill` command. The syntax is

```
kill [-signal] processid...
```

Signal:
A message, identified by a number, sent to a process that notifies the process that a specific event has occurred.

The purpose of the `kill` command is to send a *signal* to the process whose processid you specify. For example, to send signal number **9** to the process with processid **223**, enter

```
kill -9 223
```

A signal notifies a process that a particular type of event has occurred. Modern System V Unix recognizes 27 different signals, each of which is identified by a number. In practice, there are only two signals you need to know about: **15** and **9**.

Signal **15** is the `terminate` signal. It tells a process to stop. If you use the `kill` command without specifying a signal number, **15** is taken as a default. Thus, if you want to terminate the process whose processid is **223**, the following two commands are equivalent:

```
kill 223
kill -15 223
```

Under certain circumstances, a process can ignore a `terminate` signal. To stop such a process, you must send signal number **9**, the `kill` signal. Signal number **9** cannot be ignored—it provides a sure kill.

We can summarize the killing of a process as follows:

 RULE   To terminate a background process, use

kill *processid*

If this does not work, use

kill -*9 processid*

Unix allows you to kill only those processes that were started under the auspices of your own userid. The superuser, however, can kill any process in the system.

As a convenience, the Bourne shell, but not the C-shell, will allow you to specify a processid of **0** (zero) to refer to all of the processes that you started since you last logged in. Thus, with the Bourne shell, you can clear out all your background processes by entering

```
kill 0
```

Do not use the -9 option with a processid of 0:

```
kill -9 0
```

Regardless of which shell you are using, this command will instantly terminate your main shell and you will be logged off.

So far, we have mentioned signals 9 and 15. As a point of interest, when you press the intr key to stop a foreground process, you generate signal number 2. This signal is disabled for background processes.

Specifying Priorities: The nice Commands

Unix allows many processes to be active at the same time. However, only one process at a time can actually execute. Unix automatically schedules all the processes so that they share the computer. As far as you are concerned, your programs run from start to finish. In reality, Unix stops and starts your program according to a complicated scheduling system.

For example, say that you start a program that requires 10 seconds of computer time. Unix will allot those 10 seconds in many short fractions of a second. In between, other programs will have a chance to execute. So, although your program requires only 10 seconds, it may take, say, 20 seconds for it to receive that much time.

Priority:

A number from 0 to 39, assigned to a process that indicates the preference that the process should be alloted by Unix; the lower the number, the greater the preference.

Unix assigns each process a number from 0 to 39, called a *priority*. Processes with lower numbers receive preference when it comes to allocating the resources of the computer. For example, on a busy system, a process with priority 0 will finish much faster than a process with priority 39. (This can be confusing—just remember, the lower the number, the higher the preference.) Unix continually examines and changes priorities to meet the needs of the system.

When you enter a command, it is automatically started at priority 20. You can enter a command with a different starting priority by using the nice command. The syntax is

nice [-*increment*] *command*

where *increment* is a number between 1 and 19, and *command* is a Unix command.

The shell will start the command you specify at a priority of 20 + the number you specify. For example, if you specify an increment of 5, the command will start with priority 25. If you do not specify an increment, the shell will use a default value of 10. That is, the command will be started with a priority of 30 (20 + 10).

Here is an example using a command that we mentioned earlier. You want to sort a very large file named bigfile, and write the output to a file named sorted.file. Running the sort program on a large file, even in the background, can slow down the whole system. To avoid this, you can use the nice command to start sort in such a way that it receives low preference as it executes.

You enter

```
nice -19 sort bigfile >sorted.file &
```

This command starts the sort program in the background, with a priority of 39 (20 + 19). Using this priority avoids a slowdown because Unix gives preference to the other processes.

RULE

To keep a time-consuming program from tying up the whole system, run the program in the background with a high priority value (low preference).

For regular users, the nice command enables you to request a lower preference only. However, if you are the superuser, you can request a higher preference by specifying a negative increment. This results in a lower priority number, which means a higher preference.

For example, say that you are the superuser and you want to run the sort command with higher than normal preference. Enter

```
nice --15 sort bigfile >sorted.file &
```

In this case, you specified an increment of -15, which results in a priority of 20 + (-15), that is, 5. This will cause the command to execute faster than if it had started at the usual priority of 20.

Conditional Execution Using && and ||

There are three ways that you can enter a sequence of commands as part of the same command line. First, as we described in Chapter 3, you can enter more than one command separated by semicolons. The commands will be executed, one after the other, just as if you had entered them on separate lines.

For example

```
sort bigfile >temp; mv temp bigfile
```

These commands sort the contents of the file named bigfile, placing the results in a file named temp. Next, the file named temp is renamed to bigfile. The net result is that the contents of bigfile are sorted.

The second way to enter a sequence of commands is to separate the commands with && (two ampersand characters). This tells the shell to execute the second command only if the first command completed successfully.

For example, you enter

```
sort bigfile >temp && mv temp bigfile
```

This tells the shell to execute the mv command, but only if the preceding sort command has terminated successfully. If an unforeseen event occurs and the sort command encounters an error, you will not have to worry about your original file being replaced with bad data.

The third way to specify a sequence of commands is to separate them with || (two vertical bars). This tells the shell to execute the second command only if the first command fails.

For example, you enter

```
sort bigfile >temp || echo The sort command failed.
```

In this case, the echo command will display an error message, but only if the sort command terminates abnormally.

Like ; (the semicolon), you can use && and || more than once on the same command line. For instance, say that `get.data`, `process.data`, `make.report`, and `print.report` are four shell scripts that start big programs. You want to execute each script in sequence, but only if the preceding programs terminate successfully. Enter

```
get.data && process.data && make.report && print.report
```

30

Controlling Input/Output and Combining Commands

Introduction

By now, you have learned a lot about using commands. However, using Unix well involves more than entering one command after another. The real power of Unix lies in controlling the input and output and in combining commands. In this chapter, you will learn how to apply these techniques to build your own custom-designed tools.

To start, let's examine how Unix deals with input and output, and take a look at what you can do to control what happens.

Standard Input, Standard Output, and Standard Error

Standard Input:
The basic source from which Unix programs read their input.

As a general design principle, all Unix commands and programs read their input from a source that is called the *standard input*. When a program starts, the standard input is assigned to a particular file which will be the actual source of the input data.

As a default, the standard input is assigned to the special file that represents the keyboard of your terminal. (As we explained in Chapter 16, special files represent hardware devices.) In other words, by default, all Unix commands and programs read from the keyboard.

Standard Output:
The basic target to which Unix programs write their output.

With respect to output, the situation is similar. However, there are two general-purpose output targets. The *standard output* represents the usual target to which commands and programs write their output. The *standard error* represents a second target to which commands and programs write error messages.

Standard Error:
The output target to which Unix programs write error messages.

By default, the standard output and standard error both write to the special file that represents the screen of your terminal. That is, by default, commands and programs write their output to your terminal.

Most of the time, you will accept the defaults; the programs you run will read from your keyboard and write to your screen. This is what allows programs to be interactive. However, on occasion, you will want to change the input source or the output target. When you do this, we say that you *redirect* the standard input, standard output, or standard error.

Redirect:
To reassign the standard input, standard output, or standard error to a specified file.

When you change the output target, you need both standard output and standard error to make sure that you do not miss error messages. Here is an example. You run a program with the standard output redirected to a text file. This means that all of the usual output will be written to this file. Now, say that something goes wrong and the program writes an important error message. If there were only one type of output, the error message would go to the text file. However, error messages are written to the standard error file, not to the standard output; and the standard error was not redirected. Thus, no matter where the regular output goes, you will still see your error messages.

Although it is possible to redirect the standard error, most people usually leave it alone. You don't want to take a chance that you will ever miss an important message.

To redirect input and output, you specify the name of the file which will be the source or target. This file can be an ordinary file or a special file. As we explained in Chapter 16, special files represent physical devices. Thus, to send the output of a command or program to a device, simply redirect the standard output to the special file that represents that device.

Redirecting the Standard Input

To redirect the standard input for a command, type the command, followed by a < (less than) character, followed by the name of the input file.

For example, say that the file `ex.script` contains a number of `ex` commands that you want to use to edit a file named `document`. As we explained in Chapter 28, a file containing such commands is called an editing script.

Use an `ex` command with the name of the file you want to edit, and redirect the standard input to the file that holds the editing script. Enter

```
ex document <ex.script
```

`ex` will edit the file `document`. However, instead of reading commands from the keyboard, `ex` will take its input from `ex.script`.

When you redirect the standard input, the input file must already exist. If it does not, Unix will display an error message. For instance, if you enter the previous command and the file `ex.script` does not exist, you will see

```
ex.script: cannot open
```

Redirecting the Standard Output

To redirect the standard output for a command, type the command, followed by a > (greater-than) character, followed by the name of the output file.

Here is an example. You want to make a long listing of your working directory and store the output in a file named `directory`. Enter

```
ls -l >directory
```

There will be no output to your terminal. But after the command finishes, the file `directory` will contain the output. You can display the output by using the `more` or `pg` commands (see Chapter 23):

```
more directory
pg directory
```

You can redirect output to a file even if the file does not already exist. If this is the case, Unix will create the file for you. If you redirect output to a file that does exist, its contents will be replaced. Once this happens, the original contents of the file are gone for good.

Be careful; do not make a mistake and redirect output to a file that contains important data. Once you press <Return> the data is gone. Here is why:

When you enter a command line that redirects input or output, the shell sets up the input and output files before it starts the command. Thus, by the time the command starts, any data in the output file is already gone. If you do not have a backup, there is no way to get it back.

Here is an example from Chapter 23. In this example the file info contains a lot of data. The files info1, info2, and info3 each contain a small amount of data. The intention is to write the data in these three files onto the end of info.

The example uses the cat command to combine all four files and then redirect the standard output to info:

```
cat info info1 info2 info3 >info
```

What really happens, however, is that Unix first clears the output file info. Then, the standard output is redirected to this file. Thus, before the command even starts, all the data in the info is wiped out.

Appending to the Standard Output

When you use a > character to redirect the standard output, any data that is in the output file is replaced. If you want to append output to the end of the file, use >> instead. If the output file does not exist, the shell will create the file for you.

For example, say that the file directory exists and contains data. If you enter

```
ls -l >directory
```

the output of the ls -l command replaces the data in the file named directory. If you enter

```
ls -l >>directory
```

the output of the **ls -l** command will be appended to the end of the file named **directory**. The existing data will not be lost.

  In the last section, we examined the command

```
cat info info1 info2 info3 >info
```

from Chapter 23. The purpose of the command was to combine the data in all four files. Unfortunately, the command had the side effect of erasing the data in the output file **info**. However, by appending to **info**, we can achieve the desired result:

```
cat info1 info2 info3 >>info
```

  The **>>** construction is useful for accumulating data into a master file. For example, say that you have a program named **status** that checks the status of your system and generates a short report. You want to run this program at intervals and accumulate the reports in a file named **log**. Use

```
status >>log
```

The first time you enter this command, the shell will create the output file **log**. Once the file exists, each execution of the command will append data to the file. However, be careful. If you make a mistake and enter

```
status >log
```

you will wipe out all the data that has accumulated.

Redirecting Standard Error

Usually, all output from a Unix program is written to the standard output. However, some messages are so important that they should not be redirected away from your screen.

  For example, say that you are running a program whose output is to be redirected to a text file. If, in the middle of the program, the output fails—say, the disk becomes full—you would want to know about it.

For this reason Unix supports two types of output: standard output and standard error. Unix programmers write their programs so that any crucial messages are written to the standard error.

You can redirect the standard error, although it is usually not a good idea. To do so, use **2>** followed by the name of the output file. For example, say that you want to execute a program named **status**. You want the standard output to go to a file named **log**, and the standard error to go to a file named **errors**. Use

```
status >log 2>errors
```

Once the program finishes, you can check for errors by displaying the **errors** file. Use either of these commands:

```
more errors
pg errors
```

(The **more** and **pg** commands are described in Chapter 23.)

On occasion, you may want to redirect both the standard output and the standard error to the same file. In this case, use

```
2>&1
```

For example, to redirect both the standard output and the standard error to a file named **log**, use

```
status >log 2>&1
```

In this context, the "**&1**" represents the standard output. Thus, **2>&1** tells the shell to redirect the standard error to the same file as the standard output.

Like the standard output, you can append the standard error to a file by using **>>**. Here is an example:

```
status >>log 2>>errors
```

| RULE | Do not redirect the standard error unless you have a good reason. |

Redirecting to and from Devices

As we explained in Chapter 16, physical devices are represented by special files. In Chapter 17, we saw that most of these special files lie in the /dev directory.

For the most part, you will not need to use special files; they are usually used by system programs. However, you may want to reference the special files that represent the terminals. On most Unix systems, these files are /dev/console, /dev/tty00, /dev/tty01, /dev/tty02, and so on.

If you want to find out the name of the special file that represents your terminal, use the tty command. If you want to find out the names of the terminals that are currently active, use the ps or whodo commands. (All of these commands are discussed in Chapter 12.)

Using a special file, it is possible to redirect input or output to a device. Here is an example.

You are logged in as userid harley. You want to send a mysterious message to a friend whose userid is kevin. First, you need to find out if kevin is logged in. Use the who command (see Chapter 7):

```
who
```

You see

```
harley     console     Sep 12 13:55
peter      tty00       Sep 12 14:01
addie      tty01       Sep 12 16:10
kevin      tty02       Sep 12 19:48
```

kevin is logged in at terminal tty02.

One way to send kevin a message is to use the write command (see Chapter 14). However, if you do, kevin's terminal will display a line that starts with:

```
Message from harley...
```

and you want your message to be mysterious. So, you decide to write your message directly to terminal **tty02**—that way there will be no clues as to origin of the message.

To write to this terminal, you can enter a command and redirect the standard output to the special file that represents the terminal. In this case, that file is **/dev/tty02**.

The **echo** command will do the job. Here is what it looks like:

```
echo Kevin, can you guess where I am? >/dev/tty02
```

At **kevin**'s terminal, the following message

```
Kevin, can you guess where I am?
```

will appear suddenly out of nowhere, scaring Kevin into an early decline.

Note: If **kevin** has used the **mesg** command to specify that he does not want messages (see Chapter 13), the special file **/dev/tty02** will be off limits and the shell will not be able to redirect the standard output. You will see the error message

```
/dev/tty02: cannot create
```

Of course, our example is somewhat frivolous, but it does illustrate how to use a special file to access a device directly. However, be aware that reading or writing a special file directly should be done with caution. Almost all of the time, it is better to use regular commands that are programmed to deal with the idiosyncrasies of actual devices.

In particular, do not try to read or write directly to a disk. If you are a regular user, you will be denied permission. If you are the superuser, the results will be unpredictable and you may end up causing a great deal of trouble.

Using the Empty File: /dev/null

There is one special file that provides a highly useful function. The file is **/dev/null**. As the name implies, this file is empty.

How can an empty file be useful?

The **/dev/null** file is maintained by Unix and has a strange property: No matter how much data you write to the file, it is always empty. (The principle is a lot like loaning money to a relative.)

In other words, any output you send to **/dev/null** is thrown away. This is useful when you run a program that generates output that you want to ignore.

Here is an example. You have an editing script named **ex.script** that you wish to use to edit a file named **document**. Normally, you would enter

```
ex document <ex.script
```

However, as **ex** executes, it generates some messages that you would rather not see. To get rid of the messages, send them to the empty file:

```
ex document <ex.script >/dev/null
```

You can, of course, redirect the standard error to **/dev/null**. However, be careful: All your error messages will be lost.

If you are a DOS user, you may be familiar with the NUL: device. This device works much like **/dev/null**. For instance, you can copy a file without looking at the messages by using

```
COPY OLDFILE NEWFILE > NUL:
```

What is less well known is that DOS has an undocumented file that works the same as NUL:—the name of this file is \DEV\NUL. That is, the following DOS command is equivalent to the previous one:

```
COPY OLDFILE NEWFILE > \DEV\NUL
```

Even if you do not have a DOS directory named \DEV, you can still send output to \DEV\NUL. (Notice the spelling, only a single "L" in "NUL".)

Where did this name come from? From the same operating system that inspired the DOS tree-structured file system, the redirection of input and output, and many other DOS features:
Unix.

Hint
••••

DOS users:

The empty file `/dev/null` works much like the DOS NUL: device.

Filters and Pipes

Filter:

Any program that reads from the standard input and writes to the standard output.

Any program that reads from the standard input and writes to the standard output is called a *filter*. The importance of filters is that they can be combined. Data can be passed from one filter to another, each filter acting as a tool to perform a particular task. Most Unix commands are filters because, wherever possible, Unix programs are written to use the standard input and output.

Here is an example of how you might combine two filters, the `nl` (line numbering) command and the `more` command. You have two long files, `doc1` and `doc2`, that together hold one long document. You want to peruse the data in these files so you can make notes about possible changes.

First, you use the `cat` command to join the contents of the two files into one long stream of data. Next, you send the output of `cat` to the `nl` filter to number each line. Finally, you send the output of `nl` to the `more` filter so you can display the output, one screenful at a time.

Pipeline:

An arrangement in which data passes, in sequence, through a series of programs.

In other words, you combine filters by joining the standard output of one program to the standard input of the next program. Such an arrangement is called a *pipeline* (although an assembly line would be a better analogy). The mechanism that connects adjacent parts of a pipeline is called a *pipe*.

Pipe:

The mechanism that joins two adjacent programs, by connecting the standard output of one program to the standard input of the next program. (Can be used as a verb.)

One way to create a pipeline is to use temporary files to hold the data as it is passed from one program to the next. For instance, we can implement our example by using the following commands:

```
cat doc1 doc2 >temp1
nl <temp1 >temp2
more <temp2
rm temp1 temp2
```

The first command combines the two data files and stores the results in a temporary file named `temp1`. The second command reads from this file, adds line numbers, and stores the results in a second temporary file named **temp2**. The third command reads from the second temporary file and displays the data, one screenful at a time. The final command removes the two temporary files.

As a convenience, the shell makes it easy to create pipelines. It does this by handling all the details for you—including moving the data from one program to another. All you need to do is list the programs, one after the other, separated by the | (vertical bar) character. For example:

```
cat doc1 doc2 | nl | more
```

The | character is sometimes called a "pipe symbol." It tells the shell to connect the standard output of a command to the standard input of the next command. In other words, the | character represents a pipe.

The word *pipe* is often used as a verb, to describe this process. For instance, we might say, "To display the results, pipe the output of **nl** to **more**."

The Importance of Pipelines

The importance of pipelines cannot be overstated: the capability to combine tools is one of the main reasons why Unix is so powerful. Because it is so easy to create pipelines, each command can be designed to do one job only. If you want to perform a complex task, you can combine several simple tools.

For instance, when you write a Unix program, you do not need to concern yourself with how the user will display the output—just make sure that your program writes to the standard output. You know that when the user runs your program, he can display the output by piping it to **more**.

The Unix philosophy suggests that you should solve problems, whenever possible, by combining existing tools, not by writing new programs. This is one of the reasons why Unix comes with so many built-in utilities: most of the common problems have already been solved.

RULE	To solve a problem, it is better to combine existing tools than to write a new program.

Using the standard Unix utilities, it is possible to solve many, many different types of problems by constructing pipelines. To give you a feeling for how this is done, here are a few examples.

To display the number of files in a directory, use **wc** to count the number of lines in the output of the **ls** command:

```
ls | wc -l
```

If you have 10 files in your working directory, the output of this pipeline is simple:

```
10
```

In Chapter 29, we embedded this pipeline within an **echo** command by using command substitution:

```
echo This directory has `ls | wc -l` files.
```

The output of this command looks like this:

```
This directory has 10 files.
```

Here is another example. To count how many users are currently logged in on your system, enter:

```
who | wc -l
```

Finally, here is a longer, more complex pipeline that uses the **grep** and **sort** programs (which we will meet in Chapter 31.)

grep searches a file and extracts all of the lines that contain a particular pattern of characters. **sort** reads a file and writes the data, sorted alphabetically. Both of these programs are filters.

Here is the problem: You have three files that contain mailing lists: **old**, **new**, and **extra**. You want to look at all the lines in these three files that contain the word "**Albuquerque**". Use the following pipeline:

```
cat old new extra | grep Albuquerque | sort | more
```

Here is how it works: First, the `cat` command combines all the data in the three files. Next, the `grep` command extracts all the lines that contain the required word. Next, the `sort` command sorts these lines into alphabetical order. Finally, the `more` command displays the results.

Having studied these examples, let us reconsider the question, What is a filter?

A filter is a program that reads data from the standard input, does something with the data, and then writes the resulting data to the standard output. Now you can see why the idea of filters is so important and why such programs naturally fit together in a pipeline.

A related question is, What is the simplest possible filter? The answer is, Whatever program copies its data from an input source to an output target without making any changes. Do you recognize this program? It's the `cat` command.

And where did the `cat` command come from? It was created on purpose because the designers of Unix realized that, somewhere in the grand scheme, the simplest possible filter was a necessity.

By now, you should be starting to appreciate that Unix is a well-designed system of tools. The basic commands were developed to fit together and to form as complete a toolbox as most people need.

Using a Tee to Split a Pipe

TEE:

A filter that reads data from the standard input, copies the data to a file, and then writes the data, unchanged, to the standard output.

If the `cat` command is the simplest possible filter, the `tee` command is the next simplest. A *tee* is a filter that reads from the standard input, copies the data to a file, and then writes it, unchanged, to the standard output. A tee allows you to copy the data in a pipeline without disturbing the flow.

The syntax for the `tee` command is

```
tee [-a] [file...]
```

The standard input is copied to the file you specify. If you specify more than one file, `tee` will make more than one copy.

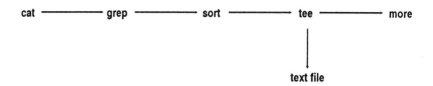

Figure 30.1 *An example of how data flows through a pipeline and a tee.*

Here is an example. In the previous section, we used the following pipeline to combine three files and then extract, sort, and display those lines that contained a certain word.

```
cat old new extra | grep Albuquerque | sort | more
```

Suppose that you want to save a copy of the sorted output before it is displayed. You want the copy to be stored in a file named **A.list**. Use the **tee** command as follows:

```
cat old new extra | grep Albuquerque | sort | tee A.list | more
```

After the data leaves **sort**, it is copied to the file **A.list** before it is sent, unchanged, to **more**.

Figure 30.1 shows how the data flows in this pipeline. Notice that the part of the diagram between **sort** and **more** has the shape of a capital "T." Hence, the name "tee."

When you use a tee to copy data to a file, the shell will create the file if it does not already exist. However, if the file does exist, its data will be overwritten. If you want to add data to an existing file, use **tee** with the **-a** (append) option.

For example, the following pipeline displays the number of userids that are currently logged in. Within the pipe, a copy of the data is appended to a file called **master.log**:

```
who | tee -a master.log | wc -l
```

Why Does Unix Have So Many More Filters Than DOS?

One of the big differences between DOS and Unix is that DOS has very few filters. DOS does have pipelines, but the operating system proper comes with only three filters, FIND, MORE, and

SORT; moreover, these filters are much less powerful than their Unix counterparts.

Within DOS, it is possible to create filters. All you have to do is design programs that read from the standard input and write to the standard output. However, it is not part of the DOS culture to design in this manner and, as a result, DOS utility programs cannot be combined.

To understand why this is so, we need to appreciate the environments in which DOS and Unix were developed.

DOS was developed as a single-user operating system for PCs. With a PC, each user has his own display, attached directly to the system unit. From the beginning, DOS programmers used the entire screen to display output. Unfortunately, the early PCs were slow; programmers found that when they wrote to the standard output it took too long for the display to be updated.

To solve this problem, DOS programmers bypassed the standard output and sent data directly to the display hardware. This made it possible to write quickly to any part of the screen. However, this practice also made it impossible for the output of one program to be connected to the input of another program.

Today, there are many wonderful DOS tools, some of which are unsurpassed in the entire world of computing. But filters are not part of the DOS culture and, for the most part, DOS tools cannot be combined.

Unix, on the other hand, was developed using terminals that printed one line at a time. From the beginning, the idea of standard output was an integral part of the operating system. Since there was no way to access an entire display screen, there was no advantage in bypassing the standard output. Thus, using standard input and standard output became the norm.

The result is an environment that provides many small tools which are designed to be combined. However, Unix tools do lack the look and feel of DOS tools. Since most Unix programs write to the standard output, they cannot take advantage of the entire screen. Even with today's high-speed computers and displays, most Unix programs write their output one line at a time, just as they did in the days of the slow, line-oriented terminals.

In Chapter 1, we explained that an operating system has two main purposes:

1. to manage the computer's hardware resources efficiently.
2. to make it easy for you to use the computer.

Operating systems are not developed in a vacuum—they are developed in order to manage specific hardware. The nature of an operating system depends a great deal on what hardware was used by the programmers who created the initial design.

What is important is that we are shaped by our tools. How we think depends on what we are thinking about. When we solve a problem with Unix, we think differently than when we solve a problem with DOS. As you learn to use the Unix tools and how to build pipelines, your approach to problem solving will change.

RULE

The fundamental relationship between our hardware and how we think can be expressed as follows:

hardware → operating system → tools → how we think

31

Searching, Sorting, and Comparing

Introduction

Unix offers a variety of commands that enable you to search and sort using the data in text files. In this chapter, we will cover these commands. You will find them to be essential additions to your toolbox.

As you read the examples, notice how the basic operations can be combined to perform many different types of tasks.

Searching for a PATTERN: The `grep` Command

Unix has a family of commands that will search text files for a specified pattern. These commands are named `grep`, `egrep`, and `fgrep`. Here is where the name comes from:

`grep` stands for "global regular expression print":

global refers to the fact that these programs search an entire file, much like `vi`'s `:g` command

regular expression tells us that we specify the search pattern by using a regular expression *print* shows us that the purpose of the command is to display all the lines that contain the search pattern (remember, in the Unix tradition, "print" means "display")

In other words, `grep` searches an entire file for the pattern specified by a regular expression, displaying each line that contains the pattern. The other two commands, `egrep` and `fgrep`, are variations of `grep`. We will discuss them in a moment.

The syntax for the `grep` command, showing the important options, is

`grep` [-cinv] *pattern* [*file...*]

where *pattern* is a regular expression, and *file* is the name of the file you want to search.

Most of the time, you will use `grep` without any options. For example, say that your userid is `harley`. You want to search the password file `/etc/passwd` (see Chapter 13) for the entry for your userid. Enter

```
grep harley /etc/passwd
```

The output will consist of all lines of the file that contain the pattern `harley`:

```
harley:x:100:1:Harley Hahn:/usr/harley:/bin/sh
```

Here is another example. You want to create a file named `sept` that contains the names of all the files in your working directory that were last modified in September. Within a long directory listing, that date associated with such files will contain the letters "`Sep`". All you need to do is use `ls -l` to generate the long directory listing. Then, search the listing for the required pattern and save the results in a file. The command is

```
ls -l | grep Sep > sept
```

If you want to look at the results at the same time, you can send the output to the file using a tee:

```
ls -l | grep Sep | tee sept | more
```

The output will look something like this:

```
drwxr-xr-x   2 harley   other   400 Sep 14 12:55 docs
drwxr-xr-x   3 harley   other   416 Sep 13 12:08 backups
-rwxrwxrwx   1 harley   other   205 Sep 11 16:57 extra
-rw-r--r--   1 harley   other    99 Sep 14 14:00 results
```

If you want to find out the number of files that were last modified in September, you can pipe the output of **grep** to the **wc** program and count the number of lines:

```
ls -l | grep Sep | wc -l
```

When you use **grep**, you can specify the name of more than one file. For example, to search for the pattern **Example** in four files named **chapter1**, **chapter2**, **chapter3**, and **chapter4**, enter

```
grep Example chapter1 chapter2 chapter3 chapter4
```

Alternatively, you can specify the file names using a regular expression (see Chapter 22):

```
grep Example chapter[1234]
```

Two of the options that are used with **grep** control how the search will be performed. Normally, **grep** will distinguish between upper and lower case as it searches. The **-i** (ignore) option tells **grep** to ignore the distinction. For example, if you want to search the files in our last command for either **Example** or **example**, you can use

```
grep -i example chapter[1234]
```

The **-v** option tells **grep** to display only those lines that do not contain the search pattern. For example, to search the file **output** and display only those lines that do not contain the pattern **Error**, use

```
grep -v Error output
```

If you want to omit all lines that contain this same word in upper- or lower-case letters, use

```
grep -iv error output
```

The rest of the options control how grep will write its output. The -c (count) option displays the number of lines on which the pattern was found, rather than the lines themselves. For example, in one of our previous commands, we searched a long directory listing for all the lines that contained the pattern Sep. We counted these lines by piping the results to the wc command:

```
ls -l | grep Sep | wc -l
```

Using the -c option, we can count the lines directly:

```
ls -l | grep -c Sep
```

The -n (number) option prefaces each line of output with a number that indicates the position of the line in the original file. For example, say that you enter the command

```
grep quack complaint
```

to search a file named complaint for the pattern quack. The output consists of three lines:

```
incessant quacking that is keeping us awake
Of course, I can appreciate quacking in its place
your attention to this quacking problem as soon as
```

If you want to find out where these lines are in the file, use

```
grep -n quack complaint
```

The output looks like this:

```
18:incessant quacking that is keeping us awake
24:Of course, I can appreciate quacking in its place
32:your attention to this quacking problem as soon as
```

The line numbers are not actually a part of the file. They are generated by grep, which counts each line during the search.

Using Regular Expressions with grep

When you specify a regular expression for which you want grep to search, you can use many of the same characters that work with the vi editor. Figure 31.1 lists the characters that grep recognizes. The rules for using these characters are the same as with vi (see Chapter 26).

When you use special characters with grep, it is a good idea to quote the entire regular expression. For example, to search the file info for all the lines that start with and or And, use

```
grep '^[Aa]nd' info
```

You might wonder, Are the quotes really necessary? Moreover, how is it that the ^, [, and] characters retain their special meaning inside of quotes? Shouldn't these characters be taken literally? The answer involves a subtle but important point.

Before a command can look at its arguments, they must be processed by the shell. As you know, the shell recognizes cer-

Within a regular expression, letters and numbers represent themselves. A few characters have special meanings.

.	match any single character except a **newline**
*	match zero or more of the preceding characters
^	match the beginning of a line
$	match the end of a line
[ ]	match one of the enclosed characters
[^]	match any character that is not enclosed

Inside [ ] , you can use - (minus sign) to indicate a range of single letters or digits.

A \ (backspace) character indicates that the following character is to be taken literally.

Figure 31.1   *Using regular expressions with* grep *to specify patterns.*

tain characters as having special meanings. For example, the *
character is used to match file names, and the < character is
used to redirect the standard input.

The shell looks for and interprets these characters before it
executes your command. When you use special characters in a
search pattern, you run the risk of having them interpreted by
the shell before they even get to grep. By quoting your search
pattern, you tell the shell to pass the characters to grep exactly
as they are. Another way of saying this is that you can quote
characters in order to protect them from the shell. (This is true
in general, not just with grep.)

The reason that grep does not take the characters literally is
that the shell removes the quotes before passing the argument.
Thus, in the last example, grep sees ^[Aa]nd rather than
'^[Aa]nd'.

Here is another example. The following command searches
the file info for lines that contain any pattern that starts with an
A, followed by any character, followed by zero or more characters, followed by a y:

```
grep 'A.*y' info
```

If you want grep to treat a special character literally, precede
the character with a \ (backslash). Thus, to search for lines in
the same file that contain the characters "A.*y", use

```
grep 'A\.\*y' info
```

To specify a \, use two \\ characters. For example, to search for
the pattern 1\2, use

```
grep '1\\2' info
```

Extended Searching: The egrep Command

The egrep program is an extended version of grep. (egrep
stands for "extended grep.") For the most part, egrep works
just like grep, only faster. Moreover, egrep has four important
advantages. The syntax of egrep is similar to grep:

```
egrep [-cinv] pattern [file...]
```

However, there is a second form of `egrep` that has an extra option, `-f`, that we will discuss in a moment.

The first advantage of `egrep` is that it supports two extra special characters within regular expressions: the `+` (plus sign) and the `?` (question mark).

The `+` character will match one or more of the preceding characters. For example, to match `s`, followed by one or more o's, followed by n, you can use

```
so+n
```

This pattern would match

```
son    soon    sooon
```

To match one or more upper-case letters, use

```
[A-Z]+
```

The `?` character will match zero or more of the preceding characters. For example, the pattern

```
so?n
```

would match

```
sn    son    soon    sooon
```

To match any upper-case letter, followed by zero or more lower-case letters, use

```
[A-Z][a-z]?
```

Notice that the meaning of the `?` character with `egrep` is not the same as when you specify file names or when you search for patterns with `vi`. With file names and with `vi`, the `?` matches any one character. With `egrep`, the `.` (period) character is used to match any one character.

The second advantage of `egrep` over `grep` is that you can enclose a regular expression within parentheses and treat it as a complete unit. Such an expression can be followed by `*`, `+`, or `?` characters.

For example, you want to search for the letter **x**, followed by zero or more occurrences of **123**, followed by the letter **y**. Use

```
X(123)*Y
```

This regular expression would match character strings like

```
XY    X123Y    X123123Y    X123123123Y
```

As with **grep**, it is best to quote such expressions on the command line. For example, to search for all the lines in the file **data** that contain the previous patterns, use

```
egrep 'X(123)*Y' data
```

The third advantage of **egrep** is that you can specify that you want to search for more than one regular expression. Simply separate each regular expression with either a | (vertical bar) character or a **newline**. To generate a **newline**, you press the<Return> key.

For example, you want to search a file named **congressmen** for all the lines that contain either **Groucho**, **Chico**, **Harpo**, or **Zeppo**. You could use either

```
grep 'Groucho | Chico | Harpo | Zeppo' congressmen
```

or

```
grep 'Groucho<Return>
Chico<Return>
Harpo<Return>
Zeppo'<Return>
Congressmen
```

If you use the second form with the Bourne shell, you will see the secondary prompt as you enter the continuation lines (see Chapter 29). The previous example would look like this on your screen as you typed it:

```
$ grep 'Groucho
> Chico
> Harpo
> Zeppo'
```

The final advantage of `egrep` over `grep` is that you can tell `egrep` to look in a file for a list of regular expressions for which to search. The syntax for this form of `egrep` is

```
egrep [-cinv] -f pattern-file [file...]
```

where *pattern-file* is the name of the file that contains the patterns for which to search, and `file` is the file to be searched. The `-f` (file) option tells `egrep` to read the regular expression from the pattern file you specify.

For example, here is an alternate way to perform the search from the last example. First, use `vi` to create a file named `names` that contains the following four lines:

```
Groucho
Chico
Harpo
Zeppo
```

Next, enter the `egrep` command with the `-f` option, and specify the pattern file:

```
egrep -f names congressmen
```

To recapitulate, the advantages of `egrep` over `grep` are

- speed
- the capability of searching for more sophisticated regular expressions
- being able to accept more than one regular expression, either on the command line or from a file

Figure 31.2 summarizes how to use regular expressions with `egrep`.

Searching for Fixed Patterns: The `fgrep` Command

The third member of the `grep` family is `fgrep`. The name stands for "fixed `grep`." This refers to the fact that `fgrep` will search for fixed character strings only, not for regular expressions.

The characters used to specify search patterns with **egrep** are the same as those used with **grep**, with the addition of the + and ? characters.

Within a regular expression, letters and numbers represent themselves. A few characters have special meanings:

.	match any single character except a **newline**
*	match zero or more of the preceding characters
+	match one or more of the preceding characters
?	match zero or one of the preceding characters
^	match the beginning of a line
$	match the end of a line
[ ]	match one of the enclosed characters
[^]	match any character that is not enclosed
( )	treat the enclosed **reg exp** as a complete unit

Inside [ ], you can use - (minus sign) to indicate a range of single letters or digits.

A \ (backspace) character indicates that the following character is to be taken literally.

To search for more than one pattern, separate the regular expressions by either a | (vertical bar) or a **newline**.

Figure 31.2 *Using regular expressions with egrep to specify patterns.*

Like **egrep**, there are two forms of the **fgrep** command:

```
fgrep [-cinvx] fixed-string [file...]
fgrep [-cinvx] -fpattern-file [file...]
```

The options and arguments work exactly the same as **grep** except that the search pattern, *fixed-string*, can be only literal characters. Like **egrep**, you can use the -**f** (file) option and specify a file of patterns for which to search.

Here is an example. To search the file **vegetables** for all the lines that contain the word **turnip**, use

```
fgrep turnip vegetables
```

When you use `fgrep`, all characters in the search pattern are taken literally—there are no regular expressions. However, as with `grep` and `egrep`, it is a good idea to quote any characters that have a special meaning to the shell.

For example, to search the file `document` for all the lines that contain a semicolon, use

```
fgrep ';' document
```

If you look at the syntax for descriptions, you will see that `fgrep` has one option that the other programs do not have. The **-x** (exact match) option tells `fgrep` to select only those lines that are exactly the same as the search pattern. For example, the command

```
fgrep -x 'it is time to leave' document
```

would select the line

```
it is time to leave
```

but not the line

```
it is time to leave the house
```

Having made the acquaintance of `grep`, `egrep`, and `fgrep`, you might ask, Why are there three search commands?

The answer is that the three commands were programmed differently to span a wide range of memory/speed trade-offs. The `egrep` program offers the most sophisticated options and search capabilities. Moreover, it is usually the fastest of the three programs. However, `egrep` will use more memory than `grep` or `fgrep`.

The `fgrep` program was designed to search only for simple strings. Within its limitations, `fgrep` uses the least amount of memory. However, contrary to what many people have been taught, it is usually no faster then `egrep`. (Some people mistakenly believe that the name `fgrep` stands for "fast `grep`.")

The `grep` program was programmed as a middle-of-the-road alternative: it will accept limited regular expressions and uses less memory than `egrep`.

At the time Unix was first developed, memory was at a premium. It made sense to develop three different search programs based on different designs. That way, you could choose the most economical program that would satisfy your needs. For instance, if you needed to search for a fixed string, you could use the less-demanding `fgrep`.

These days, memory is cheap and such considerations are far less important. Knowledgeable people usually use `egrep` all the time. The only exception to this rule is for searching for a great many fixed strings. In such cases, `fgrep` may work better.

RULE	In almost all cases, the best search program to use is `egrep`.

Introduction to Sorting

Unix comes with a built-in program, the `sort` command, to sort text files. However, before we discuss `sort`, let's take a few moments and cover the basic concepts that you will need to get the most out of this utility.

Record:

Within a text file, the largest unit of data holding one or more related items.

Sorting involves reading and processing files of data. Within a file, the data is organized into collections called *records*. Each record holds one or more related data items.

Here is an example. Consider a text file that holds information about all the employees of a company. The file might be organized so that each record holds the data relating to a single employee. If there are 250 employees, there will be 250 records.

Field:

Within a record, one item of data.

Within each record, the various data items are called *fields*. For example, in our file of employee data, each record might contain a field for the last name, a field for the first name, a field for an identification number, a field for the home address, and so on.

Sort:

To rearrange the records in a text file according to a specified ordering of one or more fields in each record.

Sorting a text file means rearranging the order of the records based on the values in one or more fields. For instance, you might sort a file of employee data based on the last name of each employee. A more technical way of saying this is that you would sort the records according to the value of the "last name" field.

When you sort a file, you usually ignore some of the fields. In our example, we are ignoring all the fields except the one that holds the last name. The parts of a record that are actually com-

Key:
The part of a record that is compared during a sorting operation.

pared to one another are called *keys*. In this case, there is only one key: the "last name" field.

When you use a sorting program, you specify which fields within each record are to be considered keys. The program will rearrange the order of the records within the file, based on the key values. For example, you might ask that the records of the employee file be arranged so that the last names are in alphabetical order.

Each time you sort, you can choose the keys you want. For instance, you might resort the employee file based on the identification number.

As a general rule, there are two ways to sort: in alphabetical order and in reverse alphabetical order. This means that the choice of "alphabet" is crucial. For most purposes, the alphabet must contain not only letters, but numbers, punctuation, and even the invisible characters such as `space` and `tab`. Moreover, it is important that the alphabet distinguish between upper- and lower-case letters.

In Chapter 4, we explained how Unix, like many computer systems, uses the standard ASCII code to represent characters. Within this code, the characters have a particular order. The `a` character comes before the `b` character, the `3` character comes before the `4` character, and so on. There are 128 characters represented by the ASCII code, and each of these characters has a well-defined position within the code.

The ASCII code is the official "alphabet" that Unix uses when it sorts data. This means that when you sort a file in alphabetical order, you are using the order defined by the ASCII code.

The Online ASCII Table: `/usr/pub/ascii`

For your reference, we have included a copy of the ASCII code in Appendix A. In addition, most Unix systems store a copy of the code within a file called `/usr/pub/ascii`. (The `pub` stands for "public.") If your system has this file, you display it by entering:

```
more /usr/pub/ascii
```

You will see the characters displayed across the screen. Each character will be preceded by a number. The number shows the position of the character within the code.

With System V Unix, the ASCII reference file contains three copies of the code. In the first copy, the numbers are in octal (base 8); in the second copy, the numbers are in hexadecimal (base 16); in the third copy, the numbers are in decimal (base 10). With BSD Unix, there are only two copies of the code, octal and hexadecimal.

Decimal, of course, is our everyday counting system. Hexadecimal and octal are counting systems particularly suited to computers. If the hexadecimal and octal numbers do not mean anything to you, you can ignore them. The important thing about these tables is that they show the order in which the characters appear.

Most of the time, you do not need to remember the exact order of each character. Just use the following guideline:

RULE   Learning Unix: Within the ASCII code

- numbers (0 to 9) are in order
- letters (A to Z; a to z) are in order
- numbers come before upper-case letters, which come before lower-case letters

---

Thus, when you sort data, 3 comes before H, which comes before h.

Sorting Text Files: The `sort` Command

The `sort` command is a powerful tool that can perform several related tasks. First, `sort` can sort the lines in a file, based on the value of all or part of each line. Second, `sort` can check a file and tell you if it is in sorted order. Third, `sort` can take several sorted files and merge them into one large sorted file.

Here is the syntax for the `sort` command. We have described only the most important options:

```
sort [-bcdfimnru] [-o outfile] [-tchar] [+pos1 [-pos2]] [file...]
```

Here *file* is the name of one or more text files that you want to sort. The values of *outfile*, *char*, *pos1*, and *pos2* are explained below.

The `sort` command reads from the file you specify, sorts it, and writes the results to the standard output. For example, the following command sorts a file named `data` and displays the results:

```
sort data
```

If the file is a large one, you can pipe the results to `more` or `pg` so you can read the output one screenful at a time:

```
sort data | more
sort data | pg
```

If you want to save the sorted data, redirect the output to a text file. The following command sorts a file named `data` and stores the results in a file named `new`:

```
sort data >new
```

Alternatively, you can use the `-o` (output) option, followed by the name of the file to which you want to write the output. For example:

```
sort -o new data
```

In general, `sort` does not change the original file. However, if you want to replace the original file with the results of the sort, use the `-o` (output) option and specify the name of the original file. For example, to replace the file `data` with the same data in sorted order, use

```
sort -o data data
```

As we explained in Chapter 30, you cannot redirect the standard output of a command to the input file. If you were to use

```
sort data >data
```

it would wipe out the contents of `data`.

If you do not specify the name of an input file, `sort` will read from the standard input. That is, you can use `sort` as a filter. For example, to display a sorted list of all the userids that are currently logged in, enter

```
who | sort
```

(The who command is explained in Chapter 7.)

If you specify more than one input file, sort will combine them before it starts to sort. Thus, the command

```
sort data1 data2 data3 data4
```

has the same effect as

```
cat data1 data2 data3 data4 | sort
```

Options to Use with sort

There are a number of options that you can use to control the operation of the sort command.

The -c (check) option reads a file and checks to see if it is in sorted order. Thus, no sorting is actually performed. If the file is in order, sort will not display a message. If the file is not in order, sort will display the word "disorder", followed by the first line that is out of order.

The -d (dictionary) option tells sort to consider only letters, numbers, and space and tab characters during the sorting process. Like a dictionary, this option ignores punctuation and special characters. For the purposes of sorting, the tab character comes before the space character, and they both come before the numbers and letters.

The -f (fold) option tells sort to consider all upper-case letters as if they were lower case. (Sometimes, the conversion from upper to lower case is called "folding.") For example, the word Pride would normally come before the word fall, because P comes before f in the ASCII code. However, when you use the -f option, the p is counted as lower case and fall comes before Pride.

The -i (ignore) option tells sort to ignore the nonprintable characters from the ASCII code. These include the control characters that we discussed in Chapter 9. Normally, these characters will not find their way into a text file, and you can safely ignore this option.

The strict definition of -i is that it tells sort to ignore any characters that do not lie in the range of 32 to 126 (040 to 176 octal) in the ASCII code. If you check with the ASCII table in Appendix A, you will see that this range includes all of the common, printable characters.

The −m (merge) option combines several sorted files into one large sorted file. For example, say that the files january, february, and march each contain sorted data. You want to merge these files into one large file called first.quarter. Use

```
sort -m january february march >first.quarter
```

or

```
sort -m -o first.quarter january february march
```

The -n (numeric) option sorts numbers by their numeric value, rather than character by character. For example, say that the file data contains one number on each line. Three of the lines are

```
888.0
  1.5
 -1.5
```

The second and third numbers have space characters in front of them in order to line up the decimal points. If you were to enter

```
sort data
```

you would see

```
  1.5
 -1.5
888.0
```

This is because sort compares character by character, and space comes before -, which comes before 8.

However, if you use

```
sort -n data
```

sort will consider each line by its numeric value. The output is

```
    -1.5
     1.5
   888.0
```

As you might expect, negative numbers come before positive numbers.

When you use the -n option, sort will ignore any space or tab characters that precede the numbers. Within the numbers, you may use minus signs or decimal points as you wish.

The -b (blank) option tells sort to ignore leading space and tab characters. When you use the -n option, -b is assumed automatically and you don't need to specify it.

The next option, -r, tells sort to write the output in reverse order. For example, if we added the -r option to the previous command:

```
sort -nr data
```

the output would be

```
   888.0
     1.5
    -1.5
```

The final option, -u (unique), tells sort to eliminate all lines that compare the same as a previous line. For example, say that you have a large file named words that contains many different words, each on a separate line. You want to display the words in sorted order, but you only want to see each word once. Use

```
sort -u words
```

Sorting with Fields

As we explained earlier, a file that is to be sorted can be considered as a collection of records, each record containing a number of fields. During a sorting operation, the part of the record that is being compared is called a key.

sort considers each line to be a complete record. Another way to put this is that sort processes a file line by line. Unless you specify otherwise, sort considers each line to be one large key. However, sort is capable of recognizing fields within lines and distinguishing between keys to be sorted and other fields. For example, you can sort a file based only on the values of the third and fourth fields. In this section, you will learn how to tell sort which parts of the lines are to be considered as keys.

Unless you specify otherwise, sort assumes that all the fields within a record are separated by either space or tab characters. For example, the following line has three fields:

```
827-23-7163    Albert    Gendeau
```

The first field has the value 827-23-7163; the second field has the value Albert; and the third field has the value Gendeau.

In order to use keys, you must specify the beginning and the end of each key in terms of field numbers. One tricky point is that sort counts fields starting at 0 (zero). Thus, the first field is field 0, the next is field 1, the next is field 2, and so on. If, for example, you wanted to refer to the sixteenth field, you would call it field 15.

To define a key, use a + character, followed by the number of the field that begins the key. Then, use a - character, followed by the number of the field that follows the key.

At first, this can be confusing so here are a few examples. You want to sort the file employees based on the value of the the third field. Use

```
sort +2 -3 employees
```

That is, the key starts at field 2 (the third field), and extends up to, but does not include, field 3 (the fourth field).

The next example uses two keys. One key consists of fields 3, 4, and 5 (the fourth, fifth, and sixth fields). The other key consists of field 9 (the tenth field) only. The command is:

```
sort +3 -6 +9 -10 employees
```

If you use a + specification without a - specification, sort assumes that the key extends to the end of the line. For example, to define a key that starts at field 7 (the eighth field) and extends to the end of the line, use

```
sort +7 employees
```

When necessary, `sort` allows you to be even more precise. You can start a key at a particular character within a field. At the end of the field number, add a period followed by the position within the field at which the keys starts.

For example, say that the field 0 (the first field) of the `employees` file consists of identification numbers in the form

```
827-23-7163
```

To sort the file according to the value of this field, use

```
sort +0 -1 employees
```

However, you want to sort according to the last four characters of the field. Use

```
sort +0.7 -1 employees
```

This means that the key starts at 7 positions past the beginning of field 0, and continues up to, but does not include, the beginning of field 1.

You can use a similar specification to define the end of a field. For example, the command

```
sort +0.7 -2.4 employees
```

means that the key starts at 7 positions past the beginning of field 0 and extends up to, but does not include, 4 positions past the beginning of field 2. In other words, the key contains the first three characters of field 2.

When you use more than one key, `sort` looks at them in the order you specify. Later keys are examined only if earlier keys have different values.

For example, say that the first three fields of the `employees` file contain an identification number (field 0), a first name (field 1), and a last name (field 2). You want to sort the file by last name. If two last names are the same, you want to compare first names. If both names are the same, you want to compare identification numbers.

The following command defines these three keys in order of priority:

```
sort +2 -3 +1 -2 +0 -1 employees
```

The question arises, what does `sort` do with lines that have equal values on all the keys that you specify? The answer is that `sort` starts from the beginning of the line and looks at the other fields. For example, say that the `employees` file has the following two records, in this order:

```
1234-56-7890    Rick    Shaw
0000-00-0000    Rick    Stout
```

You enter a command to sort on the field 1 (the second field):

```
sort +1 -2 employees
```

Since these two records have equal values in the second field, `sort` compares the rest of the fields starting from the beginning of the line. The result is

```
0000-00-0000    Rick    Stout
1234-56-7890    Rick    Shaw
```

Stable:

Describes a sorting program that maintains the relative order of records that have equal key values.

If a sorting program never changes the order of records that have equal key values, we say that the program is *stable*. If a program sometimes changes the order of records that have equal key values, we say that the program is *unstable*.

As the last example shows, the Unix `sort` program is unstable.

Unstable:

Describes a sorting program that sometimes changes the relative order of records that have equal key values.

Options to Use When Sorting with Fields

There are two options that you use when you sort with fields. In addition, there are several options that you can use to describe a particular field.

By default, `sort` considers fields to be separated by one or more `space` or `tab` characters. For example, the record

```
0000-00-0000    Rick    Stout
```

has three fields.

However, you may find yourself working with a file in which another character separates the fields. If this is the case, use the -t (tab) option, followed by that character. Do not put a `space` between the -t and the character.

Here is an example. You have a file called `people` in which the fields are separated by % characters. For instance

```
1234-56-7890%Rick%Shaw
0000-00-0000%Rick%Stout
```

To sort this file using field 1 (the second field) as a key, enter

```
sort -t% +1 -2
```

If you are using the C-shell, the % character has a special meaning, and you will have to quote it:

```
sort -t\% +1 -2
```

The other option that works with fields is the `-b` (blank) option that we mentioned earlier. This option ignores `space` and `tab` characters at the beginning of each key.

When you define keys, you can specify that one or more options should apply to a particular field. For example, you might want `sort` to ignore `space` and `tab` characters at the beginning of one particular key, rather than at the beginning of every key.

The options that apply to individual fields are

b	ignore leading **space** and **tab** characters
d	compare only letters, numbers, **space**, and **tab**
f	treat upper-case letters as lower case
i	ignore all but the regular printable characters
n	treat a field as a numerical value
r	sort in reverse order

To apply one or more of these options to a particular field, put the letters for those options directly after the specification for the field. You can do this for both + and for - specifications.

Here is an example. The following command sorts the file named `employees`. The keys are field 2 (the third field) and field 4 (the fifth field). Within field 2 only, punctuation is ignored (the `-d` option):

```
sort +2d -3 +4 -5 employees
```

The next example is similar. The only difference is that instead of the first key ending just before field 3, the key ends just before the first character in field 3 that is not a **space** or a **tab**:

```
sort +2d -3b +4 -5 employees
```

In this last example, field 2 is sorted with the punctuation ignored and in reverse order. Field 4 is sorted in the regular manner:

```
sort +2dr -3 +4 -5 employees
```

Appendix A:
The ASCII Code

Character	Decimal	Octal	Hex	Binary
	0	000	00	0000 0000
^A	1	001	01	0000 0001
^B	2	002	02	0000 0010
^C	3	003	03	0000 0011
^D	4	004	04	0000 0100
^E	5	005	05	0000 0101
^F	6	006	06	0000 0110
^G	7	007	07	0000 0111
^H (backspace)	8	010	08	0000 1000
^I (tab)	9	011	09	0000 1001
^J (newline)	10	012	0A	0000 1010
^K	11	013	0B	0000 1011
^L (return)	12	014	0C	0000 1100
^M	13	015	0D	0000 1101
^N	14	016	0E	0000 1110
^O	15	017	0F	0000 1111

Character	Decimal	Octal	Hex	Binary
^P	16	020	10	0001 0000
^Q	17	021	11	0001 0001
^R	18	022	12	0001 0010
^S	19	023	13	0001 0011
^T	20	024	14	0001 0100
^U	21	025	15	0001 0101
^V	22	026	16	0001 0110
^W	23	027	17	0001 0111
^X	24	030	18	0001 1000
^Y	25	031	19	0001 1001
^Z	26	032	1A	0001 1010
	27	033	1B	0001 1011
	28	034	1C	0001 1100
	29	035	1D	0001 1101
	30	036	1E	0001 1110
	31	037	1F	0001 1111
space	32	040	20	0010 0000
!	33	041	21	0010 0001
"	34	042	22	0010 0010
#	35	043	23	0010 0011
$	36	044	24	0010 0100
%	37	045	25	0010 0101
&	38	046	26	0010 0110
'	39	047	27	0010 0111
(	40	050	28	0010 1000
)	41	051	29	0010 1001
*	42	052	2A	0010 1010
+	43	053	2B	0010 1011
,	44	054	2C	0010 1100
−	45	055	2D	0010 1101
.	46	056	2E	0010 1110
/	47	057	2F	0010 1111

Character	Decimal	Octal	Hex	Binary
0	48	060	30	0011 0000
1	49	061	31	0011 0001
2	50	062	32	0011 0010
3	51	063	33	0011 0011
4	52	064	34	0011 0100
5	53	065	35	0011 0101
6	54	066	36	0011 0110
7	55	067	37	0011 0111
8	56	070	38	0011 1000
9	57	071	39	0011 1001
:	58	072	3A	0011 1010
;	59	073	3B	0011 1011
<	60	074	3C	0011 1100
=	61	075	3D	0011 1101
>	62	076	3E	0011 1110
?	63	077	3F	0011 1111
@@	64	100	40	0100 0000
A	65	101	41	0100 0001
B	66	102	42	0100 0010
C	67	103	43	0100 0011
D	68	104	44	0100 0100
E	69	105	45	0100 0101
F	70	106	46	0100 0110
G	71	107	47	0100 0111
H	72	110	48	0100 1000
I	73	111	49	0100 1001
J	74	112	4A	0100 1010
K	75	113	4B	0100 1011
L	76	114	4C	0100 1100
M	77	115	4D	0100 1101
N	78	116	4E	0100 1110
O	79	117	4F	0100 1111

Character	Decimal	Octal	Hex	Binary
P	80	120	50	0101 0000
Q	81	121	51	0101 0001
R	82	122	52	0101 0010
S	83	123	53	0101 0011
T	84	124	54	0101 0100
U	85	125	55	0101 0101
V	86	126	56	0101 0110
W	87	127	57	0101 0111
X	88	130	58	0101 1000
Y	89	131	59	0101 1001
Z	90	132	5A	0101 1010
[	91	133	5B	0101 1011
\	92	134	5C	0101 1100
]	93	135	5D	0101 1101
^	94	136	5E	0101 1110
_	95	137	5F	0101 1111
`	96	140	60	0110 0000
a	97	141	61	0110 0001
b	98	142	62	0110 0010
c	99	143	63	0110 0011
d	100	144	64	0110 0100
e	101	145	65	0110 0101
f	102	146	66	0110 0110
g	103	147	67	0110 0111
h	104	150	68	0110 1000
i	105	151	69	0110 1001
j	106	152	6A	0110 1010
k	107	153	6B	0110 1011
l	108	154	6C	0110 1100
m	109	155	6D	0110 1101
n	110	156	6E	0110 1110
o	111	157	6F	0110 1111

Character	Decimal	Octal	Hex	Binary
p	112	160	70	0111 0000
q	113	161	71	0111 0001
r	114	162	72	0111 0010
s	115	163	73	0111 0011
t	116	164	74	0111 0100
u	117	165	75	0111 0101
v	118	166	76	0111 0110
w	119	167	77	0111 0111
x	120	170	78	0111 1000
y	121	171	79	0111 1001
z	122	172	7A	0111 1010
{	123	173	7B	0111 1011
|	124	174	7C	0111 1100
}	125	175	7D	0111 1101
~	126	176	7E	0111 1110
(del)	127	177	7F	0111 1111

Appendix B:
Rules for Learning Unix

1. Unix is fun.

2. Anything that can be done simply can also be done with as much complexity as you like.

3. Unix is precise.

4. Unix is a culture.

5. Your user interface influences how you think when you use Unix.

6. The shell is Unix's command processor. It has a large number of powerful features that you will come to appreciate as your experience with Unix grows.

7. The Fundamental Equation of Unix shows what objects make up a Unix system:

       Host
   +   Terminals
   +   Userids
   +   Files
   +   Processes
       ———————
       UNIX

8. When you run into something that has many technical details, do not avoid it and do not try to memorize it all. Instead, try to make sure you understand the overall concepts. Later, if you need the details, you can look them up in the manual.

9. Take some time and learn about the Unix special codes:

   `eof, erase, esc, intr, kill, lnext, newline, quit, return, space, start, stop, tab, werase`

10. Get in the habit of using all three typing codes

erase	\<Backspace>
kill	Control-X or Control-U
werase	Control-W

   instead of relying only on \<Backspace>.

11. Do not confuse the `intr` code with the `kill` code.

   `intr` (interrupt) stops a program that is executing.

   `kill` cancels the line you are currently typing.

12. With programs that prompt you for input, you can quit by pressing ^D at the prompt. This sends the program an `eof` (end of file) code.

13. Place an **stty -a** command at the end of your `.profile` or `.login` file. Every time you log in, you will be reminded of your control code settings.

14. Start by learning the basics. Use Unix. As the need arises, teach yourself more.

15. Most of learning Unix is learning how to use the commands.

16. Each Unix command should do one thing only and should do it well.

17. Unix provides simple tools that can be combined, as you require, to perform complex tasks.

18. Unix is terse. Error messages are short. A command with nothing to say will say nothing.

19. Unix is difficult to learn but easy to use.

20. Most command options are designated by a single character, usually a lower-case letter. Unix commands usually have many options. You will memorize the ones you need by practice. Make a point of using the manual to expand your knowledge by learning new options.

21. The online Manual is the single most important Unix reference.

22. Section 1 of the online Manual contains a description of each Unix command. This is the most important section of the Manual.

23. Continual learning is part of the process of using Unix.

24. Put a `news -n` or `news -s` command in your startup script (`.profile` or `.login`) to keep abreast of what is happening on your system.

25. To see what other people are up to, use the `ps -af` command.

26. Don't write down your password or tell it to anyone. If you forget your password, ask the system manager for help.

27. If you have a superuser password, be sure not to forget it. If you do, you may have to reinstall the entire system.

28. To check what your current userid is, you must use the `id` command.

29. The superuser can always send messages to any userid.

30. Reading your mail: As you read each message, decide immediately whether to save or delete it. Do not let old messages accumulate.

31. The term "file" refers to any source of input or target of output, not only to a repository of data.

32. Be careful when removing files. Once a file is erased, it is gone permanently.

33. If you use more than one userid, remember that whichever userid creates a file will own it.

34. Unix system files are owned by special userids that are not used for everyday work. Do not log in with these userids (except for using `root` to become superuser).

35. Do not set execute permission for an ordinary file unless it is executable.

36. Whenever you create a shell script, remember to give yourself execute permission.

37. To keep other users from fiddling with one of your directories, restrict the execute permission.

38. There is no need to create extra groups if you do not have a compelling reason.

39. Create directories so that the structure of the tree reflects the natural organization of your data.

40. When designing a directory structure

(1) Use each directory to hold either files or subdirectories, but not both.

(2) Keep your subdirectories to within three levels of your main directory.

41. The directory name `tmp` is pronounced "temp."

42. The directory name `usr` is pronounced "user."

43. When naming files, confine yourself to lower-case letters and the period.

44. The Fundamental Equation of Directory Names:

Full Path Name = Working Directory + Relative Path Name

45. Think of your home directory as your base within the overall directory tree.

46. No matter how you set your file permissions, the superuser will always be able to read and modify your files.

47. In order to remove a directory using `rmdir`, the following conditions must hold:

1. The directory must be empty.
2. Your userid must have write and execute permission for the parent directory.
3. The directory cannot be your working directory.

48. The default file-creation mask used by Unix is 022. This withholds the following permissions:

owner:	none (0)
group:	write (2)
others:	write (2)

49. When you create data files, the default file mode assigned by Unix is 644. This represents the following permissions:

owner:	read, write (6)
group:	read (4)
others:	read (4)

50. To create files with permissions that afford the maximum privacy, use the command umask 077.

51. To create an empty file, use the touch command.

52. To create a short text file, use the command

    cat > *file*

53. To add a few lines to the end of a short text file, use the command:

    cat >> *file*

54. If you want to display file names in columns, use the lc command. Otherwise, use the ls command.

55. There is no way to get back a file that has been removed.

56. Before using a regular expression with the rm (remove) command, use the same regular expression with the ls command to check exactly which file names are matched.

57. Whenever you use a regular expression with the rm (remove) command, use the -i (interactive) option so you can approve the removal of each file.

58. To copy a file: if you want to use an option
    -a (ask)
    -n (new)
    -v (verbose)

    use the copy command; otherwise, use the cp command.

59. Get into the habit of displaying files with more or pg, rather than with cat.

60. vi is easy to use but can be difficult to learn.

61. As a habit, use \ (backslash) or a pair of ' (single quote) characters for quoting arguments.

    Use " (double quote) characters only when you specifically want to preserve the meaning of $ (dollar sign) or ` (backquote).

62. To terminate a background process, use

`kill` *processid*

If this does not work, use

`kill -9` *processid*

63. To keep a time-consuming program from tying up the whole system, run the program in the background with a high priority value (low preference).

64. Do not redirect the standard error unless you have a good reason.

65. To solve a problem, it is better to combine existing tools than to write a new program.

66. The fundamental relationship between our hardware and how we think can be expressed as follows:

hardware → operating system → tools → how we think

67. In almost all cases, the best search program to use is `egrep`.

68. Within the ASCII code

numbers (0 to 9)are in order

letters (**A** to Z, a to z) are in order

numbers come before upper-case letters, which come before lower-case letters

Appendix C:
Hints for DOS Users

1. Unix requires a great deal more system administration than DOS.

2. You can install both DOS and Unix on a PC and start either one or the other. With a PC version of Unix, it is possible to run DOS programs under Unix and to share both DOS and Unix files.

3. If you would like to run Unix on your PC, you should have at least a 286-based computer. For high performance, you will need a 386- or 486-based system.

4. You can use a PC as a terminal by running a terminal emulation program. Most terminal emulation programs emulate VT-100 terminals.

5. With the proper software, you can connect to a Unix host at the same time you are running DOS programs.

6. Unix is a lot more fun than DOS. If you enjoy fooling around with DOS, you may have a lot more fun fooling around with Unix.

7. To access a Unix system from a separate PC running DOS, you need to use a terminal emulation program.

8. Unlike DOS, Unix distinguishes between small letters and capital letters. Take care to type your commands correctly.

9. A Unix shell is similar to the DOS command processor, COMMAND.COM.

10. If you are accessing a Unix system over a phone line, you will not be able to use graphics.

11. The DOS version of the ASCII code contains special symbols not found in the Unix ASCII code.

12. If you have used Microsoft Windows or the OS/2 Presentation Manager, you will find it easy to learn how to use a Unix graphical user interface.

13. Unix shells are much more powerful and complex than the DOS command processor.

14. Unix shells offer a full programming language. Shell scripts are similar to, but a great deal more useful than, DOS batch files.

15. Unlike DOS, Unix requires routine system maintenance. If you are using a standalone Unix system, you will be your own system manager.

16. The amount of time and effort required to manage a multi-user Unix system is comparable to what is required to manage a DOS-based local area network.

17. If you are managing your own system, remember to enter the special shutdown command before turning off the power.

18. The .profile file (Bourne shell) and the .login file (C-shell) perform the same types of initialization functions as the AUTOEXEC.BAT file.

19. If you are using a PC to emulate a terminal, the <Pause> key on your PC is always handled by DOS.
    <Pause> cannot send a signal to Unix.

20. In DOS, you frequently use the <Esc> key. With Unix, <Esc> is rarely used, except from within the vi editor and the Korn shell.

21. The <Delete> key is not used to delete characters. The <Delete> key is often used to send the intr (stop a program) signal.

22. To introduce command options, Unix uses a minus sign (-), not a slash (/). Unix commands have many more options then DOS commands. Command options may be specified singly or in groups, in any order. Like DOS, most options are single characters. Be careful to distinguish lower case from upper case. Unlike DOS, options usually come directly after the name of the command.

23. The differences between versions of Unix are much more pronounced than the differences between PC-DOS and MS-DOS.

24. Unlike DOS, Unix has an extensive online manual.
    Remember to use it.

25. Many Unix experts are not familiar with PCs or DOS. You will have to learn to speak *their* language.

26. The Unix `clear` command works much like the DOS CLS command.

27. On a multiuser system, passwords are imperative to keep people from causing damage, accidental or otherwise.

28. The word "file" is used with far more generality in Unix than in DOS.

29. The type of files that are used with DOS are called "ordinary files" in Unix.

30. Where DOS uses device names to access devices directly, Unix uses special files.

31. In Unix, more than one file name can refer to the same file.

32. A Unix file is not erased until its last link is removed.

33. Unlike DOS, all Unix files have an owner, a userid that controls the file.

34. You can control who is allowed to access your files by setting file permissions.

35. Unlike DOS, Unix maintains a number of directories for its own purposes.

36. Unix file names can be up to 14 characters long and do not use extensions.

37. The parts of a Unix path name are separated by slashes, not backslashes.

38. The Unix working directory is similar to a DOS current directory.

39. Rather than store files anywhere on the disk, each Unix user has his own home directory, within which he can build his own tree structure.

40. Unlike DOS, there is no easy way to make the Unix shell prompt display the name of the working directory. Use `pwd` to see where you are.

41. Where DOS maintains separate directory systems for each device, Unix uses one large tree structure.

42. Unix users tend to stay in the part of the tree defined by their home directory.

43. Summary Of Unix Directory Commands

	Unix command	*DOS command*
change working directory	`cd`	CHDIR, CD
display working directory	`pwd`	CHDIR, CD
make directory	`mkdir`	MKDIR, MD
remove directory	`rmdir`	RMDIR, RD
rename directory	`mv`	—
move directory	`mvdir`	—
copy directory	`copy`	XCOPY

44. Unlike DOS, Unix will allow you to create empty files.

45. Creating a short Unix file by using

`cat >` *file*

is similar to creating a DOS file with

COPY CON: *FILENAME.EXT*

46. Unlike the DIR command, `ls` displays file names in alphabetical order.

47. The `ls -c` and `lc` commands are analogous to the DOS DIR /W command.

48. Unix regular expressions can be used to specify file names, like DOS wildcards.

   Regular expressions are much more powerful than DOS wildcards.

49. Within a regular expression, the ? works the same way as within a DOS wildcard; however, the * works differently.

50. Displaying a file with `cat` is like using the DOS TYPE command.

   Displaying a file with `more` or `pg` is like using TYPE | MORE.

51. The `vi` editor is much more powerful than EDLIN. You need to learn `vi`.

52. The empty file `/dev/null` works much like the DOS NUL: device.

Appendix D:
Summary of System V
Unix Commands

(There are 538 commands.)

300	special handling for DASI 300 terminals
300s	special handling for DASI 300s terminals
4014	paginate output for a Tektronix 4014 terminal
450	special handling for DASI 450 terminal
abs	Graphics command: transform—absolute value
accept	allow line printer requests
acctcms	command summary from per-process accounting records
acctcom	search and display process accounting files
acctcon1	prepare login records for accounting—step 1
acctcon2	prepare login records for accounting—step 2
acctdisk	prepare disk records for accounting
acctdusg	compute disk resource consumption
accton	turn process accounting on or off
acctmerg	merge or add total accounting files
acctprc1	process accounting records—step 1
acctprc2	process accounting records—step 2
acctwtmp	write an accounting record

`adduser`	add a new user to the system
`admin`	create and change SCCS files
`adv`	RFS: advertise a directory for remote access
`af`	Graphics command: transform—arithmetic function
`alias`	C-shell: assign a specified list of words to a name
`ar`	create and update archive files used by link editor
`as`	assembler
`as386.sed`	sed script: convert 386 assembler source to as source
`at`	execute commands at a later time
`awk`	pattern scanning and processing language
`backup`	perform various backup functions
`banner`	make signs with large letters suitable for printing
`bar`	Graphics command: translate—make bar chart
`basename`	display filename minus directory name and suffix
`batch`	execute commands later, when load level permits
`bc`	an easy to use interface to dc calculator program
`bcheckrc`	check and repair root file system
`bdiff`	same as `diff` for big files
`bel`	Graphics command: send bel to terminal
`bfs`	scan a file too big for ed
`bg`	C-shell: puts jobs in background
`brc`	initialize mounted file system table
`break`	Bourne shell: exit from `for` or `while` loop
`break`	C-shell: : exit from `foreach` or `while` loop
`breaksw`	C-shell: : exit from a `switch` construct
`bucket`	Graphics command: summarize—break into buckets
`cal`	display a calendar
`calendar`	provide a reminder service
`captoinfo`	convert `termcap` description to `terminfo` description
`case`	Bourne shell: alternative control flow
`cat`	catenate and display files
`cb`	beautify a C program using spacing and indentation
`cc`	C compiler
`ccoff`	convert a COFF file: byte-swap multibyte integers
`cd`	Bourne shell: change the working directory
`cd`	C-shell: change the working directory
`cdc`	change the delta commentary for SCCS files
`ceil`	Graphics command: transform—ceiling function
`cflow`	generate graph showing external references for programs

chargefee	charge accounting units to a specific userid
chdir	C-shell: same as cd
checkmm	check the usage of mm macros within a document
chgrp	change the group ID of a file or directory
chkshlib	check library compatibility between files
chmod	change permissions (mode) of a file or directory
chown	change the owner of a file or directory
chroot	change root directory for one command
chrtbl	generate character classification/conversion table
ckbupscd	check file system backup schedule
ckpacct	check disk space used for process accounting
clear	clear the terminal screen
clri	clear an inode
cmp	compare two files
col	filter reverse linefeeds; use with multicolumn output
comb	use deltas: create script to recreate SCCS files
comm	select or reject lines common to two sorted files
config	produce configuration information for a kernel
continue	Bourne shell: resume next iteration, for or while loop
continue	C-shell: resume next iteration, foreach or while loop
conv	convert the byte ordering of object files
convert	convert Xenix or old Unix archive to new format
copy	copy groups of files and directories
cor	Graphics command: summarize—correlation coefficient
cp	copy files
cpio	copy file archives in and out
cpp	C preprocessor (first pass) invoked by cc
cprs	compress object file, remove duplicate descriptors
crash	examine a system memory image
cron	daemon to execute commands at specified times
crontab	copy specified file to crontab directory
crypt	encode or decode text using a specified key
cscope	interactively browse through C source code
csh	the C-shell
csplit	split a file into sections based on context
ct	dialup a terminal and spawn a getty to it
ctags	create tags file for vi editor from C source files
ctrace	follow the line-by-line execution of a C program
cu	call another Unix system
cusum	Graphics command: transform—cumulative sum

cut	cut out selected fields of each line in a file
cvrtopt	Graphics command: reformat args for shell processing
cxref	generate cross-reference table from C source files
daps	print troff output on Autologic APS-5 phototypesetter
date	display or set the time and date
dc	arbitrary-precision, stack-oriented desk calculator
dcopy	copy file system while optimizing its access time
dd	copy a file while converting to another format
deluser	remove a userid from the system
delta	make permanent changes (deltas) to an SCCS file
deroff	remove nroff, troff, tbl, and eqn constructs
devnm	identify special file related to a file system
df	report free disk blocks and inodes in file systems
dfsck	run fsck on two file systems at same time
di10	print troff output on Imagen Imprint-10 laser printer
diff	show lines to be changed to make two files the same
diff3	compare three files and show differences
diffmk	mark differences between files, suitable for nroff
dircmp	compare two directories
dirname	print directory name part of a filename
dirs	display the directory stack
dis	disassemble an object file into assembly language
disable	deactivate line printers
diskadd	set up disk partitions
diskusg	generate disk accounting data by userid
displaypkg	display names of packages installed with installpkg
dname	RFS: display domain and network names
dodisk	perform disk accounting functions
dtoc	Graphics command: make TTOC of subdirectory names
du	summarize disk usage
dump	display selected parts of an object file
echo	Bourne shell: write arguments to standard output
echo	C-shell: write arguments to standard output
ed	older standard line-oriented text editor
edit	variant of ex for casual or novice users
egrep	like grep but searches for full regular expressions

`enable`	activate line printers
`env`	change environment for one command
`eqn`	format mathematical text, output suitable for `troff`
`erase`	erase screen on Tektronix 4010 terminal
`eval`	Bourne shell: read arguments, evaluate as commands
`ex`	newer, standard text editor; superset of `ed`
`exec`	Bourne shell: execute command within current shell
`exec`	C-shell: execute command in place of current shell
`exit`	Bourne shell: exit a shell, with specified exit status
`exit`	C-shell: exit a shell, with specified exit status
`exp`	Graphics command: transform—exponential
`export`	Bourne shell: mark names for automatic export
`expr`	evaluate arguments as an expression
`factor`	calculate the prime factors of a specified number
`false`	do nothing, unsuccessfully
`fdisk`	create or modify PC hard disk partition table
`ff`	list file names and statistics for a file system
`fgrep`	like `grep` but searches only for a character string
`file`	determine the type of a file
`finc`	fast incremental backup for 386-based PC
`find`	find files, then optionally perform commands
`fixperm`	correct, initialize Xenix file permissions and owners
`floor`	Graphics command: transform—floor function
`for`	Bourne shell: repetitive control flow
`foreach`	C-shell: repetitive control flow
`format`	format tracks of a diskette
`frec`	recover file from 386-based PC backup
`fsck`	check and repair a file system
`fsdb`	patch a damaged file system after a crash
`fsstat`	report on the status of a file system
`fstyp`	determine the identifier of a file system
`ftape`	read or write to a floppy tape
`fumount`	RFS: force unmount of advertised resource
`fusage`	RFS: profile disk usage
`fuser`	identify processes using a file or remote resource
`fwtmp`	convert `wtmp` connect accounting records to ASCII
`gamma`	Graphics command: transform—gamma function
`gas`	Graphics command: translate—generate add sequence
`gd`	Graphics command: display readable listing of GPS file

ged	edit GPS graphics files on Tektronix 4010 terminal
gencc	generate front-end shell script to start cc command
get	generate ASCII text g-file from SCCS file
getopt	old version of getopts
getopts	Bourne shell: parse command line options
getty	set terminal type, modes, speed, line discipline
glob	C-shell: same as echo but with no \ escapes
glossary	Help Facility: give definitions of terms and symbols
goto	C-shell: continue execution after specified line
grap	preprocessor for pic, for typesetting graphs
graph	display a graph based on specified ordered pairs
graphics	start a session with the Graphics subsystem
greek	interpret extended character set
grep	search a file for a limited regular expression
grpck	check system group file for consistency
gtop	Graphics command: transform GPS file for plot filters
hardcopy	generate hard copy at a Tektronix terminal
hash	Bourne shell: recompute command name hash table
hashcheck	from compressed spell list, recreate hash codes
hashmake	generate hash codes from spell check word list
hd	display file in hex, octal, decimal or ASCII
hdr	display selected parts of a Xenix object module
help	Help Facility: access online Help Facility
help	provide information on SCCS command or error message
helpadm	Help Facility: modify the online database
hilo	Graphics command: summarize—find high and low values
hist	Graphics command: translate—make histogram
history	C-shell: display history event list
hp	support special functions of HP 2640 terminals
hpd	translate GPS graphics string to HP 7221A Plotter
hpio	provide I/O archive facilities for HP 2645A tapes
hyphen	find all the hyphenated words in a document
i286	check if processor is Intel 286
i286emul	run 286 System V.2 or V.3 programs on a V.3 386 system
i386	check if processor is Intel 386
i552pump	download software onto Intel iSXM522/552A board
ib	place Intel vol label, bootstrap loader on tape, disk

id	display userid, groupid, and names of invoking process
idcheck	display information about system configuration
idload	RFS: build translation tables for userids, groupids
idmknod	remove nodes, read specifications of nodes
idspace	check free space in /, /usr, and /tmp file systems
idtune	set value of a tunable parameter
if	Bourne shell: alternative control flow
if	C-shell: alternative control flow
infocmp	compare, modify, or display a terminfo description
init	initialize the system to a particular run level
install	install a command into the appropriate directory
installpkg	install a software package
ipcrm	remove message queue, semaphore set, shared memory ID
ipcs	display information about interprocess communication facilities
ismpx	see if standard output is connected to window channel
%job	C-shell: place job in foreground or background
jobs	display list of active jobs
join	relational join of two files using specified field
jterm	reset a layer of a windowing terminal
jwin	display size of window layer of current process
kill	terminate a process, send signal to a process
kill	C-shell: terminate a process, send signal to a process
killall	kill all active processes
label	Graphics command: translate—label axis of GPS file
labelit	provide a label for a file system
lastlogin	update the data showing last time users logged in
layers	manage asynchronous windows on a windowing terminal
ld	link editor for common object files
lex	generates programs for simple lexical analysis of text
limit	limit consumption of resources
line	read one line, up to newline, from standard input
link	create a link; like ln but without error checking
lint	check a C program for bugs, nonportability, and waste

list	produce a C source listing from a common object file
list	Graphics command: transform—list vector elements
ln	make a link between two directory entries
locate	Help Facility: use specified keywords, find a command
log	Graphics command: transform—logarithm
login	initiate a login to the system
logname	display the login userid
logout	C-shell: terminate a login shell
lorder	check object library, show dependencies between files
lp	send or modify requests to printers
lpadmin	configure and administer printers
lpfilter	administer filters used with printers
lpforms	administer forms used with printers
lpmove	move requests from one printer to another
lprof	interpret and display information from execution profile file
lpsched	start the printing service
lpshut	shut down the printing service
lpstat	display info about status of printing service
lpusers	set limits for print queues
lreg	Graphics command: summarize—linear regression
ls	display the names of files contained in a directory
m4	general-purpose macro processor
macref	display cross-reference of macros in nroff, troff documents
mail	send or read mail
mailx	send or read mail (more sophisticated than mail)
mailq	display the contents of the sendmail mail queue
make	maintain, update, and regenerate groups of programs
makekey	generate an encryption key
man	display entries from online reference manual
mean	Graphics command: summarize—arithmetic mean
mcs	display or manipulate comment section of object file
mesg	allow or deny receiving messages at your terminal
mkdir	make a directory
mkfs	make a file system
mknod	make a directory entry and inode for a special file
mkpart	display and modify data structures used by disk driver
mkshlib	create host and target shared object libraries

mkunix	configure and create a bootable kernel
mm	format nroff documents that use the mm macros
mmt	format troff documents that use the mm macros
mod	Graphics command: transform—modulus
monacct	create monthly summary accounting files
more	display a file, one screenful at a time
mount	mount a file system or remote resource
mountall	mount multiple file systems
mt	perform special operations on a cartridge tape
mv	move or rename files
mvdir	move a directory within a file system
mvt	format troff documents that use the mv macros
nawk	new awk: pattern scanning and processing language
ncheck	display path names of files based on inumbers
ndx	create a subject-page index for a document
neqn	format mathematical text, output suitable for nroff
newaliases	rebuild the sendmail alias database
newform	reformat text changing tabs, spaces, or line length
newgrp	Bourne shell: change a userid's current groupid
news	display the system news
nice	run a command at a specified priority
nice	C-shell: run a command at a specified priority
nl	add line numbers to text
nlsadmin	administer a network listener service
nm	display the symbol table (name list) of object files
nohup	run command, ignore hangups and quit signals
nohup	C-shell: run command, ignore hangups and quit signals
notify	C-shell: notify user when job status changes
nroff	text processor, output suitable for printing
nsquery	RFS: provide information about resources available to host
nulladm	create null file used by certain accounting programs
od	dump a file in octal, decimal, hex, or ASCII
omf	convert object module from COFF to OMF (Xenix)
onintr	C-shell: control action of shell on interrupts
pack	store a file in compressed format
pair	Graphics command: transform—pair elements
passmgmt	manage the system password files

passwd	change a userid's password and its attributes
paste	concatenate lines from one file or several files
pcat	concatenate and display files compressed by pack
pd	Graphics command: display readable listing of plot file
pdp11	check if processor is DEC PDP 11
pg	display a file, one screenful at a time
pic	format simple figures, output suitable for troff
pie	Graphics command: translate—make pie chart
plot	Graphics command: translate—plot a graph
point	Graphics command: summarize—point, density function
power	Graphics command: transform—raise to a power
pr	format text, suitable for printing
prctmp	print accounting record for a session
prdaily	format report or previous day's accounting
prfdc	perform system profile data collection at intervals
prfld	initialize system profile recording mechanism
prfpr	format system profile data
prfsnap	perform onetime system profile data collection
prfstat	enable or disable system profile sampling mechanism
prime	Graphics command: translate—generate prime numbers
prod	Graphics command: summarize—internal product
prof	interpret profile file generated by monitor function
prs	display all or part of SCCS file in specified format
prtacct	format and print a total accounting file
ps	display information about active processes
ptog	Graphics command: transform plot file to GPS
ptx	make permuted index, output suitable for nroff, troff
pwck	check system password file for consistency
pwconv	create or update shadow file from password file
pwd	Bourne shell: display pathname of working directory
qsort	Graphics command: summarize—quick sort
quit	Graphics command: stop a Graphics subsystem session
rand	Graphics command: translate—generate random sequence
random	generate a pseudorandom number between 0 and 255

`rank`	Graphics command: summarize—vector rank
`rc0`	run commands to bring system to state 0: halt
`rc2`	run commands to bring system to state 2: multiuser
`read`	Bourne shell: read one line from standard input
`readonly`	Bourne shell: mark names as being not changeable
`red`	restricted version of **ed**
`regcmp`	compile regular expressions
`rehash`	C-shell: recompute internal command name hash table
`reject`	prevent line printing requests
`relogin`	rename login entry to show current windowing layer
`remcom`	Graphics command: remove comments from input text
`removepkg`	remove a software package installed with `installpkg`
`repeat`	C-shell: repetitive control flow
`restore`	restore files backup with **backup**
`return`	Bourne shell: exit function, return specified value
`rflogin`	RFS: add or remove hosts and authentication information
`rfpasswd`	RFS: update authentication for a host
`rfstart`	RFS: start Remote File Sharing
`rfstop`	RFS: stop Remote File Sharing
`rfuadmin`	RFS: used by `rfudaemon` to handle unexpected events
`rfudaemon`	RFS: listen for and handle unexpected events
`rmail`	receive UUCP mail
`rmdel`	remove a change (delta) from an SCCS file
`rmntstat`	RFS: display information on mounted resources
`rmount`	RFS: try to mount a remote resource
`rmountall`	RFS: mount specified remote resources
`rm`	remove (unlink) files or directories
`rmdir`	remove empty directories
`rmail`	process UUCP mail; pass output to **sendmail**
`root`	Graphics command: transform—take a root
`round`	Graphics command: transform—round to nearest int
`rsh`	the restricted Bourne shell
`rumountall`	RFS: unmount all remote resources
`runacct`	run the principal daily accounting procedure
`sa1`	collect and store system activity data
`sa2`	generate daily report based on system activity data
`sact`	check if an SCCS file has impending changes (deltas)

sadc	collect system activity data
sadp	display tables showing disk access information
sag	display graph based on system activity data
sar	display report, collect data about system activity
sccsdiff	find differences between two versions of an SCCS file
sdb	symbolic debugger for use with C programs
sdiff	list differences between two files, side by side
sed	perform a script of editing commands upon a file
sendmail	deliver preformatted messages over the Internet
set	Bourne shell: set flags to control operations of shell
set	C-shell: set and show value of variables
setenv	C-shell: set value of an environment variable
setmnt	establish the mount table
settime	set access and modification time of a file
setup	allow the first user to initialize the system
sh	the Bourne shell
shift	Bourne shell: shift positional parameters to the left
shift	C-shell: shift positional parameters to the left
shl	use layers: more than one shell from same terminal
shutacct	turn off accounting during a shutdown
shutdown	shut down the system and change its state
siline	Graphics command: transform—generate a line
sin	Graphics command: transform—sine
size	show section size information for loaded parts of object file
sleep	suspend execution for specified number of seconds
smail	send UUCP mail
sort	sort or merge files
source	C-shell: read commands from a file
spell	check text, display words that may be spelled wrong
spellin	from hashmake output, create compressed spell list
spline	produce smooth curve suitable for graphing
split	split a file into pieces
starter	Help Facility: start menu-driven Help Facility
startup	turn on accounting during startup
stop	stop a background job
strace	display Streams trace messages
strclean	clean up the Streams error logger directory
strerr	deamon to log Streams error messages
strings	find the printable strings within an object file
strip	strip symbol table and line number information from object file

stty	set operating options for your terminal
su	temporarily substitute different userid for yours
subj	examine document, display subjects suitable for index
subset	Graphics command: transform—generate a subset
sulogin	used by init: start single-user or multiuser mode
sum	calculate a checksum and show block count for a file
suspend	C-shell: stop the shell
swap	manage system swap areas used by the memory manager
switch	C-shell: alternative control flow
sync	update the super block on your local system
sysadm	invoke menu-driven system administration facility
sysdef	display values of all tunable system parameters
tabs	set the tabs on your terminal
tail	display the last part of a file
tar	save and restore files, to and from archive medium
tbl	format tables, output suitable for nroff or troff
tc	interpret troff output on a Tektronix 4015 terminal
td	translate GPS graphics string to Tektronix 4010 term
tee	copy standard input to standard output and to a file
tekset	reset a Tektronix terminal
telinit	direct actions of init program (tell it what to do)
test	Bourne shell: evaluate a conditional expression
tic	compile a terminfo entry from source format
time	execute a command, show elapsed time data
time	C-shell: show time summary, execute and time a command
times	Bourne shell: display accumulated system and user times
timex	execute a command: show time, account, system data
title	Graphics command: translate—title a vector of GPS
total	Graphics command: summarize—sum total
touch	update the access and modification times of a file
tpfix	prepare object file for tape by padding to block size
tplot	produce plotting output for a specified terminal
tput	initialize a terminal or query terminfo database
tr	translate or delete selected characters in text
trap	Bourne shell: execute command upon receiving signal

`troff`	text processor, output suitable for typesetting
`true`	do nothing, successfully
`tsort`	topologically sort a totally ordered list of items
`otset`	provide information needed to initialize terminal and set modes
`ttoc`	Graphics command: make table of contents in TTOC form
`tty`	display the pathname of your terminal
`turnacct`	turn accounting on or off
`type`	Bourne shell: show how command name would be executed
`u3b`	check if processor is AT&T U3B
`u3b2`	check if processor is AT&T U3B2
`u3b5`	check if processor is AT&T U3B5
`uadmin`	provide control for basic administrative functions
`ulimit`	Bourne shell: impose file size limit
`umask`	Bourne shell: set mode mask for file creation
`umask`	C-shell: set mode mask for file creation
`umount`	unmount a file system or remote resource
`umountall`	unmount multiple file systems
`unadv`	RFS: unadvertise a directory for remote access
`unalias`	C-shell: remove a name defined by `alias`
`uname`	display name of Unix system and associated information
`unget`	undo the previous `get` of an SCCS file
`unhash`	C-shell: disable use of command name hash table
`uniq`	remove adjacent repeated lines in a text file
`units`	convert quantity from one type of units to another
`unlimit`	C-shell: remove the limit on a resource
`unlink`	remove link, like `rm`, `rmdir` but without error checking
`unpack`	expand files that were compressed by `pack`
`unset`	Bourne shell: remove variable or function
`unset`	C-shell: remove variable
`usage`	Help Facility: display information about using specified command
`uucheck`	check the uucp directories and permissions file
`uucico`	transport work files as requested by uucp or uux
`uucleanup`	examine and clean up the uucp spool directories
`uucp`	copy file from one Unix system to another
`uugetty`	perform `getty` for tty lines used with uucio, cu, ct
`uulog`	query a log file of uucp or uuxqt transactions

uuname	list names of systems known to uucp or cu facility
uupick	ask user to accept or reject received files
uusched	schedule uucp file transport
uustat	cancel or provide status for uucp commands
uuto	send a file to a specified destination
uutry	use uucio to call a remote site with debugging
uux	execute command on a specified system
uuxqt	execute remote command requests sent by uux
val	validate that SCCS file meets specified criteria
var	Graphics command: summarize—variance
vax	check if processor is a VAX
vc	provide version control facility for a text file
vedit	same as vi with defaults set for beginners
vi	screen-oriented editor, based on ex
view	same as vi in read-only mode
volcopy	make a literal copy of a file system
vtoc	Graphics command: make GPS describing specified TTOC
wait	Bourne shell: await completion of background process
wait	C-shell: await completion of all child processes
wall	write a message to all users
wc	count number of words, characters, lines in a file
what	show identification info from SCCS file
whatis	Graphics command: show description of specified name
while	Bourne shell: repetitive control flow
while	C-shell: repetitive control flow
who	display info about currently logged in userids
whodo	display info about users and their active processes
write	send messages to another user's terminal
wtinit	download file to be executed by a 5620 DMD terminal
wtmpfix	correct wtmp consistency of connect accounting records
x286emul	run 286 V.2.3, V.2.3.2 Xenix progs on V.3.2 386 system
xargs	construct an argument list, then execute a command
xfsck	check and repair a Xenix file system
xinstall	install Xenix-based software

xrestor	same as xrestore command
xrestore	read backups made by the Xenix backup command
xtd	show link structure to debug with xt window driver
xts	show statistics to debug with xt window driver
xtt	show packet traces to debug with xt window driver
yacc	convert context-free grammar into set of LR(1) tables
yes	repeatedly output a specified string or a "y" char

Appendix E: Glossary

The number following each term indicates the chapter in which the term is first discussed.

ABSOLUTE MOVE COMMAND [26] with `vi`, a command that moves the cursor to a specific line

ABSOLUTE PATH NAME [17] same as a FULL PATH NAME

ADDRESS [15] a description of how to send mail to a particular recipient

ARGUMENT [10] part of a command line, specifies information that the command needs to carry out its job

ASCII [4] (American Standard Code for Information Interchange) a standard coding scheme, used by Unix, for representing a character as a pattern of 8 bits

BACKGROUND [29] describes a process that executes on its own, without input from the terminal; such processes are said to be running "in the background"

BERKELEY UNIX same as BSD [10]

BINARY FILE [16] an ordinary file that contains machine language programs

BIT [4] (contraction of "binary digit") an entity that can be thought of as existing in one of two possible states; either on or off

BLOCK [21] A unit of disk storage, 512 bytes.

BLOCK DEVICE [21] A device, such as a disk, that handles data in chunks.

BSD [10] stands for "Berkeley Software Distribution"; the version of Unix produced at the University of California at Berkeley

BYTE [4] a string of 8 bits

CHARACTER DEVICE [21] A device, such as a keyboard, that handles data one character at a time.

CHARACTER TERMINAL [4] a terminal that displays only text, not graphics

COMMAND LINE [10] when you enter a command, everything you type, up to and including the `return`

COMMAND MODE [15] in `mailx`, a mode in which the characters you type are interpreted as commands

543

COMMAND MODE [25]   in vi, a mode in which the characters you type are interpreted as commands

COMMAND SUBSTITUTION [29]   within a command line that itself contains a command enclosed in è (backquote) characters, the enclosed command is executed and replaced by its output before the entire command line is processed

CONSOLE [2]   the main terminal that is connected to a host computer

CURRENT FILE [25]   with vi, the text file that you are currently editing

CURRENT LINE [26]   with vi, the line on which the cursor is positioned

DAEMON [7]   a process that executes in the background in order to be available at all times

DEFAULT [5]   a choice that is made for you automatically

DELETE BUFFER [27]   with vi, one of 9 temporary storage areas, numbered 1 through 9, used to hold the 9 most recent deletions that involved a line, a sentence, or anything longer

DEMODULATION [2]   the process by which a telephone signal is converted to a computer signal after being received over a telephone line

DESKTOP MANAGER [5]   a sophisticated interface, based on a graphical user interface, in which you work with objects that are represented by pictures

DIAL-IN TERMINAL [2]   a terminal which connects to a host computer over a telephone line

DIRECTORY [16]   a file that contains the information needed to access other files

DUMB TERMINAL [2]   a terminal that offers only the bare minimum of facilities, a screen and a keyboard

EDITING BUFFER [25]   with vi, a working copy of the current file

EDITING SCRIPT [28]   a text file that contains ex commands

EDITOR [24]   a program used to create and modify text files

ELECTRONIC MAIL [15]   same as MAIL

E-MAIL [15]   same as MAIL

EMULATE [2]   to act like a specific device by running a program that simulates that device

ENTER [3]   to issue a command to Unix by typing the command and then pressing the <Return> key

ENVIRONMENT [8]   an area of memory in which Unix and other programs can store data that needs to be universally accessible

ESCAPE CHARACTER [9]   a character that signals a program to change from one mode to another

EXECUTABLE PROGRAM [16]   a machine-language program, ready to be executed

EXECUTE a program [1]   to follow a the instructions contained in a program

EXECUTE PERMISSION [16]   the permission that allows a userid to execute an ordinary file or special file, or to fully access a directory

EXPORT [8]   to make available the value of a variable to all subsequent processes

FIELD [31]   within a record, one item of data

FILE [16]   any source from which data can be read or any target to which data can be written

FILE-CREATION MASK [20]   a 3-digit number, each digit being from 0 to 7, that represents the permissions for a file

FILTER [30]   any program that reads from the standard input and writes to the standard output

FLAG   same as OPTION [10]

FOREGROUND [29]   describes a process that, while executing, reads from and writes to the terminal; such processes are said to be running "in the foreground"

FULL PATH NAME [17]   a path name, beginning with a / [slash], that starts from the root directory

GATEWAY [15]   a connection between two dissimilar networks, often used for delivering mail

GLOBAL VARIABLE [8]   a variable that is accessible to all the processes executing within a session

GRAPHICAL USER INTERFACE [5]   a user interface, based on graphics, that is especially easy to use

GRAPHICS [4]   data in the form of pictures composed of small dots

GRAPHICS TERMINAL [2]   a terminal that is capable of displaying pictures

GROUP [16] a collection of userids that share file permissions

GROUPID [16] the name of a group

GUI (same as GRAPHICAL USER INTERFACE) [5]

GURU [11] same as WIZARD

HARDWARE [1] the physical parts of the computer

HEADER [15] the first part of a message

HOME DIRECTORY [18] the directory to which the shell automatically sets your working directory when you log in

HOST [2] the main computer that supports a multiuser system

INDEX NODE [16] same as INODE

INODE [16] the internal representation of a file, containing all the information that Unix needs to access the file

INODE NUMBER [16] a number that represents the position of an inode within the master table of inodes

INPUT MODE [15] in `mailx`, a mode in which the characters you type are collected into a message

INSERT MODE [25] in `vi`, a mode in which the characters you type are inserted into the editing buffer

INTELLIGENT TERMINAL [2] a terminal that offers some memory and processing power as well as the minimum screen and keyboard

INTERFACE [5] hardware or software that bridges a gap

INTERACTIVE [5] describes a computer system that responds immediately to your commands

INTERNET [15] a worldwide collection of networks and sub-networks

INTERPRET [6] to execute a list of commands, one by one

KEY [31] the part of a record that is compared during a sorting operation

LINE EDITOR [24] an editor that works with and displays groups of lines

LINE PRINTER [9] the Unix term for a regular printer that prints data on paper

LINK [16] the correspondence between a file name and the inode it represents

MACRO [24] a text formatting command defined in terms of one or more other other commands

MAGIC NUMBER [23] a numeric value, stored at the beginning of most non-text files, that identifies the file type

MAJOR NUMBER [23] a number, associated with a special file, that indicates the type of device the file represents

MAIL [15] a file of textual information that is sent from one userid to another

MAILBOX [15] a file in which incoming messages are kept until they are read

MANUAL [11] known as *the* manual, the principle reference manual, part of the Unix system, usually accessible from a terminal

MASK [20] same as FILE-CREATION MASK

MENU [5] a list of choices

MESSAGE [15] a specific file of data that is to be mailed

MESSAGE LIST [15] the specification of one or more messages to be acted upon by a `mailx` command

MINOR NUMBER [23] a number, associated with a special file, that indicates which device of a particular type the file represents

MODE [8] one of a number of specific ways in which a program can behave

MODEM [2] (modulator/demodulator) a device that converts signals in both directions between a computer and the telephone line

MODULATION [2] the process by which a computer signal is converted into a telephone signal in order to be transmitted over a telephone line

MOUNT (a device) [18] connecting the directory structure stored on a device into the main tree structure

MULTI-TASKING [1] describes an operating system that can do more than one thing at a time

MULTIUSER describes an operating system that can be used by more than one person at a time

MULTIUSER MODE [8] the normal mode of operation for Unix, in which all userids may log in and use the system

NAMED BUFFER [27] with `vi`, one of 26 temporary storage areas, named `a` through `z`, available to the user to hold text

NETWORK [2] a system in which computers are connected to other computers

NEWS [12] files, containing information of general interest, that are accessible to all users via the news command

ONLINE [11]   accessible to users from their terminals

OPERATING SYSTEM [1]   the master control program that manages the resources of a computer system

OPTION [10]   part of the command line, a word beginning with a minus sign (–) that controls the operation of the command

OPTION [28]   in vi, a value that you can set to specify how you want vi to behave

ORDINARY FILE [16]   a file that stores everyday information, such as programs and data

OVERRIDE [5]   to specify your own choice rather than accept a default

OWN a file [16]   to have control over the permissions for a file

PAGE [11]   as in Manual page or man page; an entry in the Unix online reference manual that explains a specific topic

PARAMETER   same as ARGUMENT [10]

PARENT DIRECTORY [17]   with respect to a subdirectory, the directory that contains the subdirectory

PASSWORD AGING [13]   a system that automatically forces users to change their passwords at predetermined intervals

PASSWORD ATTRIBUTES [13]   values that are used to control the password system, including password aging

PATH [17]   the series of file names that shows which directories must be traversed in order to reach a particular file

PATH NAME [17]   the exact specification of a path

PERMISSION [16]   the specification of what type of operations can be performed on a file: read, write or execute

PERMUTED INDEX [24]   an index consisting of keywords within their immediate contexts

PIPE [30]   the mechanism that joins two adjacent programs within a pipeline, by connecting the standard output of one program to the standard input of the next program

PIPE [30]   as a verb, to pass data, within a pipeline, from one program to another

PIPELINE [30]   an arrangement in which data passes, in sequence, through a series of programs

PORT [1]   to modify a program from one computer system so that it works with a different system

PORT [8]   a connecting point at which data flows in or out of a computer

PRE-PROCESSOR [24]   a program to read a data file and process certain commands before the file is sent to a final processing program

PRIMARY PROMPT [29]   for the Bourne shell, the same as the regular shell prompt ($ for regular user; # for superuser)

PRINT [9]   to display data on the screen; less often, to print data on paper

PRIORITY [29]   a number, from 0 to 39, assigned to a process, that indicates the preference that the process should receive as Unix allots the resources of the computer; the lower the number, the greater the preference

PROCESS [7]   a program that has started to execute

PROCESS GROUP LEADER [12]   a process whose main purpose is to execute other processes

PROCESSID (pronounced "process-eye-dee") [7]   a unique identifier describing a process

PROGRAM [1]   a list of computer instructions, that when followed, achieves a desired result

PROMPT [5]   a signal displayed by an interactive program to indicate that the program is waiting for input

PUBLIC ACCESS UNIX [15]   a service, possibly costing money, that provides Unix to the public

QUOTE [29]   to indicate to the shell that one or more character are to be taken literally and not endowed with special meaning

READ PERMISSION [16]   the permission that allows a userid to read an ordinary file or special file, or to read the file names from a directory

RECORD [31]   within a text file, the largest unit of data holding one or more related items

REDIRECT [30]   to reassign the standard input, standard output, or standard error to a specified file

REGULAR EXPRESSION [22]   a compact way of specifying all the character strings that match a particular pattern

REGULAR FILE [16]   same as an ORDINARY FILE

RELATIVE PATH NAME [17] a path name, not beginning with a / [slash], that starts from the working directory

REMOVE (a file) [16] to eliminate the link between a file name and an inode

ROOT DIRECTORY [17] the directory that, directly or indirectly, contains all the other directories in the file system

RUN a program (same as EXECUTE) [1]

SCREEN EDITOR [24] an editor that makes use of the whole screen to allow you to see and to manipulate more than one line at a time

SCRIPT [6] a list of commands that are to be executed, one by one, by a specific program

SCROLLING [5] a method used to display data on the bottom line of a screen such that all the other lines move up one position as the new line is written

SECONDARY PROMPT [29] for the Bourne shell, a prompt (the > character) that indicates that the line you are typing is a continuation of the previous line

SESSION [2] a working connection to a host computer

SHADOW FILE [13] a file, used on some Unix systems, that holds encoded passwords and password attributes

SHELL [5] an interactive program, usually text-based, that reads and interprets a wide variety of commands, thereby providing a user interface

SHELL SCRIPT [6] a list of commands that are to be executed. one by one, by a shell

SIGNAL [29] a message, identified by a number, sent to a process, that notifies the process that a specific event has occurred

SINGLE-USER MODE [8] a special mode of operation for Unix, used for system maintenance, in which only the superuser is logged in

SOFTWARE [1] programs

SORT [31] to rearrange the records in a text file according to a specified ordering, based on the values of one or more fields in each record

SOURCE PROGRAM [16] a text file that contains a program written in a computer language

SPECIAL FILE [16] a file that represents a device

STABLE [31] describes a sorting program that maintains the relative order of records that have equal key values

STANDALONE [1] describes a computer system that is used by only one person at a time

STANDARD ERROR [30] the output target to which Unix programs write error messages

STANDARD INPUT [30] the basic source from which Unix programs read their input

STANDARD OUTPUT [30] the basic target to which Unix programs write their output

STRING OPTION [28] in vi, an option that has the value of a string of letters or numbers

SUB-DIRECTORY [17] a directory that lies within another directory

SUPERUSER [7] a user who is logged in to a system using a userid that gives him special privileges

SWITCH same as OPTION [10]

SWITCH OPTION [28] in vi, an option that is either on or off

SYNTAX [10] the formal and precise description of the format of a command

SYSTEM ADMINISTRATOR (same as SYSTEM MANAGER) [7]

SYSTEM MAINTENANCE MODE (same as SINGLE-USER MODE) [8]

SYSTEM MANAGER [7] the person whose job it is to maintain a Unix system

SYSTEM V [10] the version of Unix produced at AT&T

TEE [30] a filter that reads data from the standard input, copies the data to a specified file, and then writes the data, unchanged, to the standard output

TELETYPE [9] an electro-mechanical device that was used to send messages from one location to another

TERMINAL [2] a device which provides the input and output facilities necessary to access a host computer

TEXT [4] data in the form of separate characters

TEXT FILE [16] an ordinary file that contains ASCII-coded data

TEXT FORMATTER [24] a program that reads a text file containing embedded commands and outputs a formatted document based on those commands

TILDE ESCAPE COMMAND [15]   a `mailx` command, starting with a tilde (~), that is used in input mode

TIME-SHARING SYSTEM (same as a MULTIUSER operating system) [1]

TREE-STRUCTURED FILE SYSTEM [17]   a hierarchical system of directories, based on a single root directory, in which all directories except the root directory are subdirectories

TTY (pronounced "tee-tee-why") [7]   a terminal; the name "tty" is derived from the name "teletype"

UNNAMED BUFFER [27]   with `vi`, a temporary storage area used to hold the most recent deletion

UNSTABLE [31]   describes a sorting program that sometimes changes the relative order of records that have equal key values

UUCP [15]   abbreviation for Unix to Unix Copy; a family of programs that implements that transfer of data from one computer to another; UUCP is sometimes used as a synonym for the UUCP NETWORK

UUCP NETWORK [15]   the collection of all the computers to which mail can be sent via UUCP

UNIX [1]   an operating system whose variations run on many different types of computers

USENET [11]   a loosely administered worldwide network of discussion groups

USER [7]   a person who is using a computer

USER FILE-CREATION MODE MASK [20]   same as FILE-CREATION MASK

USERID (pronounced "user-eye-dee") [7]   a name, registered with a Unix system, that is user to identify a particular user

USER INTERFACE [5]   the interface that you use to work with a particular program

UTILITY [1]   a program that comes with an operating system and that performs a specific task

VARIABLE [8]   a named quantity whose value is stored in the environment

WHITESPACE [10]   the collective name used to describe the `tab` and `space` characters that delimit the parts of a command line

WINDOW [5]   a rectangular box, displayed by a graphical user interface, in which is displayed the output of a particular task

WIZARD [11]   a Unix expert

WORD [10]   part of the command line, a sequence of characters delimited by whitespace

WORKING DIRECTORY [17]   a designated directory that acts as a base for the specification of path names

WORKSTATION [1]   a computer that is used by only one person at a time

WRITE PERMISSION [16]   the permission that allows a userid to modify an ordinary file or special file, or to create or remove entries in a directory

ZERO OR MORE [10]   none, one, or more than one of something

Indexes

Quick Index of Unix Commands

551

Quick Index of vi Commands

General Index